D1576982

Cardiff Libraries
www.cardiff.gov.uk/libraries

Llyfrgelloedd Caerdydd
www.caerdydd.gov.uk/llyfrgelloedd

ACC. No: 03226635

THE BEER BOOK

EDITOR-IN-CHIEF
TIM HAMPSON

THE BEER BOOK

WITH CONTRIBUTIONS FROM

TIM HAMPSON • STAN HIERONYMUS • WERNER OBALSKI • ALASTAIR GILMOUR • JORIS PATTYN

LORENZO DABOVE • GILBERT DELOS • CONRAD SEIDL • RON PATTINSON • LAURA STADLER-JENSEN

BRYAN HARRELL • WILLIE SIMPSON • GEOFF GRIGGS • ADRIAN TIERNEY-JONES

LONDON • NEW YORK
MELBOURNE • MUNICH • DELHI

DK India
Senior Editor Nidhilekha Mathur
Editor Aditi Batra
Senior Art Editor Balwant Singh
Art Editors Swati Katyal, Neha Wahi
DTP Designers Satish Chandra Gaur, Sachin Singh,
Anurag Trivedi, Manish Chandra Upreti
Picture Researcher Sakshi Saluja
Managing Editor Alicia Ingty
Managing Art Editor Navidita Thapa
Pre-Production Manager Sunil Sharma

DK UK
Managing Editor Dawn Henderson
Managing Art Editor Christine Keilty
Senior Jackets Creative Nicola Powling
Pre-Production Producer Raymond Williams
Senior Producer Oliver Jeffreys
Publisher Peggy Vance
Art Director Peter Luff

2008 edition
Produced for Dorling Kindersley by
Blue Island Publishing
www.blueisland.co.uk

Publishing Director Rosalyn Ellis
Editorial Director Michael Ellis
Art Director Stephen Bere
Editor Fay Franklin
Designers Marisa Renzullo, Ian Midson
Researchers Rebecca Carman,
Jürgen Scheunemann, Katerina Cerna

For **Dorling Kindersley**
Project Editor Laura Nickoll
Senior Art Editor Isabel de Cordova
Senior Jacket Creative Nicola Powling
Managing Editor Dawn Henderson
Managing Art Editor Christine Keilty
Senior Production Editor Jenny Woodcock
Production Controller Alice Holloway

First edition published in Great Britain in 2008 by Dorling Kindersley Limited
Second updated edition published in Great Britain in 2014
by Dorling Kindersley Limited
80 Strand, London WC2R 0RL

A Penguin Random House Company

4 6 8 10 9 7 5 3
002-256551-October/14
Copyright © 2008, 2014 Dorling Kindersley Limited

All rights reserved. No part of this publication may be reproduced, stored
in a retrieval system, or transmitted in any form or by any means, electronic,
mechanical, photocopying, recording, or otherwise without the prior written
permission of the copyright owners.

A CIP catalogue record for this book is available from the British Library
ISBN 978 1 4093 5347 8
Printed and bound in China by South China Printing Co. Ltd.

Discover more at
www.dk.com

CONTENTS

INTRODUCTION

This is a book all about beer – the best long drink in the world. It is a drink that has changed and civilized us, yet too often we think that a beer is just a beer – a standard product of our industrial society. Beer is a product of the land, however, made with wonderful natural ingredients. It is the art, craft, and science of the brewer that turn these ingredients into beer.

This book is an adventure – a journey through a fascinating world of flavours, colours, and aromas. On this expedition, we spend time in the new world of brewing in the United States, then travel through the great brewing nations of Europe – Germany, the British Isles, Belgium, and the Czech Republic.

We also visit countries more often associated with their viniculture. Because wine is so much part of the culture in France, the country's rural brewing tradition is often overlooked, while that other great Old World wine nation Italy is now emerging as a force to be reckoned with in craft beer brewing.

For a beer enthusiast, trying to imagine a world without beer is like trying to imagine a world without a sky or the stars above. It is a normal part of human life for so many of us that it can all too easily be taken for granted. But we shouldn't do so. Beer is one of the oldest and most popular drinks known to man. It is thought that about 10,000 years ago, in the Middle East, nomadic peoples began to grow and harvest grain and set up settlements near the fields. Some archaeologists believe the reason man did this was to make beer.

An ancient oral poem from Babylonia called the *Gilgamesh Epic* tells the story of the civilizing influence of brewing. First told some 4,000 years ago, it is the story of Enkidu, an uncivilized man who was taught to eat bread and drink beer. Enkidu drank seven cups of beer and his "heart soared". According to the legend, he washed and became a refined human being – beer had tamed him.

EARLY BREWING

The first records of brewing are in the Middle East in Mesopotamia with the Sumerians 6,000 years ago. At least 3,000 years before the Christian era, an intoxicating drink, made from grains, was providing nutrition to people in Egypt. The writings of the Roman historian Pliny record that a fermented drink made from corn and water was drunk regularly across much of northern Europe.

As well as enjoyment, there was a religious side to early beer brewing, and around the world today in tribal communities there are still social ceremonies where an ancient form of beer is drunk. These ceremonies acknowledge gratitude to the gods. Beer in ancient times was like bread – one of life's essentials. It provided quick calories and, because it was boiled, was safer than water to drink. Wherever agriculture and the cultivation of grain went, beer followed.

BEER TODAY

The beer industry has two faces – one traditional, the other young and vibrant. Both can be found within this book. We should not decry the older industry – it has helped shape the industry as it is today. The older industry gave us refrigeration, science, and marketing – which is why we celebrate here the beers from breweries such as Anheuser-Busch InBev (AB InBev), Carlsberg, Heineken, and SABMiller. They have elevated brewing from serendipity to an art and a science, and their creations are rightly found within this book. The young brewing world is a fascinating and dynamic one, and gets due attention here too.

USA

USA is the new world of beer. From Alaska to the Mexican border, USA brewers are pushing at boundaries as never before. They brew darker beers, more bitter beers, and hoppier beers than can be found anywhere else in the world. In brewing terms, there are simply no rules anymore. European beer styles are being taken apart and put back together with barely a nod to tradition.

In the 40 years since the godfather of the USA beer renaissance, Fritz Maytag, saved the Anchor Brewery from closing, a revolution has taken place. Today there are more than 2,500 new breweries, with few settling for a limited range. Instead, they brew many styles of beers over the course of a year, some inspired by classic beer styles, others limited only by the brewer's imagination.

At the Dogfish Head Brewery in Milton, Delaware, founder Sam Calagione is brewing "off-centred ales for off-centred people". His beers use unusual ingredients or "extreme" amounts of traditional ingredients. White Muscat grapes, honey, saffron, liquorice, chicory, and coffee have all been added to the kettles.

Brooklyn Brewery's Garrett Oliver is not only pushing on the environmental front – the Brooklyn Brewery is 100 per cent wind powered – but he has also taken the pairing of beer with food to new heights. He wants every restaurant to have a beer list to stand proudly alongside its wine list. Good beer, he says, is an affordable luxury – and the pairing of it with serious food is a truly creative, life-enhancing experience.

At the Alaskan Brewery in Juneau, each of the beers produced emphasizes its regional roots. Its Smoked Porter uses malt smoked with alder at the local fishery – a local twist on the smoked beers from Bamberg in Germany, where beechwood is used. And Samuel Adams in Boston, Massachusetts, continues to push at the boundaries of strength. Utopias, at 28 per cent ABV, just keeps getting stronger.

The great beer writer late Michael Jackson and Charles Papazian have both had pivotal influences on the craft beer scene in the USA. Michael Jackson's seminal writing inspired a generation of people to brew good beer, develop new recipes, and recreate historic lost styles. Charles Papazian's writings gave people the skills to start brewing at home. He helped found the Brewers Association and created the Great American Beer Festival in 1982.

GERMANY

The great brewing nations of Europe still stand tall, with glorious tradition standing alongside intriguing innovation. All across Germany, wonderful beer gardens are to be found. Here, brimming litre steins, booming oompah bands, and exuberant celebrations help make the country a beer paradise. In the main, the country's brewing tastes remain very traditional, with even new brewpubs producing pilsner-style beers rather than being innovative.

However, the country has more than 15 classic beer styles, ranging from the rauchbier of Bamberg and Nurnberg to Cologne's soft kölsch, served by the blue-aproned köbes, and the acidic weissbier of Berlin.

At the Heller Brewery's tap, the Schlenkerla restaurant in Bamberg, brewer Matthias Trum produces world-class smoked malt beers that are unequalled anywhere else in the world. At Weltenburger Kloster, to the north of Munich, the brewers in one of the world's oldest brewing locations are showing their Barock Dunkel is a beer to be enjoyed locally and abroad – it has won gold three times in the dark lagers category at the World Beer Cup in San Diego, California.

BRITISH ISLES

Hook Norton Brewery in the British Isles is more than 100 years old and has a historic Victorian steam engine, but its beers are not stuck in the past. Brewer James Clarke is increasingly using local ingredients to make beers with new flavours.

Heineken Brewery's visitor centre in Amsterdam

Thornbridge, which opened in 2005, is one of Britain's new wave of breweries and has rapidly gained a reputation for innovative beers with an emphasis on pronounced flavour. And Richard Keene at Cotswold Brewing is showing that a small British craft brewer can make lager-style beers rather than ales.

At the Meantime Brewery in London, brewmaster Alastair Hook is on a mission to show the full flavours that beer has to offer. His Coffee Porter, which is rich with roasted cappuccino flavours, is brewed with fair-trade coffee beans from Rwanda.

Each of these breweries, in its own way, is contributing to a reinvigoration of the British brewing scene, centred on small-batch producers.

BELGIUM

Beer drinkers in Belgium probably have more choice about which beer to drink than in any other country in the world. From Flanders come pale ales and sour red ales. Add to this the gueuze, lambic, and krieks of Brussels, the country's abbey ales and *saisons*, and not forgetting its witbier, and the drinker in Belgium is spoilt for choice.

Imbued with tradition, the Cantillon Brewery in Brussels produces uncompromising and intensely sour beers. The Van Roy family has been making acetic gueuze beers (a blend of aged and newly brewed lambic beers) for over 100 years – long before the term "extreme beers" was ever coined. Brewer Jean-Pierre Van Roy went organic in 1999, and is well known for his experimentation with new ingredients and variations on the traditional wild yeast fermented lambics, gueuze, and fruit beers. Like many of today's craft beer producers,

Portland Brewing, where the MacTarnahan's beer range is brewed

he recognizes the importance of using the Internet to sell and promote his beers, and half of his production is now exported to foreign markets.

CZECH REPUBLIC

The town of Plzeň in the Czech Republic plays an important part in the history of beer. Here, in 1842, brewer Josef Groll mastered the art of triple decoction mashing, which created a golden, clear beer. And, as they say, the rest is history, as pilsner went on to become the world's dominant beer style.

The bars and beer halls of Prague are rightly renowned as being must-visit places for any beer lover. But, outside the city, many of the country's brewers have embraced beer tourism and offer fabulous visitor centres, such as can be found at Pilsner Urquell in Plzeň and Budweiser Budvar's in Česke Budějovice.

ITALY

Beer can now be produced in any country in the world. The traditional winemaking country of Italy has more than its fair share of brewing tyros. Indeed, it is not uncommon to find American brewers touring the country's more innovative new breweries, looking for inspiration.

Teo Musso lives in a part of Italy renowned for its Barolo and Barbera wines. At his Baladin Brewery he produces "his raptures" using wine and whisky yeasts. One beer, Xyauyu, is oxidized for a year to produce mouth-tingling, sherry-like flavours. Ever the nonconformist, he has placed large headphones on his fermenting vessels, convinced that the type of music played will influence the quality and characteristics of the brew.

At Bi-Du, in the tiny village of Rodero, just a few steps away from the Swiss border, brewer Beppe Vento is producing beers in his brewery that are pushing at the boundaries of conventional styles. Rodersch, for example, is a cloudy, fresh digestif, and a perfect precursor to the region's food.

Former home-brewer Agostino Arioli saw the light after a visit to the Granville Island Brewery in Vancouver, Canada. Today, production at his Birrificio Italiano, in Como, includes Fleurette, a beer brewed with barley, wheat, and rye, and flavoured with rose petals. His Tipopils, which is hopped with four hop varieties (Hallertauer Magnum, Perle, Herbsucker, and Saaz), was recently voted the world's best pilsner by Ratebeer.com.

PACIFIC RIM

In Japan, the Ise Kadoya Brewery uses soybean paste and the juice from a native aromatic citrus fruit called yuzu. Even Cabernet grapes can be found in some Japanese brewers' mash tuns and kettles.

Forget the notion that Australians only drink pale yellow lagers; that never was the case. Australians are increasingly looking for beers of distinction and invention – a demand that is being met not only by the bigger producers but also by a growing number of independent craft producers. Today, there are more than 100 brewers producing an exciting array of beer styles. The country's wine producers had better watch out!

The family-owned Coopers Brewery, which opened in 1862, continues with its exquisite range of cloudy, bottle-conditioned beers, while highly creative Little Creatures, in Fremantle, has introduced US-style, hoppy pale ales to the local market.

BEER VERSUS WINE

Wine and beer should have equal billing in the pantheon of alcoholic drinks. Yet, wine is treated by many as a cultured drink, while beer is not. In the wine world, experts can talk reverentially about the grapes used and the nuances of colour, aroma, and flavour that different varieties bring to bear. We must never forget that the same is true for beer and its ingredients, too.

To make wine, the grapes are crushed, releasing a sweet, sugary liquid, which is then fermented. The brewer has a similar, though

A fruit beer lambic (wild beer) from Belgium's Cantillon

arguably more complicated, task to perform. It requires greater skill and more artistry than will be used by a winemaker, for the brewer has to extract the sweet fermentable sugars from cereal rather than juicy grapes. The brewer garners and unleashes the magic of yeast, which converts the sugar into alcohol. And the brewer adds the hops, with their bouquet of aromas, flavours, and cleansing qualities, and decides upon the quality of the water used.

The result of all this is that drinkers today can choose from over 100 different styles of beer, covering every imaginable flavour and colour. From the simple notes of grain, yeast, hops, and water, brewers create a symphony of tastes, colours, and aromas that swirl around the glasses from which we drink.

We should drink with our eyes and noses before we take a sip to experience the spectrum of colours and burst of aromas that are all part of the experience of enjoying beer. Then, and only then, take a sip and let the beer unleash its flavours as it dances on your tongue. As you take a second sip and enjoy the lingering aftertaste of a good beer, say a silent "cheers" to the skill of the world's brewers – they are true heroes of beer, creating drinks with variety and complexity equal to the most expensive wines.

KNOWLEDGE IS POWER

With copious tasting notes and features that explain beer styles and the role of key ingredients, this book provides the information to understand what creates the complexity of vivid colours, aromas, and flavours in beer. Within these pages are the brewing innovators and creators of some of the world's greatest beers. Beers from many countries are listed, along with information

Boulevard Brewing, in Kansas City, Missouri

on their alcoholic strength (ABV) and style. It is a companion to a wonderful world in which beer is much more than just a beer.

People do not ask for a glass of wine without specifying, at the very least, whether they want it to be red or white, sweet or dry, still or sparkling. More often than not, they will decide the country of origin, and they might choose the grape variety – Chardonnay or Pinot Noir, Cabernet Sauvignon or Muscat. This book is intended for people who want to broaden their knowledge of beer and hunt down exciting brews from around the globe. It should encourage you never to ask just for a beer without first considering its style – pilsner or wheat, fruit or an American IPA, Belgian ale or a gueuze?

The great beers of the world deserve to be placed on the same high pedestal as fine wines. It is still the drink of the masses, but it is increasingly becoming appreciated like fine wines and malt whiskies.

In 10,000 years we have changed from hunter gatherers to civilized people with rich cultures. Beer was there right at the beginning and has changed with us from "liquid bread" to a sophisticated drink. Whatever the next 10,000 years bring, we can be pretty sure that beer will still be a vital component of the human experience. For there can be few better pleasures – when returning home after a long day at work or just sitting in a favourite bar – than the pleasure of a great beer. But which one? The choice is yours – enjoy the experience.

Tim Hampson

BEERS TO TRAVEL FOR

KEY NATIONS

USA • GERMANY • BRITISH ISLES • BELGIUM • CZECH REPUBLIC

WASHINGTON STATE

Boundary Bay
Diamond Knot
Redhook
Seattle
Fish
Mac & Jack's

WASHINGTON

Pelican
Portland
Full Sail

Rogue

Terminal Gravity

Deschutes

OREGON

Caldera

Seattle

Elysian
Georgetown
Hale's
Pike
Pyramid

Portland, Oregon

Bridgeport
Hair of the Dog
Hopworks
Portland Brewing
Widmer Brothers

ALASKA

ALASKA

Midnight Sun

Alaskan

MINNESOTA,

Surly
Summit
Leinenku

August Schell

MINNESOTA

IOWA

Millstream

Goose Island

NORTHERN CALIFORNIA

Lost Coast
Mad River
Eel River

North Coast

Butte Creek/
Sierra Nevada

Anderson Valley
Mendocino
Bear Republic
Moonlight
Russian River
Lagunitas
Sudwerk
Marin
Trumer
San Francisco
Drake's

Seattle

WASHINGTON

Portland
Ninkasi

OREGON

Bayern/
Big Sky

MONTANA

NORTH DAKOTA

MINNESO

IDAHO

Grand Teton
Snake River

WYOMING

SOUTH DAKOTA

NEBRASKA

IO

San Francisco

NEVADA

Gordon Biersch

Uinta/
Utah Brewers

UTAH

Denver
COLORADO
Dixie

Boulevard

KANSAS

Anchor

San Francisco

Anchor
Shmaltz
Speakeasy

Firestone Walker
CALIFORNIA

The Bruery

Ska/
Steamworks

ARIZONA

Marble

NEW MEXICO

OKLAHOMA

Four Peaks

Nimbus

TEXAS

SOUTHERN CALIFORNIA

Green Flash
Lost Abbey
Stone
Alesmith/
Ballast Point
Alpine

COLORADO

New Belgium/
Odell

Oskar Blues
Left Hand
Avery/
Boulder
Molson Coors
Tommyknocker
Denver

COLORADO

Bristol

Denver

Breckenridge
Great Divide
Wynkoop

Great Divide

COLETTE

HAWAII

HAWAII

Kona

USA

If the USA was once known as the land of bland, pale lager, those days are long gone. With more craft brewers than anywhere else on Earth, their passions feed a beer culture in which diversity of styles, flavour, and experimentation are the motivating factors – not rules and traditions.

This map shows where some of the breweries are based, with pullout boxes where a city has more than one brewery.

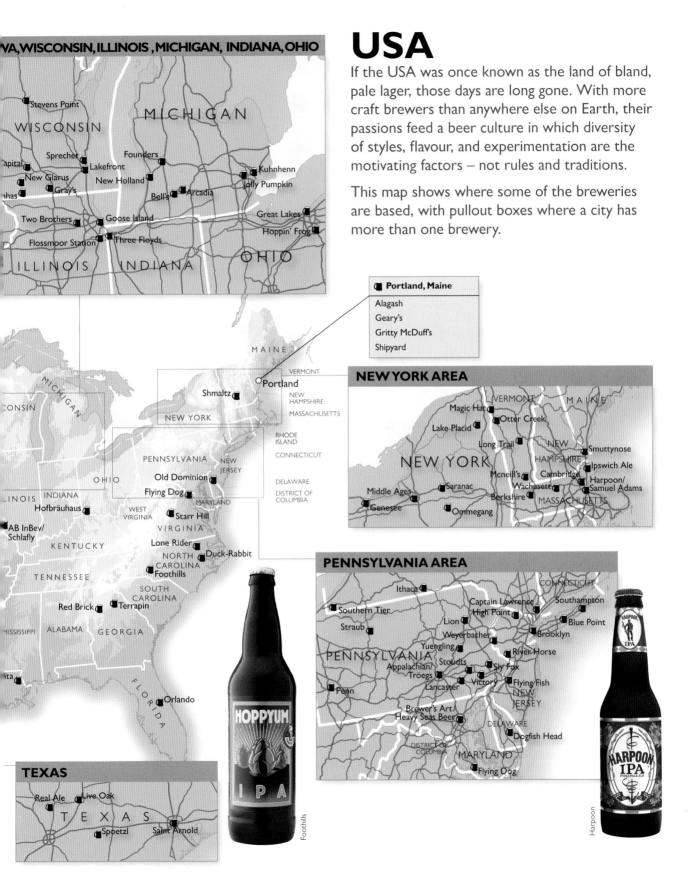

VA, WISCONSIN, ILLINOIS, MICHIGAN, INDIANA, OHIO
Stevens Point
WISCONSIN
MICHIGAN
Sprecher
Founders
Lakefront
New Glarus
New Holland
Gray's
Bell's
Arcadia
Kuhnhenn
Jolly Pumpkin
Two Brothers
Goose Island
Great Lakes
Hoppin' Frog
Flossmoor Station
Three Floyds
ILLINOIS
INDIANA
OHIO

Portland, Maine
Alagash
Geary's
Gritty McDuff's
Shipyard
MAINE
VERMONT
Portland
Shmaltz
NEW HAMPSHIRE
NEW YORK
MASSACHUSETTS
RHODE ISLAND
CONNECTICUT
MICHIGAN
PENNSYLVANIA
NEW JERSEY
OHIO
Old Dominion
Flying Dog
DELAWARE
DISTRICT OF COLUMBIA
MARYLAND
INDIANA
Hofbräuhaus
WEST VIRGINIA
Starr Hill
AB InBev/ Schlafly
VIRGINIA
KENTUCKY
Lone Rider
NORTH CAROLINA
Duck-Rabbit
Foothills
TENNESSEE
SOUTH CAROLINA
Red Brick
Terrapin
MISSISSIPPI
ALABAMA
GEORGIA
FLORIDA
Orlando

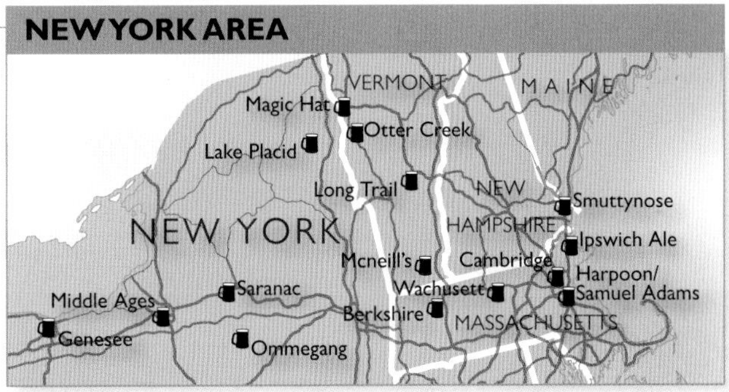

NEW YORK AREA
VERMONT
MAINE
Magic Hat
Otter Creek
Lake Placid
Long Trail
NEW HAMPSHIRE
Smuttynose
NEW YORK
Ipswich Ale
Mcneill's
Cambridge
Harpoon/ Samuel Adams
Middle Ages
Saranac
Wachusett
Berkshire
MASSACHUSETTS
Genesee
Ommegang

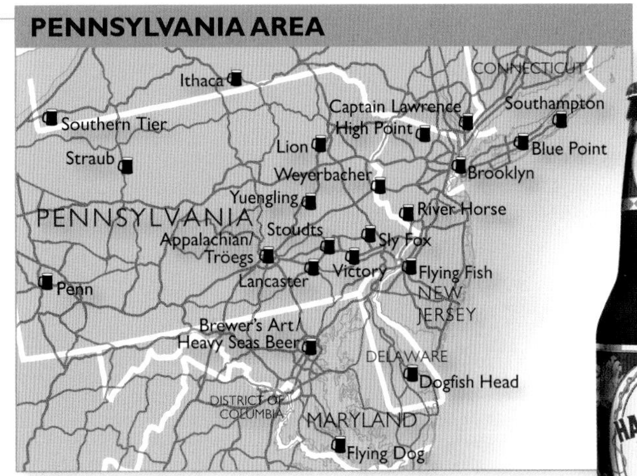

PENNSYLVANIA AREA
Ithaca
CONNECTICUT
Southern Tier
Captain Lawrence
Southampton
High Point
Straub
Lion
Blue Point
Brooklyn
Weyerbacher
Yuengling
PENNSYLVANIA
River Horse
Stoudts
Appalachian/ Tröegs
Sly Fox
Victory
Flying Fish
Lancaster
Penn
NEW JERSEY
Brewer's Art/ Heavy Seas Beer
DELAWARE
Dogfish Head
DISTRICT OF COLUMBIA
MARYLAND
Flying Dog

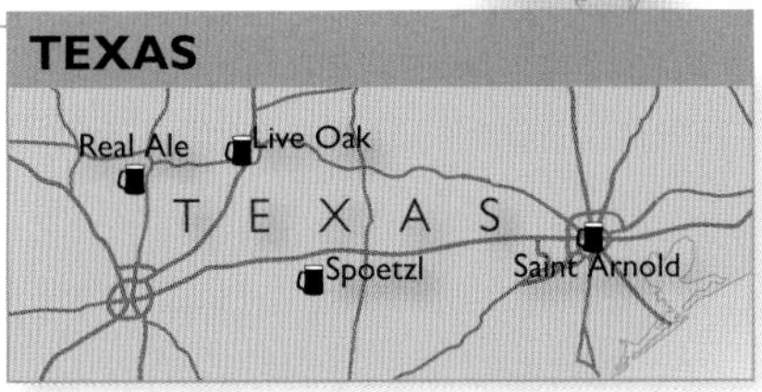

TEXAS
Real Ale
Live Oak
TEXAS
Spoetzl
Saint Arnold

HOPPYUM
IPA

Foothills

HARPOON
IPA

Harpoon

BREWERY

ABITA

PO Box 1510, Abita Springs,
Louisiana 70420, USA
www.abita.com

A sleepy town in the pinewoods north of Lake Pontchartrain, Abita Springs was best known for the healing powers of its mineral waters before Abita Brewing opened as a brewpub in 1986. Today Abita operates a fast-growing, thoroughly modern brewery, the largest speciality producer south of the Mason-Dixon line.

ALASKAN

5429 Shaune Drive, Juneau,
Alaska 99801, USA
www.alaskanbeer.com

Although it is located in a coastal community without roads connecting it to the rest of the USA, Alaskan Brewing has grown into a regional force, selling its beer over much of the nation west of the Rockies. Founders Geoff and Marcy Larson focused on native ingredients and recipes from the outset. Alaskan's first and flagship brew, Amber Ale,

is based on a beer made across the channel from Juneau back at the turn of the 20th century.

BREWING SECRET Alaskan's Smoked Porter, a beer that typifies what's new in American brewing, is made with malt smoked at a local fishery.

ALESMITH

9366 Cabot Drive, San Diego,
California 92126, USA
www.alesmith.com

One of several San Diego breweries that has pushed Southern California to the forefront of national brewing. It has a wide following for its mostly strong and often esoteric beers, many barrel aged and vintage dated.

BREWING SECRET Every employee is an award-winning home-brewer.

BEER

TURBODOG
BROWN ALE 5.6% ABV
Dark, with a rich chocolate nose, and toffee emerging on the palate; a bitter coffee finish.

PURPLE HAZE
FRUIT BEER 4.2% ABV
Wheat ale infused with raspberry purée. Mildly sweet; a refreshing remedy for southern humidity.

AMBER
ALTBIER 5.3% ABV
Clean caramel on the nose, brightened by spicy hops. Smooth and malty, with balanced bitterness.

BARLEY WINE ALE
BARLEY WINE 10.7% ABV
Cellared in a former gold mine. Rich and smooth, with dark caramel, cherries, and plums. Nicely balanced.

SMOKED PORTER
SMOKED BEER 6.5% ABV
Alder smoked. Flavours of chocolate and burnt fruit; luscious and oily on the palate. Smoky from the beginning through to a satisfying finish.

WINTER ALE
WINTER BEER 6.4% ABV
Spruce intermingles with fruit at the start. Modestly rich on the palate, woody at the finish.

IPA
INDIA PALE ALE 7.3% ABV
Brimming with hops and fruit salad aromas, including notes of ripe mango and pineapple.

SPEEDWAY STOUT
IMPERIAL STOUT 12% ABV
Coffee infused, it complements a broad imperial palate of chocolate, toffee, currants, and oily nuts.

THE BEST-KNOWN BEERS OF THE USA

Over the last 30 years, the USA has undergone a sea change in the world of brewing, though the mass market remains packed with pale light beers.

Just a few decades ago, the USA was a country with one basic style choice when it came to beer – a pale lager, generally light in body and lacking in hop flavour or aroma. Today, there are more than 2,500 breweries, producing a wider range of beers than has ever been available anywhere in the world before. However, despite this dramatic change, the overall market is still dominated by Anheuser-Busch InBev (who produce Budweiser), Coors, and Miller. The market is led by light beers. In fact, six of the top seven selling domestically produced beers are low-calorie lagers. America's brewing past can still be glimpsed on faded advertisements along the back roads, promoting brands from breweries long gone. But many of those brands are still produced under contract – such as Pabst, Schlitz, and Lone Star – and have avid fans. All are pale lagers that taste much alike.

BUD LITE (LAGER 4.2% ABV)
BUDWEISER (LAGER 5% ABV) *left*
COORS LIGHT (LAGER 4.2% ABV) *centre*
MILLER LITE (LAGER 4.2% ABV)
BUSCH LIGHT (LAGER 4.2% ABV)
MICHELOB LIGHT (LAGER 4.2% ABV) *right*
PABST (LAGER 5% ABV)
SCHLITZ (LAGER 4.7% ABV)
LONE STAR (LAGER 4.7% ABV)

ALLAGASH

50 Industrial Way, Portland,
Maine 04103, USA
www.allagash.com

Focusing on Belgian-inspired beers, Allagash draws on tradition but does not shy away from innovation. In 2007, it became the first American brewery to build a traditional "coolship" (a huge, open, shallow pan) for spontaneous fermentation by wild yeasts.

BREWING SECRET Some speciality beers are aged in oak bourbon barrels.

ALPINE

2351 Alpine Boulevard, Alpine,
California 91901, USA
www.alpinebeerco.com

This brewery is known for beers whose names describe their hoppy nature, such as Pure Hoppiness and Exponential Hoppiness ("double dry-hopped" and not always available). It also produces beers with unusual ingredients, including a honey ale with orange zest and coriander, and a wheat beer infused with vanilla pods.

ANCHOR

1705 Mariposa Street, San Francisco,
California 94107, USA
www.anchorbrewing.com

Fritz Maytag saved Anchor Brewing from closing in 1965, introduced USA drinkers to many classic styles, and launched a microbrewery revolution.

BREWING SECRET Maytag is known for preserving the USA's indigenous "steam style", which involves using bottom-fermenting yeast at high temperatures in wide, shallow, open pans.

ALLAGASH WHITE
WITBIER 5.1% ABV
Appropriately cloudy, fruity, and refreshing. Brightened by subtle coriander and Curaçao orange peel.

CURIEUX
TRIPLE 11% ABV
Allagash Tripel ale aged in Jim Beam barrels. Orchard fruits and honey meet bourbon, vanilla, and wood.

PURE HOPPINESS
INDIA PALE ALE 8% ABV
A balance of German hops for spiciness and American northwest varieties for piney and citrus flavours.

MCILHENNEY'S IRISH RED
IRISH RED 6% ABV
Brewed with 11 malts, including rye. Complex aromas, with caramel and toffee emerging on the palate. A spicy, medium-dry finish.

LIBERTY ALE
PALE ALE 5.9% ABV
A benchmark American pale ale. Fruity and floral on the nose; crisp bitterness on the palate.

ANCHOR STEAM
STEAM BEER 4.9% ABV
A signature woody, minty nose. Well-rounded caramel flavours yield to a firm, crisp finish.

BREWERY

ANDERSON VALLEY

17700 Highway 253, Boonville, California 95415, USA
www.avbc.com

Set in Mendocino County's picturesque Anderson Valley, this solar-powered brewery mixes local and international styles and techniques. Some beer names are those of local landmarks, others are in Boontling, a regional dialect.

BREWING SECRET The copper brew kettles were rescued from a closed-down German brewery.

ANHEUSER-BUSCH

One Busch Place, St. Louis, Missouri 63118, USA
www.anheuser-busch.com

Anheuser-Busch, now part of AB InBev, brews half the beer sold in the USA, including Budweiser and Bud Light, two of the world's best-selling brands. With its Michelob line, seasonal specialities, and beers produced by its regional breweries for local consumers, the company has significantly broadened the range of its beers.

APPALACHIAN

50 North Cameron Street, Harrisburg, Pennsylvania 17101, USA
www.abcbrew.com

There's room in this cavernous facility, rich in bricks and timber, for the brewery, a restaurant, and a separate speciality beer bar. It took two years to restore the century-old building. Founded in Harrisburg in 1997, the Appalachian Brewing Company has six other brewpubs, at Camp Hill and Gettysberg.

ARCADIA

103 West Michigan Avenue, Battle Creek Michigan 49017, USA
www.arcadiaales.com

Using the British Peter Austin system more common in the Northeast, and brewing with British malts, Arcadia leans toward UK-inspired ales, but made with citrussy and piney Pacific Northwest hops. Ringwood yeast gives the beers a fresh character, and they work particularly well on cask.

BEER

HOP OTTIN' IPA

INDIA PALE ALE 7% ABV
Combination of citrus, grapefruit, and pine flavours underpinned by bold, rich malt and a hint of roses.

BARNEY FLATS OATMEAL STOUT

OATMEAL STOUT 5.8% ABV
Impression of coffee and cream, sweetness balanced by roasted grains, the complexity heightened by earthy undertones.

MICHELOB ORIGINAL LAGER

MALT LAGER 4.8% ABV
Returned to its all-malt roots in 2007. Delicate, with a spicy nose, clean malt middle, and crisp, dry finish.

STONE MILL ORGANIC PALE ALE

PALE ALE 5.5% ABV
Organic beer under the Green Valley Brewing label. This ale is lightly bready with an earthy hop character.

HINTERLAND

HEFE WEIZEN 5.3% ABV
Banana, orchard fruits, and bubble-gum aromas. Fresh, tart wheat on the tongue, and a light clove finish.

JOLLY SCOT SCOTTISH ALE

SCOTTISH ALE 5.9% ABV
A straightforward session beer. Hints of rich caramel, a touch of smokiness, and a final impression of sweetness.

LONDON-STYLE PORTER

PORTER 7% ABV
Rich on the nose, flavours of coffee beans, chocolate, and dark fruit, with a lingering, dessert-like finish.

LOCH DOWN SCOTCH ALE

SCOTTISH ALE 8.5% ABV
Nuttiness and piney hops don't totally balance here. The final impression is of sweet caramel.

AUGUST SCHELL

1860 Schell Road, New Ulm,
Minnesota 56073, USA
www.schellsbrewery.com

Family-owned since August Schell
founded it in 1860, this brewery has
perhaps the most beautiful setting in
the USA, with ornamental gardens and
a former carriage house converted
into a museum. In 2002, the company
took over production of the legendary
Grain Belt Premium beer, when that
brewery failed, to save a Minnesota
icon from extinction.

AVERY

5763 Arapahoe Avenue, Boulder,
Colorado 80803, USA
www.averybrewing.com

Located near the Rocky Mountains,
though in a nondescript industrial
park, this brewery has earned a
reputation for its hoppy beers
and its astonishingly strong beers
(sometimes they are both). These
include a threesome nicknamed
the "Demons of Ale", in which the
beers average 15 per cent ABV apiece.

BALLAST POINT

10051 Old Grove Road, San Diego,
California 92131, USA
www.ballastpoint.com

This brewery started in the back
of a homebrew shop, offering a
dizzying variety of beers, including
the hop-centric kinds for which
San Diego has become known.

BREWING SECRET Their kölsch has proved
so popular that a separate production
brewery has been built to keep up
with demand.

BAYERN

1507 Montana Street, Missoula,
Montana 59801, USA
www.bayernbrewery.com

Bayern Brewing focuses solely on
the beers of Bavaria, where owner-
brewer Jürgen Knöller was born. He
is a German diploma master brewer,
who started brewing when he was
16 and joined Bayern when it opened
in 1987, buying the brewery four
years later. Still true to its Germanic
traditions, today Bayern is a pioneer
of sustainability.

SCHELL'S BOCK
BOCK 6.1% ABV
Dark amber, it is a bold blend of
10 different malt and Noble hops.
Slowly fermented and conditioned,
it has a warming smoothness.

SCHMALTZ ALT
ALTBIER 5.1% ABV
Subtle combination of biscuit and
chocolate balanced by mild, slightly
spicy hop flavours and bitterness.

INDIA PALE ALE
INDIA PALE ALE 6.5% ABV
Piney, oily nose, with grapefruit
and orange from the aroma to the
palate. Unapologetically bitter.

SALVATION
BELGIAN GOLDEN ALE 9% ABV
Fleshy fruits, particularly apricots,
mingle with sweet, spicy aromas
and flavours, and a surprising
hint of honey.

PALE ALE
KÖLSCH 5.2% ABV
Soft and sweet on the nose with a
hint of spices. Dry cracker flavours
yield to a floral, but still dry finish.

SCULPIN IPA
INDIA PALE ALE 7% ABV
Clean, crisp bitterness overlaid
with some malt sweetness, which
counterbalances swirls of fruity
hop flavours.

BAYERN PILSENER
PILSNER 5% ABV
Intially flowery, with not-quite-sweet
malt flavours, quickly followed by a
hoppy bitterness.

BAYERN AMBER
VIENNA LAGER 5.4% ABV
Created when the brewery opened;
blending a rich Oktoberfest malt
profile with Czech Pilsner hops.

THE STORY OF...

Anheuser-Busch

One Busch Place, St. Louis, Missouri 63118, USA

Anheuser-Busch is a potent image of USA and it remains so even though the company was taken over by InBev in 2008.

In the 1850s St. Louis, in America's midwest, bustled with German immigrants who had fled revolution in Europe, bringing with them their language, culture, and a love of beer. By 1870, the city had 50 breweries. St. Louis is built over limestone caves; today most are sealed up but, at that time, they were natural cold stores, where beer could be kept and conditioned (lagered) until it was ready for sale. In 1852, George Schneider opened the Bavarian Brewery. Sadly, he wasn't much of a businessman and soon went bust, but this was the beginning of a company that today brews America's best-known beer brand, Budweiser.

The company had a couple more owners before Eberhard Anheuser acquired it in 1860. A German who had emigrated to America in 1843, he made his fortune by making and selling soap. But the brewery owed him money and he took shares in it to clear the debt. He believed he could make money from the beer suds. But it was the involvement of his son-in-law Adolphus Busch in 1864 that sparked the transformation from local brewery into national icon. The company was renamed the Anheuser-Busch Brewing Association in 1879 and, a year later, when Eberhard died, Adolphus became its president. The Busch family's connection with the company ended in 2011 when August Busch IV left the AB InBev board.

◄ A NATURAL SALESMAN The biggest asset that Adolphus Busch brought to the business was his exceptional skill as a salesman. He could have sold ice to the Eskimos and coals to Newcastle – instead, he sold beer to America. Adolphus became the merchant prince of the "king of beers".

▼ DRAY HORSES Anheuser-Busch InBev used shire horses for its beer deliveries in St. Louis in the early days, and the horses are still trotted out today on special occasions.

▲ COLD BEER AND FAST TRAINS It was a combination of railways, refrigeration, and pasteurization that meant the beers of St. Louis knew no frontiers. Refrigerated railcars saw beer, which might otherwise spoil in days, carried across the country. Over the Rockies to the West Coast, up to the wind-chilled shores of the Great Lakes, across to the hot, humid, burgeoning cities on the East Coast, bottled beer was guaranteed to keep fresh in any climate, thanks to pasteurization.

▼ THE ART OF ADVERTISING

It was the marriage of brewing and the new industry of advertising that proved the real key to capturing a mass market. From the use of the American eagle icon to the use of beautiful women in advertising campaigns, Adolphus Busch knew how to market beer. Over the course of 35 years, Adolphus grew a brewery with a production of 4,000 barrels per annum into one turning out more than one million barrels by 1901.

▼ AN AMERICAN SUCCCESS

It is hard to imagine the scale of Anheuser-Busch InBev, but, as befits a company that brews nearly one in every two beers drunk in America, it is huge. The new owners have retained its current brewery and offices in St. Louis, making it the North American headquarters for the combined company.

▲ BUDWEISER

It was in 1876 that Anheuser first sold a beer called Budweiser. It didn't catch on immediately, though; for a time the locals stuck faithfully with the company's now long-gone St. Louis Lager beer.

▶ MICHELOB

Another popular Anheuser-Busch brand name Michelob was first sold in 1896, with a tiny output aimed at "connoisseurs".

BREWERY

BEAR REPUBLIC

345 Healdsburg Avenue, Healdsburg,
California 95448, USA
www.bearrepublic.com

With a brewpub located amidst the
Sonoma County wine-tasting rooms
and a brewery north of town, Bear
Republic presents a decidedly different
break for wine tourists. Founding
brewmaster (and fireman and race-
car-driver) Richard Norgrove is just
as skilled as any wine blender when
merging hops flavour and aromas.

BELL'S

8938 Krum Avenue, Galesburg,
Michigan 49053, USA
www.bellsbeer.com

The oldest surviving microbrewery
east of Colorado, Bell's (formerly
Kalamazoo Brewing) has grown nearly
700-fold since its first sales in 1985.
Founder Larry Bell has earned
a reputation as something of a
maverick. In 2006, he withdrew
his beer from sale in Illinois, one
of the brewery's top markets, in
a distribution dispute. However,

in late 2007 he launched a range of
Kalamazoo (not Bell's) beers back
into the Chicago area. Bell's has
built a new brewing facility outside
Kalamazoo, but the original brewery
remains, along with its appropriately
named Eccentric Café. Bell's beers are
famous for their intensity, although
the brewery flagship is wheat-based.

BERKSHIRE

12 Rail Road Street South, Deerfield,
Massachusetts 01373, USA
www.berkshirebrewingcompany.com

Western Massachusetts's local brewery
(although its beers are increasingly easy
to find in Boston). Berkshire Brewing
Company (BBC) handles almost all its
own distribution, guaranteeing fresh
beer with a subtle, balanced complexity
that begins with open fermentation.

BREWING SECRET These pure, unfiltered
beers must be kept refrigerated.

BEER

RACER 5
INDIA PALE ALE 7% ABV
Delightfully fresh grapefruit and
thick piney aromas, built on a
resinous, malty-sweet middle.

HOP ROD RYE
IMPERIAL INDIA PALE ALE 8% ABV
Bright, citrussy nose with spicy
alcohols. A subtle blend of biscuit
and clean rye. Incessant hops.

EXPEDITION STOUT
IMPERIAL STOUT 10.5% ABV
Begins with an intense blast of dark
fruit (figs and plums) that turns into
chocolate, roasted coffee, and port.

BELL'S TWO-HEARTED ALE
INDIA PALE ALE 7% ABV
Amplified hops, with an initial rush
of grapefruit and orange mingling
with fresh floral notes. Perfectly
balanced, with persistent bitterness.

OBERON ALE
WHEAT BEER 5.8% ABV
A summer refresher. Zesty, with
orange rind in the aroma and a
delicate spiciness behind it; has
a crisp, sharp finish.

BEST BROWN ALE
BROWN ALE 5.8% ABV
Brimming with rich flavours such
as caramel and chocolate, subtly
balanced by rustic hops.

DRAYMAN'S PORTER
PORTER 6.2% ABV
Coffee-like aromas, a complex
middle (chocolate and toffee),
and a pleasantly bitter finish.

RASPBERRY STRONG ALE
FRUIT BEER 9% ABV
Brewed with fresh berries and
released for Valentine's Day.
Scarily nicknamed "Truth Serum".

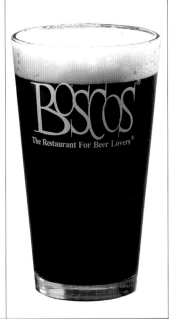

BIG SKY

5417 Trumpeter Way, Missoula,
Montana 59808, USA
www.bigskybrew.com

Three partners successfully combined
a quality ale with a clever name
(albeit one it had to defend in
lawsuits lodged by Canadian brewer
Moosehead) and an attractive label.
Big Sky has grown quickly into a
regional brewery selling beer from
Alaska to Minnesota, three-quarters
of it owing to their flagship brown ale.

BJ'S

Various locations
www.bjsbrewhouse.com

Founded in 1996, BJ's now operates
more than 130 restaurants in 17
states, each selling a wide range
of eight regular ales and lagers from
a delicate kölsch to full-bodied
imperial stout. The beers are either
brewed in its own pubs or contract
brewed elsewhere. Its beers regularly
win awards at the North American
Beer Awards.

BLUE POINT

161 River Avenue, Patchogue,
New York 11772, USA
www.bluepointbrewing.com

This microbrewery was founded
in 1998 in a former ice factory. Its
draught beer, brewed here, is on tap
across Long Island and in Manhattan;
its bottled beer is now outsourced.

BREWING SECRET Blue Point's draught
beer is brewed in a direct-fire kettle
that comes from Marylands' former
Wild Goose Brewery.

BOSCOS

Various locations
www.boscosbeer.com

Since 1992, this brewpub chain has
been a leader in promoting greater
knowledge of beer in the mid-south.
Its pubs feature English-inspired
cask-conditioned ales, with customers
invited to participate as cellarmen.

BREWING SECRET Flaming Stone's
brewing process involves red-hot
chunks of granite being plunged into
the wort to caramelize the sugars.

MOOSE DROOL

BROWN ALE 5.1% ABV
Dark fruits and nuts mingle with
chocolate; sweetness moderated by
earthy hop notes. Chocolate-brown
with a medium body.

SCAPEGOAT PALE ALE

PALE ALE 5% ABV
Biscuity, fruity, and spicy on the
palate, balanced by moderate
bitterness. Short, but dry finish.

JEREMIAH RED®

IRISH-STYLE ALE 7.3% ABV
A cross between an Irish red and an
English strong ale, with rich, clean
caramel-toffee malt. Dry finish.

HARVEST HEFEWEIZEN®

HEFEWEIZEN 4.9% ABV
Genuinely Bavarian, cloudy, with
substantial banana notes on the
nose. Fruity on the palate.

TOASTED LAGER

VIENNA LAGER 5.5% ABV
The direct-fire kettling produces
toasted-nut aromas and flavours.
A firm, medium-dry finish.

EXTRA SPECIAL BITTER

EXTRA SPECIAL BITTER 5% ABV
Full bodied, rich caramel flavours
balanced by earthy British hops.
Best on cask at the brewery.

FAMOUS FLAMING STONE BEER

STEINBEER 4.8% ABV
Brewed in the manner of German
stein beers. Caramel, toffee, and
nuts throughout. Smoky, dry finish.

HEFEWEIZEN

HEFEWEIZEN 4.8% ABV
Classic bubble-gum and banana
nose; softer fruity (more banana)
and creamy flavours, with underlying
spices including light clove notes.

BREWERY

BOULDER

2880 Wilderness Place, Boulder,
Colorado 80301, USA
www.boulderbeer.com

The first US microbrewery outside
of California, Boulder has been
something of a poster child for the
"movement" because its partners
began brewing in a goat shed and
it relied on the largesse of domestic
giant Coors to acquire ingredients.
Boulder Beer is available in much
of the US, and emphasizes its
Colorado roots.

BOULEVARD

2501 Southwest Boulevard, Kansas City,
Missouri 64108, USA
www.boulevard.com

Boulevard is all about midwestern
hospitality, starting with friendly tours
of its smokestack-topped brewery,
and including a range of beers well-
suited to Heartland dining such as
Kansas City's famous barbecue.

BREWING SECRET The brewery's
Smokestack Series is a range of
Champagne-bottle-conditioned beers.

BOUNDARY BAY

1107 Railroad Avenue, Bellingham,
Washington 98225, USA
www.bbaybrewery.com

Three brewpubs opened in this town
on Bellingham Bay during the beer
boom of the 1990s. Boundary Bay
is the survivor, and has become
one of the nation's most productive
brewpubs. Further expansion, both
in production and in distribution,
is planned. At the brewhouse, a new
cask is tapped every Thursday at 4pm.

BRECKENRIDGE

471 Kalamath Street, Denver,
Colorado 80204, USA
www.breckbrew.com

Breckenridge Brewery was founded in
the famed ski-resort of Breckenridge.
The brewery was so successful, it
eventually expanded to Denver,
opening a new brewery and attached
brewpub. Both locations still operate
successfully today, brewing a wide
portfolio of beers.

BEER

PLANET PORTER
PORTER 5.5% ABV
The brewery's original beer. Dark
fruit aromas and flavours. Subdued
roasted malts and bitterness.

HAZED & INFUSED
PALE ALE 5% ABV
As hazy as promised – hops in
suspension – supported by a bouquet
of citrus, flowers, and spices.

UNFILTERED WHEAT
AMERICAN WHEAT BEER 4.4% ABV
A remedy for Missouri humidity,
cloudy and lightly grainy, with
refreshing citrus throughout.

BULLY! PORTER
PORTER 6% ABV
Roasted coffee on the nose, with
chocolate emerging on the palate.
Slightly sweet, rich, with subtle,
balancing hop flavours and finish.

IPA
INDIA PALE ALE 6.4% ABV
Rich with Northwest hop
flavours and aromas – orange,
and grapefruit. Malt sweetness
yields to resiny, bitter finish.

IMPERIAL IPA
IMPERIAL INDIA PALE ALE 9% ABV
Thick with rich malts and hops.
A blast of oranges, grapefruit, and
pineapple, and a long, bitter finish.

AVALANCHE ALE
AMBER-STYLE ALE 4.4% ABV
Flagship ale. Fruity and tart, but
balanced with sweetness, including
caramel and honey, on the palate.

OATMEAL STOUT
OATMEAL STOUT 4.95% ABV
Rich with roasted chocolate and
a very creamy texture. Complex,
hints of smoke, pleasingly bitter
at the end.

eightmillion years of beer

BREWER'S ART

1106 North Charles Street, Baltimore, Maryland 21201, USA
www.thebrewersart.com

Housed in a grand 1902 townhouse in the Mount Vernon area, The Brewer's Art serves Belgian-inspired house beers and an outstanding selection of continental (primarily Belgian) beers in a comfortable dining atmosphere. It recently began brewing and bottling some of its beer under contract in Pennsylvania.

BRIDGEPORT

1313 Northwest Marshall Street, Portland, Oregon 97209, USA
www.bridgeportbrew.com

BridgePort Brewing holds the trademark of Oregon's Oldest Craft Brewery, and its India Pale Ale has come to define northwestern US beer character. Now owned by Belgian brewer Gambrinus, it operates independently.

BRISTOL

1604 South Cascade Avenue, Colorado Springs, Colorado 80905, USA
www.bristolbrewing.com

Since opening in 1994, Bristol Brewing has been the beer hub in Colorado Springs, as others have come and gone. It ventured into experimenting with barrels ahead of many USA breweries.

BREWING SECRET It has won awards with a beer made using wild yeast and lactic acid bacteria from raspberries picked somewhere near Cheyenne Canyon.

BROOKLYN

1 Brewers Row, 79 North 11th Street, Brooklyn, New York 11249, USA
www.brooklynbrewery.com

While Brooklyn Brewery pays homage to New York's rich brewing history, it is very much a 21st-century business, and occupies New York's first commercial building to derive all of its electricity from wind power. The brewery's bottled beers are made under contract in upstate New York. (Continues overleaf)

GREEN PEPPERCORN TRIPEL
TRIPLE 9% ABV
Effervescent and full of life. Fruity and spicy, a bit of candy sweetness, subdued pepper and a dryish finish.

RESURRECTION
DOUBLE 7% ABV
Caramel, dark fruits on the palate, and surprising citrus notes. The yeast in the first batch "died" and was "resurrected", hence the name.

BRIDGEPORT INDIA PALE ALE
INDIA PALE ALE 5.5% ABV
Citrussy from the outset. Solid malt backbone, delicate fruits (peaches and apples). Complex hoppy finish.

WITCH HUNT
ALE 5.8% ABV
A spicy, seasonal harvest ale; bold hop notes mingle with subtle notes of cinnamon and nutmeg.

LAUGHING LAB
SCOTTISH ALE 5% ABV
Medium bodied, with sweet notes of caramel and toffee and a lingering impression of smoke. Best on tap.

WINTER WARLOCK
OATMEAL STOUT 6% ABV
Toasted marshmallows and chocolate up front, creamy chocolate and roasted flavours on the palate.

LAGER
AMBER LAGER 5.2% ABV
With a floral nose, this beer is spicy with citrus notes. Solidly bitter without being harsh.

BROWN
BROWN ALE 5.6% ABV
Caramel, chocolate, and ripe plums throughout, with minerally undertones and a hint of smoke. A coffee-dry finish.

BREWERY

(*Continued*) Brewmaster and well-respected industry spokesperson Garrett Oliver regularly produces seasonals and a reserve series at the brewery, sold on draught throughout the region.

BREWING SECRET The brewery has installed a bottling line for 750ml (1¼ pints) Champagne-style corked bottles, creating a line of Belgian-inspired ales.

BUTTE CREEK
1601 Airport Road, Ukiah, California 95482, USA
www.buttecreek.com

Founded in 1996, this brewery was inspired by a neighbouring organic winery to make organic beers. In 2010, the brewery was bought by Mendocino Brewing, who continue its support of organic farming and sustainability. Its beers are the official beers of Planet Earth.

CALDERA
590 Clover Lane, Ashland, Oregon 97520, USA
www.calderabrewing.com

Although it has been around since 1997, Caldera has enjoyed increased visibility and distribution since 2005, when it became the first microbrewery in Oregon to install a small-run line for its distinctively packaged canned beers.

BREWING SECRET Caldera sets itself apart by continuing to use whole hop flowers in all its beers.

CAMBRIDGE
One Kendall Square, Cambridge, Massachusetts 02139, USA
www.cambrew.com

At the Cambridge restaurant, beer and food form a perfect partnership. Since opening in 1989, Cambridge has consistently offered beers on tap that are outside the ordinary – perhaps aged in wood in the cellar, spiced with flowers from the garden, or made with organic pumpkins that the brewers chop up themselves.

BEER

BLACK CHOCOLATE STOUT
IMPERIAL STOUT 10% ABV
Pitch black, with a viscous mixture of dark fruits, port, and, of course, bitter chocolate.

LOCAL 1
BELGIAN STRONG GOLDEN ALE 9% ABV
An explosion of aromas and flavours of fruits and spices, and a complex texture, all brought together with a chalky-dry finish.

ORGANIC PORTER
PORTER 6% ABV
Tastes as rich as it looks, with roasted malts balancing chocolate and liquorice flavours.

ORGANIC PILSNER
PILSNER 4.5% ABV
Light and crisp, with a hint of citrus hops, it has a smooth, dry, malt finish. A great American take on a pilsner.

IPA
INDIA PALE ALE 6.1% ABV
Makes a large hop impression without being heavy-handed. Citrus, pine, and grapefruit flavours from start to finish.

PILSENER BIER
PILSNER 5.2% ABV
Gets eight full weeks of lagering. Floral aroma, with just an initial hint of sulphur, with a crisp, hoppy flavour and finish.

TALL TALE PALE ALE
PALE ALE 5.7% ABV
An aromatic blast of Northwest hops. Pine and grapefruit flavours on a solid malt foundation.

CERISE CASSÉE
AMERICAN SOUR ALE 9% ABV
"Broken cherry" begins with a sour mash, aged up to nine years in oak barrels. A complex blend of sweet and sour, oak and cherries.

CAPITAL

7734 Terrace Avenue, Middleton, Wisconsin 53562, USA
www.capital-brewery.com

Capital Brewery is known for its excellent German-inspired beers – brewed in copper kettles sourced from a defunct German brewery – though some are made with a twist. Autumnal Fire, for instance, is a cross between a doppelbock and an Oktoberfest.

BREWING SECRET Island Wheat's grain is grown on an island in Lake Michigan.

CAPTAIN LAWRENCE

444 Saw Mill River Road, Elmsford, New York 10523, USA
www.captainlawrencebrewing.com

Brewmaster-owner Scott Vaccaro represents the newest generation of American brewers, with a formal education in brewing science, then on-the-job training in the USA and England. Back in his home state, he founded this brewery with the support of his family. He is at the forefront in experimention with barrel ageing.

The company's Barrel Select series, in which beer is stored in oak barrels previously used for storing bourbon, apple brandy, and rum, is much sought after.

DESCHUTES

901 Southwest Simpson Avenue, Bend, Oregon 97702, USA
www.deschutesbrewery.com

What began as a brewpub in 1988 in this outdoor-vacation town quickly expanded with a separate production facility that's grown into one of the nation's largest craft breweries. As well as selling a full line of beers with notable hop character throughout the western USA, Deschutes still operates its original brewpub in downtown Bend. (Continues on p30)

CAPITAL DARK
DUNKEL 5.4% ABV
Malt-accented, with early hints of caramel and nuts. It builds richness with its chocolate-toffee notes.

CAPITAL PILSNER
PILSNER 4.7% ABV
Light on the palate with a note of honey. Lovely floral hop aromas and a sturdy hop finish.

XTRA GOLD
AMERICAN TRIPEL ALE 10% ABV
Citrus notes from Northwest hops blend seamlessly with juicy orchard fruits and a bit of candy sweetness.

CAPTAIN'S KÖLSCH
KÖLSCH 5% ABV
Low in hoppy bitterness, this refresher is full of biscuit malt flavours.

SMOKED PORTER
PORTER 6% ABV
Smoky to start, but rich dark fruits, chocolate, and liquorice quickly emerge. Luscious palate.

BROWN BIRD ALE
BROWN ALE 5% ABV
American hops marry German hops to make a full-bodied, easy-drinking beer.

MIRROR POND PALE ALE
PALE ALE 5% ABV
Grapefruit and fresh flowers at the outset. Light, clean biscuit on the palate, with generous hop flavour.

BLACK BUTTE PORTER
PORTER 5.2% ABV
Well balanced and complex, aromas and flavours blend roasted coffee beans, chocolate, and dark fruit with signature acidic notes.

THE STORY OF...

Brooklyn Brewery

79 North 11th Street, Brooklyn, New York 11249, USA

New York was once a vibrant brewing city. Before Prohibition there were around 78 breweries here, nearly 50 of which were in Brooklyn, with its large German community. One area of Brooklyn was known as "Brewers' Row".

All that seemed gone forever when, in 1976, the Schaefer and Liebmann families closed their Brooklyn breweries, the last in the city. They were unable to compete with the rise of light American lagers produced in the midwest. "What made Milwaukee famous" had put an end to brewing in the Big Apple.

In 1984, journalist Steve Hindy returned from a six-year stint in the Middle East. He had learned much on his travels, including how to home-brew beer in Islamic countries where alcohol was not available to buy. He wanted to develop his passion for brewing great beer so, together with his neighbour, former banker Tom Potter, he set up the Brooklyn Brewery in 1987. His craft beers have since become some of the best-selling draught beers in New York City.

▲ **BROOKLYN LAGER** The original brewmaster was Bill Moeller, who developed his recipe for Brooklyn Lager from the notebooks left to him by his grandfather, who was a brewer in Brooklyn at the turn of the 20th century.

▶ **THE WILLIAMSBURG PLANT** The first Brooklyn brews were produced for them by the Matt Brewery in Utica, and it wasn't until 1996 that Brooklyn had its very own brewery.

Brooklyn LAGER 5.1% ABV
Brooklyn PILSNER
BROOKLYN BREWERY
Brooklyn BROWN ALE 5.5% ABV
Brooklyn WEISSE
Brooklyn PENNANT ALE 5.0%
Brooklyn SUMMER AL
BREWMASTER RESERVE
Brooklyn HELLES 5.0%
Brooklyn BLAST! 8.

▼ A GROWING MARKET Led by companies such as the Brooklyn Brewery, the USA has the most vibrant beer culture in the world, and good beer is an affordable luxury. While Brooklyn cannot match the advertising and marketing spend of its bigger competitors, the beers are sold well beyond New York's five boroughs. Today, Brooklyn sells beers in 25 states and 20 countries, exporting more than any other USA craft brewer.

◄ EXPANDING HORIZONS
At the outset, the company's philosophy was quite simple. Hindy wanted a full-bodied, full-flavoured beer reminiscent of those that he believed were made in New York's glory days of brewing. Today, there are no boundaries to what beer styles it brews. And it continues to expand – in 2013, it embarked upon an overseas venture, entering a partnership with Carlsberg Sweden to build a waterfront brewery in Stockholm, Norway.

◄ STEVE HINDY In 1994, co-founder Steve Hindy was joined by Garrett Oliver, former brewmaster at the Manhattan Brewery. By the time he joined Brooklyn, Garrett had already developed a reputation for his own interpretations of traditional beer styles, and for his writing and lecturing on beer. Within two years of arriving at Brooklyn, he had opened the company's very own brewery.

BREWERY TOURS
SATURDAYS 12–5PM
COMPANY STORE OPEN
DURING TOUR HOURS
FOR INFORMATION ABOUT
SPECIAL EVENTS CALL
718 486-7422
OR LOOK AT
brooklynbrewery.com
FRIDAY TASTING
PANEL 6– PM

KELLER HELLES

BROOKLYNER
SCHNEIDER
HOPFEN WEISSE
LOT #1148

▲ BEER AND FOOD The ambition of brewmaster Garrett Oliver is for every restaurant to offer a beer list as well as one for wine, in order for people to discover for themselves that beer is an honourable companion to even the finest food.

BREWERY

(*Continued from p27*) It recently opened another brewpub in Portland. A Bond Street Series of special beer releases, developed "at the pub", has further widened the brewery's portfolio.

BREWING SECRET Deschutes maintains that the character of its beer is due in part to its use of whole hop flowers.

DIAMOND KNOT

621 Front Street, Mukilteo, Washington 98275, USA
www.diamondknot.com

Diamond Knot Brewing has grown substantially since founders Bob Maphet and Brian Sollenberger, two Boeing employees, milled grain at home and hauled it to their brewery tucked in the back of a local bar. They've since bought the alehouse and opened a separate production brewery. The menu features Stonegrill™ cooking.

DIXIE

861 Southpark Drive, Suite 400 Littleton, Colorado 80120, USA
www.paulanerhpusa.com/dixie

For more than a century, Dixie beer has survived everything from Prohibition to bankruptcy. Although the brewery was destroyed in the aftermath of Hurricane Katrina in 2005, the brand perseveres. Its beers are brewed at Minhaus, Wisconsin, but the owners say they want to bring them back to New Orleans, even though there are plans to build a hospital on its original site.

DOGFISH HEAD

6 Cannery Village Center, Milton, Delaware 19968, USA
www.dogfish.com

Brewing in the spirit of founder Sam Calagione's slogan: "Off-centered ales for off-centered people", Dogfish Head has found a national audience for its "extreme beers". These have included ales developed using research from archaeologists; recipes featuring unusual ingredients, from chicory to chillies; and beers that simply have more of everything.

BEER

THE ABYSS
IMPERIAL STOUT 11% ABV
Brewed with liquorice and molasses, and partially aged in oak barrels. A cornucopia of intense flavours, held together by wonderful texture.

INVERSION IPA
INDIA PALE ALE 6.8% ABV
A swirl of hop aromas (particularly orange zest). Solid, biscuity malt holds its own against bracing bitterness.

INDIA PALE ALE
INDIA PALE ALE 6.2% ABV
Opens with a blast of hops, grapefruit, and pine that lasts through a long, juicy, not-too-bitter finish.

STEAMER GLIDE STOUT
STOUT 4.8% ABV
Careful blends throughout – coffee, cocoa, and bittersweet chocolate offset by sweetness. Irish inspired, with a rich creamy head.

BLACKENED VOODOO
SCHWARZBIER 5% ABV
In 1991, this dark lager was briefly banned in Texas because of the voodoo references on its label. Smooth and light bodied for southern drinking, with chocolate and toffee notes throughout.

MIDAS TOUCH
HISTORIC BEER 9% ABV
White Muscat grapes, honey, and saffron create layers of flavour, melded with subtle acidity.

WORLD WIDE STOUT
IMPERIAL STOUT 15–20% ABV
Not a classic rendition, but much, much stronger. Port like, with dark fruits, ripe berries, and a massive dose of alcohol.

The brewery recently installed the largest wooden brewing vessels built in America since before Prohibition. Calagione is a tireless promoter, and author of three books, including one in which he and his sommelier co-author debate the merits of beer versus wine. Dogfish still operates a brewpub in Rehoboth Beach, where Calagione started in 1995.

BREWING SECRET Pangaea ale blends ingredients from every continent, including water from Antarctica.

DRAKE'S
1933 Davis Street, Building 177, San Leandro, California 94577, USA
www.drinkdrakes.com

Operating in San Leandro, California since 1989, Drake's original owner Roger Lind, conceived it as a hands-on brewery, something it remains today, even though it has different owners. True to the style of the region, the beers feature large doses of aromatic and tongue-tingling unapologetic American hops.

DUCK-RABBIT
4519 West Pine Street, Farmville, North Carolina 27828, USA
www.duckrabbitbrewery.com

Known for darkly intense beers, this is one of several small breweries that have thrived since North Carolina changed its law to allow beer stronger than 6% ABV. Duck-Rabbit's distinctive logo is based on an illustration by philosopher Ludwig Wittgenstein.

BREWING SECRET These quirky brewers say "we sing softly to the yeast".

EEL RIVER
1777 Alamar Way, Fortuna, California 95540, USA
www.eelriverbrewing.com

Eel River had been around for less than five years when, in 2000, it became the first certified organic brewery in the USA. The brewpub added a production brewery in nearby Scotia in 2007, moving into an abandoned mill. The new brewery is 100 per cent powered by biomass – that is, mill waste, such as wood chippings, and spent grain from brewing.

60 MINUTE IPA
INDIA PALE ALE 6% ABV
Flagship session beer brewed with Warrior, Amarillo, and "Mystery Hop X"; brimming with citrus flavours.

FESTINA PECH
SOUR ALE 4.5% ABV
Labelled a "neo-Berliner Weisse" and fermented with peaches. Fruity sweetness is nicely balanced by tart wheat and slightly sour elements.

HOPOCALYPSE IPA
INDIA PALE ALE 9.3% ABV
A journey into the world of hops. Masses of hops soar out of this bready, malted beer.

EXXPEDITION
AMBER ALE 8% ABV
Hard to find, but worth the effort, the lingering hop bitterness is balanced by chocolate sweetness.

BALTIC PORTER
BALTIC PORTER 9% ABV
Perfect blend of caramel, toffee, blackcurrants, and other dark fruits. Smooth, with restrained bitterness.

MILK STOUT
STOUT 5.7% ABV
A well-integrated combination of roasted coffee beans and chocolate, held together by a creamy palate. Sweet, but not too sweet.

TRIPLE EXULTATION
OLD ALE 9.7% ABV
A complex nose of rich caramel-toffee and fruit, then piney hops assert themselves.

ORGANIC PORTER
PORTER 5.8% ABV
Malty and creamy with chocolate aromas and flavours, and lesser notes of roast coffee beans. Robust.

BREWERY

ELYSIAN

1221 East Pike Street, Seattle,
Washington 98122, USA
www.elysianbrewing.com

Elysian Brewing has four locations in Seattle, with the production facility and a restaurant at the original brewery in the Capitol Hill district. Writer-turned-brewmaster Dick Cantwell keeps an exceptionally wide range of beers available, including a seasonal pumpkin ale that provides an excuse to host a popular autumn festival.

FIRESTONE WALKER

1400 Ramada Drive, Paso Robles,
California 93446, USA
www.firestonebeer.com

In rolling out its new Union Jack IPA at the start of 2008, Firestone Walker Brewing Company intensified its focus on pale ales. Each one includes a portion of beer fermented in the patented Firestone Union barrel system, which takes inspiration from the historic Burton Union method that originated in Burton upon Trent, England.

Firestone also blends wood-fermented beer with beer from stainless steel to fashion each of its ales. To celebrate recent anniversaries, the brewers created several strong ales aged in a variety of bourbon, brandy, and untreated oak barrels, then blended them into a single release, using input from regional winemakers.

FISH

515 Jefferson Street Southeast, Olympia,
Washington 98501, USA
www.fishbrewing.com

Close to bankruptcy in 2000, Fish Brewing has redoubled its efforts in recent years on the core range of Fish Tale Organic beers (a portion of the profits from beers in this line goes for protecting aquatic habitats). It has since grown into a regional force, and also now produces German-inspired beer under the Leavenworth label.

BEER

DRAGONSTOOTH STOUT
STOUT 7.5% ABV
Dark fruit, chocolate, molasses, bitter coffee, and liquorice aromas and flavours abound and resonate.

PERSEUS PORTER
PORTER 5.4% ABV
Cocoa and roasted nut flavours, and just-right bitterness. Like toasting marshmallows by the campfire.

DOUBLE BARREL ALE
PALE ALE 5% ABV
Contains 15–20 per cent oaked beer. Spicy, rounded fermentation-based fruit, vanilla, and a woody, rich-but-not-sweet, texture.

PALE 31
CALIFORNIA PALE ALE 4.9% ABV
About 3 per cent oaked beer. Bright and citrussy aromas, with layers of fruit and malt on the palate.

VELVET MERLIN
OATMEAL STOUT 5.5% ABV
Rich, textured, and a touch oily. Pours black. Sweet chocolate notes balance roasted coffee flavour.

UNION JACK IPA
INDIA PALE ALE 7.5% ABV
Juicy hops arrive in waves of citrus, grapefruit, pine, and mangoes, complementing a solid malt base. Oak and bitterness work in tandem.

ORGANIC INDIA PALE ALE
INDIA PALE ALE 6.7% ABV
Fresh taste of Northwest hops; piney and citrussy. Crisply rich, with hops lingering beyond a bitter finish.

MUDSHARK PORTER
PORTER 5% ABV
Full of chocolate notes, it resonates with smooth, dark, and bittersweet cocoa. Its assertiveness is tempered by a late addition of hops.

Brooklyn Brewery has developed a wide range of beers, many of which are inspired by traditional Belgian, German, and British styles.

BREWERY

FLOSSMOOR STATION

1035 Sterling Avenue, Flossmoor,
Illinois 60422, USA
www.flossmoorstation.com

Brewers Matt Van Wyk and Andrew
Mason have expanded on what
barrel-ageing pioneer Todd Ashman
started at Flossmoor Station
Brewing. They offer a wide range
of award-winning beers in a pub
housed in a former railway station.
The brewery's range of wood-aged
beers is proving very popular.

FLYING DOG

4607 Wedgewood Boulevard,
Frederick, Maryland 21703, USA
www.flyingdogales.com

With labels by British illustrator Ralph
Steadman, and the "gonzo" spirit of
the late Hunter S. Thompson (both
friends of founder George Stranahan),
Flying Dog is not your average
brewery. The original brewpub
was founded in Aspen but is now
headquartered in Denver, while the
company moved brewing operations
to Frederick in Maryland in 2008.

FLYING FISH

900 Kennedy Boulevard, Somerdale,
New Jersey 08083, USA
www.flyingfish.com

Flying Fish Brewing began worldwide
and then went local. It started out
as a "virtual brewery" on the Internet
before establishing itself as a distinctly
regional brewery in 1996, now serving
a 160-km (100-mile) radius around
its South Jersey home. The brewery
recently increased capacity, with plans
to widen the range of beers on offer.

FOOTHILLS

638 West Fourth Street, Winston-Salem,
North Carolina 27101, USA
www.foothillsbrewing.com

One brewery, three different brands
– Foothills, Cottonwood, and
Carolina. The company believes its
beers should be drunk in its brewpubs
as fresh as possible. The brewer
Jamie Bartholomaus has a preference
for stronger seasonal beers.

BREWING SECRET Draught brews are
served straight from the tank.

BEER

PULLMAN BROWN ALE

BROWN ALE 6% ABV
Brewed with hand-toasted malts
and molasses. A full-bodied blend
of chocolate, toffee, and dark fruit.

DE WILDE ZUIDENTREIN

SOUR ALE 7% ABV
A Flanders brown ale aged in an
oak wine barrel on fresh raspberries
for a year, dosed with wild yeasts.

SNAKE DOG IPA

INDIA PALE ALE 7.1% ABV
Bright amber in the glass, the
white head lingers. There is malt
sweetness in the mouth, although
the balance is towards hops.

GONZO IMPERIAL PORTER

PORTER 9.2% ABV
Rummy, chocolatey, and almost
sweet before dry cocoa flavours
and solid hop bitterness kick in.

BELGIAN ABBEY DUBBEL

DOUBLE 7.2% ABV
Chocolate mingled with dark fruit,
and a pleasant whiff of alcohol.
Finishes on the sweet side of dry.

ESB ALE

EXTRA SPECIAL BITTER 5.9% ABV
Malt-accented, rich with caramel
and fruit character, and with an
underlying nuttiness. Hops are
American, but restrained.

HOPPYUM IPA

INDIA PALE ALE 6.2% ABV
Whole Simcoe hops add swirls of
pungent citrus notes. The finish is
dry, crisp, and long.

CAROLINA BLONDE

CREAM ALE 4.75% ABV
A clean, refreshing beer brewed with
American barley and a hint of wheat.
Noble hops provide a subtle nose.

FOUNDERS

235 Grandville Avenue South West,
Grand Rapids, Michigan 49503, USA
www.foundersbrewing.com

Founders was just another small
brewery until it jettisoned much of
its portfolio for a more esoteric range
of craft beers with names like Devil
Dancer and Old Curmudgeon.

BREWING SECRET Its Kentucky Breakfast
Stout is brewed with coffee and
vanilla, and aged in bourbon barrels
in mines 30m (100ft) underground.

FOUR PEAKS

1340 East 8th Street, Tempe,
Arizona 85281, USA
www.fourpeaks.com

Little surprise that UK-inspired beers
make up a good proportion of the
many award winners here. A retired
brewer from Young's in London helped
fledgling brewmaster Andy Ingram
when Four Peaks opened in 1996.
Later, Paul Farnsworth, who began
working in the breweries of Burton
upon Trent when he was 16 years old,
consulted on quality control.

FULL SAIL

506 Columbia Street, Hood River,
Oregon 97031, USA
www.fullsailbrewing.com

Full Sail represents much that is new
in American brewing. Founded in
1987, it became employee-owned
in 1999, and its beers reflect an
independent nature. Executive
brewmaster Jamie Emmerson has
overseen the brewery's productions
for 26 years and among his most
popular brews are Full Sail Amber,
IPA, Limited Lager Series, Pub Ale

Series, Session Premium, Session
Black, and Session Fest lager. The
brewery is committed to sustainable
practices and its award-winning
brews are available in 31 states.

BREWING SECRET The farmers of the
Northwest supply the brewery
with the ingredients for its beers;
99 per cent of its ingredients come
from local sources.

BREAKFAST STOUT

IMPERIAL STOUT 8.3% ABV
Espresso coffee dominates, with
complex dark chocolate notes
and a rich texture on the tongue.

PORTER

PORTER 6.5% ABV
An almost chewy texture, with
burnt caramel and chocolate
sweetness offset by solid bitterness.

KILT LIFTER

SCOTTISH ALE 6% ABV
Richly malty, with caramel emerging
on the palate. Complex, with just
a hint of smokiness.

8TH STREET ALE

BEST BITTER 4.7% ABV
Particularly mellow on cask, with
caramel and light fruitiness matched
with earthy hops, giving way to a
medium-bitter finish.

AMBER

AMBER ALE 6% ABV
Citrus and spice, quickly balanced
by underlying sweetness. Seamless
through to a clean finish.

SESSION LAGER

PREMIUM LAGER 5.1% ABV
Designed as a throwback to beer
produced before Prohibition, with
appropriately retro packaging. Clean
and malt-accented.

FULL SAIL IMPERIAL
STOUT BOURBON

BARREL-AGED STOUT 9.6% ABV
Ageing for a year in Kentucky
bourbon casks from Maker's Mark,
Four Roses, Jim Beam releases
hints of vanilla and allows the beer
to pick up flavours of oak and
bourbon. Will cellar well for years.

ALL ABOUT...
TASTING

Beer is best drunk in the company of others, whether in a pub or beer café. Take this sense of conviviality further and invite friends to a tasting session – a joyful celebration of the best of John Barleycorn.

Tasting beer involves all the senses. After all, beer has a rich variety of colours, flavours, and aromas. There are few rules, but think about the beers that you are sampling. Either choose a variety of styles, showcasing the diversity of beer, or serve different variations on a theme – a selection of American IPAs, for example, Czech pilsners perhaps, or British bitters. Whichever course you choose, begin with the most delicate beers and end with the most intensely flavoured or strongest beers. Try keeping between 6–10 beers, too many and the palate becomes dulled.

Use large wine or brandy glasses for beer tasting if you can – the shape of these helps to concentrate aromas. Also arrange for water and crackers, or plain salted crisps, which help to dry the palate between beers.

Then, enjoy!

1 POURING Use a clean tasting glass for each beer. Hold the glass at an angle of about 45 degrees at first, straightening it towards the end of the pour to let the beer acquire a head.

3 AROMA Swirl the beer in the glass to help release the aromas. Malty aromas include cereal, dried fruit, coffee beans, biscuit, Ovaltine, chocolate, toffee, and caramel. Hops produce fruity, fragrant, perfumy, spicy, resiny, peppery, citrussy, herbal, and floral notes. Yeast esters add their own character to stronger beers, with rich fruity notes redolent of tropical fruit, bananas, and ripe apricot skin. Lambic and gueuze have powerfully earthy, sweet-and-sour aromas, thanks to the presence of wild yeast.

2 APPEARANCE Look at the beer. It should have a clarity and sparkle to it. Judge the colour and condition: does it dance and shimmer in the glass? A tired beer lacks life and actually looks dull. As you drink the beer, a lacework-like trace of foam should be left adhering to the side of the glass – again, a sign of good condition.

4 FLAVOUR Taste the beer. In our mouths are an array of sensitive taste buds; these can detect salt, sweet, bitter, sour, and umami. Some beers come bearing lots of fruity gifts, while others – especially dark porters and stouts – produce roast, coffee, caramel, and chocolate flavours. Let the beer roll about the tongue, and work out the order of flavours. How does the beer feel in the mouth: smooth, thin, grainy, acidic (lambics again), oily, or chewy. A great beer is about balance and harmony. The malt and hops should be working with each other. Wine tasters always spit, but beer needs to be swallowed for the finish to be noted. Is it bitter? That's the hops. Dry? That's often the effect of the malt. It might be a long, lingering finish, or it might be short and abrupt.

5 TASTING NOTES Make notes on the beer's key aspects – appearance, aroma, taste, and finish – as you go along. On pages 340–345, you'll find charts for starting your own tasting notes.

BREWERY

GEARY'S

38 Evergreen Drive, Portland, Maine 04103, USA
www.gearybrewing.com

David Geary has followed a traditional English model since the brewery sold its first beer in 1986, focusing on a core range of beers (originally just two) and serving the New England region. Geary's still makes only seven regular and three seasonal beers.

BREWING SECRET Geary's uses yeast from Ringwood Brewery in the UK.

GENESEE

25 Cataract Street, Rochester, New York 14605, USA
www.geneseebeer.com

Genesee is still brewing old-style beers on the site where they have been made since 1878. It also makes the J.W. Dundee family of beers for the traditional ale market.

BREWING SECRET Genesee is one of the largest and oldest continuously operating breweries in the USA.

GEORGETOWN

5200 Denver Avenue South, Seattle, Washington 98108, USA
www.georgetownbeer.com

Co-founder salesman Manny Chao was the brewery's first employee at Mac & Jack's Brewery in Redmond and he was very good at this job. Georgetown, which sells only draught beer, initially focused on just one, Manny's Pale Ale. The brewery is one of many artisan businesses in the former Seattle Brewing and Malting plant, where the iconic Rainier brand was formerly brewed.

GOOSE ISLAND

1800 West Fulton Street, Chicago, Illinois 60612, USA
www.gooseisland.com

This brewery's extensive range of beers reflects the MBA (Master of Beer Appreciation) programme that it established shortly after opening as a brewpub in 1988. When Goose Island built its production brewery in 1995, brewmaster Greg Hall would launch dozens of styles during the course of a year. Goose Island still operates the original pub on

BEER

HAMPSHIRE ALE
STRONG ALE 7% ABV
Complex balance of slightly burnt caramel, light fruits, and warming alcohol. Traditional bitter finish.

PALE ALE
PALE ALE 4.5% ABV
A showcase for Ringwood yeast, fruity with some underlying caramel, just a bit slick over the tongue.

DUNDEE INDIA PALE ALE
INDIA PALE ALE 6.3% ABV
A seasonal summer beer. Relatively sweet caramel character, with more bitterness than flavour from its hops. Crisp finish.

GENESEE CREAM ALE
CREAM ALE 5.2% ABV
Pale, faintly sweet, with roast corn flavours; smooth and easy to drink.

MANNY'S ALE
PALE ALE 5.2% ABV
Begins with notes of grapefruit, then hop flavours blend with fermentation fruitiness on the palate.

LUCILLE IPA
INDIA PALE ALE 6.8% ABV
An easy drinking but heartily strong IPA. It is full of New World hops, citrus flavours, and lashings of caramel malts.

INDIA PALE ALE
INDIA PALE ALE 5.9% ABV
Pineapple and grapefruit, full of hop flavour, with a fruit and malt backbone balancing the bitterness.

312 URBAN WHEAT
AMERICAN WHEAT BEER 4.2% ABV
Typically unfiltered and hazy, with a citrussy, almost sweet, hop nose that announces it is American. Tart, fruity, with underlying creaminess.

Clybourn as well as another near Wrigley Field, and both still offer an "MBA" (it's actually a kind of loyalty card!). The company was bought by AB InBev when Greg Hall stepped down as brewmaster in 2011.

BREWING SECRET Bourbon County Stout (launched as the brewpub's 1,000th batch in 1995) arguably kicked off the USA revolution of ageing beer in bourbon (and then other spirit) barrels.

GORDON BIERSCH

357 East Taylor Street, San Jose, California 95112, USA
www.gordonbiersch.com

Gordon Biersch began as a single brewpub, grew into a chain, then split into two – a brewery in San Jose, and restaurant-breweries that produce a similar line of beers. The San Jose operation also brews private label brands for Trader Joe's and Costco.

BREWING SECRET Brewer Dan Gordon trained for five years in Bavaria.

GRAND TETON

430 Old Jackson Highway, Victor, Idaho 83455, USA
www.grandtetonbrewing.com

Founded in 1988 as Otto Brothers' Brewing – a brewpub which claims a place in American beer history by reintroducing a receptacle called the "growler" (a 1.92-litre/64-oz beer jug). The company took its new name in 2000 after building a production brewery at the base of the Teton Mountains near Yellowstone Park.

GREAT DIVIDE

2201 Arapahoe Street, Denver, Colorado 80205, USA
www.greatdivide.com

Opened in 1994, Great Divide Brewing quickly earned a reputation for carefully balanced beers. Its ales have grown bigger (in strength and hop character), and the brewery's reputation has grown, but its beers still retain that delicate equilibrium. The brewery is a short walk from Coors Field, home of the Rockies baseball team.

MATILDA
BELGIAN STRONG ALE 7% ABV
Wild, lively hopsack aroma, earthy, with rich fruits and a firm, dry, characterful finish.

BOURBON COUNTY STOUT
IMPERIAL STOUT 14.5% ABV
Vintages vary, some flashing more bourbon than others. Always a marriage of rich chocolate, dark fruit, vanilla, and certainly bourbon.

HEFEWEIZEN
HEFEWEIZEN 5.5% ABV
Banana and subdued bubblegum to start, with a pinch of spicy cloves. Refreshing, tart wheat flavours.

MÄRZEN
MÄRZEN/OKTOBERFEST 5.8% ABV
Smooth and malty with notes of crusty bread and caramel. Spice flavours add complexity. Clean, dry finish.

SWEETGRASS
AMERICAN PALE ALE 6% ABV
Crisp malt flavours are overlaid with fragrant citrus hops and lashings of spice and resins. A great food beer.

BITCH CREEK ESB
BROWN ALE 6% ABV
Hybrid, with toasted malts as well as caramel. Plenty of piney and citrussy hops. Big, but balanced.

COLETTE
BELGIAN-STYLE SAISON 7.3% ABV
Hazy in the glass, it is a mixture of fruit and tart. A harmony of complexity and refreshment.

TITAN IPA
INDIA PALE ALE 7.1% ABV
Balanced, in a big way, with plenty of caramel-sweet body to match the piney, grapefruity hops throughout.

BREWERY

GREAT LAKES

2516 Market Avenue, Cleveland,
Ohio 44113, USA
www.greatlakesbrewing.com

Selling its beer across a growing
region surrounding Ohio, this brewery
has been an industry leader in tracking
the quality of its beer on retailers'
shelves. Nonetheless, its brewing
complex near the historic West Side
Market always merits a visit. The
original brewpub, established in
1988, sits across from the production
brewery, which came online in 1998.

Visitors are directed to the taproom's
striking Tiger Mahogany bar and
shown bullet holes reputedly made
by Eliot Ness. He, of course, was the
"untouchable" Prohibition agent who
brought down gangster Al Capone.
The beer garden looks onto Ohio
City's Market Square.

GREEN FLASH

6550 Mira Mesa Boulevard, San Diego,
California 92121, USA
www.greenflashbrew.com

Green Flash refers to a rare light
phenomenon that lasts only seconds
at sunrise or sunset over water.
Green seems appropriate for a
brewery gaining a national reputation
for its hop-accented beers, although
brewer Chuck Silva has proved adept
at a wide range of styles.

GRITTY MCDUFF'S

396 Fore Street, Portland,
Maine 04101, USA
www.grittys.com

Opening in Portland Old Port in 1988,
Gritty McDuff's was one of the first
brewpubs in the northeast and an early
outpost for USA cask ale. There are
now branches in Freeport and Lewiston.

BREWING SECRET The brewery uses
traditional English methods,
equipment, yeasts, hops, and
a range of barley malts.

BEER

EDMUND FITZGERALD PORTER
PORTER 5.8% ABV
Perfectly balanced, chocolate-
mocha throughout, delightful fresh
quality, and a dry coffee finish.

ELIOT NESS
VIENNA LAGER 6.2% ABV
Bold and hoppy in the Vienna style,
with creamy, nutty maltiness and
brisk hoppiness nicely balanced.

DORTMUNDER GOLD
DORTMUNDER 5.8% ABV
Aromas of fresh grain or new-
mown hay blend with bright
Noble hops. Robust and crisp.

BURNING RIVER PALE ALE
PALE ALE 6% ABV
Borders on an India pale ale,
brimming with juicy, piney
American hops that last
through a long, dry finish.

WEST COAST IPA
INDIA PALE ALE 7.3% ABV
Northwest hops balanced on a solid
malt base. Earthy, floral, citrussy,
piney, grapefruity, and bitter.

LE FREAK
AMERICAN BELGO 9.2% ABV
Mix of sweet malt, complex fruit
flavours, and bitterness in the mouth.
A brilliant merger of fermentation
and hop-induced flavours.

BLACK FLY STOUT
STOUT 4.1% ABV
Surprising coffee aromas and flavours,
mingling with chocolate and toffee,
but light and satisfyingly dry.

HALLOWEEN ALE
EXTRA SPECIAL BITTER 6% ABV
An autumn release, brewed
stronger, aged longer, and with
more East Kent Goldings hops than
are used in Gritty's Best Bitter.

HAIR OF THE DOG

61 SE Yamhill Street, Portland
Oregon 97214, USA
www.hairofthedog.com

Chef-turned-brewer Alan Sprints founded this tiny cult brewery in 1994. His first ale, Adam, was brewed in the Adambier style of Dortmund in Germany, and based on the research of beer writer Fred Eckhardt.

BREWING SECRET Every bottle carries a batch number. Check the website to match it to brewing and bottling dates.

HALE'S

4301 Leary Way Northwest, Seattle, Washington 98107, USA
www.halesbrewery.com

First opened in western Washington State in 1983, the brewery has been a fixture in Seattle since 1995. Its English-inspired pub adjoins a "display production" brewery (visible behind glass, with mirrors on the ceiling to show the foamy fermentation in open-top vessels). Hale's believes the best beer is fresh beer, and coined the slogan "think globally, drink locally".

HARPOON

306 Northern Avenue, Boston, Massachusetts 02210, USA
www.harpoonbrewery.com

This brewery, with major facilities in Boston and Vermont, has tapped into speciality-beer-drinkers' affection for hops, with its flagship IPA accounting for 60 per cent of sales. However, its wheat-based UFO has recently been the fastest-growing brand, and its 100 Barrel Series of one-offs guarantees there's always something new.

HEAVY SEAS BEER

4615 Hollins Ferry Road, Halethorpe, Maryland 21227, USA
www.heavyseasbeer.com

Henry Sissons sold Baltimore's first brewpub in 1995 to found Clipper City, now called Heavy Seas. It has the largest programme of cask ales in the USA and is developing a series of wood-aged beers in its Uncharted Waters range.

BREWING SECRET Hop^3 (cubed) is hopped three ways – in the kettle, in the hop back, and dry-hopped.

ADAM
STRONG ALE 10% ABV
Rich and complex, with dark fruits, bread, chocolate, smoked peat, and more, all cleverly unified.

FRED
STRONG ALE 10% ABV
Named after Eckhardt, this beer defies categorization. Dark fruits and juicy ones, spices and hops – impossible to summarize.

EL JEFE WEIZEN ALE
HEFEWEIZEN 4.5% ABV
Hale's doesn't only do English styles. This is brewed in the Bavarian manner: cloudy, with banana fruity, yeasty character, and light cloves.

PALE AMERICAN ALE
PALE ALE 5.2% ABV
Nods towards the UK, with rounded biscuit malt. Well balanced by citric, earthy Northwest hops.

HARPOON IPA
INDIA PALE ALE 5.9% ABV
Floral at the outset; zestful citrus aromas. More hops in the flavour, biscuit-like palate, subdued bitterness at the end.

RICK & DAN'S
RYE INDIA PALE ALE 6.9% ABV
Hazy orange, spice, and citrus fruit aromas dance on the palate. Rye gives it a long dry finish.

LOOSE CANNON HOP^3 ALE
INDIA PALE ALE 7.25% ABV
A well-balanced cocktail of hops, with flavours of tangerine, grapefruit, and pine. Amber hues.

SMALL CRAFT WARNING
STRONG LAGER 7% ABV
An "über pils" with strong pale bock qualities. Sturdy bitterness complements the malty sweetness.

Samuel Adams, made by the Boston Beer Company, is one of USA's most successful craft brewery brands.

HIGH POINT

22 Park Place, Butler,
New Jersey 07405, USA
www.ramsteinbeer.com

High Point founder Greg Zaccardi
was an American "hophead" until he
discovered the wheat beers of Bavaria.
He branded his beers Ramstein, after
the German city that's home to the
largest US Air Force base in Europe,
and began making true-to-style
weissbiers and lagers at High Point,
even though his brewing system
was designed for British-style ales.

HIGHLAND

12 Old Charlotte Highway, Suite H
Asheville, North Carolina 28803, USA
www.highlandbrewing.com

Having moved into a large new
production facility in 2006, Highland
Brewing was perfectly positioned
for the rise in profile of North
Carolina beer after state lawmakers
eased the limit on beer strength.
Asheville is a fast-growing mountain
town, with a beer scene to match,
including five breweries.

HOFBRÄUHAUS

200 East 3rd Street, Newport,
Kentucky 41071, USA
www.hofbrauhaus.us

Hofbräuhaus Newport, across the
river from Cincinnati, was the first
licensed franchise of the state-owned
brewery of the same name in Munich.
Bavarian-style beer is brewed on site
(the Las Vegas Hofbräuhaus serves
beer brewed in Munich). The menu
and decor replicate the original,
and there's a beer garden and quiet
dining room too.

HOPPIN' FROG

1680 East Waterloo Road (Rte 224),
Akron, Ohio 44306, USA
www.hoppinfrog.com

Brewmaster-owner Fred Karm
opened this smallish brewery making
big beers in 2006. He established
his reputation for bold products while
directing operations for three Thirsty
Dog brewpubs, before the chain
went bankrupt. Thirsty Dog itself has
been revived as a production-only
microbrewery, also in Akron.

BREWERY

RAMSTEIN CLASSIC
DUNKELWEIZEN 5.5% ABV
Sweet chocolate on the nose and
palate. Orchard fruits and banana,
balanced by light clove and spicy hops.

MAIBOCK
MAIBOCK 6.5% ABV
A spring seasonal. Surprisingly dark
with subtle caramel notes. Clean,
honey maltiness, not-so-subtle
alcohol, and pleasant, herbal hops.

OATMEAL PORTER
PORTER 5.9% ABV
Chocolate to start, with roasted
coffee beans emerging, more
prominent in the mouth. Coffee and
cream impression. Dry and bitter.

GAELIC ALE
AMBER ALE 5.6% ABV
Its name and caramel character nod
towards Scotland, but the resiny
hop finish is distinctly American.

HEFE WEIZEN
HEFEWEIZEN 5.1% ABV
Properly cloudy, with subdued fruit
aromas. Banana on the palate, with
distinct cloves and crisp wheat.

DUNKEL
DUNKEL 5.5% ABV
Rich without being heavy.
Surprising caramel and toasted
flavours, mild hop presence with
just enough bitterness.

B.O.R.I.S. THE CRUSHER
IMPERIAL STOUT 9.4% ABV
As thick as motor oil, with intense
aromas of burnt liquorice, chocolate,
and roasted coffee beans.

FROG'S HOLLOW
PUMPKIN ALE 8.4% ABV
A giant of a pumpkin ale. Orange
in colour, it is full of cinnamon,
nutmeg, ginger, and clove notes.

BEER

BREWERY

HOPWORKS/HUB

2944 Southeast Powell Boulevard,
Portland, Oregon 97202, USA
www.hopworksbeer.com

Hopworks Urban Brewery is the
first brewery in Portland to offer only
organic beers, part of its commitment
to "green culture". HUB's founder-
brewmaster Christian Ettinger made
Portland's first organic beers.

BREWING SECRET HUB fires its brewing
kettle with biodiesel fuel.

IPSWICH ALE BREWERY

2 Brewery Place, Ipswich,
Massachusetts 01938, USA
www.ipswichalebrewery.com

Founded in 1991 as the Ipswich
Brewery, it had sold the rights to its
original brands before new owners
acquired the brewery in 1999 and
renamed it Mercury. Mercury later
reacquired the Ipswich brands and
has been on a fast growth track, with
Ipswich and Stone Cat ales, Mercury
old-fashioned soda pop, and even an
oatmeal stout mustard.

IRON HILL

Various locations
www.ironhillbrewery.com

Named after a Revolutionary War
landmark in Delaware, the Iron Hill
Brewery & Restaurant chain continues
to grow throughout Delaware and
Pennsylvania, offering a set line-up
at each location but also a range of
specials. Its brewers also package
an Iron Hill Reserve Line in 750ml
(1¼ pints) corked bottles for sale
at the pubs.

ITHACA

122 Ithaca Beer Drive, Ithaca,
New York 14850, USA
www.ithacabeer.com

Located in New York's Finger Lakes
region, already well known among
wine drinkers, Ithaca Beer Company
has boosted the region's beer's profile
since brewing began in 1998.

BREWING SECRET The brewery has led
efforts to re-establish New York State
as a USA centre of hop growing.

BEER

VELVET ESB

SPECIAL BITTER 5.2% ABV
A session ale by American
standards; rich in caramel, soft
on the palate, with signature
hop character throughout.

ORGANIC IPA

INDIA PALE ALE 6.6% ABV
Fresh hop aromas – pine, grapefruit,
lemon zest. Hop flavours, bitterness
matched by bright malt character.

IPSWICH ORIGINAL ALE

PALE ALE 5.4% ABV
Lightly bready with tropical fruit
on the nose. Pleasing hop flavours
meld with a biscuity palate.

IPSWICH DARK ALE

BROWN ALE 6.3% ABV
Bold, with significant citric hops to
match a full body of roasted malts,
chocolate, brown sugar, and toffee.

RUSSIAN IMPERIAL STOUT

IMPERIAL STOUT 9.8% ABV
Rich, dark chocolate aroma with
supporting coffee notes. Roasty
bitterness balances the sweetness
of the chocolate.

PIG IRON PORTER

PORTER 5.4% ABV
One of their first beers. Roasted
and rich, it is a full-flavoured blend
of coffee, prunes, and dark cherries.

NUT BROWN ALE

BROWN ALE 5.4% ABV
A deep, inviting brown pour. Nutty,
with caramel and chocolate notes,
its underlying sweetness is balanced
by herbal hops.

EXCELSIOR! OLD HABIT

STRONG RYE ALE 9% ABV
Part of a special Excelsior! series.
Made with four rye malts, with a
portion aged in rye whisky barrels.

JOLLY PUMPKIN

3115 Broad Street, Dexter,
Michigan 48130, USA
www.jollypumpkin.com

Not quite like any other brewery in
the USA, Jolly Pumpkin Artisan Ales
allows its beers to develop under the
influence of local wild yeast. All beers
are aged in barrels, and are often
blended and re-fermentated in the
bottle to deliver effervescent beer.
Though its output is small, the brewery
has developed a national following.

KONA

75-5629 Kuakini Highway, Kailua Kona,
Hawaii 96740, USA
www.konabrewingco.com

Sales are booming everywhere for
Kona Brewing, which offers mainland
drinkers "a pint of paradise". The Big
Island brewery added capacity to meet
growing demand in Hawaii, while sales
in 36 mainland states and nine other
countries have increased even faster.
Beers sold on the mainland are made
under contract at Widmer Brothers
in Oregon. More than 10 different

beer styles are now brewed and
can be found in the company's pubs.
The colours range from black as
the darkest night to sun-bleached
yellow. In some of the beers, hops
predominate, while others allow
tangy malts to come to the fore.

KUHNHENN

5919 Chicago Road, Warren,
Michigan 48092, USA
www.kbrewery.com

Brothers Brett and Eric Kuhnhenn
turned the hardware store their
father ran for 35 years into a small
brewery, winery, meadery, and
brew-on-premises (where customers
can make their own beer). The
national reputation of Kuhnhenn
shows how word of mouth – and the
Internet – can help small breweries
develop a cult following.

LA ROJA

BELGIAN-STYLE RED 7.2% ABV
Sour red berries with a hint of oak
make this a refreshing beer.

BAM BIÈRE

SAISON 4.5% ABV
The whole exceeds the sum of its
parts in this "farmhouse" ale, from
the hops (billowing head, dry finish)
to the spicy malts.

PIPELINE PORTER

PORTER 5.4% ABV
Brewed with local Kona coffee, its
flavour is well-integrated. Roasty
malt, oily, with chocolate notes.

KOKO BROWN

BROWN ALE 5.5% ABV
A dark, smooth beer, full of nutty
toffee flavours from the island-
grown toasted coconut. Pairs well
with Thai food.

FIRE ROCK PALE ALE

PALE ALE 6% ABV
Reddish orange with slightly
sweet caramel aromas and flavour;
spicy and citric hops are cleverly
integrated and balanced.

PARADISE FOUND

PALE WHEAT ALE 5.4% ABV
A seasonal golden-coloured ale
full of citrus flavours, which come
from locally grown passion fruit.

RASPBERRY EISBOCK

EISBOCK 15.5% ABV
A small-run beer. Complex, rich
with raspberries, chocolate, warming
alcohol, and a closing tartness.

PENETRATION PORTER

PORTER 5.9% ABV
Almost black, with roasted coffee,
chocolate, and dark fruits like
cherry filling the nose and the
mouth. Citrussy hop finish.

BREWERY

LAGUNITAS

1280 North McDowell Boulevard,
Petaluma, California 94954, USA
www.lagunitas.com

Always known for its hop-driven
beers, Lagunitas launched a new range
in 2006, each one commemorating
a Frank Zappa album and released
40 years after the album of the same
name. Founder Tony Magee obtained
the permission of the Zappa Family
Trust to use the original album art
on the bottle label for these beers.

LAKE PLACID

813 Mirror Lake Drive, Lake Placid,
New York 12946, USA
www.ubuale.com

Located in the Adirondack Mountains
ski resort, this brewery's flagship Ubu
Ale became famous when Bill Clinton
had "growlers" (64-oz refillable jugs)
delivered to the White House. The
company has built a new brewery
near its brewpub, offering tours and
tastings every Saturday afternoon.

LAKEFRONT

1872 North Commerce Street,
Milwaukee, Wisconsin 53212, USA
www.lakefrontbrewery.com

Lakefront Brewery, known since 1987
for a range of robust beers, recently
moved to the fore in brewing New
Grist gluten-free beer for coeliacs
who cannot tolerate the grains
traditionally used in making beer.

BREWING SECRET New Grist is brewed
from sorghum, hops, water, rice, and
gluten-free yeast grown on molasses.

LANCASTER

302 North Plum Street, Lancaster,
Pennsylvania 17602, USA
www.lancasterbrewing.com

Lancaster was once dubbed the
"Munich of the United States" and
home to 14 breweries, some of which
flaunted Prohibition. The last of the
originals closed nearly 40 years before
Lancaster Brewing opened in 1995.
The 19th-century former tobacco
warehouse also houses a restaurant
serving dishes such as mussels cooked
in ale, and beer-battered shrimp.

BEER

LAGUNITAS IPA
INDIA PALE ALE 6.2% ABV
Brimming with hop character –
orange, grapefruit, peaches,
pine – over malty sweetness.

HOP STOOPID
IMPERIAL INDIA PALE ALE 8% ABV
Hop aroma – citrus, pine, and all
you'd expect – jumps from the glass,
followed by a solid bitter punch, the
blow softened by malty sweetness.

UBU ALE
STRONG ALE 7% ABV
On the sweet side, dominated by
malt with chocolate, caramel, and
dark fruit flavours.

46'ER PALE ALE
PALE ALE 6% ABV
English malts bring tastes of grain
and biscuit to this lemon, citrus ale,
the finish is long and bitter.

NEW GRIST
GLUTEN-FREE PILSNER 5.1% ABV
A tang of citrus zest to start, then
a light palate with hints of fruit.
Mildly astringent and tart.

RIVERWEST STEIN
AMERICAN AMBER LAGER 5.6% ABV
Lightly toasted aromas with hints
of caramel. More caramel in the
mouth, and hop citrus fruitiness.
Woody undertones.

HOP HOG IPA
INDIA PALE ALE 7.9% ABV
Considerable caramel-malt character
is well balanced by hoppy grapefruit,
citrus, and spruce.

MILK STOUT
MILK STOUT 5.3% ABV
Lightly roasted coffee notes sit well
with the creamy texture. Chocolate,
dark fruits, and nuttiness.

LEFT HAND

1265 Boston Avenue, Longmont, Colorado 80501, USA
www.lefthandbrewing.com

The company takes its name from the Arapahoe Chief Niwot, his name translating as "left hand". Originally brewing English-style ales, the brewery merged in 1998 with Tabernash, known for Bavarian-inspired beers. Those beers have now been phased out, but Left Hand continues to develop a wide range of beer styles and produces many seasonal brews too.

LEINENKUGEL'S

124 East Elm Street, Chippewa Falls, Wisconsin 54729, USA
www.leinie.com

Since 1988, when Miller Brewing bought a controlling interest, the Jacob Leinenkugel Brewing Company has grown into one of the largest regional breweries in the country, distributing in almost every state.

BREWING SECRET The brewery, founded in 1867, still offers a range reflecting its German heritage.

LION

700 North Pennsylvania Avenue, Wilkes-Barre, Pennsylvania 18705, USA
www.lionbrewery.com

The Lion Brewery, founded in 1905, is a survivor – the last of dozens of breweries that once operated in northeastern Pennsylvania. Most recently the brewery has emphasized this heritage with its Stegmaier brand of good-value traditional beers, the roots of which go back to 1857.

LIVE OAK

3301 East Fifth Street, Austin, Texas 78702, USA
www.liveoakbrewing.com

Live Oak's brewmaster-owner Chip McElroy successfully merges Austin's hip culture with a traditional brewing regimen. More than ten years after opening, the brewery still sells only draught beer.

BREWING SECRET Their classic Pilz is produced with an old-fashioned method that uses a decoction mash.

MILK STOUT
MILK STOUT 6% ABV
Complex and smooth, chocolate and burnt toast in the aroma and flavour constantly balanced by creamy sweetness.

BLACK JACK PORTER
PORTER 6.8% ABV
Smooth, medium bodied. Chocolate and liquorice aromas harmonize with cherries, herbal hops, and espresso.

CREAMY DARK
AMERICAN DARK LAGER 4.9% ABV
As creamy as promised, chocolate with coffee and cream character and a dryish not-too-bitter finish.

SUNSET WHEAT
AMERICAN WHEAT BEER 4.9% ABV
Light but complex beer, almost a fruit salad of aromas and flavours, with some wheaty tartness and coriander spiciness.

DELUXE PILSNER BEER
PILSNER 4.5% ABV
Clean, crisp with a nice lemon nose, it is a refresher with a lovely bitter finish.

LIGHT
AMERICAN LAGER 3.9% ABV
Dry, with a hint of malty sweetness, it is light and reassuringly refreshing.

PILZ
PILSNER 4.7% ABV
Bright golden, with a flowery nose showcasing Saaz hops. Soft and slightly oily palate; dry, bitter finish.

HEFEWEIZEN
HEFEWEIZEN 5.2% ABV
Yeasty, full of bananas, vanilla and cloves, with a hint of bubble-gum. Lush flavours to start with, but dry at the finish. A spring/summer beer.

THE STORY OF...

THE GIANTS OF BREWING

Walk into any airport bar in the world, five-star hotel, or major supermarket and the chances are that it will sell beer from one of the big four multinational breweries. SABMiller, Anheuser-Busch InBev, Heineken, and Carlsberg stand as behemoths in the world of beer. These mega-companies straddle continents and dominate domestic markets. And while their beers are happily drunk by millions of people every day, they do ruffle the feathers of many serious beer lovers, who accuse them of stifling innovation and local and regional beer traditions.

Around the world, the big four are involved in fierce competition, battling it out for the cream of the market share. For this is no cosy cartel, but a full-bloodied battle royal to be the biggest brewer in the world. They grow their businesses organically and through acquisitions, and, now that beer is drunk worldwide, they are targeting Russia, China, and India – places far beyond their traditional markets.

Big they might be, dominated by marketing personnel and accountants they certainly are, but somewhere within each of these giant corporations there beats the heart of a brewer proud to be producing a beer made with good, natural ingredients.

CARLSBERG

Times have changed since JC Jacobsen first introduced the world to Carlsberg in 1847. Carlsberg's three key markets are Western Europe, Eastern Europe, and Asia. It has majority holdings in several large European breweries, such as Carlsberg UK, Carlsberg in Sweden, Ringnes in Norway, Feldschlösschen in Switzerland, Sinebrychoff in Finland, and Carlsberg Polska. It wholly owns the Baltic Beverages Holding, which brews beer in Russia, Ukraine, and the Baltic states. Carlsberg also has significant activities in Asia, run by its fully owned subsidiary Carlsberg Asia. It has recently upped its stake in China's Chongqing Brewery to 60 per cent and is rapidly expanding in India.

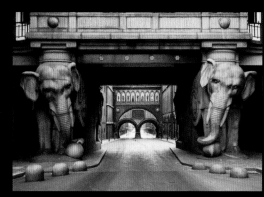

▲ Poster for Carlsberg beer from 1958.
◀ Carlsberg's original brewery in Denmark was founded in the mid-19th century in Valby.
▼ Carlsberg's original brewhouse is now used to brew the Jacobsen range of speciality beers.

ANHEUSER-BUSCH INBEV

Anheuser-Busch InBev's heritage is rooted in brewing traditions that originate from the Den Hoorn brewery in Leuven, Belgium, dating back to 1366 and the pioneering spirit of the Anheuser brewery, established in 1860 in St. Louis, USA. The company was formed in 2008 when the Belgian-based brewer InBev acquired its US rival Anheuser-Busch. The US$52bn takeover represented the largest deal in brewing history when the deal closed. InBev was formed in 2004 when the Belgian company Interbrew and the Brazilian Companhia de Bebidas das Américas combined to form a new world force in brewing. Interbrew, which styles itself as the world's largest local brewer, was formed in 1987 from the merger of Brasseries Artois, then the second largest brewer in Belgium, and Brasseries Piedboeuf, the brewer of Jupiler. Anheuser-Busch InBev employs more than 150,000 people in over 30 countries across the world, describing itself as "the Best Beer Company in a Better World".

Anheuser-Busch InBev is the leading global brewer and one of the world's top five consumer products companies. Anheuser-Busch InBev manages a portfolio of brands that includes global, flagship brands Budweiser, Stella Artois, and Beck's. Striving to be the world's greatest local brewer, the company also manages a portfolio of over 200 other beer brands including fast-growing multi-country brands like Leffe and Hoegaarden, and strong local jewels such as Bud Light, Skol, Brahma, Quilmes, Michelob, Harbin, Sedrin, Cass, Klinskoye, Sibirskaya Korona, Chernigivske, and Jupiler. It now sees India, China, and South America as markets that will become increasingly significant.

◀ Anheuser-Busch InBev's brewing headquarters in Leuven, Belgium, is home of the Stella Artois beer brand.
▼ Anheuser-Busch InBev also owns the German brewery in Bremen where Beck's is brewed. In the last 20 years, Beck's has become a major international beer brand.

▲ The drayhorses that were once used at Anheuser-Busch have become a symbol of the company's heritage; Budweiser is its most famous brand.
◀ Anheuser-Busch InBev continues to grow by acquisition and has recently completed the purchase of Grupo Modelo in Mexico — the brewer of the country's biggest brand, Corona.

SABMILLER

SABMiller has brewing operations in more than 60 countries across six continents. Its internationally marketed brands include Pilsner Urquell, Peroni Nastro Azzurro, and Miller Genuine Draft; its local brands include Aguila, Miller Lite, Snow, and Tyskie.

SAB (South African Breweries) was founded in 1895 when it launched its first brand, Castle Lager, in its home market of South Africa. The founder, a Swedish entrepreneur called Jacob Letterstedt, intended to provide beer for the thousands of miners and prospectors around Johannesburg.

In 2002, SABMiller was formed after SAB acquired Miller Brewing Company, then the second largest brewery by volume in the USA. The company is expecting growth in both its developed and developing markets. In 2013, growth was particularly strong in Tanzania, Zambia, Nigeria, and Ghana. It is continuing to invest in new breweries, most notably in Africa and Latin America.

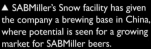

▲ SABMiller's Snow facility has given the company a brewing base in China, where potential is seen for a growing market for SABMiller beers.
▶ Among the best-known brands that SABMiller owns are Peroni from Italy, Pilsner Urquell from the Czech Republic, Grolsch from the Netherlands, and the USA's Miller Lite.
◀ Castle Lager is where it all started for the SAB part of SABMiller; South African Breweries began in 1895, and Castle Lager was its first brew.

◀ Gerard Heineken, the brewery's founder, set up Heineken in 1864, and immediately began brewing lager.

HEINEKEN

Heineken has its roots in Amsterdam, where Gerard Adriaan Heineken purchased a run-down brewery called the Haystack in 1864. Today, the Heineken brand is the largest beer brand in Europe, and the company claims it is the most valuable beer brand in the world. Heineken also owns Amstel, which is the third largest beer brand in Europe.

Operating in more than 170 countries, Heineken has the widest global presence of all international brewers, and is the world's third largest. Europe accounts for over half of Heineken's sales. Heineken owns more than 120 breweries in at least 70 countries and employs more than 85,000 people. It has recently bought breweries in Africa, India, Asia, and Latin America.

▲ Currently Heineken's main brewing facility in the Netherlands, the Zoeterwoude Brewery near Amsterdam was built in 1975.
◀ Heineken is now the largest beer brand in Europe.

HIDDEN GEMS

While the four giants might concentrate most of their marketing strategies and budget on the main brands that they produce, they all also brew gems that beer lovers should certainly seek out.

Carlsberg's Jacobsen's Vintage series are said to be the most expensive beers in the world. Barley wines, each vintage, is wood aged slowly and carefully in Côte d'Or barrels made from Swedish and French oak before bottling. They have flavours of vanilla, smoke, caramel, and port.

Anheuser-Busch InBev's Campbell's Scotch Ale (right), at 7.7% ABV, has wonderful spicy and caramel candy aromas. Full of raisin flavours, it has a slightly burnt finish.

In the USA, Anheuser-Busch InBev may be more well known for its classic Budweiser brands, but it also brews a sprightly beer in the style of a Belgian witbier. Shock Top – an unfiltered wheat beer brewed at 5.2% ABV – sports a naturally cloudy consistency and tastes of orange and spices.

Heineken bought the Żywiec Brewery in Poland in the 1990s. At the company's Bracki Brewery in Zamkowy, an aromatic Baltic Porter is brewed in open fermenters. Weighing in at a very hefty 9.5% ABV, it is full of sweet coffee notes.

SABMiller's Castle Milk Stout, at 6% ABV, is a true milk stout, in which lactose sugars have been added to the wort during the brewing process.

▶ Campbell's Scotch Ale, produced by Anheuser-Busch InBev.

BREWERY

LONERIDER

8816 Gulf Ct. Suite 100, Raleigh, North Carolina 27617, USA
www.loneriderbeer.com

Home-brewers are at the heart of this powerhouse craft brewery. Three friends moved out of their kitchens to set up the brewery in 2009 and quickly established themselves as movers and shakers within the North Carolina beer scene. The beers, whose names are inspired by the "wild west", have become favourites at the Great American Beer Festival.

LONG TRAIL

5520 Route 4, Bridgewater Corners, Vermont 05035, USA
www.longtrail.com

Long Trail Brewing is a promoter of "EcoBrewing". Among other measures, it uses only two gallons of water for each of beer made (compared to an industry average of 6:1). Although the regional brewery leans heavily on its flagship Long Trail Ale, it continues to broaden its range with seasonal beers.

LOST ABBEY

155 Mata Way, San Marcos, California 92069, USA
www.lostabbey.com

Lost Abbey beers sometimes pay homage to monastery ales, but some are unlike anything ever brewed in an abbey. Port Brewing, born out of a successful chain of brewpubs in the San Diego area, launched the brand in 2006. Lost Abbey quickly built up a devoted following, with consumers lining up outside to buy its special releases. Brewmaster Tomme Arthur

oversees the ageing room, conjuring up what are best thought of as "Wild American" ales – malt-accented beers enhanced by the barrels in which they are matured.

BREWING SECRET The wooden barrels that once held wines and whiskies now nurture wild yeasts.

BEER

SWEET JOSIE
BROWN ALE 6.5% ABV
Lashings of chocolate and aromatic malts balanced by generous hop bitterness.

SHOTGUN BETTY
GERMAN WHEAT BEER 5.8% ABV
Full-bodied, German-style wheat beer full of banana and clove flavours. A hot day refresher with a satisfying dry finish.

LONG TRAIL ALE
ALTBIER 4.6% ABV
Deep copper, smooth malt aromas, and hop spiciness, but without the hop bitterness of German altbiers.

DOUBLE BAG
STRONG ALE 7.2% ABV
Tastes like a stronger version of Long Trail Ale, particularly rich in caramel and chocolate. Earthy, somewhat pungent, hops.

RED POPPY ALE
SOUR ALE 5.5% ABV
Brown ale with sour cherries, aged in French oak wine barrels for a year. Oaky, with pleasing acidity.

CUVEE DE TOMME
BELGIAN STRONG ALE 11% ABV
Flavours of cherries, chocolate, smoke, dark fruits, dried fruits, and vanilla. Balanced by restrained sourness and an acidic finish.

JUDGMENT DAY
BELGIAN STRONG DARK ALE 10.5% ABV
Dark and powerful, with profoundly fruity aromas and palate; chocolate and whisky malt undertones.

THE ANGEL'S SHARE
BARLEY WINE 12.5% ABV
Some batches are aged in bourbon barrels, some in brandy ones. The result is an intense blend of rich malts and wood character.

LOST COAST

123 West 3rd Street, Eureka,
California 95501, USA
www.lostcoast.com

Set in a historic seaside town amidst
Victorian buildings, Lost Coast is itself
somewhat historic. The brewery was
founded in 1990 by two women, one
of them, Barbara Groom, the brewer.
"If there's a difference between male
and female brewers," Groom has said,
"it's that women brewers may make
more well-balanced beers, ones with
less bitterness".

MAC & JACK'S

17825 Northeast 65th Street, Redmond,
Washington 98052, USA
www.macandjacks.com

Mac and Jack's has grown into a
significant regional presence with
a tiny range and selling only draught
beer. Its African Amber accounts
for 90 per cent of sales and is the
best-selling draught beer in Seattle.

BREWING SECRET Each keg that leaves
the brewery contains a mesh bag
packed with hops.

MAD RIVER

195 Taylor Way, Blue Lake,
California 95525, USA
www.madriverbrewing.com

Founder Bob Smith built his brewery
in 1989 using recycled materials, and
has since received many awards for
its waste-reduction programmes.
Mad River reuses 98 per cent of its
residuals and generates just one
cubic metre/yard of waste a month
while brewing about 950,000 litres
(250,000 gallons) of beer per year.

MAGIC HAT

5 Bartlett Bay Road, South Burlington,
Vermont 05403, USA
www.magichat.net

Magic Hat's unique and sometimes
outrageous packaging and its "non-
style" beers have brought double-digit
growth year after year. It began in
2008 with construction underway
to double capacity, and plans to push
distribution into the midwest and
south. In 2010, Magic Hat was bought
by North American Breweries.

DOWNTOWN BROWN
BROWN ALE 5% ABV
Soft and smooth, caramel, nuts, and
cocoa throughout, coffee bitterness
blending with earthy hops.

8 BALL STOUT
STOUT 5.8% ABV
Creamy, full bodied, with a balance
of bitter chocolate and coffee. Brief
sweetness is swept away in the
bitter-dry finish.

AFRICAN AMBER
AMBER 5.2% ABV
Generously dry-hopped and
brimming with refreshing citrussy,
floral hop aromas and flavours.
Caramel on the palate gives way
to a medium-dry finish.

JAMAICA RED ALE
AMBER ALE 6.5% ABV
First made for the annual reggae
festival. Sweetish nose, with crystal
malts and solid, refreshing hops.

STEELHEAD SCOTCH PORTER
PORTER 6.5% ABV
Distinctly a porter, with roasted
malt and a touch of sourness.
Caramel notes and hints of smoke
add complexity.

#9
PALE ALE 5.1% ABV
Apricot infused. Subtle stone fruits
on the palate, sometimes buttery
notes. Finishes dry.

HEART OF DARKNESS
STOUT 5.7% ABV
A winter seasonal, it is inky black
with a smooth mouthfeel and
a good long, bittersweet, dark
chocolate finish.

BREWERY

MARBLE

111 Marble Avenue Northwest,
Albuquerque, New Mexico 87102, USA
www.marblebrewery.com

This new microbrewery has spun out
of the award-winning Chama River
and Blue Corn brewpubs, both part
of the same northern New Mexico
restaurant chain. Reflecting shifting
beer trends, Marble Brewery's first
batch was an assertive India pale ale.
Its beers are available throughout
the chain.

MARIN

1809 Larkspur Landing Circle, Larkspur,
California 94939, USA
www.marinbrewing.com

Marin Brewing was one of the most
honoured breweries in the early years
of the Great American Beer Festival
awards. It returned to the spotlight
in 2007, adding four gold medals to
its trophy case. A brewpub "Moylan's"
opened by its brewmaster Brendan
Moylan in nearby Novato has won
gold and silver for its Imperial India
Pale Ale.

MCMENAMINS

Various locations
www.mcmenamins.com

The McMenamin brothers seem to
have a pub in every northwestern
neighbourhood – more than 50 in all
– but each one is different, tailored
to the location or the premises they
inhabit. Some brew on site while
others serve McMenamins beer
brewed at the Edgefield Brewery,
near Portland in Oregon, as well
as a range of local beers.

MENDOCINO

1601 Airport Road, Ukiah,
California 95482
www.mendobrew.com

Mendocino Brewing was one of
the first success stories among USA
"boutique" breweries (as they were
called at the time). It opened in
1983 as the Hopland Brewery, having
acquired equipment, the house yeast,
and even a few employees from the
groundbreaking, but by then defunct,
New Albion Brewery.

BEER

MARBLE INDIA PALE ALE
INDIA PALE ALE 6.8% ABV
West-coast oriented, with an
opening rush of citrus, particularly
grapefruit. Resiny, bitter finish.

WILDFLOWER WHEAT
AMERICAN WHEAT ALE 5.6% ABV
Pale and cloudy, this unfiltered
beer is flavoured with a little
Mexican honey. Light and crisp,
it is a refresher.

SAN QUENTIN'S BREAKOUT STOUT
STOUT 7% ABV
Bittersweet chocolate and coffee at
the start and end, balanced by sweet
molasses in between. Roasty and dry.

STAR BREW TRIPLE WHEAT ALE
AMERICAN WHEAT BEER 9.2% ABV
A tongue-twister: the juicy, dark
fruit of a barley wine, spicy wheat
tartness, and intense hop flavours
and bitterness.

HAMMERHEAD ALE
PALE ALE 6% ABV
Their bestseller. Abundant caramel
sweetness balanced with a large
dose of fragrant Northwest hops.

BLACK RABBIT PORTER
PORTER 5.6% ABV
Cocoa and nutty aromas, with
sweeter chocolate and roasted nuts
in the mouth, as well as a bit of
buttery toffee.

RED TAIL ALE
AMBER ALE 6.1% ABV
An earthy nose includes hints of
orchard fruits. Layers of creamy
malt with notes of liquorice.

BLUE HERON
PALE ALE 6.1% ABV
Orange zest and lemon rind to
start, giving way to traditional
biscuity malt and a balanced,
moderate bitterness.

MIDDLE AGES

120 Wilkinson Street, Syracuse,
New York 13204, USA
www.middleagesbrewing.com

When Mary Rubenstein gave her
husband, Marc, a birthday card that
read "welcome to the middle ages",
she unknowingly named the brewery
the two home-brewers would launch in
1995. They've earned a reputation for
their cask-conditioned, or "real", ale.

BREWING SECRET Their yeast is descended
from a 150-year-old Yorkshire strain.

MIDNIGHT SUN

8111 Dimond Hook Drive,
Anchorage, Alaska 99507, USA
www.midnightsunbrewing.com

Since opening in 1997, Midnight Sun
has developed a cult following beyond
Alaska and its beers can be found
in Washington, Idaho, Oregon,
California, and New York City. The
brewery is committed to making
beers which are refreshing and
full of flavour. The beer names
are inspired by the geography of
the Pacific Northwest.

MILLSTREAM

835 48th Avenue, Amana,
Iowa 52203, USA
www.millstreambrewing.com

Millstream is located in the historic
Amana Colonies, a region established
by German-speaking European settlers
before the Civil War. Opening in 1985,
it didn't attract the same attention
as other microbreweries, but it has
an increased presence in the midwest
since a change of ownership in 2000.

MINHAS

1208 14th Avenue, Monroe,
Wisconsin 53566, USA
www.minhasbrewery.com

Ravinder Minhas was just 24 years old
when he bought the historic Joseph
Huber Brewery in 2006 to produce
his popular Mountain Creek brands,
already brewed under contract in
Monroe for Canadian distribution.
Minhas Craft Brewery still makes the
Huber brands (dating back to 1843),
Berghoff beers, and a line of grocery
store house label beers as well.

GRAIL ALE
PREMIUM BITTER 5.5% ABV
Alive on cask, with a ruby hue
and a fresh blend of floral hops and
toffee. Notes of plums and dates.

BLACK HEART STOUT
STOUT 6.6% ABV
Fresh coffee and chocolate, with
underlying smokiness. Rich yeast
character, but a dry finish.

SOCKEYE RED IPA
INDIA PALE ALE 5.7% ABV
Northwest hops upfront, grapefruit
and evergreen pine needles later.
Complemented by caramel richness.

ARCTIC DEVIL BARLEY WINE
BARLEY WINE 13.2% ABV
Aged in port, wine, or whiskey
barrels, it varies from batch to
batch. A malt base, rich with plums
and raisins, assures complexity.

**JOHN'S GROCERY GENERATIONS
WHITE ALE**
WITBIER 5.2% ABV
Cloudy and effervescent. Pepper and
coriander spices, fruity character
blending with yeast, and finally tart.

SCHILD BRAU AMBER
VIENNA LAGER 5.4% ABV
Copper with rich red highlights. A
full malt middle that's almost nutty.
Floral, spicy hops.

LAZY MUTT FARMHOUSE ALE
GOLDEN ALE 5% ABV
The first released under the Minhas
brand, billed as a "farmhouse ale"
by the brewery but more summer
ale than a *saison*.

HUBER BOCK
BOCK 5.5% ABV
Toasty and dry, with caramel notes.
Best at Baumgartner's Cheese
Store & Tavern near the brewery.

BREWERY

MOLSON COORS

1225 17th Street, Suite 3200,
Denver, Colorado 80202, USA
www.molsoncoors.com

Although it merged with Molson, and that company now partners SABMiller in the USA, Coors has continued to develop less mainstream beers. Its Blue Moon line competes with the largest craft brands, and its SandLot Brewery, within the Coors Field baseball stadium in Denver, regularly offers outstanding traditional lagers.

MOONLIGHT

PO Box 6, Fulton,
California 95439, USA
www.moonlightbrewing.com

Brian Hunt has run Moonlight Brewing as a one-man operation since 1992, sometimes calling on his family to help deliver beer (available only in kegs). He worked for former brewing giant Schlitz, before founding his farmhouse brewery in Sonoma County.

BREWING SECRET Hunt grows as many of his own hops as possible.

NEW BELGIUM

500 Linden Street, Fort Collins,
Colorado 80524, USA
www.newbelgium.com

New Belgium Brewing's fans praise its beers and the sense of environmental and social responsibility its employees represent. Once the beers were hard to find and only sold in a few states, but now they can be bought in more than 30. Jeff Lebesch and Kim Jordan started out with a system, built to Belgian specifications, in their cellar in 1991. They now operate the third largest craft brewery in the USA. Best known for Fat Tire Ale, the brewery offers quite a wide range of beers, including its outstanding Blue Paddle Pilsener.

BREWING SECRET New Belgium has more capacity for ageing beer on wood than any brewery, other than Rodenbach Brewery in Belgium.

BEER

BLUE MOON BELGIAN WHITE

WITBIER 5.4% ABV
Citrussy sweet nose, spicy with notes of celery. Some wheat sourness, finishing on the sweet side.

BARMEN PILSNER

PILSNER 5% ABV
Beautiful billowing head when poured correctly. Rich with Saaz hops, floral, and spicy. Pleasantly grainy, with a long, bitter finish.

DEATH AND TAXES

SCHWARZBIER 5% ABV
Very dark, and rich with roasted malt and chocolate flavours, but surprisingly light, clean, and smooth.

REALITY CZECK

PILSNER 4.8% ABV
Almost sweet aromas and flavours of freshly crushed pilsner malt, with new-mown hay and flowery hop notes; splendidly balanced.

FAT TIRE

AMBER ALE 5.2% ABV
Biscuity, malty nose, with toasted caramel in the middle and a balanced finish on the sweet side of dry.

MOTHERSHIP WIT

WITBIER 4.8% ABV
The brewery's first organic beer. Fruity and spicy; a creamy texture and wheat tartness on the tongue. Refreshing acidity at the finish.

LA FOLIE

SOUR BROWN ALE 7% ABV
Tart fruits on the nose, then oak and vanilla. Distinct but balanced acidity; a mouth-puckering finish.

ABBEY

DOUBLE 7% ABV
Fruity, spicy aromas of bananas and raisins, with complex chocolate and dark fruit flavours. Rich on the tongue before easing to a dry finish.

NEW GLARUS

2400 State Highway 69, New
Glarus, Wisconsin 53574, USA
www.newglarusbrewing.com

In 2008, New Glarus Brewing moved
into a $21 million plant, just outside
a picturesque village settled by Swiss
pioneers in 1845. In its rural setting,
the attractive complex is designed
to look like a Wisconsin dairy farm.
In 2002 it was a microbrewery that
made 13,700 barrels; by 2007, it
had increased this fivefold. The new
expansion will allow the brewery

to double production and keep pace
with soaring sales and the demand
for brewmaster Dan Carey's fruit
beers and limited-edition "Unplugged"
brews. It is an amazing success story
given that New Glarus does not ship
its beers outside of Wisconsin.

NEW HOLLAND

684 Commerce Court, Holland,
Michigan 49423, USA
www.newhollandbrew.com

New Holland Brewing bottle caps
carry the slogan "Art in Fermented
Form", which extends from beer
to a line of brandy-flavoured vodka,
gin, rum, and other spirits. All staff
are encouraged to improve their
knowledge of beer and are expected
to evangelize about it, especially
about its virtues with food.

NORTH COAST

455 North Main Street, Fort Bragg,
California 95437, USA
www.northcoastbrewing.com

Since opening in 1988, North Coast
Brewing has cast a larger shadow than
its production levels would suggest.
Though small for a regional brewery,
it sells beer in 36 states and exports
to Europe and the Pacific Rim too.
Brewmaster Mark Ruedrich has
further extended North Coast's
reputation by exploring beer styles
(Continues overleaf)

SPOTTED COW
CREAM ALE 5.1% ABV
Faintly fruity, tasting of fresh
peaches. Pleasantly grainy, light
on the tongue, and refreshing.

TWO WOMEN
PALE LAGER 5% ABV
Floral and spicy aroma, tinged
with citrus and a hint of graininess.
It is bready in the mouth with
fruity, spicy notes and bitterness.

FAT SQUIRREL
BROWN ALE 5.8% ABV
Hazelnuts on the nose, blending
with chocolate and caramel flavours;
nicely balanced by earthy hops.

WISCONSIN BELGIAN RED
FRUIT ALE 4% ABV
Packed with Wisconsin-grown
Montmorency cherries that dominate
the aroma and flavour, balanced
by just-right sourness and acidity.

THE POET
OATMEAL STOUT 5.2% ABV
Abundant roast, chocolate, and dark,
rummy fruits. Full bodied and creamy
enough to balance the coffee start.

BLACK TULIP
TRIPLE 8.8% ABV
Floral, with candy and honey
sweetness, and fruity notes. Sweet
but tart in the mouth, accented
by spicy, bitter hops.

OLD RASPUTIN
IMPERIAL STOUT 9% ABV
Powerful, but flavourful – bitter
and sweet chocolate, burnt barley,
rum, toffee, dried dark fruits,
and espresso.

RED SEAL ALE
PALE ALE 5.4% ABV
Fresh and citrussy. Solid dry
malt-caramel character, perfectly
balances bracing hoppy bitterness.

BREWERY

(Continued) before many others, and brewing them well. The brewery's Artisan series, packaged in corked 750ml (1¼ pints) bottles, has proved to be very successful. Part of the profits from one, Brother Thelonious, go to the Thelonious Monk Institute of Jazz for music education. That beer has earned the brewery entry into many international jazz clubs.

NINKASI

272 Van Buren Street, Eugene, Oregon 97402, USA
www.ninkasibrewing.com

One of America's fast-rising brewing stars, Ninkasi quickly moved from being a local brewer to a regional favourite; now garnering a national reputation. Named after an ancient Sumerian goddess, the company's mantra is to be connected to its community. It believes that good beer is a balance of malt and hops and plays a big role in building a healthy lifestyle.

ODELL

800 East Lincoln Avenue, Fort Collins, Colorado 80524, USA
www.odellbrewing.com

Odell Brewing opened in 1989 as a gravity-fed brewery housed in a 1915 grain elevator. It has since moved and expanded, but its dedication to traditional brewing hasn't wavered. Like its bigger neighbour, New Belgium, the company is committed to environmentally friendly brewing.

OLD DOMINION

1284 McD Drive, Dover, Delaware 19901, USA
www.olddominion.com

The brewery has made highly regarded beers since 1989. Coastal Brewing, a joint venture of Fordham in Maryland and Anheuser-Busch, purchased Old Dominion in 2007, leading to wider availability but a reduction in brands.

BREWING SECRET All Old Dominion beers are strictly kosher.

BEER

BROTHER THELONIOUS
BELGIAN STRONG DARK ALE 9.3% ABV
Spicy and candy-sweet aromas, with dark fruits, notes of banana and caramelized sugar, almost rummy.

PRANQSTER
BELGIAN-STYLE GOLDEN ALE 7.6% ABV
Complex, fruity, honeyish aromas. Medium body offers more fruit, a bit of banana candy, and a sweet, smooth finish.

BELIEVER
DOUBLE RED ALE 6.9% ABV
Soaring citrus hop flavour counterbalanced by rich malty tones. The finish is long and sweet.

TOTAL DOMINATION
INDIA PALE ALE 6.7% ABV
Citrus flavours, dominated by grapefruit. A bold malt background gives a sweetness, which works well with spicy Mexican food.

90 SHILLING
SCOTTISH ALE 5.3% ABV
A lighter version of a Scottish ale. Smoothly malty, with some nuttiness and a relatively dry finish.

5 BARREL PALE ALE
PALE ALE 5.2% ABV
Fresh, floral, and fruity (peaches). A hoppy nose, with more hops in the earthy middle, balanced perfectly against rich British malts.

DOUBLE D IPA
INDIA PALE ALE 9% ABV
A full-bodied majestical Imperial IPA. The hops exude masses of tropical flavours, which are offset by light caramel flavours.

DOMINION LAGER
DORTMUNDER 5.3% ABV
Well-balanced sweet pilsner malt and spicy hops. Bready notes on the palate; clean, and relatively dry.

BEER STYLES
AMERICAN ALES

The huge influx of German-speaking immigrants into the United States in the middle of the 19th century changed more than the ethnic mix of the country. These newcomers brought with them a tradition of beer-making that was to revolutionize the American brewing industry. Lager beers, as well as the odd weissbier, replaced porters and ales. Then, in 1920, began 13 years of Prohibition, which wiped the slate clean as far as brewing heritage was concerned. Those breweries that survived decided that the future lay in a light and neutral-tasting lager-style beer.

However, when a new wave of craft brewers emerged in the late 20th century, its vanguard looked to the beer styles of mainland Europe and the British Isles, and then went on to develop individual versions of amber ales, pale ales, India pale ales, and brown ales. There are approximately 2,500 US breweries today, and many produce ales of some description. After the long reign of pale lager, ale is back with a vengeance.

EXTREME BEERS American ales are big, bold, and inventive, intensely flavoured with hops and malt's caramel, biscuity qualities. Exceptional examples of such creativity have led to a coining of the term "extreme beers" to convey a sense of beers that are pushing boundaries and breaking the rules.

CRAFT BREWERS In 1965, Fritz Maytag bought an ailing San Francisco brewery, creating the traditionally brewed Liberty Ale and launching the microbrewery movement. Home-brewer and bicycle repairer Ken Grossman is a more recent example of what is now often called the craft brewer – his Sierra Nevada Brewery was founded in 1979. The term pays due tribute to the skill and respect for tradition of this new wave of brewers.

OLD STYLES REVIVED American brewers have been enthusiastic in replicating Old World ales, even those that had become extinct in Europe. Brown ale, somewhat taken for granted in its English homeland, has thus benefited from the magical touch of Brooklyn Brewery's Garrett Oliver, while the long-abandoned hybrid style of Cream Ale is enjoying a renaissance in the form of Honey Cream Ale from Rogue Ales of Oregon.

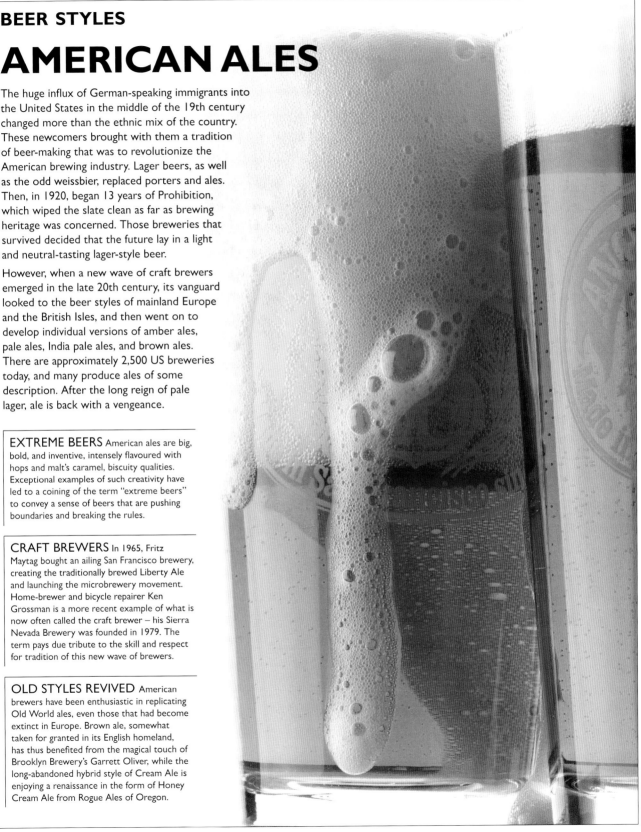

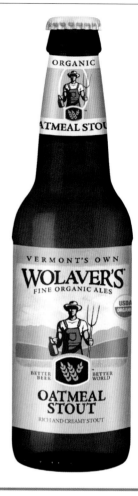

BREWERY

OMMEGANG

656 County Highway 33, Cooperstown,
New York 13326, USA
www.ommegang.com

Owned by Belgium's Duvel Moortgat,
Brewery Ommegang has brewed ales
in the Belgian tradition since 1997,
selling limited quantities across much
of the USA. It hosts one of the nation's
most outstanding beer festivals,
Belgium Comes to Cooperstown,
each summer in the picturesque
brewery grounds outside of town.

ORLANDO

1301 Atlanta Avenue, Orlando,
Florida 32806, USA
www.orlandobrewing.com

Florida's only certified organic brewery,
Orlando is trying to find a niche that
has so far eluded microbreweries in
the state. Forced to relocate because
of highway construction, it moved to
its new home on 7 April 2006, the
anniversary of the end of Prohibition.

OSKAR BLUES

1800 Pike Road, Unit B, Longmont,
Colorado 80501, USA
www.oskarblues.com

A small mountain-town brewpub,
Oskar Blues sparked a hand-canning
revolution among America's small
breweries in 2002, and has grown
more than 800 per cent as a result.
Before owner Dale Katechis won over
an audience for Dale's Pale Ale craft
beer, drinkers clung to the notion that
quality beer was not sold in cans.

OTTER CREEK

793 Exchange Street, Middlebury,
Vermont 05753, USA
www.ottercreekbrewing.com

The Wolaver family bought the
well-established Otter Creek Brewery
in 2002 in order to make its own
organic ales, which had previously
been made under contract at other
breweries. Otter Creek beers are
still produced as well, and the
"World Tour" series includes Otter
Mon (a Jamaican-style stout) and
Otteroo (an Australian-style lager).

BEER

HENNEPIN
SAISON 7.7% ABV
Spicy and peppery throughout.
Yeasty notes, citrus more apparent
on the palate. Tart and dry.

ABBEY ALE
BELGIAN STRONG DARK ALE 8.2% ABV
The flagship ale, produced in the
spirit of a Christmas beer. Rich
and chocolatey, with underlying
liquorice and festive spices.

BLACKWATER DRY PORTER
PORTER 5.4% ABV
Malt-accented, with roasting coffee
beans on the nose, and almost milky
chocolate and caramel flavours.

ORGANIC BLONDE ALE
GOLDEN ALE 4.7% ABV
Pale straw coloured, light bodied,
with subtle malt aromas turning to
apples and peaches on the palate.
Dry, but with no bitterness.

DALE'S PALE ALE
PALE ALE 6.5% ABV
Pour it from the can to release a
blast of Northwest hops, supported
by a rich, malty backbone.

OLD CHUB
SCOTTISH ALE 8% ABV
Malt-accented – even a hint of
whisky malt. Its creamy, chewy
body carries chocolate and caramel
notes well. Powerful and mellow.

WOLAVER'S OATMEAL STOUT
OATMEAL STOUT 5.9% ABV
Chocolate and roasted coffee at
the outset, blending with creamy
notes in the mouth. Full bodied,
but finishing rather dry.

OTTER CREEK COPPER ALE
ALTBIER 5.4% ABV
Rich, complex, malty aromas and
flavours, with a sneaky bitterness
that extends the finish.

PELICAN

33180 Cape Kiwanda Drive,
Pacific City, Oregon 97135, USA
www.yourlittlebeachtown.com/pelican

Set on the ocean shore, Pelican lies just south of Cape Kiwanda, one of Oregon's most photographed landmarks. Only small quantities are sold outside the pub.

BREWING SECRET Its India Pelican Ale and Doryman's Dark Ale have both been named Grand Champion Beer at the Australian International Beer Awards.

PENN

800 Vinial Street, Pittsburgh,
Pennsylvania 15212, USA
www.pennbrew.com

Operating in the former Eberhardt and Ober Brewery, with lagering caves in the adjoining hillside, the Pennsylvania Brewing Company has brewed in the German tradition since it opened in 1986. Its other links with Germany are equally strong, with Teutonic fare on the restaurant menu, a beer garden, and a *rathskeller* (cellar bar).

PIKE

1415 First Avenue, Seattle,
Washington 98122, USA
www.pikebrewing.com

A stroll through the restaurant side of Pike Brewing is like a trip to a well-kept beer museum. Owners Charles and Rose Ann Finkel have been key figures in reviving interest in traditional beer in the USA. In 1978 they founded Merchant du Vin, importing classic European styles, some for the first time, and inspiring a generation of craft brewers.

PORTLAND BREWING

2730 Northwest 31st Avenue,
Portland, Oregon 97210, USA
www.portlandbrewing.com

Portland Brewing, one of Oregon's first breweries, was acquired by Pyramid in 2004. It now brews their beers in Oregon but also the popular MacTarnahan range, named after Robert "Mac" MacTarnahan, an early investor in Portland Brewing. One of Oregon's most accomplished senior athletes, he was the public face of the brewery until he died in 2004.

DORYMAN'S DARK ALE
BROWN ALE 6.2% ABV
Complex malt qualities – roasted nuts, cocoa, coffee beans, caramel – balanced by Northwest hops.

TSUNAMI STOUT
STOUT 7% ABV
Deep black, with a creamy head. Coffee and chocolate on the nose and palate, rich and almost creamy. Pleasant acidic bite at the end.

PENN WEIZEN
HEFEWEIZEN 5.2% ABV
Bavarian all the way. Banana bubble-gum, fruity aromas enlivened by cloves and almost peppery spices.

PENN PILSNER
VIENNA LAGER 5% ABV
The flagship, with light, tasty notes that define a Vienna. A true triple-decocted northern German pils.

PIKE PALE
PALE ALE 5% ABV
Creamy, with juicy hops playing well off a fruity, biscuity medium body, and lingering, nutty dry finish.

PIKE KILT LIFTER
SCOTTISH ALE 6.5% ABV
Caramel-accented, with balancing earthy peat-smoked notes, from the opening aromas through to a just-dry-enough finish.

MACTARNAHAN'S AMBER ALE
AMBER ALE 5.1% ABV
Scottish-style caramel and brown sugar sweetness, with citrussy Northwest hops.

BLACKWATCH CREAM PORTER
PORTER 5.3% ABV
Brewed with oatmeal for a creamy mouthfeel. Cocoa and nutty aromas, with richer chocolate and dark fruits on the palate.

BREWERY

PYRAMID

1201 First Avenue South, Seattle, Washington 98134, USA
www.pyramidbrew.com

Pyramid has developed scores of ales and absorbed other breweries since opening in 1984. Today it emphasizes its wheat beer prowess. It operates several brewpubs on the West coast, with brewing facilities in Washington, Oregon, and California. In 2010 Pyramid was bought by North American Breweries.

REAL ALE

231 San Saba Court, Blanco, Texas 78606, USA
www.realalebrewing.com

The brewers at Real Ale Brewing celebrated their 2007 move from a tiny basement brewery to a new facility by doubling their output. As well as using biodiesel for its own trucks, the brewery now sells the fuel (on a not-for-profit basis) to truckers passing through Hill County.

RED BRICK BREWING

2323 Defoor Hills Road, Northwest, Atlanta, Georgia 30318, USA
www.redbrickbrewing.com

Founded in 1993, Red Brick Brewing was recently forced to abandon the iconic red-brick brewery, after which its beers are named, to make way for a highway. Since 2013, the brewery's focus has been on producing barrel-aged and high-gravity beers in its Brick Mason series.

REDHOOK

14300 Northeast 145th Street, Woodinville, Washington 98072, USA
www.redhook.com

Redhook is a part of Craft Brew Alliance. Founded in 1981, Redhook survived despite locals calling its first ale "banana beer". It was not until the introduction of Ballard Bitter in 1984 that it was certain the brewery would succeed.

BEER

APRICOT ALE

Fruit Beer 5.1% ABV
Apricot in colour. Apricot on the nose. Apricot and wheaty flavours mingle in the mouth. Clean and light.

HEFEWEIZEN

American Hefeweizen 5.2% ABV
Brewed with 60 per cent wheat. Pouring cloudy, slightly grainy, with wheat tartness on the palate.

FULL MOON PALE RYE ALE

Pale Rye Ale 5.7% ABV
Distinctively rye (almost rye bread), balanced with fruitiness in the middle and a lively citrus hop finish.

SISYPHUS

Barley Wine 10% ABV
A rich, mahogany-coloured beer that varies in strength each vintage. Complex and viscous with toffee notes, it improves with age.

LAUGHING SKULL

American Amber Ale 5.3% ABV
The late addition of Willamette hops adds an earthy and mild piquancy to the bready malt. Amber in colour, it is easy drinking.

RED BRICK BROWN ALE

American Brown Ale 6.5% ABV
Surprisingly strong. Caramel and toffee throughout, with underlying notes of chocolate and coffee.

ESB

Extra Special Bitter 5.8% ABV
Caramel on the nose, and a slightly grassy palate, with fruit, honey, and butterscotch notes.

LONG HAMMER IPA

India Pale Ale 6.2% ABV
Medium bodied and crisp. Distinctive citrus bitterness comes from handfuls of hops added to the beer throughout the production process.

RIVER HORSE

2 Graphics Drive, Ewing,
New Jersey 08628, USA
www.riverhorse.com

Founded in 1996, in this historic
river town, by three brothers who
converted a former oyster cracker
plant into a brewery. A Philadelphia
investment firm bought control of the
brewery in 2007, leaving the brothers
in charge of brewing but committing
to expand distribution and the
product range.

ROCK BOTTOM

Various locations
www.rockbottom.com

The Rock Bottom chain operates
more than 30 brewery-restaurants,
together producing more than 40,000
barrels annually. They also have over
50 Old Chicago restaurants that
offer more than 30 beers each on
tap. Each Rock Bottom brewery
restaurant location usually features
similar core beers but the recipes
may vary from pub to pub.

ROGUE

2320 OSU Drive, Newport,
Oregon 97365, USA
www.rogue.com

Rogue Ales brewmaster John Maier
joined the company a year after it
opened in 1988. He has earned an
international reputation for brewing
envelope-pushing beers by creating
a well-structured malt foundation on
which to layer massive hop additions.
This approach has won hundreds of
awards and fostered the growth of the
"Rogue Nation" – loyal fans who
eagerly await the release of
limited-edition Johns Locker Stock
beers. Beyond its home bases of
Newport and Portland, Rogue Ales
operates brewpubs and restaurants
along the west coast, calling them
"micro-meeting halls". There's even
one at Portland International Airport.

BREWING SECRET Rogue beers are
top-fermented using their own
PacMan yeast which is well-suited
for bottle conditioning.

HOP HAZARD
PALE ALE 6.5% ABV
Hop-accented, citric and grassy
aromas, with caramel flavours
meeting slightly abrasive hops.

TRIPEL HORSE
TRIPLE 10% ABV
Sweet and spicy nose with vanilla
esters, and fresh fruit flavours
with satisfying hoppy bitterness.
A substantial alcohol bite.

TERMINAL STOUT
STOUT ABV VARIABLE
Reflecting local preference, it might
be deemed an Imperial Stout at one
location, Oatmeal, or Dry elsewhere.

MOLLY'S TITANIC BROWN ALE
BROWN ALE 5.6% ABV
Brown ales vary from pub to pub.
This version from Denver is
malt-driven. It is an award winner
in the "brown porter" category.

DEAD GUY ALE
HELLER BOCK 6.6% ABV
Complex, clean malt aroma, rich and
fruity, becoming toastier on the palate.
Bright bitter hops; dry and spicy.

BRUTAL IPA
EXTRA SPECIAL BITTER 5.8% ABV
Aromatic and flowery hops become
juicier on the palate, braced against
fermentation fruit and bready malt.
Bitter to the end.

SHAKESPEARE OATMEAL STOUT
STOUT 6% ABV
Dark, roasty, chocolate, and coffee
mingle with dark fruits and husky
malt. Substantial, balanced hops
and an oily/creamy smooth finish.

HAZELNUT BROWN NECTAR
BROWN ALE 6.2% ABV
Inspired by a home-brewer's recipe,
with a solid dose of hazelnuts
saturating a robust brown ale.

BEER TRAIL

OREGON

The term "Beervana" is often used to describe Oregon's culture of craft beer. The state also offers spectacular outdoor recreation from the Pacific Ocean on the west to Hells Canyon on the east, and up and down the Cascade Mountains in the centre. Beer touring opportunities abound, and it would be possible to spend weeks travelling and never drink the same beer twice. This three-day trail starts in the seaside town of Newport, which is home to the iconic Rogue Ales brewery. It continues the next day with scenic stops on the way to Portland, then concludes with a full day in the Rose City. For more information, visit www.oregoncraftbeer.org.

Rogue's Dead Guy Ale

1 DAY 1: HOUSE OF ROGUE BED AND BEER

Rogue Ales Public House is located on OSU Drive, right in the centre of the working seaport of Newport. There are plenty of bed and breakfasts to choose from in this friendly town, including Rogue's "Bed and Beer" apartments, above the public house. The public house is also the place to book in for one of the brewery tours, which commence at 3pm daily. *2320 OSU Drive, Newport (www.rogue.com)*

JOURNEY STATS
3 days
230km (142 miles)

2 DAY 2: PELICAN PUB AND BREWERY

The scenic 77-km (48-mile) drive from Newport to Pacific City easily occupies a morning, so you should arrive just in time for lunch at the Pelican Pub & Brewery. The brewery-restaurant is located on the shoreline of Pacific City, where there are outstanding views of the oft-photographed Haystack Rock and Cape Kiwanda. *33180 Cape Kiwanda Drive, Pacific City (www.yourlittlebeachtown.com/pelican)*

3 DAY 2: GOLDEN VALLEY BREWERY AND PUB

The scenic route to McMinnville passes through the Willamette Valley, one of the nation's premier wine-growing regions. The Golden Valley Brewery & Pub offers ales, sometimes aged in wine barrels. *980 East 4th St, McMinnville (www.goldenvalleybrewery.com)*

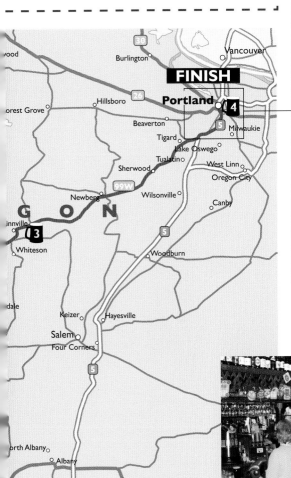

4 DAY 3: PORTLAND

With more than 50 breweries in the metropolitan region, it is little wonder that residents of Portland like to say they live in "Beervana". Here are some you could visit on Day 3 of this trail.

HAIR OF THE DOG

This tiny brewery uses equipment not originally designed for brewing. Visits by appointment. *61 SE Yamhill Street, Portland (www.hairofthedog.com)*

WIDMER BROTHERS *(see p78)*

Visit the brewery's Gasthaus restaurant to sample the full line-up of beers – including the Alt intended to be the brewery flagship before its Hefeweizen became an American standard. The brewery offers tours on Fridays and Saturdays. *929 North Russell, Portland (www.widmerbrothers.com)*

BRIDGEPORT *(see p25)*

Oregon's oldest surviving brewery helped turn the Pearl District into a hip locale. *1313 Northwest Marshall Street, Portland (www.bridgeportbrew.com)*

HIGGINS RESTAURANT AND BAR

Greg Higgins uses local produce for his widely praised menu, which pairs well with Oregon beers and wines. *1239 Southwest Broadway, Portland (www.higginsportland.com)*

GREEN DRAGON BISTRO AND PUB

This relative newcomer quickly became an instant hit with a trendy crowd. Offers a constantly changing selection of beers not necessarily found elsewhere, served by a knowledgeable staff. *928 Southeast 9th Avenue, Portland (www.pdxgreendragon.com)*

HORSE BRASS PUB

A Portland institution since 1976, the Horse Brass is a sprawling tribute to both the English pub and Oregon beer, offering 52 selections on draught. The pub is especially popular with the late-night crowd. *4534 Southeast Belmont Street, Portland (www.horsebrass.com)*

The Flanders Street
Brewpub in Portland, Oregon, has helped the city gain its reputation for fine beers.

TODAY'S SPECIAL

guine w/dill

am sauce, prawns

veggies

$7.96

ON CASK

Stout H

Clam Chowde

PORTLAND · BREWING · COMPANY

NOW FEATURING

ODSTOCK IPA

AVARIAN WE

MER PALE A

NDER

STO

BEER:
So much more
than just a
Breakfast Drink.

BREWERY

RUSSIAN RIVER

725 4th Street, Santa Rosa,
California 95404, USA
www.russianriverbrewing.com

Owner-brewmaster Vinnie Cilurzo's
creative use of hops, yeasts, and wine-
barrel-ageing make it seem incredible
that all his beers come from the same
brewery. He was the first to brew an
Imperial India Pale Ale commercially,
when he was at Blind Pig Brewing.
That beer is now called Pliny the
Elder and has become the benchmark
for the style. Cilurzo and his wife,

Natalie, have built a production
brewery separate from their popular
downtown brewpub, giving more
space for a wider range of barrels and
ageing. Each variety (the base beer
and barrel type differ) spends at least
a year on wood.

BREWING SECRET Cilurzo uses varieties
of wild yeast in his beers. They need
careful handling by a master brewer,
but give great results.

SAINT ARNOLD

2000 Lyons Avenue, Houston,
Texas 77020, USA
www.saintarnold.com

The oldest surviving and largest craft
brewery in Texas was founded in
1994. Saint Arnold grew out of its
"micro" status in 2007, although it
continues to sell its beer only within
the state borders. Austrian-born
St. Arnold is one of the patron saints
of beer; the brewery's fermenters
are named after other saints.

SAMUEL ADAMS

30 Germania Street, Boston,
Massachusetts 02130, USA
www.samueladams.com

The name Samuel Adams has been
synonymous with craft beer since
Boston Beer Company was one
of just a few speciality beer sellers
in the country. The company launched
the brand in 1984, when it contracted
production to mainstream producers
with excess capacity. Boston Beer
has since purchased some of those
breweries and produces much of

BEER

PLINY THE ELDER

DOUBLE INDIA PALE ALE 8% ABV
Hoppy aroma, hoppy flavour, and
a hoppy bitterness – all supported
by a firm malt base.

BEATIFICATION

SOUR ALE 5.5% ABV
A spontaneously fermented
blended beer. Complex, tart mix
of fruit and wood. Just-right acidity
at the finish.

TEMPTATION

BELGIAN STRONG ALE 7.5% ABV
Aged in Chardonnay barrels with
wild yeast. Complex and vinous.
Sharp nose; Chardonnay and oak
emerges as it warms.

BLIND PIG IPA

INDIA PALE ALE 6.1% ABV
Explosive floral, citrus, and pine
aromas. Sturdy malt accents the
fruit character. Clean, tangy finish.

AMBER

AMBER ALE 5.5% ABV
Caramel and fermentation fruit,
with bright, spicy hops providing
balance. Excellent on cask.

ELISSA IPA

INDIA PALE ALE 6.6% ABV
Delightfully hoppy throughout,
brimming with grapefruit character.
Big and juicy, with rich malt to
match the decided bitterness.

BOSTON LAGER

VIENNA LAGER 4.9% ABV
Complex flowery/piney nose.
Full bodied, with caramel in the
middle, and a satisfyingly dry finish.

SCOTCH ALE

SCOTTISH ALE 5.5% ABV
Rich with caramel and molasses
aromas and flavours. Underlying
earthy and smoky notes come
from the peat-smoked malt.

its own beer. The company holds an employees' homebrew contest each year, with the winner's beer being sold commercially, alongside winning brews from a national amateur competition.

BREWING SECRET Today almost one out of five craft beers sold in the USA is a Samuel Adams.

SARANAC
830 Varick Street, Utica,
New York 13502, USA
www.saranac.com

Matt Brewing moved the Saranac line to the fore in the 1990s, emphasizing craft beers at the expense of family brands brewed since 1888. Saranac core beers and varietals have thrived, while Matt's historic Utica Club brew remains as a retro favourite.

BREWING SECRET "UC" was the first beer back on sale after Prohibition.

SCHLAFLY
2100 Locust Street, St. Louis,
Missouri 63103, USA
www.schlafly.com

The Saint Louis Brewery makes beers packaged under the Schlafly brand at a suburban location, but the original downtown brewpub, The Taproom, is the location tourists seek out. Co-founder Tom Schlafly wrote a book called *A New Religion in Mecca* about "sharing" the St. Louis market with international giant AB InBev.

SHIPYARD
86 Newbury Street, Portland,
Maine 04101, USA
www.shipyard.com

British-born Shipyard brewmaster Alan Pugsley is one of the best-known figures in craft brewing, having trained under Peter Austin and established breweries around the world, including Geary's in 1984. Shipyard's beers reflect his philosophy of putting drinkability first. While not necessarily drawing huge public attention, this has driven annual double-digit growth.

BLACK LAGER
SCHWARZBIER 4.9% ABV
Roasted but smooth, with caramel and nuts on the palate. Coffee notes throughout, providing a pleasing closing bitterness.

UTOPIAS
STRONG ALE 28% ABV
Aged in brandy and port barrels, it soars with ever-changing vinous flavours. Sip like a rare cognac.

PALE ALE
ENGLISH PALE ALE 5.5% ABV
Fruity yeastiness is complemented by crisp, citrussy hops. Building bitterness extends a long dry finish.

WHITE IPA
BELGIAN-STYLE IPA 6% ABV
Waves of orange and citrus notes from Citra hops emanate from this unfiltered wheat beer.

SCHLAFLY PALE ALE
ENGLISH PALE ALE 4.4% ABV
Biscuit and fruit, with a dry, not-too-bitter finish. The brewpubs serve a strong, dry-hopped version.

SCHLAFLY OATMEAL STOUT
OATMEAL STOUT 5.7% ABV
Breakfast in a glass. Coffee and cream are balanced with a slight oiliness from the oatmeal. Smooth, with hints of smoky chocolate.

OLD THUMPER
EXTRA SPECIAL BITTER 5.6% ABV
Brewed under exclusive license from Peter Austin's Ringwood Brewery in England. Richly fruity with well-balanced bitterness.

EXPORT ALE
GOLDEN ALE 5.1% ABV
The flagship ale. Sweet honey and fruit nose continues on the palate.

BREWERY

SHMALTZ

6 Fairchild Square, Clifton Park,
New York 12065, USA
www.shmaltzbrewing.com

Since Jeremy Cowan started selling
HE'BREW beer in 1996 from the back
of his grandmother's car, it has grown
exponentially and trades nearly 15,000
barrels of over 20 beer styles to
35 states through over 4,000 retailers.
Shmaltz continues to roll out new
high-alcohol kosher beers as well as
creating the Coney Island Lagers.

SIERRA NEVADA

1075 East 20th Street, Chico,
California 95928, USA
www.sierranevada.com

Sierra Nevada Brewing has been
introducing beer drinkers to citrussy,
piney Northwest hops since former
home-brewers Ken Grossman and
Paul Camusi launched their flagship
Pale Ale in 1981. Although many
other more bitter beers have since
emerged, the brewery continues to
act as a matchmaker between beer
drinkers and hops. Sierra Nevada is
also an industry leader in good
environmental practice. It has
commissioned the first phase of
one of the country's largest private
solar installations, which will bring
it close to its goal of generating
100 per cent of its energy needs.

SKA

225 Girard Street, Durango,
Colorado 81301, USA
www.skabrewing.com

Bill Graham and Dave Thibodeau
named their brewery for the Jamaican
music they played while home-brewing
in college, reflecting their motto "it
takes characters to brew beer with
character". When they founded Ska
in 1995, they had day jobs and brewed
at night. By 2008, they couldn't keep
up with the demand and had to build
a new brewery.

BEER

BITTERSWEET LENNY'S R.I.P.A.
IMPERIAL INDIA PALE ALE 10% ABV
A tribute to Lenny Bruce. Thick
with rich malt, long hops; three
different rye malts add spiciness.

MESSIAH NUT BROWN ALE
BROWN ALE 5.6% ABV
"The beer you've been waiting for."
Complex, without being demanding,
with coffee, toffee, nuts, and earthy
hops in the flavour and aroma.

PALE ALE
PALE ALE 5.6% ABV
Piney, grapefruity Cascade hops play
against malt fruitiness on both the
nose and the palate.

HARVEST FRESH HOP ALE
INDIA PALE ALE 6.7% ABV
Made with "wet" hops, harvested
and brewed on the same day. Oily
and aromatic, like picking and using
herbs straight from the garden.

BIGFOOT ALE
BARLEY WINE 9.6% ABV
Earthy and chewy, with prominent
citric hops and whisky-like rich
malts. Boldly bitter when young.

CELEBRATION ALE
INDIA PALE ALE 6.8% ABV
A winter seasonal, full of citrussy
hop flavours, notably of tangerines.
A balanced, fruity-caramel malt
backbone and persistent bitterness.

TEN PIN PORTER
PORTER 5.5% ABV
Chocolate and caramel throughout,
with a strong roasted coffee flavour.
Eases into bitterness.

TRUE BLONDE ALE
GOLDEN ALE 5.3% ABV
Brewed with honey made just north
of town. Light biscuity malt, hints
of honey, and a touch of citric hops.

SLY FOX

331 Circle of Progress Drive, Pottstown, Pennsylvania 19464, USA
www.slyfoxbeer.com

Since opening its doors in 1995, Sly Fox Brewing has mirrored many other success stories by bottling special beers in 750ml (1¼ pints) bottles, packaging beer in cans, judicious expansion, and distinctive promotions.

BREWING SECRET Come here on Incubus Friday (the first of each month) for the tapping of a new barrel of Triple.

SMUTTYNOSE

225 Heritage Avenue, Portsmouth, New Hampshire 03801, USA
www.smuttynose.com

Although Smuttynose Brewing has earned a reputation for its carefully balanced offerings, the brewery was also one of the first to embrace "extreme beers", launching a Big Beer Series in 1998. Succeeding on all fronts, it has outgrown its current site and has recently built a new brewery nearby.

SNAKE RIVER

265 South Millward Street, Jackson, Wyoming 83001, USA
www.snakeriverbrewing.com

Located in central Jackson, with a view of Snow King Mountain and standing but a few miles from the Jackson Hole ski resort, Snake River brewpub occupies an old cinder-block warehouse. It has won the Small Brewery of the Year award twice at the Great American Beer Festival. Most of its beers are sold on draught from its restaurant above the basement brewery. As part of its commitment to being a sustainable business, it stopped using bottles in 2011 and moved to cans.

PIKELAND PILS
PILSNER 4.9% ABV
Fresh and crisp. Delicate pilsner malt is interwoven with grassy, floral hops – spicy and firmly bitter.

SAISON VOS
SAISON 6.9% ABV
Spicy, fruity, and hoppy nose, very lively on the tongue, tart fruit and bitterness emerging. Satisfyingly dry.

SHOALS PALE ALE
PALE ALE 5.6% ABV
First made at the Portsmouth pub. Pleasant fruity/biscuit palate gives way to a crisp American hop finish.

ROBUST PORTER
PORTER 6.2% ABV
Rich dark fruits and chocolate, well blended throughout. Rich, roasty flavours leave a strong impression for a medium-strength beer.

ZONKER STOUT
STOUT 6% ABV
Roasted barley sets a bold tone, with chocolate (almost sweet) underneath. Pleasingly dry finish.

PAKO'S EYE-P-A
AMERICAN IPA 6.8% ABV
A bold malt beer which explodes with bold citrus flavours from a blend of Simcoe and Columbus hops.

SNAKE RIVER LAGER
VIENNA LAGER 4.8% ABV
Golden, with a thick white head. Malt-accented, clean toasted and caramel flavours, drying hop finish.

OB-1
BROWN ALE 4.9% ABV
Soft caramel and toffee flavours with a hint of ripe fruit can be found in this organic brew.

BREWERY

SOUTHAMPTON

40 Bowden Square, Southampton,
New York 11968, USA
www.publick.com

Southampton Publick House's busy
brewmaster, Phil Markowski, routinely
travels to three breweries in New
York State and Pennsylvania to make
Southampton-branded beer. As well
as the eclectic range he's created
for the brewery-restaurant on
Long Island, he also brews specials,
packaged in 750ml (1¼ pints) corked
bottles, and oversees the production

of Double White and Secret Ale.
Since early 2008, the Southampton
range of beers has been marketed
by Pabst.

BREWING SECRET Markowski is the
author of *Farmhouse Ales*, a definitive
guide to the *saison* and *bière de garde*
styles of Wallonia in Belgium.

SOUTHERN TIER

2072 Stoneman Circle, Lakewood,
New York 14750, USA
www.stbcbeer.com

When Southern Tier Brewing opened
in 2004, it was expected to sell a
conservative range of beers. Instead
success came with an assertive IPA,
followed by other beers that showed
an equal ability to deliver great flavour.

BREWING SECRET They continue to push
envelopes, as evidenced by a trio of
11 per cent imperial stouts.

SPEAKEASY

1195 Evans Avenue, San Francisco,
California 94124, USA
www.goodbeer.com

Two big eyes peering suspiciously out
of the darkness decorate the brewery
loading dock at Speakeasy Ales &
Lagers, a nod to Prohibition days.
Since Speakeasy opened in 1997 local
sales have been its core business, and
it remains a San Francisco brewery
first and foremost. Its Big Daddy IPA
is named after venerable local publican
David Keene of the Toronado.

BEER

DOUBLE WHITE

WITBIER 6.6% ABV
Bright floral, citric, and sweet notes
from the start. Rich textures cut by
wheat and orange tartness.

IMPERIAL PORTER

BALTIC PORTER 7.2% ABV
Rich, intoxicating aromas of dark
fruit and chocolate, joined by
coffee on the palate. Pleasantly
bitter finish.

SAISON DELUXE

SAISON 6.5% ABV
An endorsement for *Farmhouse
Ales* – fruity, peppery, slightly tart,
earthy, and refreshing.

KELLER PILS

PILSNER 5% ABV
With a slight haze, it is a sweet,
crisp German-style pilsner with
a light carbonation.

IMPERIAL PUMKING

PUMPKIN BEER 8.2% ABV
Big, bold, and full of spicy
complexities. Little bitterness, with
notes of pecans, butter, and vanilla.

INTIQUITY

IMPERIAL BLACK ALE 9% ABV
As black as a winter's night, the
heavily hopped ale exudes dark
fruits, coffee malt, and citrus flavours.
A big beer, it's almost chewy.

BIG DADDY IPA

INDIA PALE ALE 6.5% ABV
Hop driven – juicy citrus and pine.
Lightly caramel, enough sturdy malt
to stand up to persistent bitterness.

PROHIBITION ALE

AMBER ALE 6.1% ABV
Their flagship, best on draught in
San Francisco. Long hop flavours,
particularly citrus, playing against
a definite caramel sweetness.

SPOETZL

603 Brewery Street, Shiner,
Texas 77984, USA
www.shiner.com

Founded in 1909, the Spoetzl Brewery has ridden the success of Shiner Bock into national prominence. In 2004 it began counting down toward its 100th birthday by releasing a special new beer every year, each one reflecting a German heritage that dates back to the original Shiner Brewing Association.

SPRECHER

701 West Glendale Avenue, Glendale, Wisconsin 53209, USA
www.sprecherbrewery.com

Randy Sprecher started his brewery in downtown Milwaukee in 1985 aiming to do more than brew the German-style beers typical of Milwaukee breweries. He insisted on authenticity, such as using real fruit in fruit beers.

BREWING SECRET Bananas are used in their Mbege African-style beer.

STARR HILL

5391 Three Notched Road, Crozet, Virginia 22932, USA
www.starrhill.com

Starr Hill Brewing became the second small-scale Virginia brewery in which Anheuser-Busch bought a stake during 2007, when it struck a deal that could lead to national distribution. The brewery has produced well-received traditional beers since taking over a failed brewpub in 1999 and later adding a production facility.

STEAMWORKS

801 East 2nd Avenue Durango, Colorado 81301, USA
www.steamworksbrewing.com

Although Steamworks Brewing sells a full range in its two brewery-restaurants (the other is in Bayfield), it has found the greatest success in an expanding southwestern market with its German-inspired beers. The brewery takes its name from the steam-powered tourist train that runs between Durango and Silverton.

SHINER BOCK

AMERICAN DARK LAGER 4.4% ABV
A dark lager, rather than a true German bock, with hints of caramel sweetness. Low on hops.

WILD HARE

AMERICAN PALE ALE 5.5% ABV
A subtle blend of aromatic hops that provide a fresh floral aroma and pair well with its toffee malt flavour.

BLACK BAVARIAN

SCHWARZBIER 5.9% ABV
Dark sweet molasses nose, with hints of coffee, chocolate, and caramel. Medium bodied and clean.

HEFE WEISS

HEFEWEIZEN 4.2% ABV
Yeasty, subdued banana and spices on the nose, more banana and honey on a soft palate, brightened by spicy cloves.

JOMO

VIENNA LAGER 4.6% ABV
Bready, even toasty to start with. Toastier and full malts in the mouth with a hint of Noble hops and clean, balancing bitterness.

DARK STARR STOUT

STOUT 4.2% ABV
Even the nose leaves an impression of dryness. Roasted malt and rich chocolate in a pleasantly light body.

STEAM ENGINE LAGER

AMBER LAGER 5.1% ABV
Pours a bright copper, with sweet malt on the nose. More caramel in the flavour, even honey.

COLORADO KÖLSCH

KÖLSCH 4.8% ABV
Not as bright or crisp as you'd find in Cologne, but popular as a light lager with lingering sweetness.

BREWERY

STEVENS POINT

2617 Water Street, Stevens Point,
Wisconsin 54481, USA
www.pointbeer.com

The Stevens Point Brewery gained a
measure of fame when, in 1973 (at
a time when American beer choice
was at its lowest), *Chicago Daily News*
columnist Mike Royko named Point
Special as the best beer in the USA.
Founded in 1857, Stevens Point is the
fifth-oldest continuously operating
brewery in the country.

STONE

1999 Citracado Parkway, Escondido,
California 92029, USA
www.stonebrew.com

Although some find the "You're not
worthy" campaign, used to promote
Arrogant Bastard Ale, off-putting,
CEO Greg Koch's argument in favour
of particularly full-flavoured beers
is the opposite of elitist. He doesn't
think beer appreciation takes special
skill: "If you want to turn people on
to great beer, use great beer to do it",
he says. That philosophy has resulted

in 30 per cent annual growth year
after year. After building a larger
brewery in 2006, the company added
the Stone Brewing World Bistro &
Gardens, serving local organic "slow
food" dishes and featuring a large,
lovely beer garden landscaped
with boulders and dry-stone walls,
reflecting the brewery's name.

STRAUB

303 Sorg Street, St. Marys,
Pennsylvania 15857, USA
www.straubbeer.com

Straub is a family-run throwback
to 1872, when it was founded. The
brewery enjoyed record sales in
2007 although its flagship beer is a
pale lager brewed with shaved corn.
It sells 60 per cent of its beer in its
home town, and offers visitors an
"Eternal Tap" (pour-your-own beer).

BEER

POINT SPECIAL
AMERICAN LAGER 4.7% ABV
Has a loyal regional following. Pours
bright and drinks smooth, with
sweet malt and hints of grassy hops.

POINT BEYOND
INDIA PALE ALE 6.5% ABV
Golden in colour, with a clean
biscuit malt character, it is topped
with passion fruit flavours from
the fragrant Galaxy hops.

IPA
INDIA PALE ALE 6.9% ABV
Starts with fruity hop aromas and
firm malt character, then develops
complexity. Finish is bitter but bright.

SMOKED PORTER
PORTER 5.9% ABV
Smoke plays a supporting role,
joining roasted coffee beans on
the nose, and chocolate on the
palate, adding depth throughout.

ARROGANT BASTARD ALE
STRONG ALE 7.2% ABV
Promises to be aggressive and
certainly lives up to it. Juicy hops
matched throughout by rich malt.
Lingering bitter finish.

IMPERIAL RUSSIAN STOUT
IMPERIAL STOUT 10.6% ABV
Intense, full of chocolate, roasted
coffee and dark fruits. All balanced
by a brooding bitterness.

STRAUB AMERICAN LAGER
AMERICAN LAGER 4.1% ABV
Fresh and grainy, light and clean on
the tongue. Minimal hoppiness, slight
bitterness that balances the beer.

STRAUB AMERICAN AMBER LAGER
AMBER LAGER 4.1% ABV
Based on a bock, but lighter. Sweet
malt on the palate, with caramel
and a touch of spiciness.

SUDWERK

2001 Second Street, Davis, California 95618, USA
www.sudwerk.com

Officially Privatbrauerei Sudwerk Hübsch, this brewery-restaurant focused on German-style beer and food when it opened in 1990. The restaurant has since been sold, and the menu now features "California cuisine", but beer from the separate Sudwerk Brewery remains old world. In 2013, one of the founder's grandson took over the brewery.

SUDWERK LAGER/HELLES

HELLES 4.9% ABV
Aromas and flavours of sweet malt. Complex texture on the palate; firm but unimposing hops.

SUDWERK PILSNER

PILSNER 5% ABV
Sweet malt brightens the nose, mixed with spicy hops. Full bodied. Bread-dough yeastiness balanced with lingering bitterness.

SUMMIT

910 Montreal Circle, Saint Paul, Minnesota 55102, USA
www.summitbrewing.com

Focusing on its Twin Cities market and a small core of beers, Summit Brewing has grown into one of the country's largest craft breweries, eventually building Minnesota's first brand new production brewery since the 1930s. It is expanding distribution to 17 states and has begun to offer special release beers.

EXTRA PALE ALE

PALE ALE 5.2% ABV
Distinctive, but not overpowering, citrus nose, firm fruity middle and dry finish with a scent of lemon.

SAGA IPA

INDIA PALE ALE 6.4% ABV
Tropical fruit flavours from a cocktail of American hops are in harmony with a clean, assertive bitterness.

SURLY

4811 Dusharme Drive, Minneapolis, Minnesota 55429, USA
www.surlybrewing.com

Surly Brewing sold its first beer in February of 2006, and by December the *Minneapolis St. Paul City Pages* had named founder Omar Ansari as one of its "artists of the year". Packaged in cans and sold only in Minnesota, the brewery's often intense, and seldom "to style", beers have developed a national following.

BENDER

BROWN ALE 5.5% ABV
Brewed with oatmeal, adding creamy texture to a blend of chocolate, dark fruit, and nuts.

FURIOUS

INDIA PALE ALE 6.2% ABV
Only for those favouring the most aggressive of hopping. Piney and oily, only somewhat balanced by caramel. Flat out bitter.

TERMINAL GRAVITY

803 Southeast School Street, Enterprise, Oregon 97828, USA
www.terminalgravitybrewing.com

The brewpub that Steve Carper and Dean Duquette literally built themselves in 1997 in Northeast Oregon has expanded into a microbrewery. When it opened, they leased space to a baker and installed a kitchen that turns out great sausages. "We're the brewer, the baker, and the sausage maker," Duquette said at the time.

IPA

INDIA PALE ALE 6.9% ABV
Rich malts against citrus hops. Thick on the tongue, but cut by grapefruit. Citrus lingers.

EXTRA SPECIAL GOLDEN/ESG

PALE ALE 5.4% ABV
Noteworthy for its peach-tinged fermentation flavour, mingling nicely with light malt sweetness, and citrussy hops.

BREWERY

TERRAPIN

265 Newton Bridge Road, Athens,
Georgia 30607, USA
www.terrapinbeer.com

Spike Buckowski and John Cochran
began shipping beer from their own
brewhouse early in 2008, almost
six years after the Terrapin Beer
Company started selling contract-
brewed Rye Pale Ale. That beer was
an immediate hit, as was the Monster
Beer Tour, a series of strong beers
released after Georgia raised its
6 per cent ABV cap on beer.

THREE FLOYDS

9750 Indiana Parkway, Munster,
Indiana 46321, USA
www.3floyds.com

Beginning with its flagship Alpha King
in 1996, Three Floyds Brewing had
lived by the philosophy of brewmaster
Nick Floyd: "I love the smell of hops
in the morning. It smells like victory."

BREWING SECRET The annual release of
Dark Lord Russian Imperial Stout sells
out in one day, with customers driving
hundreds of miles to buy it.

TRUMER

1404 Fourth Street, Berkeley,
California 94710, USA
www.trumer-international.com

Trumer Brauerei is a partnership
between Texas-based Gambrinus,
which bought and remodelled a closed
brewery in 2004, and the Trumer
Brauerei in Austria. The Pils is brewed
to the same recipe at each brewery.

BREWING SECRET Bottles for taste-testing
are regularly exchanged between
breweries to ensure consistency.

TWO BROTHERS

30W315 Calumet Avenue, Warrenville,
Illinois 60555, USA
www.twobrothersbrew.com

Brothers Jim and Jason Ebel opened
their brewery in 1997 with a
brewhouse designed to produce
traditional hefeweizen, supplemented
with recycled equipment. For
instance, their grandfather donated
bulk milk tanks from his dairy farm.
Recently, a line of stronger beers
has fuelled the growth of all brands.

BEER

RYE PALE ALE
PALE ALE 5.5% ABV
Rye blends with bright grapefruit,
adds texture to fruit fermentation,
and complements late bitterness.

**WAKE 'N' BAKE COFFEE
OATMEAL STOUT**
IMPERIAL STOUT 9.4% ABV
It is all in the name, along with
chocolate-covered dark fruits.

ALPHA KING
PALE ALE 6.6% ABV
Opens with a rush of citrus fruits.
Firm malt backbone, matched by
hop oils. Prolonged bitterness.

GUMBALLHEAD
AMERICAN WHEAT BEER 5.6% ABV
Citrus and orchard fruits on the
nose, followed by wheat tartness
and hops throughout.

TRUMER PILS
PILSNER 4.9% ABV
Grassy and grainy fresh, a lovely
blend of pilsner malt and noble
hops. Slightly sweet palate,
Noble hop flavour and a lively
mouthfeel. Refreshing dry finish.

DOMAINE DUPAGE
BIERE DE GARDE 5.9% ABV
Sweet malts, including caramel on
the nose. More caramel-toffee
on the palate. Clean smooth finish.

EBEL'S WEISS
HEFEWEIZEN 4.9% ABV
Banana and cloves, maybe lemon
too, from the outset. Bready and
wheat-tart in the mouth, moving
on to a smooth, light finish.

UINTA

1722 South Fremont Drive, Salt Lake City, Utah 84104, USA
www.uintabrewing.com

Uinta Brewing actively promotes Utah's outdoor culture and the environment, using slogans like "Keeping Utah the way we found it – except with beer". The brewery joined Utah Power's Blue Sky Programme in 2002, when it installed a new brewhouse and became 100 per cent wind powered.

UTAH BREWERS

1763 South 300 West, Salt Lake City, Utah 84115, USA
www.utahbeers.com

The Utah Brewers Cooperative is the production and packaging facility for Squatters Craft Beers and Wasatch Beers. The shared production facility opened in 2000. Their beers are now available beyond the pubs they operate.

BREWING SECRET Utah law limits beers to 4 per cent ABV, except for those sold in state stores.

VICTORY

420 Acorn Lane, Downingtown, Pennsylvania 19335, USA
www.victorybeer.com

Victory Brewing founders Ron Barchet and Bill Covaleski – who met on a school bus in 1973 – travelled much of the beer world, apprenticed in Germany, and worked in USA microbreweries before starting their own in 1996. The breadth of their interests is reflected in the range of their beers, and their new brewhouse is designed to produce almost any style in a traditional manner. They earned an early reputation for hoppy American beers, and their Belgian-inspired ales are among their most popular.

BREWING SECRET Victory has long-term contracts with German hop-growers to assure the availability of authentic ingredients for their lagers.

BABA ORGANIC BLACK LAGER
LAGER 4% ABV
Pitch black in colour, it is a full-flavoured malty beer with hints of citrus hops.

KING'S PEAK PORTER
PORTER 4% ABV
Coffee and cream sweetness, restrained dark fruit on the palate, with a pepper and cocoa dry finish.

SQUATTERS PROVO GIRL PILSNER
PILSNER 4% ABV
Flowery hops freshen a bready nose. A mild sweetness yields to a dry bracing finish. Light bodied.

WASATCH POLYGAMY PORTER
PORTER 4% ABV
"Why have just one?", the brewery asks. Chocolate dominates, with some roast and a short dry finish.

PRIMA PILS
PILSNER 5.3% ABV
Fresh flowery aromas, cookie-like palate, and a solidly bitter-rough finish. Sturdy yet delicate.

GOLDEN MONKEY
TRIPLE 9.5% ABV
Spicy, with hints of banana followed by light pepper. Candy-sweet on the palate, with a dry finish.

HOPDEVIL ALE
INDIA PALE ALE 6.7% ABV
Spicy hop aromas, hop flavours, and woody bitterness throughout, laid on a firm malt base.

WHIRLWIND WITBIER
WITBIER 5% ABV
Assertive orange, peppery spices, and cloves on the nose. Silky in the mouth, quickly matched by a spicy bite and tart wheat.

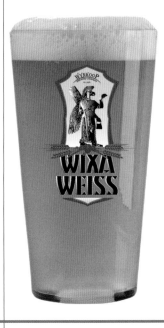

BREWERY

WACHUSETT

175 State Road East, Westminster,
Massachusetts 01473, USA
www.wachusettbrew.com

Wachusett founders Ned, Kevin, and Peter concentrate on delivering fresh beer close to home, and 70 per cent of sales are in Worcester County, central Massachusetts. They have set up a programme to enable students from their alma mater of Worcester Polytechnic to earn college credit while working at the brewery.

WEYERBACHER

905 Line Street, Easton,
Pennsylvania 18042, USA
www.weyerbacher.com

Since opening in a livery stable, with a nod toward English-inspired ales but using the original spelling of his German name, founder Dan Weirback has changed directions a few times. The company briefly tried the brewpub business, but then moved to a larger facility, and has thrived by making big, bold "New American" beers.

WIDMER BROTHERS

929 North Russell, Portland,
Oregon 97227, USA
www.widmerbrothers.com

More than two decades old, the US-centric Hefeweizen (cloudy but accented by yeast rather than hops) that the Widmer brothers basically invented continues to drive double-digit growth. Widmer and Redhook have merged to form a single company called Craft Breweries Alliance, but Widmer maintains its own brewery.

WYNKOOP

1634 18th Street, Denver,
Colorado 80202, USA
www.wynkoop.com

The first brewpub in the Rockies, Wynkoop settled into Denver's "LoDo" area before it was trendy, and co-founder John Hickenlooper later became the city's mayor. A gathering spot after hours during the Great American Beer Festival each fall, the pub sponsors an annual search for America's Beer Drinker of the Year.

BEER

COUNTRY PALE ALE
GOLDEN ALE 5% ABV
The partners' first creation strikes a balance between floral hops and bready, toasted malts.

BLUEBERRY
FRUIT BEER 4.5% ABV
This wheat-based beer plays to mixed reviews, with natural blueberry the dominant note, particularly on the nose.

IMPERIAL PUMPKIN ALE
SPICED BEER 8% ABV
Seasonal. An alcohol-infused slice of pumpkin pie – loaded with plenty of nutmeg and cinnamon.

BLITHERING IDIOT
BARLEY WINE 11.1% ABV
A European-style, slow-sipping barley wine. A sweet biscuit maltiness slips into layers of dark red fruits.

HEFEWEIZEN
AMERICAN HEFEWEIZEN 4.9% ABV
Citrus, particularly lemon zest, is matched against clean, bready-yet-tart wheat. Finale of grapefruit.

OMISSION
PALE LAGER 4.6% ABV
Refreshing lemony notes on the nose and a touch of malt sweetness. Flavours are clean, but muted. The hops provide more citrus notes.

WIXA WEISS
HEFEWEIZEN 4.8% ABV
Begins with aromas of bananas, orchard fruits and bubble-gum. Tart wheat on the tongue, while clove lingers in the back of the throat.

PATTY'S CHILE BEER
SPICED BEER 4.4% ABV
A light, German-style beer with a punch delivered by heaps of Anaheim chillies added to every barrel.

MORE BEERS OF

THE USA

The USA is the home of craft brewing, with more small batch producers than anywhere else in the world. These are often very regional operations, with their beers travelling no further than the local and neighbouring towns.

THE BRUERY

715 Dunn Way, Placentia,
California 92870, USA
www.thebruery.com

Former home-brewer and law student Patrick Rue turned a passion for wood-aged beers into business, fusing his family name with "brewery" to get the brewery's name. His beers are neither pasteurized nor filtered, and rely on natural carbonation for conditioning. Rue aims to make beers with character and depth using the purest of means.

GRAY'S

2424 West Court Street, Janesville,
Wisconsin 53548, USA
www.graybrewing.com

The Gray family has been brewing in Janesville since 1856, but not always alcoholic beer. The brewery focused on making soda between 1912 (when it quit beer production just ahead of Prohibition) and 1994, when Gray's was forced to rebuild its plant after an arson attack and decided to return to its beer-making heritage.

MCNEILL'S

90 Elliot Street, Brattleboro,
Vermont 05301, USA

Founder Ray McNeill, a classically trained cellist, has prided himself on careful research into traditional styles since opening his brewpub in 1991. The names of his beers, however, are sometimes less than traditional, or even appetizing.

BREWING SECRET The brewpub specializes in cask-conditioned beers.

NIMBUS

3850 East 44th Street, Tucson,
Arizona 85713, USA
www.nimbusbeer.com

Nimbus has made ales since 1997, first using equipment scavenged from Vermont and later modernizing and expanding. The name comes from founder-brewer Nimbus Couzin.

BREWING SECRET The water profile here is much like that of Burton upon Trent in England – hard and rich in sulphur.

BREWERY

SAISON RUE
SAISON 8.5% ABV
The addition of rye adds some dryness to this USA interpretation of a Belgian favourite. Full in warming alcohol, it is an ideal partner for bold cheeses.

HUMULUS LAGER
LAGER 7.4% ABV
Aromatic hop flavours dominated by citrus, pine, and herbal flavours.

OATMEAL STOUT
OATMEAL STOUT 5.21% ABV
Flavours of roasted coffee beans and chocolate, with caramel and sweet creaminess. Lightly bitter, dry finish.

WISCO WHEAT
GERMAN ALE 4.4% ABV
A softly hopped beer with a distinctive citrus fruit aroma. Pale in colour. Unfiltered and easy drinking, it is a summer's day thirst quencher.

DEAD HORSE INDIA PALE ALE
INDIA PALE ALE 5.7% ABV
Floral and earthy, East Kent Goldings hops on a sturdy base of rich English malts. Woody, dry finish.

CHAMP ALE
AMERICAN PALE ALE 5.5% ABV
A West-coast-style pale ale, it marries English and American malts with overlays of citrus hops.

NIMBUS PALE ALE
PALE ALE 5.5% ABV
Abundant Northwest hop aroma, and flavours of citrus and pine. Best quaffed close to the brewery.

OLD MONKEY SHINE
OLD ALE 8.2% ABV
Rich malts and British hops give this beer an old-world feel. Full bodied, with caramel, chocolate, and even Christmas-cake flavours.

BEER

STOUDTS

2800 North Reading Road, Route 272,
Adamstown, Pennsylvania 19501, USA
www.stoudtsbeer.com

Founders Carol (the brewer) and Ed Stoudt founded their brewery and adjoining steakhouse with a focus on German-inspired beers, and for more than 20 years they have balanced European tradition and American innovation. The Stoudt's adjoining antiques mall is one of many in the "Antiques Capital of America".

TOMMYKNOCKER

1401 Miner Street, Idaho Springs,
Colorado 80452, USA
www.tommyknocker.com

Tommyknocker Brewing's name stems from the town's mining background – after gold was discovered in 1859 the Argo mine supplied the Denver mint with half its gold needs. The Cornish miners who worked here were firm believers in pixies called Tommyknockers who lived in the mines and could bring good luck and protection.

TRÖEGS

200 East Hersheypark Drive, Hershey,
Pennsylvania 17033, USA
www.troegs.com

In 2007, just one year after Tröegs Brewing tripled the size of its plant, brother-owners John and Chris Trogner added equipment to double their production capacity. Although its core beers sustain growth, specials such as Mad Elf, brewed with cherries, and a "Scratch" series of one-offs, have created demand well beyond Pennsylvania.

YUENGLING

5th and Mahantongo Streets, Pottsville,
Pennsylvania 17901, USA
www.yuengling.com

The oldest brewing company in the USA, operating since 1829, Yuengling brews with adjuncts, but has set itself apart from more mainstream producers. The brewery has thrived right along with craft, all-malt beers. It has built a second brewery (the original is in Pottsville) and bought a large, idle Florida brewery to help keep up with demand.

BREWERY

STOUDTS PILS
PILSNER 5.4% ABV
A crisp expression of Saaz hops, flowery up front, spicy in the middle, long and dry at the finish.

FAT DOG STOUT
IMPERIAL STOUT 9% ABV
An oatmeal stout, but brewed to Imperial strength. Thick and rich with molasses, prunes, and bittersweet coffee flavours.

BUTT HEAD BOCK
DOPPELBOCK 8.2% ABV
Caramel and toasted malts on the nose. Richer on the palate, warming, with surprising berry fruitiness.

PICK AXE IPA
INDIA PALE ALE 6.2% ABV
Hop-spicy nose with noticeable malt fruitiness, biscuit on the palate as well as earthy hops.

TROEGENATOR DOUBLE BOCK
DOPPELBOCK 8.2% ABV
Malt-driven, with sweet caramel and toffee aromas joined by toasted bread crust in a medium body.

HOPBACK AMBER ALE
AMBER ALE 6% ABV
Caramel-sweet fruit character with bright, floral-spicy hops. The amped-up version is called Nugget Nectar.

TRADITIONAL LAGER
AMERICAN LAGER 4.4% ABV
Amber colour and light body. Slightly sweet, floral aromas, and sweet again on the palate. Crisp at the end, with subtle bitterness.

ORIGINAL BLACK & TAN
BLENDED BEER 4.7% ABV
A blend of Yuengling Premium and Porter. Pours quite dark, with chocolate and caramel flavours.

BEER

Pyramid Breweries, based in Seattle, is a characterful brewery with a bar-restaurant.

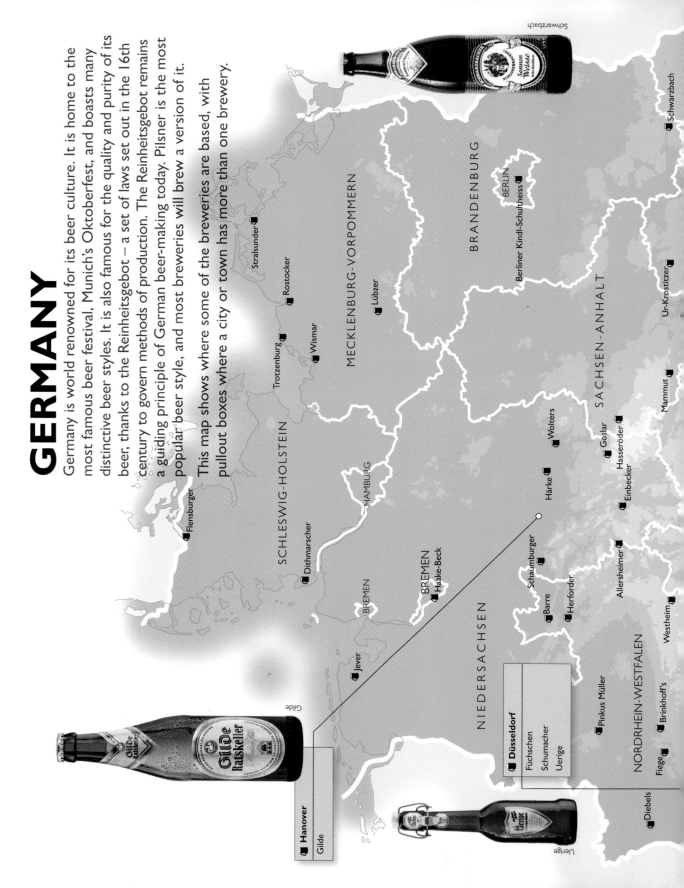

GERMANY

Germany is world renowned for its beer culture. It is home to the most famous beer festival, Munich's Oktoberfest, and boasts many distinctive beer styles. It is also famous for the quality and purity of its beer, thanks to the Reinheitsgebot – a set of laws set out in the 16th century to govern methods of production. The Reinheitsgebot remains a guiding principle of German beer-making today. Pilsner is the most popular beer style, and most breweries will brew a version of it.

This map shows where some of the breweries are based, with pullout boxes where a city or town has more than one brewery.

Schwarzbach

Schwarzbach

SCHLESWIG-HOLSTEIN

MECKLENBURG-VORPOMMERN

BRANDENBURG

BERLIN

SACHSEN-ANHALT

HAMBURG

BREMEN

NIEDERSACHSEN

NORDRHEIN-WESTFALEN

Flensburger

Dithmarscher

Jever

Stralsunder

Rostocker

Wismar

Trotzenburg

Lübzer

Berliner Kindl-Schultheiss

Ur-Krostitzer

Mammut

Wolters

Goslar

Hasseröder

Einbecker

Härke

Schaumburger

Barre

Herforder

Allersheimer

Westheim

Pinkus Müller

Fiege

Brinkhoff's

Diebels

Haake-Beck

Gilde

Hanover

Gilde

Düsseldorf

Füchschen

Schumacher

Uerige

Uerige

Braustolz

Chemnitz
Braustolz
Reichenbrand

Freiberger Brauhaus

Schlenkerla

Bamberg
Fässla
Schlenkerla

Weltenburger

Regensburg
Bischofshof
Kneitinger
Thurn & Taxis
Weltenburger

Jandelsbrunner

Hutthurmer

Bucher Bräu

Arco
Grünbach
Aldersbacher
Schlossbrauerei Au/Hallertau

Röhrl
Weideneder

Erl

Traunstein

Schonram

Altenburg

Camba Bavaria
Jettenbach
Altöttinger

THÜRINGEN

Sternquell
Gottsmannsgrüner

Rosenbrauerei Pössneck

Lang-Bräu

Friedenfelser

Braugold

Papiermühle

Saalfeld

Nailaer Wohn

Kulmbacher

Knoblach

Maisel

Bruckmüller/
Schloderer

Schneider

Kuchlbauer

Felsen Bräu

Weihenstephan
Erdinger
Grünbach
Schweiger

Maxlrain
Auer
Unertl

Reutberg

Ayinger

B A Y E R N

Leikeim

Göller

Rittmayer
Kesselring
Kauzen

Döbler
Landwehr-Bräu

Neumarkter Lammsbräu

Fürstlichen Ellingen

Scheyern

Riegele

König Ludwig

Andechs
Dachsbräu Weilheim

Nesselwang

Streck

Würzburger Hofbräu

Lohrer

Schlappeseppel

Faust

Distelhäuser

Fürst Wallerstein

Ankerbräu Nordlingen
Dinkelacker-Schwaben Bräu

Gold Ochsen

München
Airbräu
Augustiner
Hacker-Pschorr
Hofbräu München
Löwenbräu

Augustiner

HESSEN

Licher

Binding
Michelsbräu
Darmstädter

Schmucker

Glaab

Weldebräu

Bischoff

Kulturbrauerei Heidelberg

Biermanufaktur Engel

Lindenbräu

BADEN-WÜRTTEMBERG

Berg

Schussenrieder

Leibinger
Krone Tettnang

Zötler

Aktien

Weilheim

Fürstenberg

Alpirsbacher

Krombacher

Maximilians

Königsbacher

Kirner

RHEINLAND-
PFALZ

Bitburger

Mettlacher Abteibräu

SAARLAND

Alpirsbacher

Kleiner Mönch

BREWERY

AIRBRÄU

Münchner Airportcenter, Terminalstraße Mitte 18, 85356 München, Germany
www.allresto.de

This brewery has a unique location: set between the two terminals of Munich airport. It opened in 2004 at the same time as the airport's new Terminal 2, and it includes a much-frequented restaurant and beer garden. Two brewing kettles are situated right in the middle of the restaurant.

AKTIEN

Hohe Buchleute 3, 87600 Kaufbeuren, Germany
www.aktienbrauerei.de

The origins of brewing at the Aktien brewery in Kaufbeuren can be traced back to the early 14th century. In more recent times, Aktien has taken over the Löwen and Rosen breweries.

BREWING SECRET Aktien still brews its beer strictly according to the Bavarian Purity Law set in 1516.

ALDERSBACHER

Freiherr-von-Aretin-Platz 1, 94501 Aldersbach, Germany
www.aldersbacher.de

The modern operation seen today grew out of a small brewery attached to a monastery dating from the 13th century. The range of beers has grown over the centuries; white beer started to be brewed in 1928, and today the company produces 13 different styles of beer.

ALLERSHEIMER

Allersheim 6, 37603 Holzminden, Germany
www.brauerei-allersheim.de

Founded in 1854, this brewery was, for Otto Baumgarten, merely a sideline to farming. He harvested the grain in his own fields, but had to buy in the hops. Production grew over the years, though, and today the brewery has 40 employees.

BREWING SECRET The beers are brewed to suit discerning local palates.

BEER

FLIEGERQUELL
LAGER 5.2% ABV
Deep golden, finely structured, and classically dry. It is brewed for international palates.

KUMULUS
WHITE BEER 5.4% ABV
Typical yellow colour; a sparkling, very fresh white beer, refreshing and full bodied.

NATURTRÜBES KELLERBIER
KELLERBIER 5.1% ABV
Unfiltered and naturally cloudy out of the cellar. The slightly sweet taste is typical of one of the oldest styles of beer in Bavaria.

FENDT DIESELROSS-ÖL
MÄRZEN 5.9% ABV
A malty, aromatic structure and a full-bodied, slightly bitter taste. Goes well with venison dishes.

FREIHERRN PILS
PILSNER 5.1% ABV
Mild bitterness in the hopping. The lightly malted grain results in a dry, fine taste.

KLOSTER DUNKEL
DUNKEL 5% ABV
Full bodied and malty, with a typical dark mahogany colour; the roasted flavour is due to the dark malts.

LANDBIER
PILSNER 5% ABV
A pilsner with a mash bill from light and dark malt. Soft in taste, with a typical malty aroma.

ALLERSHEIMER 1854
PILSNER 4.8% ABV
Naturally cloudy, it has a distinctive hop aroma, a bold malt character, and a pleasant bitter finish.

THE BEST-KNOWN BEERS IN GERMANY

There are more than 1,300 breweries in Germany today, mostly in the south. Bavaria alone has 700 breweries.

Internationally, the most famous German beer is Beck's, which is owned by the global drinks giant Anheuser-Busch InBev. Another world-famous German brand is Holsten, which is a subsidiary of the Danish Carlsberg Group. Löwenbräu was the first German export beer to become famous after World War II; it is now part of Anheuser-Busch InBev. However, these international brands are not on the huge scale of Anheuser-Busch InBev's Budweiser in the USA, nor are they the top-selling beers in Germany itself. In fact, they are relatively small in comparison with the biggest names in the German domestic market, such as Krombacher, Veltin's, Warsteiner, and Bitburger. Most of the large German breweries produce pilsner as their main product. In terms of speciality beers, the German No.1 is Erdinger Weissbier (wheat beer), and Clausthaler is widely popular for low-alcohol beers. However, the majority of successful German breweries proudly keep themselves relatively very small, limiting their distribution to a regional market; indeed, many are home breweries that have become famous in association with a single village or even a single restaurant.

BECK'S (PILSNER 4.8% ABV) *left*
BITBURGER (PILSNER 4.8% ABV)
CLAUSTHALER (LOW ALCOHOL 0.45% ABV)
ERDINGER (WHEAT 5.3% ABV) *centre*
HOLSTEN (PILSNER 4.8% ABV) *right*
KROMBACHER (PILSNER 4.8% ABV)
VELTINS (PILSNER 4.8% ABV)
WARSTEINER (PILSNER 4.8% ABV)

ALPIRSBACHER

Alpirsbacher Klosterbräu, Marktplatz 1, 72275 Alpirsbach, Germany
www.alpirsbacher.de

A railway was constructed through the Black Forest at the end of the 19th century, which brought many visitors to the village of Alpirsbach. Johann Gottfried Glauner helped to cater for them by reopening the old village brewery. Sales were good, and today the beer from Alpirsbacher is produced by the fourth generation of the family.

KLEINER MÖNCH
LAGER 5.2% ABV
The golden colour promises a fresh, young beer. It is full bodied with a flavour of caramel from the malt.

SCHWARZES PILS
PILSNER 4.9% ABV
Deep red-black colour and a strong taste, with a roasted malt aroma that is unmistakable.

ALTENBURG

Brauereistr. 20, 04600 Altenburg, Germany
www.brauerei-altenburg.de

Founded in 1871, this brewery produced its first beer in 1873 and soon became successful. The company was taken over by the Communists after World War II. Since the 1990 Reunification of Germany, however, the Altenburg story has started anew, and it is again the biggest brewery in the region.

ALTENBURGER SCHWARZE
SCHWARZBIER 4.9% ABV
This mahogany-coloured beer has an aromatic, malty taste with an intense note of hops.

FESTBIER
BOCK 6% ABV
Amber-coloured beer, full bodied, with a taste of mild hops. It is brewed specially for local festivals.

ALTÖTTINGER

Altöttinger Hell-Bräu, Herrenmühlstraße 15, 84503 Altötting, Germany
www.altoettinger-hellbraeu.de

The Bavarian town of Altötting is home to the Altötting Madonna, a world-famous pilgrimage site. In 1890, Georg Hell expanded production at a local brewery to help cater to thirsty pilgrims. Today the brewery produces eight different beers.

BREWING SECRET The finest hops and best German malts are used.

ALTBAYRISCH HELL
LAGER 5% ABV
Golden yellow, this beer is fresh and vibrant, with a pleasing long, refreshing finish.

FEIN-HERB
LAGER 5% ABV
The best malts, combined with a careful selection of hops, produce an exceptionally dry, fine taste.

BREWERY

ANDECHS

Klosterbaruerei Andechs, Bergstraße 2, 82346 Andechs, Germany
www.andechs.de

The Benedictine monks of Andechs began to produce beer in 1455. The monastery updated its brewery in 1972, investing in modern equipment. Still closely associated with the holy mountain pilgrimage site southwest of Munich, Andechs is an internationally known brand name today.

ANKERBRÄU NORDLINGEN

Ankergasse 4, 86720 Nördlingen, Germany
www.ankerbrauerei.de

The brewery's history can be traced to 1608, when several beers were brewed here for a festival. It was acquired by the Grandel family at the end of the 19th century.

BREWING SECRET The beers are made with local malts, mineral water from the Ries, and hops from Spalt.

ARCOBRÄU

Schlossallee 1, 94554 Moos, Germany
www.arcobraeu.de

Arco has been owned by the Counts of Arco-Zinneberg for 450 years. The castle and brewery belonging to the family are situated in Moos, a small town in the heart of Niederbayern in Bavaria, where the rivers Isar and Donau converge. The current Count Arco personally launched the beers in the USA in 2004.

AUER

Münchner Str. 80, 83022 Rosenheim, Germany
www.auerbraeu.de

Between 1887 and 1920, Johann Auer acquired several plots of land and some breweries around the town of Rosenheim, southeast of Munich. Since then, the company has expanded considerably.

BREWING SECRET When it was founded, this was one of the most modern breweries in Bavaria.

BEER

BERGBOCK HELL
BOCK 7% ABV

A strong beer, but it tastes mild and aromatic. Its typical light sweetness gives it a full body.

DOPPELBOCK DUNKEL
BOCK 7% ABV

This world-famous beer has a really strong taste. The dark malts give it an unmistakable character, with a light aroma of hops in the finish.

NÖRDLINGER PREMIUM PILS
PILSNER 4.6% ABV

A very flowery hop aroma turns slightly bitter and a bit sparkling on the tongue.

RIESLER LANDBIER
LAGER 4.8% ABV

A full-flavoured clear, yellow beer; pleasant and full bodied, with a fine aroma at the beginning.

SCHLOSS HELL
LAGER 4.9% ABV

With its soft but full-bodied taste and golden colour, Arco's Schloss Hell typifies Bavarian lager.

URFASS
LAGER 5.2% ABV

Slightly more bitter than the Schloss Hell, and especially spicy, this is a real premium lager of Bavaria.

BAJUWAREN DUNKEL
DUNKEL 5.5% ABV

Brewed in old-fashioned Bavarian style, this beer has a malty aroma and a full-bodied character.

WEIZENBOCK
WHEAT BOCK 7% ABV

A strong, spicy speciality. A good accompaniment to hearty cheeses or sweet desserts.

AUGUSTINER

Landsberger Str. 31-35, 80339 München, Germany
www.augustiner-braeu.de

Founded in 1328, this is the oldest brewery in Munich and one of only two in the city (along with Hofbräu München) that do not belong to a giant of the global brewing industry. The site as it is today was constructed In 1885. Augustiner beer has become famous around the world even though the brewery does not advertise itself.

AYINGER

Muenchener Straße 21, 85653 Aying, Germany
www.ayinger.de

Johann Liebhard founded this brewery in Aying in 1876, at a time when there were about 6,000 breweries in Bavaria. That number has dropped to about 700 today, but Ayinger has survived and was renovated by the Inselkammer family in 1999. It has since become more widely known.

BARRE

Berliner Str. 122-124, D-32312 Lübbecke, Germany
www.barre.de

Family-owned since 1842, the Barre Privatbrauerei lies in the Westphalian region between the rivers Wester and Rhine. Barre's special beers are well known and loved in the region.

BREWING SECRET The company uses its own spring to supply fresh water to the brewery.

BERG

Berg Brauerei Ulrich Zimmermann, Brauhausstraße 2, 89584 Ehingen-Berg, Germany
www.bergbier.de

Berg, founded in 1757, is family-owned and one of the smallest breweries in Germany.

BREWING SECRET Berg makes use of corn in brewing, which is supplied by an organic farm nearby.

EDELSTOFF
EXPORT 5.6% ABV
The unusual dark golden colour displays its special character. A sweet and obvious hop taste guides you to a very malty finish.

WEISSBIER
WHEAT BEER 5.4% ABV
Golden and cloudy, this is a full-bodied wheat beer with a citrus taste and light bitters in the finish.

JAHRHUNDERT-BIER
EXPORT 5.5% ABV
A honey-like aroma with light flowery hops leads on to a harmonious finish.

CELEBRATOR
DOPPELBOCK 6.7% ABV
The taste of malt dominates this nearly black, strong beer. It is not as sweet as other doppelbocks of the same quality.

BARRE PILSENER
PILSNER 4.8% ABV
The clear golden-yellow colour is typical of a pilsner, as is the fine taste of hops and the malty finish. Medium bodied.

BARRE DUNKEL
DUNKEL 4.8% ABV
Fine aromas of malt, strongly flavoured, and with a finish of light bitters.

BERG ORIGINAL
LAGER 5% ABV
Its smooth, dry taste makes this beer the most popular brand offered by the brewery.

BERG MÄRZEN
MÄRZEN 6.1% ABV
A typical strong beer. The taste is very hearty, not least because of its high dose of hops.

Revellers clink glasses during Oktoberfest — the world-famous annual 16-day festival of beer that has been staged in Munich since 1810.

BREWERY

BERGQUELL

Weststraße 7, D-02708 Löbau/Sa, Germany
www.bergquell-loebau.de

With its long brewing tradition, the Bergquell Brauerei Löbau has played an important role in the Lausitz region since 1846. It is also one of the most advanced breweries in the whole of Germany and is well known for its wide range of special beers.

BREWING SECRET The special beers have an international following.

BERLINER-KINDL-SCHULTHEISS

Indira Gandhi Str. 66–69, 13053 Berlin, Germany
www.berliner-kindl.de

The union of the Berliner Kindl and Berliner Schultheiss breweries in 2006 was symbolic for Germany, whose breweries had declined through post-War division. The merger has generated a great many new brands, produced in one of the most modern brewing facilities in Germany.

BIERMANUFAKTUR ENGEL

Haller Str. 29, 74564 Crailsheim, Germany
www.engelbier.de

When this brewery was founded by Georg Fach in 1738, Crailsheim had 4,000 inhabitants and 13 breweries. Fach was not to know that his company would become one of the most successful in the country.

BREWING SECRET A survey of what women like in a beer led to the creation of the First Lady brand.

BINDING

Darmstädter Landstraße 185, 60598 Frankfurt, Germany
www.clausthaler.de

Conrad Binding started in the year 1870 with a small brewery in the ancient city of Frankfurt am Main. The other big brewery of the city, Henninger, was acquired by Binding in 2001. Since 2002 the company has been a member of the Radeberger group. The Clausthaler brands are a low-alcohol speciality of Binding.

BEER

KIRSCH PORTER
PORTER 4.2% ABV
A black beer with a cherry flavour and typical porter qualities. Malty and full bodied.

LAUSITZER PORTER
PORTER 4.4% ABV
Typical porter with a dry, roasted malt taste. It is full bodied and not too heavy; dark coloured and a little bit sweet.

MÄRKISCHER LANDMANN
SCHWARZBIER 4.9% ABV
Black and highly malty, but without any bitterness. A genuine original of the Märkish region.

BOCKBIER
BOCK 7% ABV
Golden, strong, and not too sweet; pleasant, with a smooth finish – a typical bock.

KELLERBIER DUNKEL
DUNKEL 5.3% ABV
Beautiful mahogany colour; aromas of malt and yeast; full bodied, with a taste that is both sweet and pleasantly bitter.

FIRST LADY
DUNKLER BOCK 5.9% ABV
Mild, lightly bitter, and with a harmonious malty aroma.

CLAUSTHALER CLASSIC
LOW ALCOHOL 0.45% ABV
Full bodied, with a fresh and pleasant taste, and light aromas of fine hops; golden coloured.

CLAUSTHALER EXTRA HERB
LOW ALCOHOL 0.45% ABV
This fresh, golden-coloured beer is very strong and spicy. It has a pleasant bitterness of hops and a malty finish.

BISCHOFF (WINNWEILER)

An den Hopfengärten 6, 67722
Winnweiler, Germany
www.bischoff-bier.de

Located in a famous hop growing area, the brewery has been owned by the same family since 1865. The current chief executive, Dr. Sven Bischoff, is a fifth generation member of the founding family. Production ceased during World War II but reopened in 1948 with a "peace beer". Today more than 20 beers are produced.

FALKENSTEINER UR-WEISSE
WHEAT BEER 5.2% ABV
Fresh and tangy, it has light, fruity flavours with a pleasant bitter and soft sweet finish.

BISCHOFF PILS
PILSNER 4.7% ABV
Light, sparkling, and refreshing, with light aromas of fine hops.

BISCHOFSHOF

Heitzerstr. 2, 93049 Regensburg,
Germany
www.bischofshof.de

The Bischofshof brewery started life attached to Regensburg Cathedral. Records show that it was brewing in 1230 for the Bishop. At the beginning of the 20th century, it moved to a new location in order to expand. Nowadays, Bischofshof beer is produced in one of the most modern facilities in the brewing industry.

HEFE-WEISSBIER HELL
WHEAT BEER 5.1% ABV
An old Bavarian speciality: fresh, clear, sparkling, and slightly sweet – in a pleasant way.

PILS
PILSNER 4.7% ABV
Creamy foam and a light, sparkling start. Good bitter taste; light aromas of fine hops.

BITBURGER

Römermauer 3, 54634 Bitburg,
Germany
www.bitburger.de

Founded in 1817, Bitburger is a pilsner specialist. It is well known through international sponsorship of sporting events, and is widely regarded as the best brewery for pilsner on draught.

BREWING SECRET The company always uses two-row summer barley, and its testing brewery is unique in Germany.

PREMIUM PILS
PILSNER 4.8% ABV
A clear, typical pilsner with a light, bitter taste; smooth, but very dry. On draught, it is fresh and elegant.

BITBURGER LIGHT
PILSNER 2.8% ABV
The light sister of the premium. Though only 2.8 per cent ABV, it is full bodied, with a fresh cask taste.

BRAUGOLD

Schillerstr. 7, 99096 Erfurt, Germany
www.braugold.de

The brewery was founded in 1822, and acquired other breweries over time – up until 1948, the point at which it was nationalized by the GDR. After Reunification in 1990, Braugold was purchased by the Licher Privatbrauerei.

BREWING SECRET The brewers follow recipes from the famous Thüringer brewery.

BRAUGOLD SPEZIAL
PILSNER 4.9% ABV
Has the typical golden colour and dryness of a pilsner; highly aromatic with a balanced bitterness of hops on the palate.

BRAUGOLD BOCK
BOCK 6.5% ABV
Its balanced, bitter aroma and strong flavour are typical of a bock.

BREWERY

BRAUSTOLZ

Am Feldschlösschen 18, 09116 Chemnitz, Germany
www.braustolz.com

A farmer founded this brewery in 1868. The company was modernized after World War I, nationalized in 1945, and renovated in 1991. Today it employs more than 50 people and produces many different styles of beer.

BREWING SECRET A 1991 investment of €40 million for modern equipment ensured the brewery's future.

BRINKHOFF'S

Steigerstr. 20, 44145 Dortmund, Germany
www.brinkhoffs.de

From its humble origins in 1844 as a small home brewery, Brinkhoff's has had more than 160 years of success, to become a brand known far beyond its home town of Dortmund, one of the beer capitals in the world. Brinkhoff's No. 1 is a notable name for every lover of the special pilsners from this region.

BUCHER BRÄU

Elsenthaler Str. 5-7, 94481 Grafenau, Germany
www.bucher-braeu.de

A medium-sized brewery that moved to the heart of the Bavarian Forest in 1982 after outgrowing its premises in the centre of Grafenau. It has been owned by the Bucher family since 1863 (now in its fifth generation).

BREWING SECRET The natural cloudiness of the Hefeweizen comes from the yeast added at the time of bottling.

CAMBA BAVARIA

Muhlweg 2, 83376, Truchtlaching, Germany
www.cambabavaria.de

Inspired by US craft beer, Camba Bavaria has shown the conservative drinkers of Bavaria that there is a lot more to beer than their traditional helles, lager, and weisse. Aromatic hopped ales and barrel-aged specialities have become favourites at this bustling brewpub. Brewer Markus Lohner produces some fantastic interpretations of many German brews.

BEER

BRAUSTOLZ LANDBIER
EXPORT 5.2% ABV
Golden, smooth, malty, and with a fine aroma of hops – an earthy beer.

BRAUSTOLZ PILS
PILSNER 4.9% ABV
A classic pilsner with a very dry and fresh taste accompanied by obvious aromas of bitter hops.

BRINKHOFF'S NO. 1
PILSNER 5% ABV
Typical bitter aromas of a pilsner. Smooth, slightly sparkling, with a golden-yellow colour.

BRINKHOFF'S RADLER
BEER BLEND 2.5% ABV
Honey coloured, sparkling, and pleasant, with citrus aromas; very refreshing and not too sweet.

HEFE WEIZEN HELL
WHEAT BEER 5.2% ABV
Fresh and sparkling. The light taste of yeast is fine and aromatic. There is a little sweetness.

HELLES
LAGER 4.9% ABV
Clear yellow beer, slightly bitter, with a reasonable sweetness and a taste of the finest hops. A rather strong but rounded finish.

BOURBON BARRELS
DOPPELBOCK 8.5% ABV
Aged in former whisky barrels, it has the aroma of cherries, bourbon, and vanilla.

INDIA PALE ALE
INDIA PALE ALE 8% ABV
Dark orange with lots of honey, orange, and grapefruit hop flavours, it has a long, warming, bitter finish.

DACHSBRÄU WEILHEIM

Murnauer Straße 5, 82362 Weilheim, Germany
www.dachsbier.de

It was a master brewer from Munich who founded the Dachsbräu on a farm in Weilheim in 1879. Georg Dachs began to produce wheat beer, and the family-owned brewery has since grown ever bigger.

BREWING SECRET The most significant characteristic of the beer is that it is traditionally hand-crafted.

DARMSTÄDTER

Goebelstraße 7, 64293 Darmstadt, Germany
www.darmstaedter.de

The brewery was founded in 1847, near the first Darmstadt's railway station – hence the steam engine in the company's logo. The engine represents dynamism and energy, attributes the company says it still has today as it has recently undergone a major refurbishment of its brewing equipment.

DIEBELS

Brauerei-Diebels-Str. 1, 47661 Issum, Germany
www.diebels.de

Diebels was privately owned until 2001, when the brewery was taken over by global drinks giant InBev, now AB InBev. The Düsseldorfer Alt is the brewery's most famous brand and is sold all over Germany. Other, newer brands include a pilsner and a cola-blended beer called Dimix.

DINKELACKER-SCHWABEN BRÄU

Tübinger Str. 46, 70178 Stuttgart, Germany
www.privatbrauerei-stuttgart.de

Carl Dinkelacker was the first to brew pilsner in Stuttgart at the end of the 19th century, and his contemporary Robert Leicht was the first to deliver beer by motorcar. Today, their breweries are in partnership and together form the biggest player in Baden-Württemberg.

ULIMATOR
DOPPELBOCK 7.5% ABV
Strong and sweet, this typical doppelbock has malt aromas from the start, and is very full bodied.

URHELL
LAGER 5.5% ABV
A kellerbier – unfiltered, cloudy, and yellow – it tastes very mild at the beginning, has light aromas of fine hops, and is fresh and pleasant.

BRAUSTÜB'L
PILSNER 4.8% ABV
A clear and elegant beer. A large amount of fine hops make this a typical pilsner: fresh and dry with a good bitter aroma.

FESTBIER
BOCK 5.6% ABV
Full-bodied malt harmonizes with a bold bitterness and yeasty notes in this festive brew.

DIEBELS ALT
ALTBIER 4.9% ABV
Roasted malt aromas harmonize with a sweet caramel taste; the finish is slightly bitter from hops.

DIEBELS PILS
PILSNER 4.9% ABV
The full body, light bitterness, and malt aromas are typical of a pilsner, as is the dark golden colour.

DINKELACKER PRIVAT
LAGER 5.1% ABV
A fine, smooth, and clear golden lager with a mild aroma of hops and a light note of malt.

DINKELACKER CD-PILS
PILSNER 4.9% ABV
Noble dry pilsner with strong aromas of hops and light malts; very harmonious and pleasant.

BREWERY

DISTELHÄUSER

Grünsfelder Str. 3, 97941
Tauberbischofsheim, Germany
www.distelhaeuser.de

The Bauer family has owned this
brewery since 1876. It is situated
on the famous "Romantic Street" in
Tauberbischofsheim, which is closely
associated with the German Romantic
period. The long-standing success of
the brewery is due to its attention to
quality over the course of its history.

DITHMARSCHER

Oesterstr. 18, 25709 Marne Holstein,
Germany
www.dithmarscher.de

This brewery, on the east coast of
Schleswig-Holstein, has been operating
for more than 230 years. It started
as a small home brewery; today it is
bigger, but the beers are still handmade.

BREWING SECRET The sparkle comes
from using the charmant method of
pressurized fermentation, and the
addition of dry, fresh carbonic acid.

DÖBLER

Kornmarkt 6, 91438 Bad Windsheim,
Germany
www.brauhaus-doebler.de

Döbler celebrated its 145th
anniversary in 2012. Production
was traditional until 1950, after
which the brewery switched to
creating young-styled beers using
technologically advanced equipment.

BREWING SECRET The barley has come
from sustainable sources since 1986.

EICHHORN

Dörfleinstr. 43, 96103 Hallstadt,
Germany
www.brauerei-eichhorn.de

Eichhorn was originally called
the Schwarzer Adler (Black Eagle)
brewery. The family handcrafts
its beers – always using the
latest equipment.

BREWING SECRET The beers are given
extra time to mature, and their
adherence to the Bavarian Purity Law
won't be changing in the near future.

BEER

FRÜHLINGSBOCK
BOCK 6.9% ABV
A full-flavoured, strong beer, with
a long bittersweet finish. Golden
yellow in colour, it is topped with
a large foaming head.

DISTELHÄUSER PILS
PILSNER 4.9% ABV
Topped by a snow-white foam, this
beer has a harmonious bitterness
and a great aroma of hops.

DITHMARSCHER DUNKEL
DUNKEL 4.9% ABV
This beer has a full-bodied
charmant character and a spicy
taste with notes of roastiness.
A typical colour: dark mahogany.

DITHMARSCHER PILSNER
PILSNER 4.8% ABV
A mild and spicy beer, golden
yellow in colour, slightly sparkling.

LAND MÄRZEN
MÄRZEN 5.4% ABV
A very light märzen; dark yellow,
with a pleasant taste, not too
sweet, but full bodied with a nice
yeast finish.

REICHSSTADTBIER
KELLERBIER 5% ABV
Full bodied, unfiltered, and cloudy,
with a taste of yeast. It is available
on draught.

KELLERBIER NATURTRÜB
LAGER 5% ABV
Yellow and naturally cloudy, the
kellerbier does not have much
carbon acidity, so it has a slight,
but well-balanced, hop bitterness.

EICHHORN PILS
PILSNER 5% ABV
Clear golden, dry pilsner, with a
fine bitterness of hops accompanying
light aromas of malt.

EINBECKER

Papenstr. 4-7, 37574 Einbeck, Germany
www.einbecker.de

The story goes that, in 1521, Martin Luther said that Einbecker's beer was his favourite. In 1612, Bavarian dukes engaged a master brewer from Einbeck, whose beer eventually became known as bock, in a corruption of the name Einbeck.

ERDINGER

Lange Zeile 1 and 3, 85435 Erding, Germany
www.erdinger.de

This is the biggest and most famous specialist wheat beer brewery in the world. The first mention of a brewery at Erding was in 1886, but it was not until 1949 that the name Erdinger Weissbräu was used.

BREWING SECRET Fresh spring water and hops from the Hallertau region are used in brewing.

ERL

Straubinger Str. 10, 94333 Geiselhöring, Germany
www.erl-braeu.de

The owners, Ludwig IV and his brother Günter, are the 11th generation of the Erl family at the helm of this brewery. Everything about the family and their beers is steeped in tradition.

BREWING SECRET The family farm supplies the finest raw materials for the beers made here.

FÄSSLA

Obere Königstr. 19-21, 96052 Bamberg, Germany
www.faessla.de

In 1649, just a year after the end of the Thirty Years' War, master brewer Hans Lauer founded this brewery in Bamberg. In modern times, 1986 was a turning point, when the Kalb family took over control. Fässla's speciality beers are well known in the region.

BREWING SECRET Bambergator is the strongest beer brewed in Bamberg.

UR-BOCK HELL
BOCK 6.5% ABV
The pale malt and fine hops give this classic bock a hearty taste.

LANDBIER SPEZIAL
EXPORT 5.2% ABV
Has the typical golden-yellow colour of an export beer. Has a fine, slightly sweet flavour.

ERDINGER DUNKEL
WHEAT BEER 5.3% ABV
Smooth and well matured, this dark, malty beer has a spicy hue and a satisfying alcoholic finish.

ERDINGER PIKANTUS
DARK WEIZENBOCK 7.3% ABV
The beer is not as sweet as a normal wheat bock. Watch out for the ABV on this one.

ERL "BOCKERL" BOCK
BOCK 7% ABV
A clear, elegant bock with a fine bitter taste and harmonious finish.

ERL DUNKEL
DUNKEL 5.3% ABV
One of Erl's oldest beer styles, chestnut in colour, and with a rather strong taste. A nice, light bitterness of hops in the finish.

LAGERBIER
LAGER 5.5% ABV
Strong yellow in colour; fine, compact foam; sparkling. Full bodied and slightly malty with a light bitter taste.

BAMBERGATOR
DOPPELBOCK 8.5% ABV
A dark brown, full-bodied, and very strong doppelbock, bursting with harmonious hop bitters.

ALL ABOUT...
MALT

Beer is an agricultural product that begins its life in a field of golden, swaying grain – usually barley. After the harvest the grains are taken to a malt house, or maltings, where the commencement of the magical journey that ends in the glass takes place. In brewing lore, malt, or malted barley, was known as the "soul" of beer – a raw material that has an alchemical power to provide colour and aroma, as well as the rich and distinctive array of flavours. There can be no beer without malt: it provides the sugars essential for yeast to feed on during fermentation, the by-products of which are carbon dioxide and alcohol.

COLOUR Though it doesn't tell the whole story, the colour of a beer gives an indication of the malts that have been used. Black malt is used in the very darkest beers, such as stouts; amber ales will often contain brown malt or crystal malt; pilsner-style beers often use caramalt for lightness and a sweet note.

GROWING BARLEY The barley grown for brewing is either two- or six-row barley. Two-row is common in Europe, while American brewers have traditionally used six-row; this is partly due to cost, but also because it works well with rice or corn, common adjuncts in beers produced by the larger brewers.

SELECTING THE GRAIN There are several strains of barley. In the UK, as well as with some selective American brewers, Maris Otter is the chosen one, while others include Golden Promise and Optic. Just as beer divides into styles, barley has its variations too. In Britain and Belgium, winter-sown barley is used, because of its robust flavour, while German and Czech brewers prefer lighter and sweeter tasting spring-sown barley.

GERMINATION The first step of the malting process is to kick-start germination in the grains. This helps produce enzymes that break down the starch into the essential soluble malt sugars. This process involves steeping the grains in water and then laying them out to dry. The grains are turned over several times each day to ensure that the emerging rootlets don't link up with each other. The skill of the maltster is to know when to stop the germination – after that it's off to the kiln for drying.

KILNING Shorter kilning times produce lightly cured malts that give a golden sparkle to ale and lager. Pale malt usually forms the majority of the grain in the mash tun – this is because it has the highest level of starch and the enzymes that convert starch into fermentable sugars. A longer rest in the kiln means darker malts and a deeper colour, body, and flavour.

THE MALT STORE A visit to a brewery's malt store will unlock the mysteries of this magical grain: expect sacks of pale malt, chocolate malt (so-called because it tastes like chocolate), black malt, rye malt, lager malt, brown malt, and caramalt. You may also find roasted barley, which is unmalted and a vital constituent of Irish dry stout, such as Guinness or Murphy's. Stewing malt, a process similar to making toffee, produces crystal malt, which adds body and a rich spiciness to beer.

BREWERY

FAUST

Hauptstr. 219, 63897 Miltenberg, Germany
www.faust.de

A typical regional family-run company. The brewery is about 350 years old and changed hands many times in the first 200 years of its history. The Fausts took over in 1895, and still own it. There are many different styles of beer produced, some of which have won prizes.

FELSEN BRÄU

Felsenweg 2, 91790 Thalmannsfeld, Germany
www.solarbier-felsenbraeu.de

These handcrafted beers come from one of the loveliest parts of Bavaria, between the Altmühltal and Franconia. The third generation of the family guides the brewery and uses traditional recipes.

BREWING SECRET The energy for production comes from solar power.

FIEGE

Moritz Fiege, Scharnhorststr. 21-25, 44787 Bochum, Germany
www.moritzfiege.de

"We are a classic regional brewery", says Hugo Fiege, the boss of the company. He sees his brewery as an ambassador for the Ruhr region. It is an institution offering typical local beers – inhabitants of the Ruhr love their beer. There is little chance of a big global player acquiring Fiege.

FLENSBURGER

Munketoft 12, 24937 Flensburg, Germany
www.flensburger.de

Five citizens of Flensburg founded this brewery in 1888. During the 1970s, the brewery's reputation was enhanced when a comedian kept referring to a "Flasch Flens" in his act. The term came to be used for a bottle of Flensburger, which at the time was the only German beer to use clip-top bottles.

BEER

SCHWARZVIERTLER

DUNKEL 5.2% ABV
Dark, roasty, and slightly smoky. There is also caramel and a little bitter chocolate on the tongue. It is full bodied and has a dry finish.

FAUST KRÄUSEN

KELLERBIER 5.5% ABV
A mild, full-bodied beer with a light note of honey; it is very fresh.

MÄRZEN

EXPORT 5.4% ABV
A typical märzen: dark yellow and with a strong taste and aromas of barley malt. Light scent of hops in the finish.

FELSENTRUNK

LAGER 4.9% ABV
A light, sweet taste; it sparkles a little; very fresh and with a nice bitter aroma in the finish.

MORITZ FIEGE PILS

PILSNER 4.9% ABV
A classic pilsner with bitter aromas of good hops, a light malty taste, and a fine dry structure.

MORITZ FIEGE SCHWARZBIER

SCHWARZBIER 4.9% ABV
Elegant and with a malty sweetness, this coffee-coloured beer has light bitter aromas of fine hops.

FLENSBURGER PILSENER

PILSNER 4.8% ABV
A typical golden pilsner – malty, refreshing, and with slightly bitter aromas of hops in the finish.

FLENSBURGER KELLERBIER

KELLERBIER 4.8% ABV
Amber and cloudy, like all kellerbiers, the Flensburger version is full bodied and tastes naturally fresh, slightly sweet, and has a dry finish.

FREIBERGER

Am Fürstenwald, 09599 Freiberg,
Germany
www.freibergerpils.de

This brewery was the first in Sachsen
to produce a pilsner. Other exclusive
beers followed: Freiberger Silberquell
(1903) and a wheat beer (1909). The
Eichbaum brewery in Mannheim has
acquired Freiberger and is focusing on
making it one of the most modern
beer producers in Germany.

FRIEDENFELSER

Kolpingplatz 1, 95688 Friedenfels,
Germany
www.friedenfelser.de

The brewery is situated in the
southern part of the largest forest in
Europe, between Oberpfälzer Wald
and Fichtelgebirge. Friedenfelser is
the leading brewery of the region.

BREWING SECRET The pure springs
of the national park have helped
Friedenfelser to produce excellent
beers for more than 100 years.

FÜCHSCHEN

Ratinger Str. 28, 40213 Düsseldorf,
Germany
www.fuechschen.de

Altbier has been a favoured brew at
Füchschen since 1848. The fourth
generation of the family is in charge.
There have been some changes since
1995, including the installation of
new brewing equipment.

BREWING SECRET The Düsseldorf
carnival in February is a good
opportunity to sample the altbier.

FÜRSTLICHEN ELLINGEN

Schloss-Str. 10, 91792 Ellingen,
Germany
www.fuerst-carl.de

Owner Carl Friedrich Fürst von
Wrede is a direct descendant of
Napoleon's field marshal Carl Philipp,
Prince of Wrede. The brewery
opposite his castle in Ellingen was
founded in 1690, but the brewing
history of Ellingen is certainly older.
The beer has been called Fürst Carl
for about 200 years.

FREIBERGISCH FESTBIER
MÄRZEN 5.8% ABV
With aromas of malt and a very
fine taste of hops, this amber-
coloured beer is pleasant and
full bodied.

FREIBERGISCH SCHWARZBIER
SCHWARZBIER 4.9% ABV
Deep black, with fresh, malty
aromas. Full bodied and precisely
balanced between malts and hops.

FRIEDENFELSER PILS LEICHT
LIGHT BEER 2.8% ABV
This reduced-alcohol beer is golden
and on the dry side, with aromas of
fine hops in the finish.

FRIEDENFELSER WEIZEN LEICHT
LIGHT WHEAT BEER 2.7% ABV
This light beer is fermented in the
bottle. Its taste is a mixture of
bitter hops and sweet barley and
wheat – typical of the style.

FÜCHSCHEN ALT
ALTBIER 4.5% ABV
Dark mahogany in colour, this
typical Düsseldorfer is malty
with a very intense aroma of hops.
Slightly carbonated and fresh.

SILBERFÜCHSEN
WHEAT BEER 5.4% ABV
A northern-style wheat beer, less
sweet than its Bavarian counterpart.
Smooth, fruity, and sparkling.

FÜRST CARL JOSEFI BOCK
BOCK 7.5% ABV
A creamy, malty, and full-bodied
beer, with a velvety and silky texture.

FÜRST CARL URHELL
LAGER 4.9% ABV
The clear yellow colour is typical
for a lager; the taste is pleasant
and not too dry, with very
little sweetness.

BREWERY

FÜRST WALLERSTEIN

Berg 78, 86757 Wallerstein, Germany
www.fuerst-wallerstein.de

The success of this brewery spans 400 years under the same family, who have always employed skillful brewers. In 2008 Alexander Jesina was appointed; he started his brewing career in the famous monastery of Andechs.

BREWING SECRET It's a family tradition that consistency is more important than short-term success.

FÜRSTENBERG

Postplatz 1-4, D-78166 Donaueschingen, Germany
www.fuerstenberg.de

Count Heinrich I von Fürstenberg was granted the right to brew beer in 1283, but it was not until 300 years later that a proper brewery was built. A substantial force regionally, Fürstenberg is now part of Heineken.

BREWING SECRET The beers are made with water from the Black Forest and yeast from Donaueschingen.

GANTER

Schwarzwaldstr. 43, D-79117 Freiburg, Germany
www.ganter.com

Ganter was founded more than 140 years ago and is still family-owned. The brewery buildings were damaged in World War II and had to be rebuilt. The 1950s and '60s were successful, but beer-drinking in the region has since declined. After some years of struggling, however, Ganter is finding a new lease of life in broader markets.

GILDE

Hildesheimer Str. 132, Hanover, Germany
www.gildebrau.de

It was about 500 years ago that Cord Broyhan presented his beer to the people of Hanover. *Broyhan* – a pale style of wheat beer – was popular for centuries in the city. Gilde, Hanover's longest-surviving brewery, now owned by AB InBev, was founded in 1870.

BREWING SECRET A modern version of *broyhan* is exported to the USA.

BEER

ZWICKEL
LAGER 4.8% ABV
The Wallerstein Zwickel is a cloudy golden speciality beer with a really natural quality to it.

WEISSBIERPILS
PILSNER/WHEAT BEER BLEND 5.1% ABV
Sparkling and golden with some cloudiness; yeasty in flavour, with some citrus notes and a dry finish.

FÜRSTENBERG HEFEWEIZEN
DUNKEL 5.4% ABV
Chestnut in colour and sparkling; harmonious with a malty aroma and light caramel sweetness, yet strong in the mouth.

FÜRSTENBERG GOLD
LAGER 4.9% ABV
Smooth, with few aromas of hops. This clear golden beer is a bit sweeter than the usual lager.

WODAN
DOPPELBOCK 7.5% ABV
Roasty aromas; malty-sweet at the start, but the finish is mild and slightly bitter.

MAGISCH DUNKEL
DUNKEL 5.8% ABV
A dry, bitter beer with a floral aroma from the Noble hops.

RATSKELLER PREMIUM PILS
PILSNER 4.9% ABV
A dry, golden-yellow pilsner; full bodied, typical bitterness of hops, and a nice finish.

LINDENER SPECIAL
EXPORT 5.1% ABV
The most successful export beer of Niedersachsen has a golden colour and tastes pleasant with smooth yeast-flower flavours in the mouth.

GLAAB

Frankfurter Str. 9, 63500 Seligenstadt, Germany
www.glaabsbraeu.de

For more than 250 years, this brewery has been owned by the Glaab family. It was founded in 1744 and became known for its wide variety of beers and for Vitamalz, the biggest German brand of pure malt drinks. The company is the only private brewery in the Offenbach region, to the south of Frankfurt.

GOLD OCHSEN

Veitsbrunnenweg 3-8, 89073 Ulm, Germany
www.gold-ochsen.de

It was in 1597 when the brewery-restaurant Zum Goldenen Ochsen was opened in the ancient city of Ulm. The brewery has been in the hands of one family since 1868.

BREWING SECRET The current, fifth generation, of owners are moving with the times and employing eco-friendly processes.

GÖLLER

Wildgarten 12, 97475 Zeil am Main, Germany
www.brauerei-goeller.de

Joseph Göller acquired this brewery and restaurant in 1908. Both have grown steadily over the years. In 1998 the renovated restaurant was leased by the Zeiler family.

BREWING SECRET Göller strives to make high-quality beers using modern, environmentally friendly techniques.

GOSLAR

Marktkirchhof 2, 38640 Goslar, Germany
www.brauhaus-goslar.de

Goslar, by the Gose river, has been famous for its beer since the year 995. Gose beer was popular for centuries, but fell out of favour in the early 20th century. However, Goslar launched "The Gose" again in 2004.

BREWING SECRET Gose contains coriander and salt, and therefore does not follow the Purity Law.

1744
KELLERBIER 5.2% ABV
This cloudy, amber-coloured beer is Glaab's youngest product. The taste of fine malt is typical.

DUNKLES
DUNKEL 5.3% ABV
Clear amber-coloured beer in which the light bitterness of hops is prominent. A great dunkel with a nice malty finish.

GOLD OCHSEN ORIGINAL
LAGER 5.1% ABV
Light bitterness with the aromas of fine hops. A very rounded and smooth taste, with some sweetness in the finish.

GOLD OCHSEN RADLER
SHANDY 2.6% ABV
The mixture (50 per cent beer, 50 per cent lemonade) is sparkling and full bodied, fruity, and fresh.

GÖLLER RAUCHBIER
SPECIAL BEER 5.6% ABV
This amber-coloured regional speciality has light aromas of fine hops and a smoky, roasted malt taste.

GÖLLER LAGER
LAGER 5.2% ABV
A clear golden lager with a light, malty taste and fine aromas of hops. The recipe is an ancient one.

HELLE GOSE
WHEAT BEER 4.8% ABV
Naturally cloudy and golden, this beer is pleasant, with light bitterness from the hops and malt aromas.

DUNKLE GOSE
DUNKEL 4.9% ABV
Light reddish brown in colour; smoky with malt aromas. The brewers add a special third malt.

The Hofbräuhaus in Munich is arguably Germany's best-known beer hall, offering lots of beer, traditional food, and occasional live music.

BEER STYLES

GERMAN BEER

Even though pilsner-style beers dominate the German market, the country has a good range of breweries that continue to produce distinctive, traditional types of beer. Altbier (see p132) and kölsch (see p123) are perhaps the most influential with brewers and beer enthusiasts elsewhere in the world, but the smoky rauchbier, sweet black schwarzbier, and subtle gose testify that there is much more to explore in the world of German beer.

In northern Germany, in the former industrial city of Dortmund, Dortmunder export is a style of lager drier and slightly stronger than the average pils or helles. This golden beer was popular with factory workers but, sadly, it is now becoming less easy to find.

Other hard-to-find variations on the lager theme include kellerbier, steinier, spezial, roggen (rue beer), and zoigl, which is a communally brewed beer found in northeastern Bavaria. One of the rarest German beer styles is gose, a wheat beer flavoured with a little salt and coriander. It can only be found in Leipzig and the nearby town of Goslar, from where the name of the beer originated.

SMOKY BEERS In Franconia, a neighbour of Bavaria, the beautiful and ancient town of Bamberg is the centre for rauchbier, or smoke beer. Here, malt is kilned over beechwood fires to give the beer its smoky character. Despite their smokiness, these beers are very appealing, dry, and moreish, and go well with robust dishes and smoked foods.

DARK BEERS German dark beers come in two varieties – schwarzbier ("black beer") and dunkel (meaning "dark"). The former was a dying beer style until given a new lease of life in the old East German province of Thuringia. Expect a pitch-black and luscious beer, with mocha coffee, vanilla, and burnt toffee notes.

BAVARIAN DUNKELS Bavarian dunkels are deep reddish brown in colour. One of the best examples of this style is Weltenburger Kloster's Barock Dunkel – a firm, well-bodied beer, with chocolate and cocoa on the palate and nose.

GOTTSMANNSGRÜNER

Von-Koch-Str.2, 95180 Berg, Germany
www.gottsmannsgruener.com

Gottsmannsgrüner was granted the right to brew in 1535. Caroline Freifrau von Waldenfels is the current head – the daughter of Ernst-Albrecht who retired in 2005. The brewery was awarded the silver medal at the European Beer Awards in 2006 for its schwarzbier.

GREIF

Serlbacher Str. 10, 91301 Forchheim, Germany
www.brauerei-greif.de

Kapuzinerwirt, a famous restaurant in Forchheim, was founded in 1848, a year of revolution in Germany. This incarnation of the company lasted for more than 100 years. During the 1990s there was investment in new production equipment, and today the brewery is one of the most technologically advanced in the region.

GRÜNBACH

Kellerberg 2, D-85461 Grünbach, Germany
www.schlossbrauerei-gruenbach.de

Grünbach has had a host of owners, including the famous Paulaner and Erdinger breweries. Alexander Noll is currently at the helm.

BREWING SECRET Grünbach's Benno Scharl wheat beer carries the name of an 18th-century Bavarian master brewer who wrote an influential textbook on brewing techniques.

HAAKE-BECK

Am Deich 18/19, 28199 Bremen, Germany
www.haake-beck.de

Founded in 1826, the Haake-Beck brewery is one of the most famous in northern Germany. Milestones in the company's history include the creation of Haake-Beck Kräusen Pils and the first Maibock in 1950. It is part of the AB InBev stable today.

BREWING SECRET Haake-Beck's sister is the famous Beck's label, which is exported by AB InBev around the world.

BREWERY

WEISSE
WHEAT BEER 5.4% ABV
Full of soaring fruit aromas, it is an easy-drinking refresher.

PILS
PILSNER 4.8% ABV
A golden, sparkling yellow, it has a fine aroma of Noble hops and notes of fresh bread.

DUNKLE WEISSE
WHEAT BEER 5.4% ABV
A dark amber, full-flavoured wheat beer with some sweetness and light malt in the finish.

ANNAFESTBIER
EXPORT 5.5% ABV
Amber in colour and sporting a fine, smooth foam. Sweet, full bodied, and with delicate aromas of dried fruits and banana.

ALTWEIZEN GOLD
WHEAT BEER 5.3% ABV
Clear golden and finely balanced between yeast and carbonic acid, with a lightly sparkling, dry freshness.

BENNO SCHARL
WHEAT BEER 5.3% ABV
Yellow and clouded with yeast, Benno Scharl tastes mild and sweet, pleasant and well balanced.

HAAKE-BECK 12
EXPORT 5% ABV
This is a new Haake-Beck. A harmonious golden beer, with a level of sweetness that is often liked by women.

EDEL HELL
LAGER 4.7% ABV
A mild alternative to the pilsner: not so dry, a little bit sweet, and golden like a typical lager.

BEER

BREWERY

HACKER-PSCHORR

Hochstr. 75, 81541 München, Germany
www.hacker-pschorr.de

Hacker-Pschorr is one of the most
traditional breweries in Munich, and
its restaurant is a tourist attraction,
especially during the Oktoberfest.
Beer production was mentioned for
the first time here in 1417.

BREWING SECRET The Purity Law
and principles of long lagering
are followed; no preservatives
or additives are used.

HÄRKE

Am Werderpark 5, 31224 Peine,
Germany
www.braumanufaktur-haerke.de

Härke has been a family-owned
brewery since 1890, but the first
beer was brewed here much earlier,
in 1666. The Härkes constructed
a new building for the brewery in
1927, and it has been enlarged and
renovated in subsequent decades.

BREWING SECRET Organic produce is
used in some beers.

HASSERÖDER

Auerhahnring 1, 38855 Wernigerode,
Germany
www.hasseroeder.de

Hasseröder, known around the world
for sports sponsorship, is owned by AB
InBev. Production started in 1882 and
was an immediate success. It was the
best-selling beer in East Germany – and
the pilsner lovers in the west did not
wait long after Reunification to try it.

BREWING SECRET Water from the Harz
mountains imparts a smoothness.

HERFORDER

Gebr.-Uekermann-Str. 1, 32120
Hiddenhausen, Germany
www.herforder.de

The brewery was founded in 1878
as Gebrüder Uekermann, Brauerei
zum Felsenkeller. Since then there
have been many innovations in
production, bottling, and styles
of beer. The latest chapter began
in 2007, following integration
within the Warsteiner Group,
but Herforder is still a family-
run company.

BEER

ANNO 1417
KELLERBIER 5.5% ABV
Naturally cloudy, unfiltered, with
a dull golden colour. Low carbonic
acid makes it very smooth.

SUPERIOR
MÜNCHNER SPECIAL 6% ABV
The clear, amber-coloured Superior
is based on an old recipe and has a
malty, aromatic taste, without too
many hops. Highly drinkable.

HÄRKE PILS
PILSNER 4.9% ABV
Nice bitter taste of organic hops
and malt. A real pilsner with a dry
taste and pleasant finish.

HÄRKE DUNKEL
DUNKEL 4.9% ABV
Dark barley malt gives this
beer a fulsome and satisfying
sweet flavour.

HASSERÖDER PREMIUM PILS
PILSNER 4.9% ABV
Full-bodied pilsner taste; well-
balanced bitter aromas of fine
hops and malty flavours.

HASSERÖDER PREMIUM EXPORT
EXPORT 5.5% ABV
Smooth, with some sweetness and
a harmonious bitter aroma of hops
with malty notes; golden colour.

HERFORDER HEFEWIZEN
WHEAT BEER 5.4% ABV
Yellow and turbid, with a bold,
white head. It's refreshing and light.

LANDBIER
LAGER 4.8% ABV
Darkish in colour and low
in bitterness, it has a full
malty flavour.

Proud of its natural raw ingredients and brewing methods, the company says its motto is "quality trumps profit". A wide range of beers are produced by the company which are revered by many across the German region of Westphalia.

HOFBRÄU MÜNCHEN

Hofbräuallee 1, 81829 München, Germany
www.hofbraeu-muenchen.de

The Hofbräuhaus in Munich is a very famous restaurant, frequented by visitors from around the world. It was founded in 1897 by Wilhelm V on a site where brewing began in the year 1607. The linked brewery is situated in Riem, outside of the city.

BREWING SECRET The brewing water is drawn from a depth of 150m (490ft).

HÜTT

Hütt-Brauerei Bettenhäuser, Knallhütte, 34225 Baunatal, Germany
www.huett.de

Beer has been brewed at this site since 1752, and the family-owned company is now in its ninth generation. The brewery has always been linked with the Knallhütte restaurant here.

BREWING SECRET Hütt brews its beers to suit local tastes, but they also appeal to a much wider market.

HUTTHURMER

Marktplatz 5, 94116 Hutthurm, Germany
www.hutthurmer.de

The beers from the Bavarian Forest are well known far beyond regional borders. The local Raiffeisenbank has been the owner since 1914.

BREWING SECRET Consistently using the traditional arts of brewing since 1577 is the secret of this Bavarian brewery's success.

SCHWARZBIER
DARK LAGER 5.2% ABV
A well-balanced dark beer with a fine balance between sweet malt flavours and hop bitterness.

HOFBRÄU ORIGINAL
MÜNCHNER HELLES 5.1% ABV
This clear golden beer is refreshing and dry, with a harmonious balance of malt and hops.

HOFBRÄU DUNKEL
DUNKEL 5.5% ABV
This is the oldest type of Bavarian beer, dark amber in colour, and full of fine flavour and enticing malt aromas.

SCHWARZES GOLD
DUNKEL 4.9% ABV
Smooth brown colour, dry, and very fresh; sweet-tasting and with aromas of malt and fine hops.

LUXUS PILS
PILSNER 4.9% ABV
Bitter aromas of fine hops, very elegant, malty taste, and a clear golden colour: a high-quality pilsner.

TRADITION-EXPORT
EXPORT 5.4% ABV
The gold export beer is full bodied and not too sweet. A light aroma of hops is significant in the finish.

TRADITION-DUNKEL
DUNKEL 5.3% ABV
Dark malt gives this beer its typical colour and aroma. The light hoppiness makes it a pleasant drink.

BREWERY

JANDELSBRUNNER
Hauptstr. 17, 94118 Jandelsbrunn, Germany
www.jandelsbrunner.de

The Langs have owned this brewery since 1810. In the 20th century there was renewal of equipment, such as new filling machines, and the construction of new production plants and maturing cellars.

BREWING SECRET In 2004, photovoltaic equipment was added to harness the power of the sun for brewing.

JETTENBACH
Am Schlossberg 1, 84555 Jettenbach am Inn, Germany
www.brauerei-jettenbach.de

The history of brewing in Bavaria has been closely associated with the story of the dukes of Toerring for more than 700 years. The Toerrings fought for the right to found breweries to produce beer for themselves and the local pubs and restaurants. The master brewers of the family have also become famous in their own right.

JEVER
Elisabethufer 18, 26441 Jever, Germany
www.jever.de

Jever is one of the top breweries in Germany. Established 166 years ago, the company started producing its export beer in the 1950s. The pilsner as we know it took off during the "pils-wave" of the 1960s. Radeberger bought Jever in 2005.

BREWING SECRET Jever is famous for making one of the driest pilsners in existence.

KAUZEN
Uffenheimer Str. 17, 97199 Ochsenfurt, Germany
www.kauzen.de

The most remarkable time in the history of Kauzen was its survival between 1919 and 1945, and the time after World War II, when it had problems getting hold of equipment, malts, and hops to produce beer. Today, Kauzen is one of the most modern breweries in Bavaria with a good position in the market.

BEER

DOPPELBOCK
DOPPELBOCK 8% ABV
The colour of this doppelbock is mahogany, the taste malty, flowery, and slightly sweet, with a nice bitter note when finishing.

UR-WEIZEN
WHEAT BEER 5.3% ABV
Amber coloured and cloudy from the yeast, this malty beer tastes flowery with a mild, sweet finish.

GRAF IGNAZ PREMIUM
PILSNER 4.9% ABV
A real pilsner – clear, golden, and lightly sparkling; strongly flavoured with fine, balanced bitters of hops.

GRAF IGNAZ LAGER
LAGER 4.9% ABV
This golden beer is dry and has nice aromas of fine malt. There is some sweetness on the tongue.

JEVER FUN
LOW ALCOHOL 0.5% ABV
Almost alcohol-free, but with a similar taste to the pilsner. Hop-bitters and a pilsner taste pervade this golden beer.

JEVER PILSNER
PILSNER 4.9% ABV
The master brewers use a lot of hops at Jever, and their bitterness makes this pilsner very dry.

KÄUZLE
LAGER 4.8% ABV
A modern, clear golden beer with sweet, malty aromas, and a light bitter taste of fine hops at the end.

KAUZEN ORIGINAL 1809
LAGER 5.2% ABV
With its golden-yellow colour, this beer is a typical lager; it tastes less dry than usual – indeed, a bit sweet.

KESSELRING

Leithenbukweg 13, 97342 Marktsteft,
Germany
www.kesselring-bier.de

This brewery was founded in the
19th century and became sucessful
after 1914, when Adolf Kesselring
took over the management. By the
early 1960s, Kesselring was producing
3 million litres (650,000 gallons) of
beer and half a million litres (110,000
gallons) of soft drinks each year; the
quantities have doubled since then.

KIRNER

Kallenfelser Str. 2-4, 55606 Kirn,
Germany
www.kirner-bier.de

The Andres family became part of the
beer world in the mid-17th century,
a time when every restaurant in Kirn
was brewing its own beer. By the end
of the century, however, the Andres
were supplying to other restaurants,
and this was the beginning of a success
story that continues to this day.

KITZMANN

Südliche Stadtmauerstr. 25, 91054
Erlangen, Germany
www.kitzmann.de

The Kitzmann brewery in Erlangen
near Nuremberg began brewing beer
in 1733, but it took another 100 years
for the business to really take off.
Subsequent generations have ensured
the loyalty of drinkers by adhering
to the old traditions of this great
brewing city through the years.

KNEITINGER

Kreuzgasse 7, 93047 Regensburg,
Germany
www.kneitinger.de

Kneitinger is one of the best-known
traditional restaurants in the city of
Regensburg. Master brewer Johann
Kneitinger acquired the brewery and
farmland in 1865 to assure the best
raw materials for brewing.

BREWING SECRET Johann Kneitinger
developed the strong bock beer
that the brewery still produces.

URFRÄNKISCHES LANDBIER
LAGER 5.3% ABV
A fresh beer with a clear golden
colour. The taste is a rounded
combination of hops and malt.

KESSELRING SCHLEMMER
SCHWARZE
WHEAT BEER 5.3% ABV
Very sparkling and fresh; a light
aroma of hops in the finish.

KIRNER KYR
PILSNER LIGHT 2.8% ABV
This clear golden-yellow beer has
less alcohol than most, but it tastes
like a real pilsner. Elegant, dry, with
a light touch of fine hops.

KIRNER PILS
PILSNER 4.8% ABV
Cloudy and yellow, this pilsner is
natural, unfiltered, and full bodied,
with a light taste of yeast.

KITZMANN KELLERBIER
KELLERBIER 4.9% ABV
This is a really old-fashioned beer:
unfiltered, cloudy, with fine aromas
of hops and a malty finish.

KITZMANN URBOCK
BOCK 7.1% ABV
A rounded fine bock, which is
rather heavy in taste, but well
balanced between hops and malt,
and with a smooth foam.

KNEITINGER BOCK SAISONBIER
BOCK 6.8% ABV
Black-brown in colour, full bodied,
with a creamy foam, and tasting of
malt – this is a perfect bock.

KNEITINGER DUNKEL EXPORT
EXPORT 5.5% ABV
This dark, ancient beer is malty
with light hops and a creamy foam
– visitors from all over the world
love this typical beer of Regensburg.

BEER STYLES

LAGER

Lager beer is the drink that conquered the world. From the Baltic to the Bahamas, from Australia to Iceland, if you ask for a beer you are most likely to be handed a German or Czech lager facsimile going under the name of pils, pilsner, pilsener, or just plain lager. However, if you went into a bierkeller in Germany and asked for a lager, you'd be met with a puzzled look. Lager in German means "to store" and the long conditioning time of German beers is called "lagering" – a process that was accidentally discovered by medieval Bavarian brewers after they began storing their beers in deep cold caves over the winter. The first golden lager – the type so familiar to us today – only emerged in 1842 from the town of Plzen (see pp236–237).

LAGER STYLES In Germany and Central Europe, lagered beers come in a variety of styles: märzen, bock, dunkel (dark lagers), festbier or Oktoberbier, pilsner, helles, Budweis, schwarzbier, and Dortmunds. A true pilsner is a wonderful beer: crisp and fresh, with a rounded palate of soft, biscuity malt and a delicately hoppy, subtly bitter finish, though the north German Jever Pils has an uncommonly ferocious, bitter finish.

FERMENTATION The fermentation process for lager differs from that of ale in that the yeast works in a much cooler temperature. It has always been called bottom fermentation. However, as the yeast works its way through all the fermenting liquid, it would be more correct to call it cold fermentation.

LAGERING Once the first fermentation is completed, lager beers are put into conditioning vessels, or lagering tanks, for several weeks – nearly 3 months in the case of Budvar's Bohemian lager. This "long sleep" gives the lager a smooth, soft character.

KÖNIG LUDWIG

Augsburger Stre. 41, 82256
Fürstenfeldbruck, Germany
www.royal-bavarian-beer-selection.com

The history of the Bavarian royal
family, the Wittelsbachers, is closely
connected with the art of beer-
making. Today, HRH Luitpold
Prince of Bavaria continues the
family business successfully with his
brands König Ludwig and Kaltenberg.
The latter brand name refers to
the brewery at Kaltenberg Castle.

KROMBACHER

Hagener Str. 261, 57223 Kreuztal-
Krombach, Germany
www.krombacher.de

The brewery was first mentioned in
records in 1803, but it was not until
1908 that the Krombacher brand
was truly established. Business flagged
between the wars, then began to
rise again in the 1990s. Since 2005,
Krombacher has become the leading
premium brand in Germany, making
500 million litres (100 million gallons)
of beer each year.

KRONE TETTNANG

Bärenplatz 7, 88069 Tettnang, Germany
www.krone-tettnang.de

Krone Tettnang is a small craft
brewery that has been owned by the
Tauscher family for seven generations.
It is a member of "Brewers with Body
and Soul" – a group of 10 small
companies who aim to produce beer
"in another, but traditional, way...".

BREWING SECRET The first organic beer
of the Bodensee region was made
here in 1993.

KUCHLBAUER

Römerstr. 5-9, 93326 Abensberg,
Germany
www.weissbierbrauer-kuchlbauer.de

Bestowed the right to brew beer
in 1300, this is one of the oldest
official breweries in the world. The
Kuchlbauers were from Regensburg,
but in 1751, they acquired a property
in Abensberg, where they have been
brewing ever since.

BREWING SECRET Their success stems
from focusing on brewing wheat beers.

BREWERY

KÖNIG LUDWIG DUNKEL

DUNKEL 5.1% ABV
Amber coloured, with a smooth
taste of dark malt and fine hops, it is
the most popular dunkel in Germany.

KÖNIG LUDWIG WEISSBIER

WHEAT BEER 5.5% ABV
One of the most popular wheat
beers in Bavaria; cloudy yellow,
with fine hops in the finish. A very
traditional, non-filtered speciality.

KROMBACHER PILS

PILSNER 4.8% ABV
The taste is elegant, fresh, and
dry, with light bitters of hops in
the finish. Golden in colour.

KROMBACHER WEIZEN

WHEAT BEER 5.3% ABV
Very new: an unfiltered, naturally
cloudy, yellow beer. Sparkling, with
a smooth taste, a little bit sweet,
fruity, and full bodied.

KELLER-PILS

PILSNER 4.7% ABV
The famous first organic beer of
the region. Unfiltered and cloudy, it
has the typical pilsner bitterness of
hops and some sweetness of malt.

KRONENBIER

LAGER 4.9% ABV
Richly flavoured traditional beer
with the finest possible malt aroma
and a light finish of fine hops.

KUCHLBAUER WEISSE

WHEAT BEER 5.4% ABV
One of the most famous and
typical wheat beers – slightly
cloudy, sparkling, and sweet.

ALTE LIEBE DUNKLE WEISSE

WHEAT BEER 5.4% ABV
Dark mahogany and very aromatic
with malts. Rather sweet; not
much bitterness, but fine hops
are present on the tongue.

BEER

BREWERY

KULMBACHER

Lichtenfelser Str. 9, 95326 Kulmbach, Germany
www.kulmbacher.de

The name of Kulmbacher, a brewery now owned by Heineken, is known to beer-lovers throughout the world. Its fame began with the offerings of beer master Wolfgang Reichel in 1846. Since his time, many other brands have joined the company, and production is now about 300 million litres (70 million gallons) of beer each year.

KULTURBRAUEREI HEIDELBERG

Leyergasse 6, 69117 Heidelberg, Germany
www.heidelberger-kulturbrauerei.de

The practice of beer-making was first established here in 1235, but the region was an economic backwater, and the brewery had to struggle through the centuries. Since 1999, however, it has had a rebirth as the Kulturbrauerei in the city of Heidelberg.

LANDSKRON

An der Landskronbrauerei 116, 02826 Görlitz, Germany
www.landskron.de

Founded in 1869, the Landskron brewery in eastern Germany was always one of the most important in the region. Owned by the state under the GDR, it was only after the Reunification in 1990 that the beers were brewed according to the rules of the Purity Law in Germany.

LANDWEHR-BRÄU

Reichelshofen 31, 91628 Steinsfeld, Germany
www.landwehr-braeu.de

The Landwehr brewery is a modern, yet traditionally minded, company. Beer has been produced at this site since 1755, and from 1913 it has been owned by the Wörner family.

One of the highlights of the brewery is a beer festival organized in its grounds during the first week of August, which many cycling groups

BEER

MÖNCHSHOF SCHWARZBIER
SCHWARZBIER 4.9% ABV
Dark roasted malts and fine hops. The deep, dark colour and fine aroma are typical of schwarzbiers.

KAPUZINER WEISSBIER
WHEAT BEER 5.4% ABV
Naturally cloudy, sparkling, and with a sweet and fruity taste; this unfiltered beer is typical of the wheat-beer style.

HELLES HEFEWEIZEN
WHEAT BEER 5.2% ABV
The beer is yellow to the eye, naturally cloudy if full bodied, and full of fruit flavours.

KRÄUSEN
HELLES 5.2% ABV
The Kräusen from Heidelberg is unfiltered, slightly cloudy, and golden. It is mild and similar to a pilsner.

PREMIUM PILSNER
PILSNER 4.8% ABV
Golden yellow, this beer has a very fresh and dry taste. Light in malt, it has an aromatic hop bitterness.

LANDSKRON EXPORT
EXPORT 5.2% ABV
A traditional dark-golden beer, naturally strong, brewed with a light malty taste, and a fine finish of hops.

DUNKLER BOCK
BOCK 6.6% ABV
Reminiscent of hazelnuts, this beer is a typical bock with its aromas of malts, and fine bitter taste of hops.

WINTERFESTBIER
BOCK 5.4% ABV
Red in colour, this is a warming beer with a fine malty aroma, a hint of honey, and a subtle hop nose.

choose to visit. It includes Franconian food, a display of hops, traditional Bavarian music, and a full range of its beers.

BREWING SECRET Brewing and filling technologies are as advanced as possible – important factors in the guarantee of quality.

LANG-BRÄU

Bayreuther Straße, 18-19, D-95632 Wunsiedel-Schönbrunn, Germany
www.lang-braeu.de

Schönbrunn, near Wunsiedel, is home to this small brewery, which produces 13 different styles of beer. Production levels are relatively low, yet this company is world famous because of the wide distribution of its Benedikt XVI ("The Pope's beer", 7.5% ABV). Interestingly, they also brew an "Erotic beer" (5.5% ABV).

LEIBINGER

Friedhofstr. 20-36, 88212 Ravensburg, Germany
www.leibinger.de

This brewery was founded in 1894 in Ravensburg by Max Leibinger I. Max Leibinger II took over in 1959 and began the modernization of the brewery. Michael Leibinger is now at the helm.

BREWING SECRET 100 per cent of the ingredients in Leibinger beers are sourced locally.

LEIKEIM

Gewerbegebiet 4, 96264 Altenkunstadt, Germany
www.leikeim.de

About 120 years old, the brewery is still owned by the Leikeim family, now in the fourth generation. Today, after several renovations, the company is the second largest in Germany selling beer in clip-top bottles. Dieter Leikeim, who runs the operation, has largely been responsible for turning Leikeim into a premium brewery.

ALTFRÄNKISCH DUNKEL

DUNKEL 5.2% ABV
With a rich roasted malt, almost toffee flavour, it has hints of coffee and a satisfying bitter finish.

PILSNER

PILSNER 4.9% ABV
With a gentle floral hop aroma, it is a crisp, easy-drinking beer.

SCHÖNBRUNNER SPEZIAL

EXPORT 5.5% ABV
Clear gold and full bodied, with a malty finish and notes of fine hops.

URBOCK DUNKEL

DUNKEL 7.5% ABV
A deep brown colour, it is full of warming, dark fruit flavours and mocha coffee notes.

MAX

SPECIAL 5.2% ABV
This mix of malts from wheat, barley, and fine hops has a subtle taste. A very successful beer.

EDEL PILS

PILSNER 4.9% ABV
The taste is markedly of hops, which is typical for a pilsner. It is sparkling, with delicate hop-flower notes and dryness in the mouth.

LEIKEIM RADLER

BEER BLEND 2.6% ABV
Very clear, yellow beer with a distinct lemon taste and only a few traces of bitterness. Sparkling and very fresh.

LEIKEIM PREMIUM

PILSNER 4.9% ABV
Dry and with more fine aromas of hops than most other pilsners. The finish has only light aromas of malt.

BEER TRAIL

BAMBERG

Can there be a better place in the world to drink beer? This beautiful, baroque island city, on the banks of the River Regnitz and the Main-Donau Canal is in the Upper Franconia region of Bavaria. It is built on medieval foundations and is home to 70,000 people and 11 breweries. The city is a base for many US army personnel and their families – and they have helped, no doubt, to take the fame of this beer paradise around the world.

Many of Bamberg's beers have a smoky secret. To malt a cereal, the grain has to begin to germinate, converting complicated sugars into simpler ones, which can then be broken down even further in the mash tun. But the process has to be stopped before it goes too far and the grain's goodness is lost to the brewer. Heat is normally used to arrest germination, but, in Franconia, maltsters have developed a smoky technique of stopping the grain's growth. The germinating grain is heated over beechwood fires, which imparts marvellous wood fire and peaty aromas and flavours to the finished beers.

1 BRAUEREI-GASTSTÄTTE KLOSTERBRÄU
Beer has been brewed at Klosterbrau since 1533. Down a cobbled street, time seems to slip away in this fairytale of a brewery tap. The range includes a schwarzbier, braunbier, weizen, pils, and a bock. *Obere Mühlbrücke 1-3, Bamberg (www.klosterbraeu.de)*

JOURNEY STATS
30 mins, plus drinking time
3km (2 miles)

2 OLD TOWN HALL
The river is never far away in Bamberg. The stroll to Brauerei Spezial's passes the spectacular medieval stone-and-timbered Old Town Hall, which seems precariously balanced on the footings of an ancient bridge. Take a moment to admire it before heading on to the Brauerei Spezial.

3 THE BRAUEREI SPEZIAL
The Brauerei Spezial is very much a locals' bar, decorated with laughter and conversations. Its Spezial Rauchbier has subtle, soft toffee flavours and even a hint of burnt straw. Spezial uses smoked malt in at least four of its other beers. By the bar is a serving hatch, where locals come to fill containers with beer for drinking at home. *Obere Königstraße 10, Bamberg (www.brauerei-spezial.de)*

4 BRAUEREI FÄSSLA

Directly opposite Brauerei Spezial is Brauerei Fässla. Brewing started here in 1649. The brewery tap has a comfortable, wood-panelled, country-style room, and above it is a small hotel. The brewery's logo – a dwarf rolling a barrel of beer – decorates the glasses and dark furniture. Fässla's easy-drinking Lagerbier melds malty flavours with a fresh, soft bitterness. *Obere Königstraße 19–21, Bamberg (www.faessla.de)*

5 SCHLENKERLA

Vibrant and friendly, Schlenkerla is Bamberg's best-known bar and restaurant. The warmth of its world-famous rauchbier, with its smoked whisky and cheese overtones, is as warm as the welcome. Tables are often shared, and the atmosphere is highly convivial. Beer is the social lubricant and the perfect accompaniment to robust Bavarian dishes such as onions stuffed with beery meatballs. *Dominikanerstraße 6, Bamberg (www.schlenkerla.de)*

6 AMBRÄUSIANUM

Opposite Schlenkerla is the Ambräusianum. Here, the brewing vessels can be seen, which makes it seem more like a modern brewpub than one of Bamberg's traditional establishments, and it is a relative newcomer, being open only since 2004. Weekend breakfasts comprise a glass of wheat beer with three locally made Bavarian veal sausages and a pretzel. *Dominikanerstr. 10, Bamberg (www.ambraeusianum.de)*

7 WEINSTUBE PIZZINI

The exterior of the Weinstube Pizzini is somewhat unprepossessing, and do not be deterred by its name – it is neither a wine bar nor a pizza restaurant. Inside this small, brown, decorated and time-worn bar, you get a warm-hearted welcome and the opportunity to try Fässla and Spezial beers, as well as a dunkel from Andechser. *Ober Sandstr. 17, Bamberg*

Rauchbier - Gaststätte ✦Kachelofen✦ - Kellerbier

The bars of Bamberg are known for their rauchbier (smoked beer), which uses beechwood-smoked malt.

BREWERY

LICHER

In den Hardtberggärten, 35423 Lich, Germany
www.licher.de

Tradition is an important concept at this brewery, which has been around since 1854. There is a philosophy of quality at Licher that is obvious when you drink their beers.

BREWING SECRET The basics for making good beer – malt, hops, and water – are all from sustainable sources.

LINDENBRÄU

Stuttgarter Str. 43, 76337 Waldbronn, Germany
www.lindenbraeu-waldbronn.de

Lindenbräu can look back to a history spanning three centuries. In 2000 it had a major renovation, which involved stripping the old buildings back to a shell, then creating a very modern interior. The old barn was turned into a covered beer garden.

KEILER BRAHAUS

Ludwigstr. 3, 97816 Lohr am Main, Germany
www.keilerbier.de

Keiler was founded in the late 19th century to produce beer specifically for a restaurant. The restaurant has now been rebuilt in a modern way, with the brewery as its bright, shining copper star. The brewery is now a subsidiary of Würzburger Hofbräu.

BREWING SECRET Keiler has a history of the judicious introduction of new beers.

LÖWENBRÄU

Nymphenburger Str. 7, 80335 München, Germany
www.loewenbraeu.de

Löwenbräu is one of the most famous brands in the world. The company is more than 500 years old. In 1948, only three years after the end of World War II, Löwenbräu began exporting again: first to Switzerland, then further afield. In 1997, there was a marriage between Löwenbräu and Spatenbräu; today both are part of the global player AB InBev.

BEER

LICHER WEIZEN
WHEAT BEER 5.4% ABV
A favourite of the brewery: fine yeast and hops give the beer a special note, while the sweetness gives it a full-bodied taste.

LICHER LAGER
LAGER 4.9% ABV
Clear and golden, hints of citrus shine through the bready malt notes. Clean and refreshing.

LINDENBRÄU PILS
PILSNER 5% ABV
A real pilsner: clear, golden, and with a strong but smooth taste, and a bitter aroma of fine hops.

LINDENBRÄU ORIGINAL
LAGER 5% ABV
An amber-coloured beer with a very aromatic, malty taste, and a slightly stronger bitterness than usual. The sweetness is like a märzen.

KEILER WEISSBIER
WHEAT BEER 4.9% ABV
Naturally cloudy, dark amber coloured, and unfiltered, the Keiler is balanced between wheat and barley malts. Slightly sweet, with a fine aroma of hops in the finish.

KEILER LAND-PILS
PILSNER 4.9% ABV
A golden, bubbly yellow, it has hints of floral herbs and malted bread.

LÖWENBRÄU TRIUMPHATOR
DOPPELBOCK 7.6% ABV
Dark brown in colour, the Triumphator has a strong flavour of malt, but only a subtle aroma of hops. Sweet.

LÖWENBRÄU URTYP
EXPORT 5.4% ABV
A balanced flavour with fine aromas of malt; full bodied, pleasant, and fresh, with mild hops in the finish.

LÜBZER

Eisenbeissstr. 1, 19386 Lübz, Germany
www.luebzer.de

Beer has been produced in Lübz for 130 years. Today the brewery is a part of Carlsberg A/S Denmark, and the company has a capacity of 100 million litres (20 million gallons) of beer annually. In eastern Germany, Lübzer Pils is one of the biggest brands and popular, even with beer aficionados.

MAISEL

Hindenburgstr. 9, D-95445 Bayreuth, Germany
www.maisel.com

Hans and Eberhardt Maisel founded the brewery in the city of Richard Wagner in 1887. The family decided to concentrate the production on wheat beer in 1955, and Maisel became a trendsetter for this style.

BREWING SECRET Their success is the result of a high level of ability in the handcrafting of beers.

MAXLRAIN

Schlossbrauerei Maxlrain, Aiblinger Str. 1, D-83104 Maxrain, Germany
www.maxlrain.de

Emperor Karl the Great was the founder of the castle of Maxlrain in the year 804. The current owner of the castle and its attached brewery – Leo, Count of Hohenthal von Bergen – is proud of his tradition and the high quality of his ingredients.

METTLACHER ABTEI-BRÄU

Bahnhofstr. 32, 66693 Mettlach, Germany
www.abtei-brauerei.de

Mettlacher specializes in natural, unfiltered beer. Guests can watch the brewing process from the attached restaurant. The brewers promote the beer styles of the region and run courses on beer production.

BREWING SECRET High-quality basic products, modern techniques, and the energy of the brewers ensure success.

LÜBZER URKRAFT

LAGER 6% ABV
This amber-coloured beer has a bit more alcohol than usual, a full-bodied taste, and plenty of aroma.

LÜBZER LEMON

PILSNER AND LEMON 2.5% ABV
Fresh lemons, limeade, and only 2.5 per cent ABV give this clear yellow mixture a really refreshing taste.

MAISEL'S WEISSE

WHEAT BEER 5.2% ABV
The colour is typical for Maisel: a gleaming red. Fermentation in the bottle gives the beer fruity notes and mild nuttiness in the finish.

MAISEL'S DAMPFBIER

SPECIAL BEER 4.9% ABV
A very old-fashioned beer: the mix of different malts gives it a really special, fine character.

JUBILATOR

DOPPELBOCK 7.5% ABV
A dark-coloured beer with a strong but satisfying taste, rounded and smooth with fine roasty malts in the finish.

AIBLINGER SCHWARZE

DARK EXPORT 5% ABV
Mahogany, with a fine, malty aroma and smooth taste. Full bodied and not too sweet.

ABTEI-BOCK

BOCK 6.1% ABV
Strong-roasted bock with obvious roasty aromas and an even more intense flavour of fine hops.

ABTEI-JOSEF-SUD

WHEAT BEER 5.1% ABV
The dark amber-coloured wheat beer is sparkling and has typical aromas from the mash of wheat and barley malts.

BREWERY

MICHELSBRÄU

Fahrstr. 83-85, 64832 Babenhausen, Germany
www.michelsbraeu.de

The brewery is situated in the heart of the small city of Babenhausen. It was founded in 1815 and has been managed by the Schuberts since 1925. The production is handcrafted, and the master brewer uses the best malts and hops available.

BREWING SECRET The water comes from a spring in the vicinity of the brewery.

NESSELWANG

Postbrauerei Nesselwang, Hauptstr. 25, 87484 Nesselwang, Germany
www.post-brauerei-nesselwang.de

In the second half of the 17th century there were five breweries in Nesselwang. For 200 years, this one was called the Adler brewery; its incarnation as Nesselwang began in 1883, and it has enjoyed continuous success since World War II.

NEUMARKTER LAMMSBRÄU

Gebr. Ehrnsberger KG, Amberger Str.1, 92318 Neumarkt in der Oberpfalz, Germany
www.lammsbraeu.de

Family-owned since 1800, the company turned to organic beer production in 1987 and now has about 19 types.

BREWING SECRET Neumarkter Lammsbräu works with about 100 organic farmers to ensure the quality of its ingredients.

PINKUS MÜLLER

Kreuzstr. 4-10, 48143 Münster, Germany
www.pinkus-mueller.de

The story of the Müller family began in 1816 in Münster. The company expanded over the years. Today, Pinkus Müller is the last of about 150 traditional breweries in Münster, and an attraction in the town. Its restaurant serves regional specialities.

BREWING SECRET The raw materials for its unfiltered beers are all organic.

BEER

MICHELSBRÄU HEXE
EXPORT 5.2% ABV
This special beer has a malty aroma and fine bitters of hops. It is amber yellow and a delight to drink.

MICHELSBRÄU PILS
PILSNER 4.9% ABV
The golden pilsner is fresh with a fine and gleaming foam. It has a balanced aroma of hops, and tastes lightly bitter, dry, and elegant.

POSTWIRT'S DUNKEL
DUNKEL 4.9% ABV
A dark brown speciality that tastes of roasted malts. It is slightly sweet and finishes with a whisper of hop bitterness.

POSTILLON
WHEAT BEER 4.9% ABV
A typical amber wheat beer: sparkling, with a fresh taste of light hops and malts, and a sweet finish.

URSTOFF
LAGER 4.7% ABV
Brewed with fewer hops than a pilsner, so it tastes less bitter; it is pleasant and has a nice finish.

DINKELBIER
SPECIAL BEER 5.2% ABV
Dinkel is similar to wheat beer but is a much older style. It has balanced basic ingredients and the sparkle of a wheat beer, and tastes strong.

PINKUS PILS
PILSNER 5.2% ABV
A colour like straw; it tastes dry and has a medium aroma of hops in the finish.

ORIGINAL ALT
ALTBIER 5.1% ABV
The wine-like character comes from an extra-long period of maturation. Dark golden, with light bitter aromas in the finish.

REICHENBRAND

Zwickauer Str. 478, 09117 Chemnitz, Germany
www.brauerei-bergt.de

Reichenbrand is located in the city of Chemnitz. The brewery first opened in 1874, but went bankrupt 21 years later. Joachim Bergt then took over and guided the company through difficult times. The GDR nationalized it; after Reunification, the family took it back. It has been renovated and is now enjoying more prosperous times.

CLASSIC PILSNER
PILSNER 4.8% ABV
Aromatic German hops and a nice crisp malt finish dominate this drinkable pilsner.

PREMIUM
EXPORT 5.5% ABV
Typically dark yellow, this beer is as full bodied as its sibling, but more aromatic from hops, and it has a fine, dry, and bitter finish.

REUTBERG

Klosterbrauerei Reutberg, Am Reutberg 2, 83679 Sachsenkamm, Germany
www.klosterbrauerei-reutberg.de

The monastery at Reutberg started brewing its own beer in the 17th century. In 1924, the Franziskaner monks stopped brewing, but the local people protested. Production started again, within months, with a new company. In 1987, a proposed merger with Holzkirchen failed, and Reutberg continues to brew its own beer independently.

EXPORT DUNKEL
DUNKEL 5.2% ABV
Dark malt gives the beer its typical dark amber colour. The smell is malty and the texture full bodied, with a harmonious finish.

JOSEFI BOCK
BOCK 6.9% ABV
This strong amber beer has a mild taste with a pleasant, malty aroma: a well-balanced beer.

RIEGELE

Frölichstr. 26, 86150 Augsburg, Germany
www.riegele.de

The history of brewing here goes back to 1386. Sebastian Riegele bought the small company in 1884, and developed it so well that in 1911 a new brewery was built outside central Augsburg. Today Riegele is still family-owned and operates several restaurants as well as the brewery.

BREWING SECRET Riegele has its own malt-producing company.

COMMERZIENRAT RIEGELE PRIVAT
EXPORT 5.2% ABV
Golden and gleaming, with aromas of malt and hop flowers; the taste is smooth and mild, with a lovely bitterness of hops.

SEBASTIAN RIEGELE'S WEISSE
WHEAT BEER 5% ABV
Unfiltered, cloudy, and yellow. A yeast-flower taste with fruitiness and fine bitters of hops.

RÖHRL

Heerstr. 13, 94315 Straubing, Germany
www.roehrlbraeu.de

Straubing in Niederbayern is home to the brewery that Josef Röhrl founded in 1881. From the beginning, it was family-owned. After difficulties at the end of World War II, the family managed to re-establish it as a very successful company.

BREWING SECRET The introduction of their wheat beer in 1976 brought them widespread recognition.

GÄUBODEN LANDBIER
LAGER 4.8% ABV
The name comes from the famous beer festival in Straubing. It has a light barley and hoppy taste with a nice, very slightly bitter finish.

STRAUBINGER WEISSE NASTURTRÜB
WHEAT BEER 5.3% ABV
Full bodied, fresh, sparkling, and very fruity, with a mild hoppy aroma.

The Früh brewery tap, close to Cologne cathedral, is the perfect place to drink a glass of kölsch.

BEER STYLES
KÖLSCH

Although the appearance of a glass of golden kölsch might suggest the lager method of bottom- or cold-fermentation, the unique beer of Cologne (Köln) is a member of the ale family. It might have the hue of a pilsner, and spend a month in cold maturation (or lagering), but it is a beer made with top- or warm-fermenting yeast. This marks it out as a survivor from the time when Germany was home to all sorts of unusual beers, many of which would qualify as ales. It is also one of those rare beers with its own appellation: since 1985, no brewery outside the city of Cologne or a handful of nearby villages can call its beer a kölsch. It's for this reason that American craft brewers, many of whom are keen supporters of the beers of Cologne, have to call their brews "kölsch-style".

Naturally, the citizens of Cologne are extremely proud of their beer. Sample kölsch at its best in the atmospheric brewery taps of Früh (close to the cathedral) and Dom on the Alteburger Strasse.

LIGHT AND SUBTLE This is not a big bruiser of a beer: expect delicate fruit and malt flavours on the palate, with hints of berry fruit, followed by a subtle sweetness and a quick, clean finish. It's a refreshing style of beer, easily drinkable, and normally around 5% ABV. It makes a wonderful apéritif or social drink, and is also ideal for serving at the dining table with light salads or delicate white fish.

KÖBES OF KÖLN Just like its close rival alt, from the neighbouring Rhineland city of Dusseldorf, kölsch is delivered by wandering bands of blue-apron-wearing waiters called köbes. The beer arrives in small, cylindrical glasses called stange; they are carried on round trays, with each glass sitting in its own hole.

BREWERY

ROSENBRAUEREI PÖSSNECK

Dr.-Wilhelm-Külz-Straße 41, 07381 Pössneck, Germany
www.rosenbrauerei.de

Brewing has been taking place in Pössneck since the 16th century. The company was nationalized in 1951 and had fallen into a state of disrepair by the time of Reunification. By 1994, however, the Rosenbrauerei was back on course for success.

ROSTOCKER

Doberaner Str. 27, 18057 Rostock, Germany
www.rostocker.de

In 1878, the engineers Mahn and Ohlerich acquired the Julius Meyer'sche Bierbrauerei. There followed a highly successful era until the outbreak of World War II. After several changes of ownership, the brewery is now a 100 per cent owned subsidiary of Radeberger Gruppe, the largest private brewery in Germany.

ROTHAUS

Badische Staatsbrauerei Rothaus AG, Rothaus 1, 79865 Grafenhausen-Rothaus, Germany
www.rothaus.de

The Rothaus brewery was founded in 1791 by the Benedictine monastery St. Blasien. Today it is owned by the State of Baden-Württemberg and is one of the most profitable regional breweries in Germany. Although the brewery does not advertise, the Tannenzäpfle has become a cult brand in bars throughout Germany.

SAALFELDER

Bürgerliches Brauhaus Saalfeld, Pössnecker Str. 55, 07318 Saalfeld, Germany
www.brauhaus-saalfeld.de

The tradition of brewing beer is more than 100 years old in Saalfeld. In the 1950s the brewery was partially renovated, but many machines were still old fashioned. New owners have since invested €7 million to modernize the equipment.

BEER

ROSEN KELLERBIER
SPECIAL BEER 4.8% ABV
This traditional beer has a cloudy yellow colour; it is full bodied and aromatic with a light malty aroma.

SCHWARZE ROSE
SCHWARZBIER 4.9% ABV
Sparkling and almost black, with a nice roasted malt aroma and some bitterness in the finish.

ROSTOCKER PILS
PILSNER 4.9% ABV
Mild in malt flavours and easy drinking, its quick-ending bitterness leaves you wanting more.

ROSTOCKER BOCK DUNKEL
BOCK 6.9% ABV
More bitter than other bocks. Full bodied with malt aromas and a rich caramel taste.

ROTHAUS PILS TANNENZÄPFLE
PILSNER 5.1% ABV
Tannenzäpfle ("little fir cones") is a crisp, elegant, well-rounded pilsner with a slight final bitterness.

ROTHAUS HEFEWEIZEN
WHEAT BEER 5.4% ABV
Refreshing top-fermented beer, with a mild fruity finish.

UR-SAALFELDER
MÄRZENBIER 5.6% ABV
Golden-amber in colour, it is rich and malty, with a floral bitterness from the Noble hops.

SAALFELDER PILSNER
PILSNER 4.8% ABV
This classic pilsner has a fine, dry taste with a light sparkle at the beginning and a harmonious bitter aroma at the finish.

SCHAUMBURGER

St. Annen 11, 31655 Stadthagen,
Germany
www.schaumburger-brauerei.de

The brewery was founded in 1873
in Stadthagen. Production stopped
during World War II, but the beer
was on sale again from 1948.

BREWING SECRET The brewery uses
water from the Bornan spring, which
has similar qualities to water from
Pilsen in the Czech Republic – where
the original pilsner was made.

SCHEYERN

Schyrenplatz 1, 85298 Scheyern,
Germany
www.klosterbrauerei-scheyern.de

The monks of Scheyern started
brewing beer in 1119. Later, the
brewery was leased to a producer
in Augsburg, but the monastery (one
of the oldest in Bavaria) has recently
started beer production again.
The brewery is in the middle of the
famous Hallertau region – the biggest
area of hop cultivation in the world.

SCHLAPPESEPPEL

Aschaffenburger Strasse 3-5 63762
Grossostheim, Bavaria, Germany
www.schlappeseppel.de

When King Gustav Adolf of Sweden
conquered the city of Aschaffenburg
(south of Frankfurt) in the year 1631,
there was not a drop of beer at the
castle. The only person available to
brew beer was a lame soldier called
Shlappe Seppel ("flabby Joseph").
The Schlappeseppel was born.

SCHLENKERLA

Dominikaner Str. 6, 96049 Bamberg,
Germany
www.schlenkerla.de

This legendary brewery was known by
1405. Today it is still a relatively small
company, run by a family in its sixth
generation. The so-called "smoked
beer" is a speciality of Bamberg.

BREWING SECRET The distinctive smoky
aroma of Schlenkerla's beers comes
from beechwood smoke that pervades
the malt as it dries above the oven.

SCHAUMBURGER PRIVAT-BOCK
BOCK 6.5% ABV
Typical bock with a light malt
aroma, strong flavour, and a nice
finish from fine hops.

SCHAUMBURGER LÜTTJE LAGE
LIGHT BEER 3% ABV
A special light beer that is drunk
together with corn schnapps in
northern Germany. It is low in
alcohol and delightfully light.

KLOSTER-GOLD HELL
LAGER 5.4% ABV
Golden in colour, and with a mild
flavour of hops.

HOPFAZUPFABIER
MÄRZEN 5.6% ABV
Hopfazupfa is Bavarian for "the man
who harvests hops", and it was for
such men that this golden-coloured
beer was originally produced. Fine-
flavoured with light aromas of hops.

SCHLAPPESEPPEL SPECIALITÄT
MÄRZEN 5.6% ABV
Amber rather than gold, it has
an intriguing malt note and a
light, bitter finish.

SCHLAPPESEPPEL KELLERBIER
KELLERBIER 5.5% ABV
Naturally cloudy, the depth of
the malt flavours are in harmony
with bitter hops and some pleasant
yeast notes.

RAUCHBIER URBOCK
BOCK 6.5% ABV
A traditional dark bock with
Schlenkerla's trademark smoky
and roasty aromas; dry, malty taste
and a good sweetness in the finish.

AECHT SCHLENKERLA RAUCHBIER
MÄRZEN 5.1% ABV
A very dark, dry beer. It has smoky
and roasted malt aromas and a
finish of light hops. A pure pleasure.

BREWERY

SCHLODERER BRÄU

Rathausstr. 4, 92224 Amberg, Germany
www.schlodererbraeu.de

The Schloderer Bräu is a typical brewery-restaurant situated in the ancient city of Amberg. While dining, guests can watch the brewing of beer in action. There are standard brands and also seasonal ones such as wedding beer or "the beer of the witches". To accompany the beers is an array of regional dishes and special menus.

SCHLOSSBRAUEREI AU/ HALLERTAU

Schlossbrauerei Au in der Hallertau, Schlossbräugasse 2, 84072 Au, Germany
www.auer-bier.de

Au is at the heart of the largest hop-growing area in the world. It was linked with the master brewer Schweiger in 1590 and, since 1846, has been owned by six generations of the Earls Beck of Peccoz. A modern approach is an essential feature of the management at Au in der Hallertau.

SCHMUCKER

Hauptstr. 89, 64756 Mossautal, Germany
www.schmucker-bier.de

Founded in 1780, this brewery is still a private company. The beer is considered as regional, but dealers transport it around the country, and there are even exports to Italy, Spain, France, South Korea, and the USA. The brewery has 90 employees.

BREWING SECRET The hardness of the local spring water is a key factor in the character of Schmucker beers.

SCHNEIDER

Private Weissbierbrauerei Schneider, Emil-Ott-Str. 1-5, 93309 Kelheim, Germany
www.schneider-weisse.de

The Schneider brewery has been a family-owned company since it was founded. From its original location in Munich, Schneider moved to Kelheim after World War II. The former brewery in central Munich has since become a world-famous restaurant.

BEER

SCHLODI KULT
LAGER 5.2% ABV
Naturally cloudy and yellow, the Kult tastes dry and fine-flavoured. It is slightly sparkling, and very fresh.

SCHLODERER DUNKEL
DUNKEL 4.9% ABV
Dark amber in colour, naturally cloudy, and slightly smoky with malt aromas and some sweetness.

AUER DUNKLES
DUNKEL 5.2% ABV
Aromatic dark malts give this beer a sweet, chewy character, with a bitter finish.

HOLLEDAUER LEICHTES
WHEAT BEER 3.3% ABV
A cloudy yellow, light wheat beer, fresh and lightly sparkling; not too heavy a taste, and with a slightly bitter finish.

SCHMUCKER MEISTER PILS
PILSNER 4.8% ABV
Clear yellow and gleaming, this typical full-bodied pilsner has a strong aroma of hops; it is smooth with a strong bitterness.

SCHMUCKER HEFEWEIZEN
WHEAT BEER 5% ABV
Deep yellow and cloudy, full bodied; a smooth taste accompanied by a smell of fruits and yeast.

SCHNEIDER WEISSE ORIGINAL
WHEAT BEER 5.4% ABV
People call it "liquid amber", and they are right: the amber-mahogany colour is beautiful. Fresh, full bodied, and with a light bitter finish.

AVENTINUS
STRONG WHEAT BEER 8.2% ABV
Almost black, legendary beer, with chocolate and dried-fruit aromas; full bodied, very thick, and fresh.

SCHÖNRAM

Salzburger Strasse 17, 83367 Petting/
Schönram, Germany
www.brauerei-schoenram.de

Being run by eight generations of
the same family doesn't stop the
brewery from being at the forefront
of Germany's craft beer movement.
The US brewer, Eric Toft, likes to play
tunes with hops in his beers and floral,
citrus, and piney notes can be found
in the beers from the use of American
hops. The company's IPA was one of
the first brewed in Germany.

SCHUSSENRIEDER

Wilhelm-Schussen-Str. 12, 88427 Bad
Schussenried, Germany
www.schussenrieder.de

The first brewers in the region were
monks at a monastery in the 12th
century. The modern story started in
1906, when master brewer Josef Ott
acquired the brewery. The Ott family
are still the owners.

BREWING SECRET The brewery is a
traditional one and only uses barley
and hops from the region.

SCHWARZBACH

Schleisinger Str. 27, 98673 Schwarzbach,
Germany
www.schlossbrauerei-schwarzbach.de

The owner of the Schwarzbach
restaurant was the first to brew beer
on this site – during the occupation
of the Würzburg bishop's troops in
1400. During wars and revolutions
the brewery was destroyed and
rebuilt. It was nationalized by the
GDR in 1949. The story has begun
afresh since the Reunification of
Germany in 1990.

SCHWEIGER

Ebersberger Str. 25, 85570 Markt
Schwaben, Germany
www.schweiger-bier.de

Ludwig Schweiger was by trade a
miller but in the 1930s he somehow
founded a brewery, which is now
managed by his descendants.
Their best-known beer today
is the Schmankerl-Weisse.

BREWING SECRET The brewery has used
its own malt since 1963, and also
sold its malt to other brewers.

HELL
HELLES 5% ABV
Clear, light, and golden, it has
aromas of honey with a hint of
citrus. The finish is well balanced.

PILS
PILSNER 5.4% ABV
A complex aroma of geranium
and herbs. Very bitter. Its finish
is long and refreshing.

ORIGINAL NO.1
LAGER 4.7% ABV
A natural, unfiltered, cloudy yellow
beer full of malt aromas and a light
finish of fine hops.

MÄRZEN NO.1
MÄRZEN 5.5% ABV
A golden beer with a hint of red, its
light malt character is offset by the
caress of aromatic Hallertau hops.

SONNEN WEISSE
WHEAT BEER 5% ABV
Sparkling fresh with a typical taste
of yeast, sweetness, and fine hops.
The appearance is golden yellow
and slightly cloudy.

RAUBRITTER DUNKEL
DUNKEL 5% ABV
Dark and malty, this beer is full
bodied, smooth, and the favourite
of more than just the knights.

**ORIGINAL SCHMANKERL-WEISSE
DUNKEL**
WHEAT BEER 5.1% ABV
Naturally dark and cloudy, this beer
is light and sparkling on the palate.

HELLES EXPORT
EXPORT 5.1% ABV
A classic beer with a light, dry
taste. It is pleasant, with a nice
bitterness of hops in the finish.

THE STORY OF...

Weltenburger Kloster

Asamstrase 32,
93309 Kelheim, Germany

In a courtyard, where giant chestnut trees shade visitors from the sun, the church of the Weltenburg Monastery and the Kloster brewery stand side by side. Set on a bend in the Danube, this must be one of the most dramatic and magnificent brewery locations in the world. The beautifully decorated baroque Benedictine abbey is hewn from the 150-million-year-old Jurassic limestone that forms towering cliffs on both sides of the river. Brewery and river usually co-exist harmoniously, but lines and dates on an exterior wall bear witness to the power of the river in full flood. The most recent inundation, in 2013, nearly closed the brewery.

Weltenburg Monastery was founded in the 7th century by two monks, Eustasic and Agilus, followers of St. Columbanus, one of the patron saints of brewing. Manuscripts in the monastery's library show that beer has been brewed here for over 1,000 years, with production only being halted from 1803 to 1846. This makes it the oldest abbey brewery in the world. But, although the ancient site is redolent with tradition, this is a forward-looking, hi-tech, automated brewery.

Each year many visitors take a tour of the brewery's visitor centre, where they can learn more about the 1,000-year-old history of the Benedictine Abbey and its brewery.

▲ ANCIENT AND MODERN
This monastic brewery may be the world's oldest working brewery, but behind its elegant baroque facade is a sparklingly modern brewery with state-of-the-art equipment.

▲ LUDWIG MEDERER
Weltenberg's brewmaster is mindful of the monastery's long brewing tradition but, nevertheless, embraces a technologically advanced approach to beer production at Weltenberg. Time also plays an important part in the process – a long lagering allows the beers to develop their depth of taste and flavour.

▲ THE BEER RANGE The brewery produces seven beers. Its Weissbier Hell, Urtyp Hell, Barock Hell, and Pils are top-fermented at 8°C (46°F) for seven days. Weissbier Dunkel, Barock Dunkel, and Asam Bock are bottom-fermented at 22°C (72°F) for four days.

► LAGERING The Weltenburger Kloster lager store is located beneath 40m (130ft) of limestone rock. Here, the Dunkel is stored at 0°C (32°F), and sometimes lower, for at least three months. This slowly releases the Barock Dunkel's aromatic, malty flavours and well-balanced richness. The beer was presented with the Gold Medal in the Dark Lagers category at the World Beer Cup 2008 in San Diego, USA.

◄ QUALITY INGREDIENTS Miller prides himself on the brewery's close links with local Bavarian farmers. Each June he visits the barley fields to choose the grain, which will then be malted in Bamberg. The sweet and spicy Perle Hallertau hops, used in pellet form at the brewery, come from three farms near Munich.

▲ THE BEER GARDEN Visitors should not miss the opportunity of sampling the beer, which is pumped directly to its own bar. The beer garden is open throughout the year and is renowned not only for its beer, but also for its extensive range of traditional Bavarian dishes, including suckling pig, boiled beef, and Klosterwurst, a spicy home-made sausage. The brewery is open to the public on weekends

BREWERY

STERNQUELL

Dobenauer Str. 83, 08523 Plauen, Germany
www.sternquell.de

The Aktienbrauverein in Plauen was nationalized after World War II and given a new name – Sternquell. After Reunification, the brewery quickly enjoyed success and is now in the top three of the East German territories.

BREWING SECRET A pre-Reunification program of investment was the basis for its future success.

STRALSUNDER

Greifswalder Chaussee 84-85, 18439 Stralsund, Germany
www.stralsunder.de

The art of brewing has been closely connected with the city of Stralsund for centuries. This brewery was founded in 1827. After nationalization it faced increasing difficulties but, since 1997 it has been enjoying success again.

BREWING SECRET When the brewery relaunched in 1997, it reintroduced a well-loved traditional beer from its past.

STRECK

Ludwig-Jahn-Str. 11 9745 Ostheim, Germany
www.streckbier.de

In 1718, Peter Streck started brewing beer, mainly for his own family. Soon, though, other people clamoured to buy his brews. In 1884, the brewery began to acquire technical equipment. By 2000, the 10th generation was in control of the company. The Strecks are already planning how to celebrate their 300th anniversary in 2018.

THURN & TAXIS

Fürstliche Brauerei Thurn & Taxis Vertriebsgesellschaft, Am Kreuzhof 5, 93055 Regensburg, Germany
www.thurnundtaxisbiere.de

The story of the princes of Thurn and Taxis is closely connected with both the development of the German postal service and the brewing of beer.

BREWING SECRET The family was the first in Germany to promote pilsner, to brew rye beer, and to offer wheat beer on draught.

BEER

STERNQUELL SIEBZIGER

PILSNER 4.9% ABV
Light and golden, with an aromatic, hoppy nose. The finish has a crispy, malt biscuit dryness.

STERNQUELL KELLERBIER

DUNKEL 5% ABV
A naturally cloudy beer, its taste is full bodied with yeasty hints of fresh bread.

STRALSUNDER LAGER

LAGER 4.7% ABV
Fine malts give a full body. The beer is smooth and mild, with some sweetness in the finish.

STRALSUNDER PILS

PILSNER 4.9% ABV
A typical pilsner – clear golden, full bodied, pleasant, with the dry aromas of fine hops, and some bitterness.

OSTHEIMER DUNKEL

DUNKEL 4.5% ABV
Dark amber from special malts, this beer has a malty aroma and is full bodied and pleasant.

BURGHERREN PILS

PILSNER 4.8% ABV
A long, cold fermentation helps release a refined malt taste and the flowery aromas from the Hallertau hops. The finish is refreshing and dry.

ST. WOLFGANG DUNKEL

DUNKEL 4.8% ABV
Dark coloured from the fine dark malts, this typical full-bodied dunkel has a roasted aroma and tastes malty.

ROGGENBIER

RYE BEER 5.3% ABV
A top-fermented dark beer, with an intriguing spicy, dry finish from the rye malt.

TRAUNSTEIN

Hofbräuhaus Traunstein, Hofgasse 6-11, 83278 Traunstein, Germany
www.hb-ts.de

From its date of founding in 1612, the brewery had centuries of difficulties, including near-destruction by firestorms. Its luck changed in 1975, when Hofbräuhaus Traunstein was decorated with eight gold medals for its regional beers. Today the company has about 60 employees.

TROTZENBURG

Ostsee Brauhaus AG "Trotzenburg", Strandstr. 41, 18225 Kühlungsborn, Germany
www.brauhaus-trotzenburg.de

In 1839 a certain Herr Moll opened a tavern in an old forester's house, which developed into a brewery-restaurant. The name changed to Trotzenburg in 1913. By the end of the 1980s, it had grown dilapidated, and was closed down. It has since reopened, and is part of the Ostsee Brauhaus AG.

TUCHER

Schwabacher Str. 106, 90763 Fürth, Germany
www.tucher.de

The Tucher story began in Nuremberg in 1672, with the production of wheat beer. After the brewery was modernized in 1855, two-thirds of the beers were exported. Today Tucher is a part of the Radeberger Group.

BREWING SECRET This brewery is the most traditional in northern Bavaria.

UERIGE

Bergerstr. 1, 40123 Düsseldorf, Germany
www.uerige.de

The brewery, attached to a famous restaurant in Düsseldorf, is situated in the heart of this historic town, near to the river Rhine. Since 1862 it has produced the city's famous beer – altbier. Michael Jackson, the famous beer and whisky critic, once awarded Uerige's beer four stars – a rare high judgement from the specialist.

FÜRSTENTRUNK

EXPORT 5.7% ABV
From start to finish, the aroma of hops plays an important role in the structure of this speciality beer.

1612ER ZWICKELBIER

TRADITIONAL EXPORT 5.3% ABV
Unfiltered and straight from the cellar; cloudy, golden, fresh-tasting, and not too sparkling.

TROTZENBURGER SPEZIAL

LAGER 4.9% ABV
Copper coloured, full bodied, and dry enough to exude the aroma of fine hops without being too dry.

TROTZENBURGER ORIGINAL

LAGER 4.9% ABV
Amber coloured, with a light bitterness and a malty finish. Very pleasant because of its fine yeast.

DUNKLES HEFE WEIZEN

WHEAT BEER 5.2% ABV
Dark colour and a strong taste with clear malt aromas; a very smooth beer with a little sparkle at the beginning.

HELLES HEFEWEIZEN

WHEAT BEER 5.2% ABV
Cloudy yellow, with a refreshing taste of yeast and some sweetness. A sparkling pleasure.

UERIGE ALT

ALTBIER 4.7% ABV
This nearly black beer has lots of bitter aromas. It is full bodied with a nice roasty aroma and sweet finish.

UERIGE STICKE

BOCK 6% ABV
Tastes heavy but is nevertheless elegant. The black colour signifies a large amount of malts and hops, and the taste bears this out.

Blue-shirted beer waiters with blue aprons, known as köbes provide drinkers with a steady supply of altbier in the bars of Düsseldorf.

BEER STYLES

ALTBIER

"Alt" is the German word for old, and it's an apt term for the altbiers of the Rhineland – not because they are aged (they're drunk fresh) but because the "old" top-fermented style dates back to a period before lagered beers swept all before them. Düsseldorf is the home of altbier, although examples are also found in Hanover, Munster, Holland, and the USA. A Düsseldorfer alt is clear copper bronze in colour, with a bright white head. It's a biscuity, gritty beer, closer to British bitter than to lager, but with its rough edges smoothed out by a period of cold maturation.

Diebels and Frankenheim are the big sellers, but a visit to the old town (Altstadt) of the beer's native city reveals a quartet of small brewpubs considered by connoisseurs to be the beating heart of this venerable beer style: Schumacher, Schlüssel, Füchschen, and Uerige. Within these hallowed halls, waiters called köbes, in blue shirts and aprons, weave their way through the crowds, looking for empty glasses to be replenished. With tray in hand, topping up the thirsty (until asked to stop!), and posing for pictures, they take great pride in their profession and deserve their exalted place in the hierarchy of the pub.

SCHUMACHER AND SCHLÜSSEL
Just as with British bitter, there are subtle differences and nuances that distinguish one alt from another. Schumacher Altbier (4.6% ABV) is light amber in colour, with a fruity, nutty palate. Schlüssel Altbier (5% ABV) is delicately fragrant on the nose, biscuity, and has a lingering, dry finish.

FÜCHSCHEN AND UERIGE
Füchschen Altbier (4.5% ABV) has a biscuity nose with hints of resiny hops in the background. Uerige Altbier (4.5% ABV) is richly malty on the nose, underpinned by the subtle resin of hops; it is fragrant and fruity, with a dry and bitter finish.

BREWERY

UNERTL
Lerchenberger Str. 6, 83527 Haag, Germany
www.unertl.de

This wheat-beer specialist was established at the beginning of the 20th century. Production levels have remained almost constant over the years. However, the increasing popularity of this style, coupled with special bottlings, have given Unertl a rarity value.

UR-KROSTITZER
Brauereistr. 12, 04509 Krostitz, Germany
www.ur-krostitzer.de

A portrait of the 17th-century Swedish King Gustav II Adolf graces the Ur-Krostitzer labels. The story goes that, in 1631, during the Thirty Years' War, the king came to Krostitz, parched by a hot, dry wind. He was given a glass of the town's festival beer to quench his thirst, and declared it excellent. The brand is now part of the Radeberger Group.

WALDSCHLÖSSCHEN
Am Brauhaus 8b, 01099 Dresden, Germany
www.waldschloesschen.de

In 1836, a group of important Dresden citizens met to discuss the foundation of a brewery to produce "beer of Bavarian style". Two years later the plan became reality at a location named Waldschlösschen. The brewery is Germany's oldest joint-stock brewery that still brews.

WEIDENEDER
Marktplatz 43, 84367 Tann, Germany
www.weideneder.com

Brewing has been a tradition in Tann since the 14th century. The name Weideneder first appeared in the 15th century. The company currently produces 11 different beers and 16 non-alcoholic beverages.

BREWING SECRET The village produces its own malt, and a spring owned by the brewer's family has been supplying water to the company for 100 years.

BEER

UNERTL WEISSBIER BOCK
WHEAT BEER BOCK 6.7% ABV
A dark colour for a white bock, but with a strong and pleasant taste. The alcohol is packed with fine malts and hops.

UNERTL WEISSBIER
WHEAT BEER 4.9% ABV
The flagship wheat beer of this brewery is aromatic with yeast and banana notes.

FEINHERBES PILSNER
PILSNER 4.9% ABV
A brilliant pilsner with a lightly sparkling attitude, a dry aroma of hops, and a very elegant taste.

SCHWARZES
SCHWARZBIER 4.8% ABV
Ur-Krostitzer's Schwarzes is the most famous black beer in the country. It has a fine malty taste and a nice, light hoppy finish.

ZWICKELBIER
LAGER 5.5% ABV
A golden, cloudy appearance, as the beer is unfiltered. It is full bodied and pleasant, with an enticing aroma of hops.

WALDSCHLÖSSCHEN DUNKEL
DUNKEL 5.5% ABV
Malty taste. Light, bitter aromas from fine hops at the finish round off a very harmonious beer.

PRIVAT HELL
LAGER 5.1% ABV
A clear golden classic helles beer, full bodied and mild, with a light aroma of hops and malt.

WIEDEN BRÄU
WHEAT BEER 4.3% ABV
A fresh, golden, unfiltered wheat beer, which soars with fruity flavours. It's a summer favourite.

WEIHENSTEPHAN

Postfach 11 55, D-85311 Freising,
Germany
www.brauerei-weihenstephan.de

This brewery is not only the oldest in
existence (dating from 725), it is also
the most technologically advanced.
Weihenstephan is the world's foremost
centre for brewing technology, and
hundreds of master brewers around
the world have trained here. Not
surprisingly, the beer offerings are
of the highest order.

WEILHEIM

Schillerstr. 3, 78604 Rietheim-Weilheim,
Germany
www.lammbrauerei-weilheim.de

Beer has been produced on this site
for 360 years – it is one of the oldest
and smallest breweries in the area,
and has been family-owned since
1882. The brewery has been partly
renovated, with new cellars.

BREWING SECRET The Storz family
describe their product as a naturally
matured beer.

WELTENBURGER

Heitzerstr. 2, 93049 Regensburg,
Germany
www.weltenburger.de

The Benedictine abbey of Weltenburg
houses the oldest abbey brewery
in the world, founded in 1050. The
location is delightful, close to the
scenic Donau-Durchbruch gorge.
The abbey's restaurant is famous.

BREWING SECRET Despite its history, the
beer is made with the most advanced
equipment, but is long-matured.

WESTHEIM

Kasseler Str. 7, 34431 Marsberg-
Westheim, Germany
www.brauerei-westheim.de

The first Count of Stolberg bought
Westheim in 1840. It was enlarged
in 1876 by Count Herman, the
great-grandfather of the owner today.
The company also owns Westheim
farm, but has leased it out since 1994.

BREWING SECRET The water for brewing
comes from Westheim's own spring.

ORIGINAL
LAGER 5.1% ABV
The mild and pleasant taste is a
result of a longer-than-usual period
of storage and maturation.

HEFEWEISSBIER DUNKEL
WHEAT BEER 5.3% ABV
This beer is very well balanced.
Its dark colour is typical of the
style, as is the soft, malty, and
full-bodied taste.

WEILHEIMER BOCKBIER
BOCK 9% ABV
Gleaming black with a roasty malt
aroma and sweet taste.

SCHWARZES WÄLDLE
SCHWARZBIER 5.8% ABV
Amber coloured from its malt,
this beer tastes mild, yet fun on
the palate.

ASAM BOCK
BOCK 6.9% ABV
A dark mahogany doppelbock. Very
pleasant, it tastes slightly sweet
with nice malty aromas in the finish.

ANNO 1050
EXPORT 5.5% ABV
The abbey's anniversary beer has
a distinctive mix of malt aromas
balanced with hops.

GRAF STOLBERG DUNKEL
DUNKEL 4.8% ABV
Has fine malt aromas from dark,
roasted malt. Light bitters of hops
are very typical of this amber beer.

WILDSCHÜTZ KLOSTERMANN
LAGER 4.8% ABV
Unfiltered and naturally cloudy,
with a fine taste of malt, this beer
is smooth with some bitter aromas.

BREWERY

WISMAR

Kleine Hohe Str. 15, 23966 Wismar, Germany
www.brauhaus-wismar.de

In the early 15th century, there were about 180 breweries registered in Wismar, and the town was well known all over Europe. The Brauhaus Wismar was opened in 1452. Today it is the last brewery remaining in the city and, since 1995, it has brewed beer in the style of the medieval Hanseatic League breweries of northern Europe.

WOLTERS

Hofbrauhaus Wolters, Wolfenbütteler Straße 39, 38102 Braunschweig, Germany
www.hofbrauhaus-wolters.de

The brewery was founded in 1627 in Braunschweig. Wolters' beers are well known in the region and much further afield. In 2005, InBev, the owner at the time, tried to put the brewery into liquidation, but a group of former CEOs acquired it instead.

WÜRZBURGER HOFBRÄU

Höchberger Straße 28, 97082 Würzburg, Germany
www.wuerzburger-hofbraeu.de

In 1840, the Werner family acquired this brewery in Poppenhausen. It was one of the first breweries in Bavaria to produce a pilsner beer. By 1991, it was selling 16 million litres (3.5 million gallons) each year and had about 100 employees. In 1999, it was bought by Würzburger Hofbräu.

ZÖTLER

Grüntenstr. 2, 87549 Rettenberg, Germany
www.zoetler.de

The oldest family-owned brewery in Germany, the brewery was founded in the year 1447. The descendants of the original families are still involved in the brewery. Today the company is run by Herbert Zotler III.

BREWING SECRET Zötler's Vollmond Bier is brewed only on nights with a full moon.

BEER

WISMARER MUMME

LAGER 4.8% ABV
An old-fashioned, golden beer with lovely aromas of malt, light hops on the tongue, and a long, sweet finish.

ROTER ERIC

SPECIAL BEER 4.8% ABV
The light red colour comes from the malt; the beer is smooth and aromatic, with a sweet finish.

WOLTERS PILSENER

PILSNER 4.9% ABV
Gold in colour, it is a light, crisp easy-drinking beer, with an aromatic hop character.

MÄRZEN

EXPORT 5.4% ABV
Full-bodied märzen with a fine, mild aroma of hops. It is very pleasant and has an attractive clear golden-amber colour.

WÜRZBURGER HOFBRÄU PILSNER

PILSNER 4.9% ABV
The clear golden colour is typical of pilsner; the taste is elegant, with a fine, dry aroma of hops and malt.

JULIUS ECHTER

WHEAT BEER 4.9% ABV
Bubbly, fresh, and full of banana flavours, it is naturally cloudy with a sweet malt finish.

ST. STEPHANS BOCK

DOPPELBOCK 7.1% ABV
A strong and noble beer; the roasted barley-malt exudes wonderful aromas.

VOLLMOND BIER

LAGER 5.1% ABV
This beer has a smooth malt aroma and tastes strong, with a light bitterness in the finish.

MORE BEERS OF

GERMANY

In Germany the tradition of regional brewing is still very strong, and communities are justly proud of their local beers. Many such beers are available only on draught and are seldom seen outside of their home towns.

BRUCKMÜLLER

Vilsstr. 4, 92224 Amberg, Germany
www.bruckmueller.de

Beer has been produced by this company for more than 500 years. The story began with the Franziskaner monks in the year 1490, under the name Prewhaus der Parfusser. The Bruckmüller family has continued the tradition since 1803 and is now in its seventh generation. Soft drinks are produced, too.

KNAPPENTRUNK
DUNKEL 5.3% ABV
Malty, but not too sweet, with a clear aroma of hops, which is unusual for a dunkel. Full bodied.

KELLERBIER
LAGER 5.3% ABV
Unfiltered and naturally cloudy. The taste is strong and full bodied, with aromas of fine malts and a lightly bitter hop finish.

HERRENHAUSEN

Herrenhäuser Straße 83-99, Hanover, Germany
www.herrenhaeuser.de

Herrenhäuser Premium Pilsener is sold in pubs and restaurants throughout the region – guests order a "Herry". This is a traditional but forward-thinking company that has been guided through the last 140 years by five generations of one family.

BREWING SECRET "Herry" uses lots of malt and hops, and mineral water.

PREMIUM PILSENER
PILSNER 4.9% ABV
Golden, dry, malty, and with the rather strong, bitter pilsner aroma of fine hops.

WEIZENBIER
WHEAT BEER 5.2% ABV
Unfiltered, yellow, and naturally cloudy. There is a bit of sparkle, and the taste is harmonious, pleasantly sweet, and fresh.

KNOBLACH

Kremmeldorfer Straße 1, Litzendorf-Schammelsdorf, Germany
www.brauerei-knoblach.de

Founded in 1880, the pub and brewery are still owned by the Knoblach family. The current brewmaster is Michael Knoblach, and his son, Johannes, has just qualified as a brewer, too. The brewery is famed for the beer it serves at the village of Schammelsdorf's beer festival, where local rival football teams vie to be named the region's best.

UNGSPUNDETE LAGERBIER
LAGER 5.2% ABV
A bottom-fermented, unfiltered, golden-yellow beer, which is low in carbonation and not overwhelmed by foam.

RÄUSCHLA
MARZ BIER 5% ABV
Bubbling with carbonation, it is full of rich, malt spice flavours and rounded off by a swirl of Hallertau hops.

MAXIMILIANS

Didierstr. 25, 56112 Lahnstein, Germany
www.maximilians-brauwiesen.de

A relative baby on the German brewing scene, Maximilians is a restaurant and brewery in Lahnstein that opened in 1995. It is housed in a charming, fairytale pink castle overlooking the Rhine.

BREWING SECRET The beer is brewed with top-quality natural ingredients, according to old recipes.

WIESENWEIZEN
WHEAT BEER 5.1% ABV
A huge dose of wheat-malt gives this beer a smooth and mild taste. It is sparkling and refreshing, with light aromas of hops in the finish.

BRAUWIESEN SPEZIEL
LAGER 5.4% ABV
Caramel sweet, with typical aromas of malt and bitters of hops. Golden-yellow colour.

PAPIERMÜHLE

Braugasthof, Papiermühle, Erfurter Straße 102, 07743 Jena, Germany
www.papiermuhle-jena.de

A pub has been on this site since 1737. In 1995, the Kanz family took on the challenge of running the business and installed a brand new brewhouse and distillery. The brewery produces five different beers, which are available on tap in the bar. As well as being used for lagering beers, the pub's cellar is home to several casks of slowly maturing whisky.

JENAER DEUTSCHES PILSENER
PILSNER 4.5% ABV
An easy-drinking, lightly malted and hopped beer. The malt sweetness of the brew is offset by some bready notes.

JENAER PREMIUM DUNKEL
DUNKEL 5.2% ABV
Spicy hop flavours soar above the dark malt fullness. A ruby black to the eye, it is sweet on the tongue.

RITTMAYER

An der Mark 1, 91352 Hallerndorf, Germany
www.rittmayer.de

Founded in 1422, the family-owned business is one of the most successful in Upper Franconia. Owner and master brewer, Georg Rittmayer, is committed to making his production sustainable and is minimizing his use of fossil fuels. As well as brewing classic German beer styles, he is experimenting with a Vintage Edition and a cask-matured Oak Reserve.

RITTMAYER LANDBIER
HELLES 4.9% ABV
A soft, floral hop aroma dominates the nose. It has a creamy mouthfeel, flavours of breaded malt, and a refreshing bitter finish.

SMOKEY GEORGE
SMOKED BEER 5% ABV
Dominated by whisky malt flavours, it is not a typical Franconian smoked beer. Intense flavours.

SCHUMACHER

Brauerei Ferdinand Schumacher, Oststr. 123, 40210 Düsseldorf, Germany
www.schumacher-alt.de

Altbier is the classic beer in Düsseldorf, and the Schumacher brewery, founded in 1838, is one of the most famous producers, serving it in its adjoining restaurant.

BREWING SECRET In the 1980s the brewery was completely renovated with the newest technology.

SCHUMACHER ALT
ALTBIER 4.6% ABV
A dark beer with a smooth and sweet, roasted malt taste, and a finish accompanied by fine aromas of hops.

SCHUMACHER LATZEN
ALTBIER 5.5% ABV
A bit stronger than the normal altbier; it is aromatic with malt, but sweet as well.

WELDEBRÄU

Brauereistr. 1, 68723 Plankstadt, Germany
www.welde.de

The brewery dates from 1746, but it was not until 1846, when master brewer Heinrich Seitz took over, that the story started to be one of success. The brewery was reconstructed in 1934, and enlarged in the 1980s. Today, Welde is a modern company with a portfolio of interesting beers.

WEIZEN HEFE HELL
WHEAT BEER 4.9% ABV
The beer has both dryness and sweetness. A fine yeast ensures a balance in the taste.

JAHRGANGSBIER SÜDAFRIKA
AMERICAN INDIAN PALE ALE 6.8% ABV
A beer of some complexity, it is dark golden to the eye and has notes of banana, apricots, and ripe plums.

BREWERY

BEER

Paulaner, like so many German breweries, was founded by an order of monks. The company now has franchises around the world.

BRITISH ISLES

In world beer terms, the reputation of the British Isles rests on ales that are packed with flavour yet only moderately strong. The beer culture is still centred on the pub, though there is a growing trend towards drinking bottled beer at home. Draught beer from cask is seen as a cut above bottled beer in terms of quality and flavour, but most pub chains favour Continental-style lagers. The good news for beer lovers is that craft brewing is on the up, both in terms of the numbers of micros now actively producing, and the beers being sought out and drunk.

This map shows where some of the breweries are based, with pullout boxes where a city or town has more than one brewery.

Innis & Gunn

🍺 **Edinburgh**
Caledonian
Innis & Gunn

Darwin

🍺 **Sunderland**
Darwin
Maxim

Jarrow

🍺 **Newcastle**
Big Lamp
Hadrian & Border
Mordue
Jarrow
Wylam

Brewdog

Belhaven

Harviestoun
Traditional Scottish Ales
William Brothers

Traquair

Inveralmond

Broughton

Orkney

Orkney

Atlas
Fyne Ales

Black Isle

Cairngorm

Isle Of Arran

S C O T L A N D

Isle Of Skye

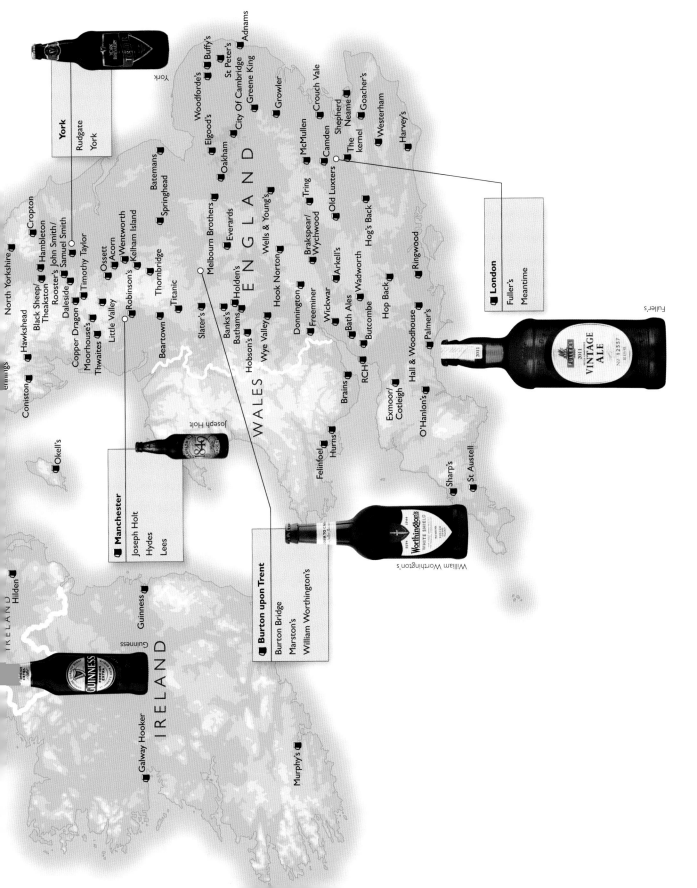

BREWERY

ACORN

Aldham Industrial Estate, Mitchell Road, Wombwell, Barnsley, England S73 8HA
www.acorn-brewery.co.uk

One of the newer microbreweries in England, Acorn was set up in 2003 and doubled capacity in its first four years. It now produces 40 barrels (6,500 litres) every week.

BREWING SECRET The yeast strain from the 1850s Barnsley Brewery has been reintroduced, coinciding with the company gathering significant awards.

ADNAMS

Southwold, Suffolk, England IP18 6JW
www.adnams.co.uk

Its "Beers from the Coast" have been brewed in the classic English seaside town of Southwold since 1872. In recent years, technological innovation has driven refurbishment, while an emphasis on traditional methods has been studiously maintained. An eco-friendly distribution centre – complete with living grass roof – summarizes

the dynamic approach. The company has now embarked on a programme of making short-run innovative beers using beer styles from around the world.

BREWING SECRET At every stage of the brewing process, from the farm to the glass, Adnams is committed to being the most environmentally friendly brewer in the United Kingdom.

ARKELL'S

Swindon, Wiltshire, England SN2 7RU
www.arkells.com

John Arkell returned from Ontario, Canada – where he had founded the village of Arkell – to grow barley and to brew beer. The brewery has been owned by family members since its establishment in 1843. The building is Grade II-listed (indicating its historical and cultural importance), and the whole site has been designated an Urban Conservation Area.

BEER

BARNSLEY BITTER
BITTER 3.8% ABV
Ripe chestnut in colour, with a rounded, rich flavour that lingers in the bitter finish.

BARNSLEY GOLD
STRONG BITTER 4.3% ABV
Beautifully golden, with citrus fruit hop aromas orchestrating the ensemble through to its dry finish.

ADNAMS BROADSIDE
STRONG BITTER 6.3% ABV
Rich fruitcake aromas dominate initially, giving way to an elegant hop and malt association.

JACK BRAND DRY HOPPED LAGER
LAGER 5% ABV
Adnams' first lager is dry-hopped with Galaxy hops, adding fruitiness to this crisp, dry beer.

ADNAMS SOUTHWOLD BITTER
BITTER 4.1% ABV
Aromatic hop and biscuit malt fragrances introduce a lingering dry and refreshingly bitter flavour.

TALLY HO
BARLEY WINE 7.2% ABV
Dark and red, it is a fruity Christmas pudding in a glass, with a long, warming finish.

WILTSHIRE GOLD
GOLDEN ALE 4% ABV
An easy-drinking sweet beer, with a floral hop aroma.

ARKELL'S 3B
BITTER 4% ABV
Sweetly scented malt is perceptible beneath a distinct hoppy aroma. Delicate, well-balanced nutty flavour.

BANKS'S

Brewery Road Wolverhampton, West
Midlands, England WV1 4NY
www.bankssbeer.co.uk

The brewery, built in 1875, occupies
a traditional, handsome site in the
centre of Wolverhampton and has
been part of the Marston's Beer
Company (formerly Wolverhampton
& Dudley) since 2007. More than
24 million litres (50 million pints)
are brewed every year. Innovative
marketing initiatives include a
campaign to protect local dialects

from extinction. The brewery's
best-known beer is Banks's Mild.
The beer is a fine example of a
West Midlands mild ale, a style once
favoured by factory workers keen
for refreshment after a long day's
work who would pop into a pub,
usually situated by the factory gate,
before going home for tea.

BATEMANS

Wainfleet, Lincolnshire,
England PE24 4JE
www.bateman.co.uk

One of the country's oldest and most
picturesque family breweries – with a
windmill towering high above – it has
a well-deserved reputation for "good
honest ales". A family split almost
destroyed the business in the 1980s,
but it survived, blossomed, and has
developed a new brewhouse and
engaging visitor centre.

BANKS'S MILD
BITTER 3.5% ABV
An easy-drinking beer, full of biscuit
malt and bitter hop flavours.

BANKS'S BITTER
BITTER 3.8% ABV
Full-flavoured, with winey, fruit
overtones and a malt and hop
influence on the palate.

BANKS'S SUNBEAM
BLONDE ALE 4.2% ABV
Zesty, citrus hops underpinned
by a sweet malt base star in this
easy-drinking, refreshing blond ale.

MANSFIELD CASK ALE
BITTER 3.8% ABV
Once brewed in Mansfield, this is
a full-bodied, sweet, malty ale with
hints of barley sugar.

XXXB
STRONG BITTER 4.8% ABV
Classic russet-tan ale, with a
well-constructed blend of malt,
hops, and fruitiness.

XB BITTER
BITTER 3.7% ABV
Finely balanced, with an apple-
influenced hop aroma that lingers
alongside the malty flavour.

BEST-KNOWN BEERS IN THE BRITISH ISLES

In the multi-layered global
business that is vast-volume
brewing, the Molson Coors
Brewing Company owns
several British Isles' brands.

Among the well-known brands
now owned by Molson Coors
are Worthington, Caffrey's, and
Carling, which produces the
British Isles' biggest-selling lager.
In the high-volume market,
huge emphasis and budgets
are concentrated on sports
sponsorship and promoting
chilled beers, served through
advanced "extra cold" and
"extra fast" bar technology.
The global giant Carlsberg is a
big player too, and has production
plants in Northampton – for its
own lagers, such as Carlsberg
Export – and Leeds, where it
brews the Tetley range of beers.
Tetley has been fully owned by
Carlsberg since 1998. Britain's
largest brewer, Scottish &
Newcastle – which produces
brands such as Newcastle Brown
Ale, John Smith's (the British Isles'
biggest-selling bitter), and
international brands such
Fosters and Kronenbourg – finally
lost its independence in 2008,
when it was bought out in a
Carlsberg/Heineken joint venture.
Closure of its Reading plant by
2010 had already been announced,
leaving three UK sites: Newcastle
Federation; John Smith's in
Tadcaster; and Royal in Manchester;
it also retains a small stake in
Edinburgh-based Caledonian.

CARLING (LAGER 4.1% ABV) *left*
NEWCASTLE BROWN
(BROWN ALE 4.7% ABV) *centre*
JOHN SMITH'S (EXTRA SMOOTH
3.6% ABV) *right*

BREWERY

BATH ALES

Warmley, Bristol, Hare House, Southway Drive, England BS30 5LW
www.bathales.com

The founders' brewing backgrounds and insistence on traditional methods operating alongside cutting-edge technology has resulted in Bath Ales' reputation for distinctive, characterful, and flavoursome ales. The success of the business has led to the brewery outgrowing its premises twice since it was established in 1995. A bottling plant and shop continue the growth.

BATHAMS

Delph Road, Brierley Hill, West Midlands, England DY5 2TN
www.bathams.com

The brewery's frontage – actually the Vine Inn – is emblazoned with a quotation from Shakespeare's *Two Gentlemen of Verona*: "Blessing of you: You brew good ale". Five generations of the Batham family have been involved since the brewery was established in 1877, each nurturing its reputation for classic Black Country mild ales.

BEARTOWN

Bromley House, Congleton, Cheshire, England CW12 1QN
www.beartownbrewery.co.uk

Bear baiting was a popular pastime in Elizabethan Congleton, where the senior public offices were Mayor, Aletaster, and Bear Warden. A traditional song suggests the town even sold a rare bible in order to pay for a more aggressive combatant. The town's brewery today was founded in 1994 and supports charities such as Asian bear rescue centres.

BELHAVEN

Spott Road, Dunbar, East Lothian, Scotland EH42 1RS
www.belhaven.co.uk

Records show that 14th-century Benedictine monks brewed in the coastal town, and water is still drawn from the wells they sunk. Austrian Emperor Francis I favoured Belhaven beers, referring to them in 1827 as "the burgundy of Scotland". The brewery lost its independence in 2005, when taken over by Greene King.

BEER

GEM
BEST BITTER 4.8% ABV
Rich and full-textured, with a malt, fruit, and bittersweet hop quality throughout.

SPECIAL PALE ALE (SPA)
PALE ALE 3.7% ABV
A prominent hop aroma and bitter malty touch complement its light-bodied character.

BATHAMS BEST BITTER
BEST BITTER 4.3% ABV
Straw-coloured ale, with an initial sweetness, soon overtaken by a complex dry, hoppy flavour.

BATHAMS MILD ALE
MILD 3.5% ABV
A fruity, dark brown mild; sweet and well balanced, with a hoppy fruit finish.

KODIAK GOLD
BITTER 4% ABV
A straw-coloured quencher, with a citrus fruit nose, some biscuit malt on the palate, and a sharp bitterness.

BLACK BEAR
MILD 5% ABV
A strong mild ale, dark ruby in colour, with a subtle roast malt profile rising to a sweet finish.

ST. ANDREWS ALE
STRONG BITTER 4.9% ABV
Alternating in flavour between roasted malt, caramel, and tart fruit, while spicy hop aromas persist.

BELHAVEN 80 SHILLING
SCOTTISH HEAVY 4.2% ABV
Classical Scottish "heavy" with a huge malt profile, then some hop and fruit flavours emerging.

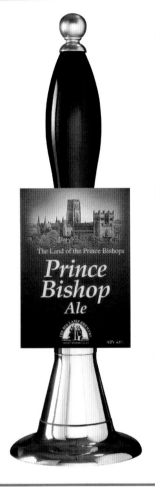

BIG LAMP

Grange Rd, Newburn, Newcastle upon
Tyne, Tyne and Wear, England NE15 8NL
www.biglampbrewers.co.uk

Northeast England's oldest
microbrewery was established in
1982. It relocated in 1997 to a listed
Victorian water-pumping station near
the Tyne Riverside Country Park.
There, The Keelman, a popular
on-site pub and restaurant, along
with accommodation in Keelman
Lodge, have won it prestigious
tourism awards.

BLACK ISLE

Black Isle, Scotland IV8 8NZ
www.blackislebrewery.com

The mission of this small independent
operation, which lies in the heart of
the Scottish Highlands, is to produce
a range of top-quality organic beers,
packaged in recycled materials. No
artificial fertilizers or herbicides are
applied to the hops and barley it uses.

BREWING SECRET The brewery's water
for its organic beers comes from its
own borehole.

BLACK SHEEP

Wellgarth, Masham, North Yorkshire,
England HG4 4EN
www.blacksheepbrewery.com

The Theakston family has brewed
in Masham, North Yorkshire, for
six generations, but a loss of
independence led to Paul Theakston
stepping aside. Far from leaving
brewing though, he then established
Black Sheep in a former maltings
sitting high above the River Ure. Since
1992, and through one of the most
challenging periods of British brewing

history, Black Sheep has enjoyed
continuous growth, physically and
in reputation, resulting in a £5m
doubling of capacity in 2006 and the
installation of an extra brewhouse,
new fermenting vessels, conditioning
tanks, and a cask racking plant. A
magnificent visitor centre and bistro
are important attractions too.

BREWING SECRET Generous amounts
of Goldings hops are essential to
the Black Sheep character.

PRINCE BISHOP ALE
STRONG BITTER 4.8% ABV
An easy-drinking, golden bitter
with a full fruity hop aroma and
a spicy bitterness.

SUMMERHILL STOUT
STOUT 4.4% ABV
A savoury, dark stout with a
roasted malt nature and malty,
long-lasting piquancy.

YELLOWHAMMER
GOLDEN ALE 4% ABV
A pale golden-coloured hoppy
bitter with a sharp grapefruit aroma
and refreshing yeasty finish.

ORGANIC BLONDE
PREMIUM LAGER 4.5% ABV
A premium, continental-style lager
beer with a light biscuit palate, and
fresh grassy aroma.

BLACK SHEEP ALE
BITTER 4.4% ABV
Full-flavoured, with a rich, fruity
aroma, bittersweet malty taste,
and a long, dry finish.

BEST BITTER
BEST BITTER 3.8% ABV
This bestseller is well hopped, light
golden in colour, with a distinctive
dry, refreshing tang.

RIGGWELTER
PREMIUM BITTER 5.7% ABV
A strong, complex, fruity bitter,
with dashes of pear drops and
hints of liquorice.

GOLDEN SHEEP
GOLDEN ALE 3.9% ABV
Refreshing, crisp aromas of citrus
hops partner with a clean, dry,
malty finish.

BREWERY

BRAINS

Crawshay Street, Cardiff,
Glamorgan, Wales CF10 5DN
www.sabrain.com

A major force in regional brewing,
Brains is tremendously proud of its
Welsh heritage. Ales are produced in
a traditional fashion at the company's
landmark Cardiff Brewery. It was
relocated in 2000 from the nearby
Old Brewery, where the famous
"pint of Brains" had been produced
for more than 100 years.

BRAKSPEAR

The Bull Courtyard, Bell Street, Henley
on Thames, England Oxon, RG9 2BA
www.brakspear.co.uk

The long-established Brakspear
Brewery closed its Henley operation in
2002, but the production of its beers
was taken on by Wychwood Brewery.

BREWING SECRET Wychwood uses
Brakspear's original equipment to brew
these beers, including the unique
"double drop" wooden fermenting
vessels, and its complex yeast strain.

BREWDOG

Balmacassie Industrial Estate, Ellon,
Aberdeenshire, Scotland AB41 8BX
www.brewdog.com

A new shining star in Britain's brewing
firmament. Established in 2007, the
founders Martin Dickie and James
Watt have been at the forefront
of UK's brewing renaissance. Bold,
full-flavoured beers are matched with
an acute understanding of how to
market them to a younger audience.

BROUGHTON

Main Street, Broughton Village, Biggar,
Peeblesshire, Scotland ML12 6HQ
www.broughtonales.co.uk

A small, independent brewery situated
in the Scottish Borders, Broughton
draws heavily on local history and
legend for its full range of styles.
Production includes 18 cask ales,
11 different bottled beers for the
domestic and export markets, two
own-label beers for selected
supermarkets, and one keg beer.

BEER

SA GOLD
GOLDEN ALE 4.7% ABV
A late addition of hops gives the
beer a refreshing finish with lots
of citrus notes.

BRAINS BITTER
BITTER 3.5% ABV
Rich amber colour, with subtle
malt and crisp hop aromas. Well
balanced, with some bitterness.

BRAKSPEAR BITTER
BITTER 3.4% ABV
An initial malt and well-hopped
bitterness develops into a
bittersweet and fruity finish.

OXFORD GOLD
GOLDEN ALE 4% ABV
The late addition of Goldings
hops gives this beer an incredible
lemon zesty finish.

PUNK IPA
PALE ALE 5.6% ABV
A beer with a modern complexity,
as passion fruit and crisp, bready
malt flavours vie for attention.

TOKYO*
IMPERIAL STOUT 18.2% ABV
A strong, dark beer with swirling
complexities of dark fruits, strong
coffee, and cigar smoke.

GREENMANTLE ALE
BITTER 3.9% ABV
Dark copper-coloured, with a rich
fruit and bittersweet encounter,
and hop-bitter finale.

BLACK DOUGLAS
PREMIUM BITTER 5.2% ABV
Dark ruby-red with a rich, full-
bodied maltiness and overtones
of preserved fruit.

BUFFY'S

Mardle Hall, Rectory Road, Tivetshall St. Mary, Norwich, England NR15 2DD
www.buffys.co.uk

A 15th-century residence, a home-brewing insurance executive, and a beer-loving piano tuner combined to establish this dynamic enterprise in 1993, when Roger and Julie Abrahams first brewed in outbuildings at Mardle Hall. Various upgradings and expansion have followed, together with local and national awards for their beer.

BURTON BRIDGE

24 Bridge St Burton upon Trent, Staffordshire, England DE14 1SY
www.burtonbridgebrewery.co.uk

In 1984, a brewery engineer and a technical manager put one and one together to make two – pub and brewhouse. Equipment was sourced from other breweries and a local farmyard, as well as parts that were found languishing in an old garage. As for the pub seating, that was salvaged from a Methodist church.

BUTCOMBE

Cox's Green, Wrington, Bristol, England BS40 5PA
www.butcombe.com

The philosophy here is simple: "Beer is a natural product, let's keep it that way." This much-expanded brewery – established in farm buildings in 1978 – now produces almost seven million pints annually from its four brands, none of which contains added sugars, colourings, or preservatives. The brewery also operates 15 pubs.

CAIRNGORM

Aviemore, Highlands, Scotland PH22 1ST
www.cairngormbrewery.com

Scotland's most dramatic scenery forms the backdrop to the brewery, which was established in 2001 within the Cairngorms National Park. Its portfolio of 18 beers has attracted numerous industry awards.

BREWING SECRET Cairngorm makes innovative use of local ingredients, such as the emblematic thistle, which is added for bitterness.

NORWICH TERRIER
BITTER 3.6% ABV
A pale, refreshing ale, with a sturdy body and solid bite – just like the dog after which it is named!

BUFFY'S BITTER
BITTER 3.9% ABV
Bestseller, with a distinct hoppy nose and traces of roast malt on the palate.

GOLDEN DELICIOUS
BITTER 3.8% ABV
Originally a summer special, this delicately hopped bitter is evenly tempered, dry, and lingering.

XL BITTER
BEST BITTER 4% ABV
Malty nosed, enveloped in fruity hops, with a hint of chocolate caramel and an astringent finish.

BUTCOMBE BITTER
BITTER 4.5% ABV
Noticeably bitter, with a citrus hop, slight sulphurous nose; light fruit notes and dry finish.

HAKA
BITTER 4.5% ABV
Light golden and easy drinking, it's full of fruity passion fruit and citrus-flavoured New Zealand hops.

TRADE WINDS
WHEAT BEER 4.3% ABV
Multi-award-winning golden wheat beer, with intense hop and elderflower aromas and fruity palate.

BLACK GOLD
STOUT 4.4% ABV
Silky bodied, award-winning stout, with subtle bitterness, roast barley assurance, and late sweetness.

ALL ABOUT...
HOPS

If malt is traditionally known as the soul of beer, charged with the duty of providing colour, sweetness, and, last but not least, sugars on which yeast will feast to produce alcohol and CO_2, then hops provide the razzmatazz – the rich, spicy, floral notes that give so much character and pizzazz to beer. Think of a glass of British bitter, with its tangy, fruity counterpoint to the sweetness of the malt – that's the work of the hops. Even with a glass of delicately hopped golden ale, hops are providing a gentle, breezy hint of summer blossom, while the hop's forthright character is right to the front of a pungent and well-hopped IPA. As well as yielding aroma and bitterness, hops also have preservative qualities, helping to keep beer fresh for longer.

In the British Isles, hopped beer was initially seen as fit only for foreigners such as Flemish merchants. Ironically, it was the latter group who brought their favourite hopped beer over the Channel in the 1400s. It found favour with the locals and, by the late 16th century, it was in the ascendancy.

BEFORE HOPS Prior to hops becoming the common currency of brewing, people drank ale – a strong brew of fermented malted barley flavoured with spices and herbs. The Williams Brothers' Alba Scots Pine Ale is a rare example today of an ale brewed without hops, but with pine needles instead.

CULTIVATION Seen in their natural state, hops grow in what looks like a vineyard, with the plants draping themselves downwards from 6-m (18-ft) high lines, the bright green hop cones hanging like fruit.

FORM Fresh hops are pale green in colour. For use in the brewery, hops come in various guises, including dried cones and small pellets. Occcasionally, hop oil is used to infuse the brew.

DRYING

In England, hops are traditionally grown in Kent, Herefordshire, and Worcestershire, and September's harvest finds the hop yards heavy with the scent of picked hops on their way to the dryer. Drying used to be carried out in oast houses, and those still standing bear witness to the industry of the past. Hops would have been dried in a kiln known as an oast; typically this would have been housed in a building with a conical roof for drawing out the humid air.

VARIETIES If names such as Pinot Noir and Syrah have lovers of the grape cooing with pleasure, then those in the world of beer lick their lips in anticipation at the mention of hop varieties such as Goldings, Fuggles, Cascade, First Gold, and Saaz. The hop is truly a noble creature.

CZECH HOPS The Žatec region in Bohemia and the Yakima Valley in Washington in the USA are home to notable hop fields. The Yakima Valley used to be dominated by Cluster hops, but today many varieties are grown, including the Saaz or Žatec hops. The Czech town of Žatec gives its name to a region that produces highly prized aromatic hops, the flowery bouquet of which can be found in many great pilsners.

TIMING Bittering hops are added to the wort at the start of the boil, while the more delicate aromatic hops are thrown into the kettle during the middle and end of the boil. The skill of the brewer is to add the right hops at the right time.

BREWERY

CALEDONIAN

42 Slateford Road, Edinburgh,
Scotland EH11 1PH
www.caledonianbeer.com

The Caledonian attitude to brewing beer is similar to that of drinking it – the longer you've been doing it, the better quality you demand. The sole survivor of some 40 breweries that once resided in Edinburgh, it is now part of Heineken.

BREWING SECRET Caledonian is one of the last breweries to use traditional direct-fired coppers to boil the wort.

CAMDEN TOWN

55-59 Wilkin Street, Mews, Kentish Town, London, England NW5 3NN
www.camdentownbrewery.com

One of the brightest and newest stars of London's brewing scene, Camden, since opening in 2010, has quickly won an international reputation for the quality of its beers. Its brewing repertoire includes styles that draw on inspiration from craft beers worldwide, while reproducing old British styles such as its London Stout Ink.

CAMERONS

Waldon Street, Hartlepool, County Durham, England TS24 7QS
www.cameronsbrewery.com

Camerons has been brewing under various ownerships since 1865. Its brewing hall is remarkable, with magnificent Italian marble walls and fine wrought-iron detailing, while the water is drawn from its own well.

BREWING SECRET A microbrewery for cask ale experimentation and short runs also operates at the site.

CITY OF CAMBRIDGE

Rookery Farm, Silver Street, Besthorpe, Attleborough, Norfolk, England NR17 2LD
www.cambridge-brewery.co.uk

An environmentally conscious brewery, City of Cambridge was set up in 1997 and relocated three years later due to the popularity of its beers. An innovative system copes with brewery waste by filtering out pollutants through a series of reed beds, marsh plants, and ponds. Awards for beer quality and conservation have followed.

BEER

CALEDONIAN 80/-
SCOTTISH HEAVY 4.1% ABV
Russett brown and typically malt-led, with an underlay of raspberry and suggestion of chocolate.

DEUCHARS IPA
INDIA PALE ALE 3.8% ABV
A strident hop aroma, with citrus notes and a degree of maltiness that never wavers.

CAMDEN USA HELLS
UNFILTERED LAGER 4.6% ABV
A British beer with an American accent. Lots of citrussy hops partner with crisp, dry malt flavours.

CAMDEN INK
STOUT 4.4% ABV
Full of chocolate and dark fruit flavours, it has a dry, coffee-roasted finish.

STRONGARM
STRONG BITTER 4% ABV
Well-rounded ruby-red ale, with a malt and hop balance, developing a fruity flavour.

TROPHY SPECIAL
ALE 4% ABV
A copper-coloured ale, with a fruity sweet finish and a swirling flourish of aromatic hops.

HOBSON'S CHOICE
BITTER 4.1% ABV
A light golden ale; distinctly hoppy on the nose, and with a refreshingly bitter finish.

BOATHOUSE BITTER
BITTER 3.8% ABV
A rich, chocolatey nose is underpinned by citrus hoppiness and a malt and fruit flavour.

CONISTON

Coppermines Road, Coniston, Cumbria, England LA21 8HL
www.conistonbrewery.com

The brewery was set up in 1995 behind a 400-year-old coaching inn, residents of which have included artist JMW Turner, poet Samuel Taylor Coleridge, and Donald Campbell. Campbell's ill-fated attempt on the world water speed record on Coniston Water in 1967 is commemorated by the brewery's flagship beer, Bluebird.

COPPER DRAGON

Snaygill Industrial Estate Keighley Road Skipton, North Yorkshire, England BD23 2QR
www.copperdragon.uk.com

Two years studying the UK brewing industry preceded the formation of Copper Dragon at the former Skipton Brewery in 2002. A new German-style, steam-powered brewhouse was soon needed, and continued growth has demanded another expansion in 2008, with the commissioning of a 60-barrel (9,800 litres) operation.

COTLEIGH

Ford Road, Wiveliscombe, Somerset, England TA4 2RE
www.cotleighbrewery.co.uk

Life for Cotleigh began in 1979 in a farmhouse stable block, and the business has changed hands twice since. Each owner has built upon its previous successes and expanded the operation to meet demand.

BREWING SECRET The New Harvest Ale is brewed with Herefordshire hops just a day after picking.

CROPTON

Cropton, Pickering, North Yorkshire, England YO18 8HH
www.croptonbrewery.com

Brewing started in 1984, and a purpose-built plant was installed 10 years later, before being greatly expanded in 2006 in order to produce 100 barrels (16,000 litres) a week. Virtually all beers are available bottle-conditioned, all are additive-free, approved by the Vegetarian Society, and are suitable for vegans to boot.

BLUEBIRD BITTER
BITTER 3.6% ABV
Its single varietal hop (Challenger) creates an inviting aroma and influences a light, clean palate.

OLD MAN ALE
BEST BITTER 4.2% ABV
Exuberant in its aroma of fruit, coatings of roasted chocolate malt, and tart hoppiness.

GOLDEN PIPPIN
BITTER 4.2% ABV
Light, refreshing, and blonde, with citrus fruit flavours appealing to ale and lager drinkers alike.

BEST BITTER
BEST BITTER 4% ABV
An amber-coloured, well-balanced, malty, and hoppy session ale, brewed for the northern palate.

TAWNY OWL
BEST BITTER 3.8% ABV
Well balanced, light copper coloured, with a subtle hop palate and sweet malt flavour.

BARN OWL PREMIUM ALE
BEST BITTER 4.5% ABV
Dark copper, with hints of toffee and nut that swoop to a smooth, malty, bittersweet finish.

TWO PINTS BITTER
BITTER 4% ABV
A crafty balance of hop flavours, caramel sweetness, and malty aftertaste creates a classic bitter.

MONKMAN'S SLAUGHTER
PREMIUM BITTER 6% ABV
Full bodied, with distinct malty, chocolate, caramel, and autumn fruit flavours; subtle hoppy bitterness.

BREWERY

CROUCH VALE

23 Haltwhistle Road, South Woodham Ferrers, Essex, England CM3 5ZA
www.crouchvale.co.uk

Crouch Vale is one of the great microbrewing success stories of recent years. The small, independent company has twice won the ultimate cask beer accolade: the Campaign For Real Ale Supreme Champion Beer of Britain (2005 and 2006) for its Brewers Gold. Needless to say, the brewery has expanded into a new site since.

DALESIDE

Camwal Road, Harrogate, North Yorkshire, England HG1 4PT
www.dalesidebrewery.co.uk

The Victorian spa town of Harrogate is renowned for its restorative waters, so it is no surprise to discover an impressive range of beers brewed there. Heritage-rich recipes have been revived, with a philosophy that demands the highest quality of raw ingredients are allied to the latest methods of production.

DARWIN

Unit 1, West Quay Court, Sunderland, Tyne & Wear, England SR1 2QE
www.darwinbrewery.com

The Darwin setup is unique in that its commercial operation is complemented by a test brew plant based at the University of Sunderland. There, students on the Brewlab brewing sciences course are able to trial some 40 new beers each year. The best of them are then produced at the award-winning site.

DONNINGTON

Stow-on-the-Wold, Cheltenham, Gloucestershire, England GL54 1EP
www.donnington-brewery.com

Thomas Arkell bought an idyllic 13th-century watermill in 1827, and brewing began on the premises in 1865. The mill passed through direct descendants of Thomas to the redoubtable Claude Arkell, who died in 2007. His cousins took up the challenge to continue and develop the brewery, which still uses the waterwheel for some of its power.

BEER

BREWERS GOLD
BITTER 4% ABV
Pale, refreshing, and perfumily hoppy, with aromas of sweet, tropical fruits and a bitter finish.

ESSEX BOYS BEST BITTER
BITTER 3.8% ABV
Pale brown, with noticeable malt and citrus hops on the nose and a dry finish.

DALESIDE BLONDE
BITTER 4.3% ABV
Distinctively hoppy, with sherbet and citrus flavours culminating in a bitter, but short, finish.

OLD LEG OVER
BITTER 4.1% ABV
An admirable balance of nut and fruit on the palate, and a suggestion of herbs in the aroma.

EVOLUTION
BITTER 4% ABV
Light, clean, and satisfying, with a dry, hoppy character and layers of malt throughout.

GHOST ALE
BITTER 4.1% ABV
Golden and richly hopped, with citrus aromas dominating, followed by a well-balanced fruit piquancy.

DOUBLE DONN
BEST BITTER 4.4% ABV
Dark, well-balanced bitter with a fruit and malt dalliance and dry, malt-hinted finish.

S.B.A.
BITTER 4.4% ABV
Sweet malt flavours with a touch of fruit dominate this lightly hopped beer.

DURHAM

Unit 6a, Bowburn North Industrial Estate, Bowburn, County Durham, England DH6 5PF
www.durhambrewery.co.uk

A home-brewing hobby evolved into a business in 1994, when two former music teachers faced redundancy. Award after award has followed, principally through attention to detail and the production of beers that wring expressive flavours and aromas out of every ingredient. Beer names celebrate Durham's ecclesiastical culture.

ELGOOD'S

Wisbech, Cambridgeshire, England PE13 1LN
www.elgoods-brewery.co.uk

The Georgian facade of this 1795 brewery may speak of its history, but significant technical advances lie behind, and Elgood's is now one of the UK's most progressive producers. The fifth generation of the Elgood family does, however, incorporate traditional values and time-honoured methods into its forward-looking approach.

EVERARDS

Castle Acres, Narborough, Leicestershire, England LE19 1BY
www.everards.co.uk

After brewing his first pint in 1849, William Everard stated his intention, and one that the fifth-generation family is proud to uphold: "No effort shall be found wanting in the production and supply of genuine ale of first-rate quality". Integrity remains king today.

BREWING SECRET Fuggles and Goldings are the key hops here.

EXMOOR

Wiveliscombe, Somerset, Taunton, England TA4 2NY
www.exmoorales.co.uk

Exmoor was among the first wave of microbreweries in the early 1980s. Its fundamentals have never altered from a reliance on skills, investment in innovation, and adherence to the principles of small-batch brewing. Being Somerset's largest brewery positions it as a regional producer, and the potential of its backbone brands is still to be fully capitalized upon.

MAGUS

BITTER 3.8% ABV
A pale session bestseller, with aromatically complex continental lager qualities and citrus undertones.

EVENSONG

STRONG BITTER 5% ABV
A 1937 recipe. The deep ruby colour unveils luscious toffee notes and a generous hop bitterness.

BLACK DOG

MILD 3.6% ABV
Well-balanced mild, with a roasted malt integrity, reinforced by a single hop variety.

GOLDEN NEWT

GOLDEN ALE 4.1% ABV
Light in malt, the beer is dominated by floral hop flavours.

TIGER

BITTER 4.2% ABV
Some spicy hop and caramel on the nose. Classically bittersweet palate, with a rounded toffeeness.

ORIGINAL

STRONG BITTER 5.2% ABV
Copper hued and full bodied. A toasted caramel aroma beckons port wine and fruit flavours.

EXMOOR GOLD

BITTER 5% ABV
Powerful earthy hop, lemon, and juicy malt aromas; fruity, butterscotch sweetness and a memorable finish.

EXMOOR ALE

BITTER 3.8% ABV
Medium bodied, with some malt and hop in the aroma and bitter hop aftertaste.

BREWERY

FELINFOEL
Farmers Row, Lanelli, Wales SA14 8LB
www.felinfoel-brewery.com

Sitting astride the River Liedi and leaning heavily on the industrial traditions of south Wales – and its workers' thirsts – Felinfoel Brewery has been in existence since 1878. It is famed for producing Britain's first canned beer in 1935. Extensive modernization came in the 1970s, but Felinfoel is still family owned.

FREEMINER
Whimsey Industrial Estate, Whimsey, Cinderfor, England GL14 3JA
www.freeminer.com

Anyone born in the Forest of Dean who has worked in a coal mine for a year and a day may open his own mine. Few such mines remain, but Freeminer celebrates this heritage with its ales.

BREWING SECRET Freeminer ales are made from traditional malt varieties and whole Worcestershire hops in open-topped fermenters.

FULLER'S
Chiswick Lane South, London, England W4 2QB
www.fullers.co.uk

London's last remaining traditional family brewer, Fuller's has been based at the historic Griffin Brewery near the River Thames in Chiswick since 1845. Brewing on the site, however, goes back 350 years. Despite its global prominence, Fuller's retains a small company spirit and formidably energetic outlook. Its beers, among the country's most consistent, have received countless awards, notably the Campaign For Real Ale Champion Beer of Britain, which it has won five times. Although firmly at the forefront of British ale production, Fuller's remains resolutely true to traditional brewing techniques. The company bought Hampshire brewer George Gale in 2005, and its beers are now brewed at Chiswick.

BEER

DOUBLE DRAGON
BITTER 4.2% ABV
Invitingly rich in colour, malty and subtly hopped, with an evenly balanced, full-drinking nature.

BEST BITTER
ALE 3.8% ABV
A good balance of malt and hops make this an easy-drinking, refreshing beer.

SPECULATION
STRONG BITTER 4.8% ABV
An initial chocolate sweetness is replaced by a hoppy rush and rich malt flavour layer.

FREEMINER
BITTER 4.8% ABV
Distinctly bitter and abundantly hoppy, balanced by a malt character that denotes "no-nonsense" beer.

DOUBLE STOUT
STOUT 7.4% ABV
Dark brown and creamy, this beer balances a rich fruity aroma with smoky, bittersweet chocolate notes.

LONDON PRIDE
BITTER 4.1% ABV
A fruity sweet malt nose and a floral spiced hop presence with marmalade undercurrents.

VINTAGE ALE
BARLEY WINE 8.5% ABV (VARIABLE)
Annually produced using different malt and hop varieties. Each vintage is different, all are intriguing.

CHISWICK BITTER
BITTER 3.5% ABV
A fresh citrus hop nature with a touch of malt sweetness on the palate. Pleasingly dry finish.

FYNE ALES

Cairndow, Argyll, Scotland PA26 8BJ
www.fyneales.com

Given that this brewery was set up in a redundant milking parlour as recently as 2001, it seems all the more remarkable that Fyne Ales has already begun winning national brewing awards.

BREWING SECRET Brewed with soft water from Loch Fyne, the brewery's Jarl was named Champion Golden Ale of Britain in 2013.

GALWAY HOOKER

Roscommon Town, Galway, Ireland
www.galwayhooker.ie

Launched in 2006, Galway Hooker is brewed by two proud "hopoholics" who believe in the joy and variety of experimentation. An online beer-naming competition came up with the Galway Hooker name, which refers to a traditional West Irish sailing boat. The philosophy is that beer is like any quality foodstuff – the fresher and less processed, the better.

GOACHER'S

Unit 8, Tovil Green Business Park, Maidstone, Kent, England ME15 6TA
www.goachers.com

The plant was purpose-built in 1983 and revived the art of brewing in Maidstone after an 11-year hiatus. It is constructed along classic lines, with full-mash brewing and open fermenters in stainless-steel vessels.

BREWING SECRET Whole Kentish hops and 100 per cent malted barley produce ales with a distinct character.

GRAIN

South Farm, Alburgh, Harleston, Norfolk, England IP20 0BS
www.grainbrewery.co.uk

From a small idea, the brewery has grown into one that is making a big impression in Norfolk for its well-made beers. Founded in 2006 by Geoff Wright and Phil Halls in a former farm dairy, the brewery has tripled since it opened. With the beers being bottled now, their reach is far beyond Norfolk.

JARL

GOLDEN BITTER 3.8% ABV
An easy-drinking golden beer with a pronounced citrus hop character.

HIGHLANDER

SCOTTISH HEAVY 4.8% ABV
A strong traditional Scottish-style ale, with intense malt properties and a citrus hop aroma.

GALWAY HOOKER IRISH PALE ALE

PALE ALE 4.3% ABV
Balanced tangy bitterness and understated biscuit flavours complement a floral aroma and citrus dry finish.

BEST DARK ALE

BEST BITTER 4.1% ABV
The original Goacher's derives its complex, full-bodied nature from a bittersweet malty infusion.

FINE LIGHT ALE

BITTER 3.7% ABV
A consistent and rewarding floral hop tang and moderate malt palate from aroma to aftertaste.

BLONDE ASH

WHEAT BEER 4% ABV
Brewed with a wheat beer, yeast banana notes are clearly present in this sunburst-yellow beer.

BLACKWOOD STOUT

STOUT 5% ABV
Based on the 18th-century Whitbread recipe, it is full of dark roasted barley and fruit flavours.

BREWERY

GREENE KING

Bury St. Edmunds, Suffolk,
England IP33 1QT
www.greeneking.co.uk

After more than 200 years, Greene
King has developed into a formidable
and dynamic force in the highly
competitive British brewing industry.
All beers are brewed at Bury St.
Edmunds, where ale has featured
since the 11th century. Benjamin
Greene opened his brewery in
1799 and it merged with the rival
King Brewery in 1887. The company

has in recent years acquired several
of its competitors – namely, Morland,
Ruddles, Ridley's, and Hardy & Hanson
– and closed them amid some
controversy. Belhaven of Dunbar,
which was bought in 2005, was
another recent acquisition.

BREWING SECRET Greene King's flagship
Abbot Ale spends "two sabbaths"
under fermentation, as master
brewers' ideal practices demand.

GROWLER

The Street, Pentlow, Essex,
England, CO10 7JJ
www.growlerbrewery.com

Founded in 1986 as the Nethergate
Brewery, the popularity of its eight
permanent, seasonal, and speciality ales
necessitated the brewery's expansion,
then relocation, in 2005. Significant
awards have been gathered, including
the Great British Beer Festival and the
Chicago International Beer Festival.
The brewery was awarded Brewery of
the Year 2012 by the Good Pub Guide.

GUINNESS

St James's Gate, Dublin 8, Ireland
www.guinness.com

When you can make a virtue out
of the time it takes to pour a pint –
119.5 seconds to be precise – you
know you have no ordinary beer in
your hands. Guinness defines stout,
Ireland, and Irishness, but it is also
inextricably linked with innovation
in physics, chemistry, packaging, and
advertising. The St. James's Gate
Brewery – occupying a 25-hectare

BEER

ABBOT ALE
STRONG BITTER 5% ABV
A biscuit malt and spicy hop aroma,
with a tangy and bittersweet fruit
and malt palate.

GREENE KING IPA
INDIA PALE ALE 3.6% ABV
Distinctly copper coloured, with
a clean, fresh hop savouriness and
subtle, sweetish malty nose.

OLD SPECKLED HEN
PREMIUM BITTER 5% ABV
Rich and intense, with a savoury,
spicy malt flavour, allied with a
fruity sweetness.

RUDDLES COUNTY
BEST BITTER 4.3% ABV
A premium ale that displays a
fruity sweetness and a definite
hoppy, dry finish.

OLD GROWLER
PORTER 5.5% ABV
A complex and distinctive porter,
with roast malt, liquorice, and fruit
layers; powerful, hoppy finish.

UMBEL ALE
BITTER 3.8% ABV
Freshly toasted coriander seeds are
added to the boil for an explosion
of spicy flavours.

GUINNESS ORIGINAL
STOUT 4.2% ABV
The packaged version's coffee
and cream aroma highlights fruit,
chocolate, and some late hoppiness.

DRAUGHT GUINNESS
STOUT 4.1% ABV
Some hop aroma apparent, then
fruit, cream, and dark toffee flavours
develop with liquorice tinges.

(25,000-square metre) prime slice of Dublin – is often likened to a citadel, but it is very much a living, working space and, 250 years after young Arthur Guinness's first mash, it is brewed in 50 countries worldwide and enjoyed in 150.

BREWING SECRET The amount of hops used is instrumental to the dry quality of Guinness Stout; Brettonamyces yeast also contributes to its dry style.

HADRIAN & BORDER

Unit 5, The Preserving Works, Newburn Industrial Estate, Shelley Road, Newcastle upon Tyne, England, NE15 9RT
www.hadrian-border-brewery.co.uk

Born out of a "marriage" between Border Brewery of Berwick upon Tweed and Hadrian of Newcastle upon Tyne, the company continues to grow, year on year, throughout a distribution area that reaches from Edinburgh to North Yorkshire. Its award-winning ales are brewed in a 40-barrel (6,500-litre) plant.

HALL & WOODHOUSE

Blandford St. Mary, Dorset, England DT11 9LS
www.hall-woodhouse.co.uk

An independent family firm, Hall & Woodhouse is owned and run by fifth-generation Woodhouses, who remain loyal to the brewery's dictum: "Dorset ales with real character". Its visitor centre is a major tourist attraction, and a new, environmentally friendly brewery is planned to sit at the heart of the local community.

HAMBLETON

Keld Close Barker Business Park, Melmerby Green Ln, Melmerby, Ripon, United Kingdom HG4 5NB
www.hambletonales.co.uk

A million-pound investment has resulted in a completely new brewery for Hambleton, with state-of-the-art bottling facilities. Innovation has been at the heart of the operation since 1991, as evident in the label designs and bespoke brewing equipment. Several awards, including one for a gluten-free range, have been well deserved.

FOREIGN EXTRA STOUT
SPECIAL STOUT 7.5% ABV
Leafy hop aroma, with burnt toast, rich malt, bitter coffee, and liquorice flavours ripening effortlessly.

GUINNESS RED
IRISH RED ALE 4.1% ABV
Rather than the familiar black and white, lighter roasted barley gives it a rich red colour.

TYNESIDE BLONDE
BLONDE ALE 3.9% ABV
Clean tasting and easy drinking, it is full to the brim with bittering and citrus hops.

FARNE ISLANDE
BITTER 4% ABV
An amber-coloured, well-rounded bitter, with a heightened sense of malt and a hoppy finale.

FIRST GOLD
BITTER 4% ABV
An exceptional golden ale, using a single hop, First Gold, for character and a distinctive flavour.

TANGLEFOOT
STRONG BITTER 5% ABV
Light golden, with a noticeable floral dry hop aroma that contrasts with biscuit and fruit notes.

STALLION
BITTER 4.2% ABV
For some, a true Yorkshire bitter, with its malty character, nuttiness, and enhanced hopping rate.

NIGHTMARE
PORTER 5% ABV
An extra-stout porter that uses a combination of four malts for a massively complex flavour.

THE STORY OF...

Guinness

St James's Gate, Dublin 8, Ireland

Ask for a pint of the "black stuff" wherever you are in the world and the likelihood is you will be served a glass of Guinness. With a body seemingly as dark as the blackest night and topped with a snow white flourish of foam, it is one of the world's most recognizable beers. Guinness is a dry stout, its flavour unerringly roasty, with a hint of smokiness. Its dark hue and distinctive creamy flavour come from the use of an abundance of barley, which is roasted in a giant drum within the St James's Gate Brewery, filling the air around with luscious, burnt coffee aromas.

The Guinness story began more than 240 years ago, when Arthur Guinness built a brewery in Dublin, the keystone of which was decorated with a relief of Ceres, the Roman goddess of grain. By 1900 the brewery's fame and its beer had travelled far and wide, and Guinness had become the biggest brewer in the world, producing more than one million barrels a year.

Today, with a number of variations, Guinness is brewed in more than 40 countries. Drinkers in Britain and Ireland commonly see it sold on draught. However, in many other parts of the world, including Nigeria and Indonesia, it is sold in bottles in a variety of different strengths from 4.1 per cent to 8 per cent ABV.

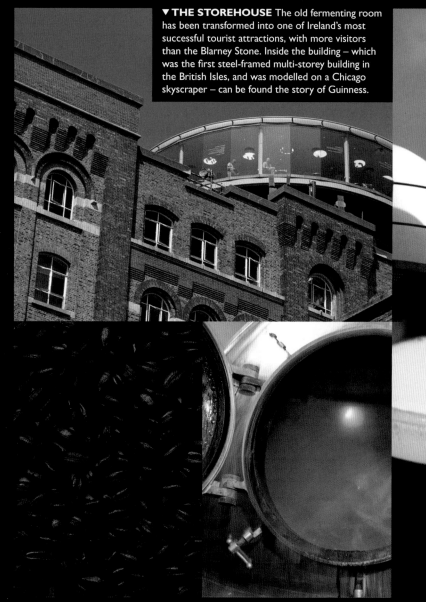

▼ THE STOREHOUSE The old fermenting room has been transformed into one of Ireland's most successful tourist attractions, with more visitors than the Blarney Stone. Inside the building – which was the first steel-framed multi-storey building in the British Isles, and was modelled on a Chicago skyscraper – can be found the story of Guinness.

▲ ROASTED BARLEY Like most beers, Guinness is made from barley, hops, and yeast. But it is the addition of flaked barley and dark roasted barley that gives Guinness its unique colour and smooth bitterness. Roasted barley forms part of the mash bill, though additional quantities are added to the wort during the boil (*right*).

THE CREAMY HEAD ▶
The famous Guinness creamy white head is created from the surging of bubbles from nitrogen and carbon dioxide gas as the beer is poured. It is actually the nitrogen that causes the tight white creamy head. To pour the perfect creamy Guinness takes time and perhaps a little patience. It requires a double, slow pour that can take nearly two minutes. It is not unknown for pubs in Ireland to have a line of partially filled glasses on the bar at opening time waiting for customers to arrive, when the final pour is made.

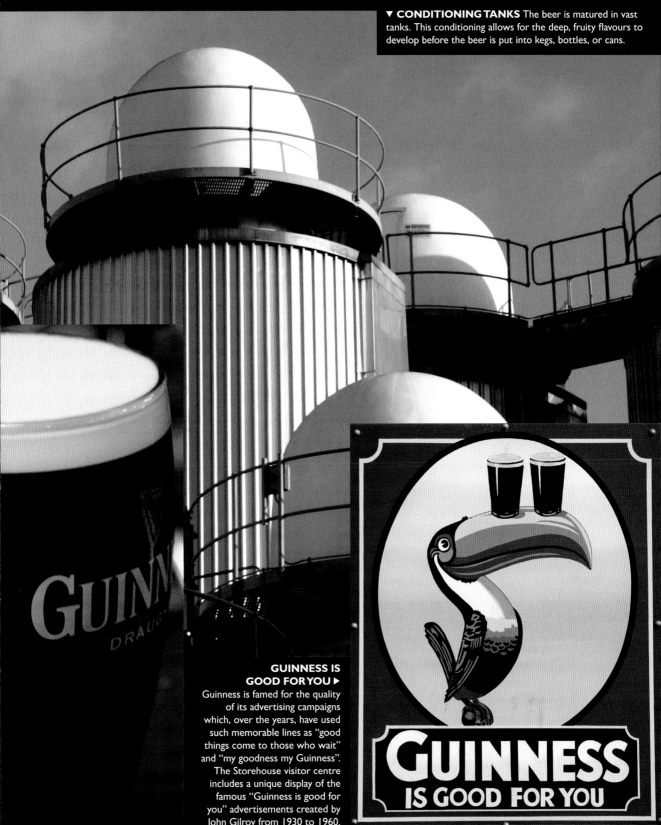

▼ **CONDITIONING TANKS** The beer is matured in vast tanks. This conditioning allows for the deep, fruity flavours to develop before the beer is put into kegs, bottles, or cans.

GUINNESS IS GOOD FOR YOU ▶

Guinness is famed for the quality of its advertising campaigns which, over the years, have used such memorable lines as "good things come to those who wait" and "my goodness my Guinness". The Storehouse visitor centre includes a unique display of the famous "Guinness is good for you" advertisements created by John Gilroy from 1930 to 1960.

GUINNESS IS GOOD FOR YOU

BREWERY

HARVEY'S

6 Cliffe High Street, Lewes, East
Sussex, England BN7 2AH
www.harveys.org.uk

The seventh generation of John
Harvey's descendants are still involved
in this prime example of Victorian
Gothic-style brewery grandeur. The
tower and brewhouse dominate the
skyline, and the fermenting rooms and
cellars remain structurally unaltered,
although they now house a modern
plant with equipment that has
increased production enormously.

HARVIESTOUN

Alva, Clackmannanshire,
Scotland FK12 5DQ
www.harviestoun.com

The brewers of Harviestoun say they
can't pretend it's a job – it's their work,
but also their play and their passion.
Curiosity towards flavours and aromas
wrung from natural ingredients was the
brewery's mission in 1985, when the
business was originally set up, and a
move to a purpose-built plant with
fresh investment has resulted
in national accolades.

HAWKSHEAD

Mill Yard, Staveley, Cumbria,
England LA8 9LR
www.hawksheadbrewery.co.uk

The focus at Hawkshead is on
traditional beer styles that have been
given a modern twist. A new 20-barrel
(3,200-litre) brewhouse was fitted out
in 2006 – an integral feature is a farm
gate for leaning on contemplatively.
The brewery's public beer hall, where
award-winning ales are served, is a
magnificent showcase for the beers
and their provenance.

HIGH HOUSE

Matfen, Newcastle upon Tyne,
Northumberland, England NE20 0RG
www.highhousefarmbrewery.co.uk

The 2001 foot-and-mouth crisis
persuaded farmer Steven Urwin that
diversification was necessary. Being a
keen home-brewer, he undertook
a course at Sunderland University's
Brewlab. He requisitioned listed farm
buildings for brewing, and success
since then has led to national and
regional brewing awards – all displayed
in the visitor centre.

BEER

BLUE LABEL
BEST BITTER 3.6% ABV
Deliciously full bodied, though fairly
low in alcohol, with a whiff of leafy
hop and sweet malt counterbalance.

ARMADA ALE
PALE ALE 4.5% ABV
Amber coloured, with a well-
balanced combination of fruit
and hops on the palate.

OLA DUBH 12
BARREL-AGED BEER 8% ABV
Dark black in colour, whisky
flavours of leather, spice, and cigars
soar through this exotic beer.

BITTER & TWISTED
BITTER 4.2% ABV
Ripe grapefruit and lemon-
influenced hop aromas are
anchored by a distinct maltiness.

LAKELAND GOLD
BEST BITTER 4.4% ABV
Hoppy and uncompromisingly bitter,
with complex fruit flavours from its
English and American hop blend.

HAWKSHEAD RED
RED ALE 4.2% ABV
A bittersweet red ale, malty and
spicy on the palate, with juicy,
woody aromas.

NEL'S BEST
BEST BITTER 4.2% ABV
Full bodied, golden, and easy on the
palate, with a delightful hoppiness
and mantle of malt.

AULD HEMP
BITTER 3.8% ABV
A rewarding, fresh malty aroma
precedes malt and fruit flavours.
Named after a farm sheepdog.

HILDEN

Lisburn, County Antrim,
Ireland BT 27 4TY
www.hildenbrewery.co.uk

This family-run microbrewery sparked
something of a revolution when it
was set up in 1981, reintroducing
cask-conditioned beer to Ireland.
The brewhouse – a former stable
belonging to a leading linen
manufacturer – now produces
seven regular ales, including a stout,
a porter, a blonde, a premium red,
and two amber-style ales.

A range of seasonal beers are also
produced, as are some one-off
brews. The beers can now be
found on sale in many parts of
the United Kingdom.

HOBSONS

Tenbury Road, Cleobury Mortimer,
Worcestershire, England DY14 8RD
www.hobsons-brewery.co.uk

Success has evolved out of a
hand-to-mouth existence, a steadily
growing reputation, brewery expansion,
relocation, and a sprinkling of single-
mindedness. At the heart of all this
has been a determination to brew
a mild at a time when the style was
perceived to be in freefall. Yet in 2007
it was judged Supreme Champion
Beer of Britain.

HOGS BACK

Tongham, Surrey, England GU10 1DE
www.hogsback.co.uk

Established in 1992, the Hogs Back
brewhouse takes up part of an
18th-century farm. Steady expansion,
extensions to storage facilities, and
re-equipping the fermenting room
have continued since, and many awards
have been gathered along the way.

BREWERY SECRETS "Late hops" are added
at the end of the boil, contributing
additional fragrance to the beer.

HILDEN IRISH STOUT
STOUT 4.3% ABV
A dry, full-bodied stout with lots of
roasted barley and chocolate notes.

HILDEN HALT
IRISH RED ALE 6.1% ABV
Named after a local rail station, it
is full of sweet biscuit malt flavours
and some bitterness.

TWISTED HOP
GOLDEN ALE 4.7% ABV
Soft malt tones allow the
abundant bittering and citrus
hops to shine.

MOLLY'S CHOCOLATE STOUT
STOUT 4.2% ABV
Hints of dark chocolate underpin
this full-bodied beer.

TOWN CRIER
BEST BITTER 4.5% ABV
Pale and straw coloured, with
some malt sweetness, an earthy
hop impression, and dry finish.

CHAMPION MILD
MILD 3.2% ABV
Traditional, with a clever wringing
of roasted malt and nutty flavours
from its ingredients.

TEA/TRADITIONAL ENGLISH ALE
BEST BITTER 4.2% ABV
Well-crafted, with delicate fruity
aromas, some bittersweet malt
flavouring, and a long, dry finish.

HBB/HOGS BACK BITTER
BITTER 3.7% ABV
A biscuit-influenced session bitter,
with a fragrantly aromatic citrus
fruit and light malt afterglow.

BREWERY

HOLDEN'S

George Street, Woodsetton, Dudley, West Midlands, England DY1 4LN
www.holdensbrewery.co.uk

Third- and fourth-generation family members are very much involved in the Holden's business, which started life in the 1920s with a brewpub, before expanding next door into a neatly tiled brewery on two floors.

BREWING SECRET The mild uses a mix of amber malt, caramalt, and black malt, along with Fuggles hops.

HOOK NORTON

Brewery Lane, Hook Norton, Oxfordshire, England OX15 5NY
www.hooky.co.uk

A particularly striking example of a Victorian tower brewery, Hook Norton is partly powered by steam, via a series of belts, cogs, and shafts. Drays pulled by shire horses deliver to local pubs, further demonstrating how the brewery likes to preserve traditional practices. While doing this, Hook Norton also produces some of the country's most outstanding ales.

HOP BACK

Batten Road Industrial Estate Downton, Salisbury, Wiltshire, England SP5 3HU
www.hopback.co.uk

Having soon outgrown its humble 1980s pub-cellar beginnings at the Wyndham Arms in Salisbury, Hop Back developed and expanded through a series of premises for brewing and drinking its beers, picking up significant awards along the way. At the core of the range is the multi-award-winning Summer Lightning.

HURNS

Unit 3, Century Park, Swansea Enterprise Park, Wales SA6 8RP
www.hurns.co.uk

The Hurns beer distribution and pub company moved into brewing in 2002 with the acquistion of the liquidated Tomos Watkin Brewery, which had built an enviable reputation in its short life. Since then, the enterprise has developed considerably, with little assistance from a dose of wholehearted Welsh passion.

BEER

HOLDEN'S GOLDEN
BITTER 3.9% ABV
Fuggles hops and Maris Otter malt combine in this medium-bodied, straw-hued pale ale.

HOLDEN'S BLACK COUNTRY MILD
MILD 3.7% ABV
Bold chestnut red, with nutty biscuit notes and wrappings of chocolate, caramel, and earthy hops.

OLD HOOKY
STRONG BITTER 4.6% ABV
Beautifully poised, with a piquant, fruity nature and malt character rounding off a bitter finish.

HOOKY
BITTER 3.5% ABV
Subtly hoppy on the nose, then malt and fruit appear, before a returning hop finish.

SUMMER LIGHTNING
STRONG BITTER 5% ABV
Intensely bitter, with a grassy, fresh, hoppy aroma and some malt lingering on the palate.

CROP CIRCLE
BITTER 4.2% ABV
Cleverly blended aroma and bittering hops combine with corn nuances for a delicate fruity crispness.

CWRW HAF
BITTER 4.2% ABV
Refreshingly zesty, with citrus flavours emerging from a clever blend of three distinct hop varieties.

CWRW BRAF
BITTER 4.2% ABV
Amber coloured, with a gentle hop aroma easing in a light bitterness and temperate maltiness.

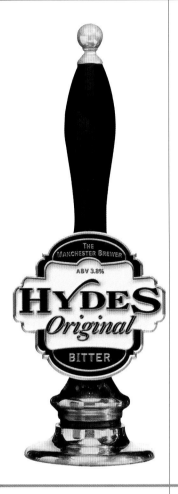

HYDES

30 Kansas Avenue, Salford, Manchester, England M50 2GL
www.hydesbrewery.com

Hydes is another of those remarkable family-owned breweries that has carved out a niche in its home region. Hydes Original has persevered with the same recipe and exacting standards that were applied on day one – back in 1863. The business continues to face the future with enthusiasm and confidence.

INNIS & GUNN

6 Randolph Crescent, Edinburgh, Midlothian EH3 7TH, Scotland
www.innisandgunn.com

Whisky distiller William Grant & Son commissioned a special beer to season oak casks for an ale cask-finished whisky. It was then discovered that the disgorged ale had taken on novel and exciting flavours. The possibilities for a new beer style were realized, and it is now produced by Innis & Gunn, which bought the concept from Grants to develop the brand further.

INVERALMOND

22 Inveralmond Place, Perth, Perthshire, Scotland PH1 3TS
www.inveralmond-brewery.co.uk

Several bottled waters available nationally are sourced from Perthshire's natural mineral springs, and it is little wonder that world-renowned whisky distilleries and this award-winning brewery put them to even better use. Plans are well advanced for increasing the production capacity at Inveralmond, with the craft keg market a major focus.

ISLE OF ARRAN

100 Wellington Street, Glasgow, North Lanarkshire, Scotland, G2 6DH
www.arranbrewery.com

Arran is often described as "Scotland in miniature", and its high-tech brewery, set among the stunning surroundings of castles, mountains, and an extraordinary shoreline, reflects tradition, substance, and native inventiveness. The plaudits it gets are matched by awards for design.

BREWING SECRET Gulf Stream-driven rainfall is a factor in the beer's character.

HYDES ORIGINAL
BITTER 3.8% ABV
A northwest classic: copper coloured, full bodied, with a distinctive bittersweet flavour.

OWD OAK
MILD 3.5% ABV
A fruit and malt nose and complex flavourings that meander through berry fruits, malt, and chocolate.

INNIS & GUNN ORIGINAL
SPECIALITY STRONG BITTER 6.6% ABV
A butterscotch sweet aroma crosses into the beer's flavour, blending with vegetable and banana notes, and a green apple sourness.

OSSIAN
GOLDEN ALE 4.1% ABV
Spicy and spritzy orange aromas blend with malt flavours and develop through further fruit notes.

SUNBURST PILSNER
PILSNER 4.8% ABV
A Scottish take on a Bohemian classic, it is crisp and easy drinking.

ARRAN BLONDE
STRONG BITTER 5% ABV
New-mown grass and floral aromas slip into citrus fruit and tangy, succulent malt flavours.

ARRAN DARK
SCOTTISH HEAVY 4.3% ABV
Rich, ripe fruit aroma, with full malt bittersweet flavours typical of a traditional Scottish "heavy".

BEER TRAIL

COTSWOLDS

The village of Hook Norton in north Oxfordshire is the perfect base for any visitor exploring the Cotswolds or the city of Oxford. For the traveller, three of the village's pubs – the Sun, the Pear Tree, and the Gate Hangs High – all offer accommodation.

Pear Tree, Hook Norton

JOURNEY STATS
3 days
160km (100 miles)

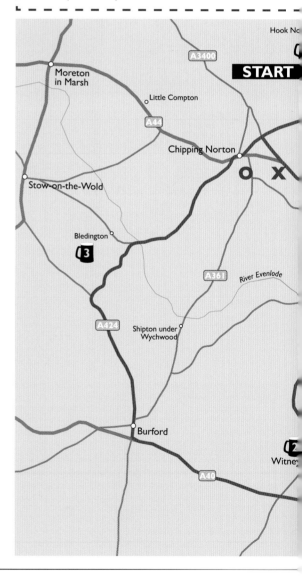

🍺 DAY 1: HOOK NORTON BREWERY

This is a near-perfect example of a Victorian tower brewery, which is home to a steam engine installed in 1895. The making of Hook Norton's beers is a tactile, aural, and visual experience. Only the finest malted barley is used in the mash tun, and this needs to be manually removed when the wort is drained off the grist. The seemingly magical transformation of turning sweet wort into alcohol takes place in the brewery's hard-working open fermenters. A horse-drawn dray still delivers beer to local pubs. The Visitor Centre is open from Monday to Saturday, though tours of the brewery must be booked beforehand via the website. The tour is followed by some sampling of Hook Norton beer. *Brewery Lane, Hook Norton (www.hooky.co.uk)*

🍺 DAY 2: WYCHWOOD BREWERY

The drive from Hook Norton to Witney takes in some glorious countryside, and at the end of the journey is the Wychwood Brewery. Tours of the brewery can be booked online. They last for two hours and go through the brewing process for Wychwood and Brakspear beers, from raw ingredients to the finished product. The tour takes in Brakspear's famous "Double Drop system" fermenting vessels. *Eagle Maltings, The Crofts, Witney (www.wychwood.co.uk)*

3 DAY 2: THE KING'S HEAD INN

On the way back to Hook Norton, the journey passes by many fine, historic pubs. One of the best is the King's Head Inn, situated on the village green at Bledington. With a meandering stream at its side, it is the perfect place to drink a glass of Hook Norton beer or even an English lager from Cotswold Brewing. *The Green, Bledington (www.thekingsheadinn.net)*

0m — 10 miles
0km — 23km

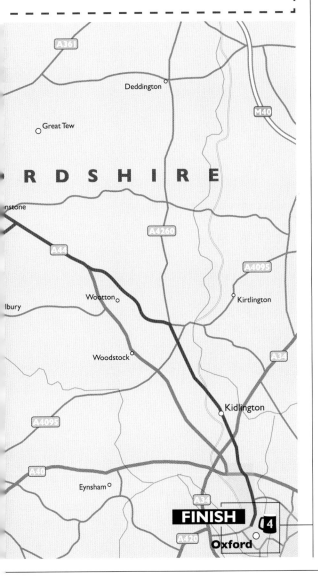

4 DAY 3: OXFORD

The third day of the trail offers a chance to sample some of the fabulous pubs in the historical city of Oxford – a place where good beer, culture, and a convivial atmosphere sit cosily together.

TURF TAVERN

Hard to find but worth the search, the Turf Tavern is built on the only remaining part of the city wall. It sells a fabulous collection of British beers. *4-5 Bath Place, Holywell, Oxford (www.theturftavern.co.uk)*

KING'S ARMS

The King's Arms sits at the end of Broad Street, which is famous for its colleges and bookshops. The large pub is a warren of rooms and is much loved by locals and students. *40 Holywell Street, Oxford (www.kingsarmsoxford.co.uk)*

THE BEAR INN

Small and friendly, The Bear Inn is on a narrow lane between Christ Church and Oriel colleges. It claims to be the oldest pub in Oxford, and is built on the site of a former bear-fighting pit. The walls are decorated with a collection of 5,000 ties. *6 Alfred Street, Oxford (www.bearoxford.co.uk)*

EAGLE & CHILD

Close to Oxford's dreaming spires and the Ashmolean museum, Eagle & Child was a frequent haunt of writers JRR Tolkein and CS Lewis, who were part of a literary group in the 1930s and 40s called the Inklings. *49 St Giles, Oxford*

Traditional pubs, such as the Eagle in Oxford, offer temporary "guest" beers, as well as serving a range of regular beers.

BREWERY

ISLE OF SKYE
Uig, Isle of Skye, Scotland IV51 9XP
www.skyebrewery.co.uk

The ferry terminal serving the Outer Hebrides also boasts an award-winning ale producer in the form of the Isle of Skye Brewery. There, a former teacher has been joined in beer-making duties by two ex-chefs – one of them Scotland's only female brewer.

BREWING SECRET These beers make the most of traditional Scottish produce, such as barley, oats, and honey.

JARROW
Primrose Hill, Jarrow, Tyne & Wear, England NE32 5UB
www.jarrowbrewery.co.uk

Set up in 2002, originally to supply the owners' two pubs, Jarrow met immediate success, and its soaring reputation meant its beers were soon more widely available. Jarrow's well-structured ales reflect Tyneside's industrial and social importance – Old Cornelius, for example, was named after the last surviving member of the Jarrow March protesters of the 1930s.

JENNINGS
Cockermouth, Cumbria, England CA13 9NE
www.jenningsbrewery.co.uk

John Jennings had already been brewing for 46 years when he built his own brewery in 1874 in the shadow of Cockermouth Castle. The brewery stands at the confluence of the rivers Cocker and Derwent, and has been owned by Marstons since 2005.

BREWING SECRET Pure Lakeland water is a key ingredient in Jennings ales.

JOHN SMITH
Tadcaster, North Yorkshire, England LS24 9SA
www.johnsmiths.co.uk

John Smith (from the same family as Samuel Smith) began brewing in 1847 to cater for the local mill trade. The enterprise was taken over by the Courage group in 1970, then absorbed by Scottish & Newcastle. John Smith's is the top-selling bitter in the British Isles, selling more than a million pints a day.

BEER

HEBRIDEAN GOLD
BEST BITTER 4.3% ABV
Softly fruity, using porridge oats for exceptional body smoothness and a full, creamy head.

RED CUILLIN
BITTER 4.2% ABV
Malt-laced, with nut and caramel fillings developing evermore malt all the way to a bittersweet finale.

RIVET CATCHER
BITTER 4% ABV
A subtle hoppiness and light malt veil persist throughout this consistently award-winning bitter.

JOBLINGS SWINGING GIBBET
BITTER 4.1% ABV
Superbly composed, with prominent hop aromas and fruit developing throughout the palate.

CUMBERLAND ALE
BITTER 4.7% ABV
Florally hoppy, its intense, full flavour and firm creamy body slide into a dry aftertaste.

SNECK LIFTER
STRONG BITTER 5.1% ABV
Dark and fascinating, with complex aromatics, and generous flavours of fruit and roasted malt.

JOHN SMITH'S MAGNET
BITTER 4% ABV
Balanced bittersweet flavours, including caramel and liquorice, head an easy-drinking, full-flavoured beer.

JOHN SMITH'S ORIGINAL
BITTER 3.8% ABV
A moderate-bodied and fruity-flavoured bitter, possessing a short, hoppy finish.

JOSEPH HOLT

Empire Street, Cheetham, Manchester,
England M3 1JD
www.joseph-holt.com

A family business survivor in an
increasingly corporate sector, Holt's
admits – with some pride – to being
unashamedly old-fashioned. That
does not mean backward-looking,
however, and its well-structured
projects and clear vision have brought
steady expansion to the brewery
and to its portfolio of 127 pubs.

KELHAM ISLAND

23 Alma Street, Sheffield, South
Yorkshire, England S3 8SA
www.kelhambrewery.co.uk

Since Kelham Island opened in 1990,
Sheffield's four large breweries have
closed down, which makes Kelham's
success all the more remarkable. An
astonishing range of awards has been
collected along the way.

BREWING SECRET Pale Rider and Easy
Rider both make great use of highly
fragrant American hops.

THE KERNEL

Arch 11, Dockley Road, Industrial
Estate, London, England SE16 3SF
www.thekernelbrewery.com

Evan O'Riordain founded the brewery
in 2010 and his big, bold beers have
quickly found favour with fans of
craft beers. The brewery's focus
is on innovation and not mass
production, and beers can vary
in taste, but not quality, between
different brews. The Kernel makes
big beers with lots of hops.

LEES

Greengate Brewery, Middleton Junction,
Manchester, England M24 2AX
www.jwlees.co.uk

Established by the far-sighted John
Lees in 1878, when Manchester was
becoming the "workshop of the world",
Lees expanded rapidly, matching the
growing local thirst. Sixth-generation
family members currently run the
brewery and pub estate, and they
remain faithful to the brewery's
maxim: "We think of ourselves as
old-fashioned and cutting-edge".

1849 TRADITIONAL ALE
BEST BITTER 4.5% ABV
A 150-year anniversary ale, with a
vibrant and generous celebratory
hop flavour to match.

JOSEPH HOLT BITTER
BITTER 4% ABV
Spicy hops dominate the aroma
with tart fruitiness tempered by
biscuit malt and bittersweet fruit.

PALE RIDER
STRONG BITTER 5.2% ABV
Strong but delicately fruity multi-
award winner, which profits from an
adventurous use of American hops.

EASY RIDER
BITTER 4.3% ABV
A subtle pale ale, its initial crisp
bitterness surrendering only to
a lingering fruity palate.

INDIA PALE ALE (CITRA)
INDIA PALE ALE 8.1% ABV
American hops and English malt
combine to produce a beer of
some stature. Expect tropical fruits
and a long finish.

EXPORT STOUT
STOUT 7.3% ABV
Prunes, plums, and other dark fruits
mingle with rum and coffee flavours.

MOONRAKER
STRONG ALE 6.5% ABV
Powerfully fruity on a rich roast
malt base, with a sweet tendency
and dryish finish.

JW LEES BITTER
BITTER 4% ABV
Classic amber-coloured northern
bitter, with layers of malt in the
mouthfeel and a citrus finale.

BREWERY

LITTLE VALLEY

Turkey Lodge Farm, New Road, Cragg Vale, Hebden Bridge, West Yorkshire, England HX7 5TT
www.littlevalleybrewery.co.uk

All beers made by master brewer Wim van der Speck are certified as 100 per cent organic. Awards have followed Wim's career in his native Holland, then Germany, Scotland, and now England.

BREWING SECRET Wim has a flair for extracting spicy, fruit, chocolate, and cereal flavours from malts and hops.

MARSTON'S PLC

Burton upon Trent, Staffordshire, England DE14 2BW
www.marstonsbeercompany.co.uk

The company operates three sites: the Park Brewery in Wolverhampton, which brews Banks's, Hanson's, and Mansfield beers; Jennings Brewery at Cockermouth in the Lake District; and the Albion Brewery in Burton upon Trent – "the home of British beer". Throughout its long existence – which stretches back to 1834 – it has acquired several of its

competitors in the Midlands, Cumbria, and Wales. In 1999, Marston's itself was taken over by Wolverhampton & Dudley Breweries, which changed its name to Marston's PLC in 2007. It brews the famed Draught Bass for AB InBev.

BREWING SECRET The brewery still uses the fabled Burton Union fermenting system for its classic Pedigree beer, capitalizing on the renowned hard and sulphur-rich local water.

MAXIM BREWERY

1 Gadwall Road Rainton Bridge Hughton Le Spring, Sunderland, England DH4 5NL
www.maximbrewery.co.uk

After several years' contracting out the company's eponymous beer, a new brewery was opened in 2007 to cope with demand. Bottling facilities are planned for the near future.

BREWING SECRET Double Maxim uses an original Vaux Brewery recipe, which head brewer Jim Murray used when he worked at Vaux in 1968.

BEER

STOODLEY STOUT
STOUT 4.8% ABV
Rich and roasted flavours, with chocolate malt, oat, and wheat chasing orange and berry aromas.

CRAGG VALE BITTER
BITTER 4.2% ABV
Three complementary hop varieties manipulate lemon aromas around a full, rounded, crisp, fruity body.

PEDIGREE
PALE ALE 4.5% ABV
A British institution – sweetly hop-laden, with the vague sulphur aroma that's characteristic of Burton ales.

BURTON BITTER
BITTER 3.8% ABV
Malty biscuit flavours counterbalance a delicate hop nature; distinctive sulphurous aroma.

OLD EMPIRE
INDIA PALE ALE 5.7% ABV
A stylish India Pale Ale, with hop and fruit flavours and a dry extra-hop finish.

DRAUGHT BASS
PREMIUM BITTER 4.4% ABV
Beautiful fruit aromas diffuse into hoppy sweetness, with a touch of malt and a lingering bitterness.

DOUBLE MAXIM
BROWN ALE 4.7% ABV
Caramel in the aroma; continues through bittersweet flavours, then expands into toffee notes.

SAMSON
BEST BITTER 4.6% ABV
A dependable northeast English bitter, with a whiff of hop and a malt-infused body.

MCMULLEN

26 Old Cross Hertford, Hertfordshire,
England SG14 1RD
www.mcmullens.co.uk

Peter McMullen started his business
in 1827. Several breweries and three
artesian wells later, the brewery today
is now more compact, but no less
efficient, dependable, and successful.
Emphasis on training, in the brewhouse
and throughout the 50-strong pub
estate, encourages the team to work
to exacting standards.

MEANTIME

Blackwall Lane, London, England SE7 8RX
www.meantimebrewing.com

Preferring to be known as the brewery
that can't be pigeonholed could be
self-regarding, but master brewer
Alastair Hook's approach is purposeful
– to demonstrate the exciting flavour
potential that beer has to offer.
BREWING SECRET Research into, and
recreation of, beers from the past is
an abiding passion here, as exemplified
by Meantime's India Pale Ale.

MOORHOUSE'S

Burnley, Lancashire,
England BB11 5EN
www.moorhouses.co.uk

Mineral water and low-alcohol "hop
bitters" were William Moorhouse's
forte. He started his business in 1865,
but his successors failed to achieve a
great deal in terms of brewing beer
until fresh investment in infrastructure
arrived in 1988. Further improvements
and additions accelerated growth and
helped create the admirable reputation
that Moorhouse ales have today.

MORDUE

North Shields, Tyne & Wear,
England NE29 7XJ
www.morduebrewery.com

When two enterprising home-brewing
brothers discovered the house they
shared was formerly owned by
19th-century brewer Joseph Mordue,
there was no doubting what to call
their business. Several expansions, high
customer demand, large investment,
award upon award, and relocation have
since brought the brewplant virtually
back to Joseph Mordue's roots.

MCMULLEN AK
BITTER 3.7% ABV
Its soft biscuit palate stems from a
carefully targeted blend of pale and
chocolate malts.

MCMULLEN COUNTRY BITTER
BEST BITTER 4.3% ABV
A distinct fruitiness combines with
nutty layers to create a complex
but refreshingly balanced palate.

INDIA PALE ALE
INDIA PALE ALE 7.4% ABV
Massively hoppy, with herbal, spice,
and grass tiers grasping the strength
of the original IPAs.

CHOCOLATE PORTER
SPECIALITY STRONG BEER 6.5% ABV
Complex malt structure, with dark
chocolate releasing vanilla notes to
create a rich, memorable infusion.

PENDLE WITCHES BREW
STRONG BITTER 5.1% ABV
Distinctive and amber coloured,
the beer has a full malty palate
and a resonant fruity hop finale.

BLACK CAT
MILD 3.4% ABV
Full, dark, and complex, with
distinctive chocolate malt and
liquorice flavours, and a hoppy finish.

WORKIE TICKET
BEST BITTER 4.5% ABV
A well-constructed bitter, with an
intricate malt and hop blend, and
a long, satisfying finish.

NORTHUMBRIAN BLONDE
GOLDEN ALE 4% ABV
An easy-drinking beer, it is
dominated by lemon, grapefruit,
and orange hop flavours.

BEER STYLES

PORTER AND STOUT

Porter is the beer that came back from the dead. A revolutionary citizen of the turbulent 18th century, it was a dark, strong, restorative thirst quencher, and a favourite of London's market porters, hence its name. Porter was the rock on which the British brewing industry was built – massive vats of it once matured in the cellars of brewers such as Whitbread. Yet porter sales declined in the 19th and 20th centuries, and it seemed dead and buried by the 1970s. Recently, it has been resurrected by American craft brewers, with British microbrewers following suit.

Unlike porter, stout has never been away. In the early 19th century, Irish brewer Arthur Guinness made porter but, by using roasted barley in the mash tun, he created a beer with a dry, roasted edge. Irish dry stout was born, and Guinness bestrode the world. Modern stouts retain a smoky and acrid dry edge, though some stray into porter territory with a more luscious touch – excellent examples include Titanic Stout, Porterhouse's Wrasslers, Murphy's, and Rogue's Shakespeare Oatmeal Stout. Other variations on a dark theme include milk stout (sweetish and low in alcohol), imperial stout (ideal as an after-dinner drink and, for historical reasons, often called Imperial Russian Stout), and oatmeal stout (smooth and silky). Imperial stout was originally brewed with lots of hops and to a high alcohol content to withstand lengthy journeys on which an even temperature would be impossible to maintain. Samuel Smith's makes a good example, though, for intensity of flavour, it is hard to beat Rogue's Imperial Stout.

DARK MALTS Porter and stout use highly kilned dark malts that contain more caramelized sugar than lighter malts, and carry notes of bitter chocolate and coffee.

MODERN STOUTS Stouts such as the USA's Rogue Brewery expression feature lots of malty and fruity flavours, and notes of mocha coffee, chocolate, and even condensed milk.

BALTIC PORTER Baltic porters tend to be very strong, with an almost medicinal quality, as exemplified by the Polish Okocim Porter.

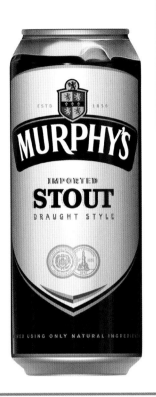

MURPHY'S

Lady's Well, Leitrim Street, Cork, County Cork, Ireland
www.murphys.com

The story has it that James J Murphy's 1856 brewery was financed by his Paris-based aunt, Marie-Louise Murphy, after she posed nude for painter Francois Boucher. Profound success followed, but trading difficulties arose in the 1970s. They were resolved only in 1983, when Heineken bought and proceeded to develop the Murphy's brand.

NORTH YORKSHIRE

Pinchinthorpe Hall, Pinchinthorpe, Guisborough, North Yorkshire, England TS14 8HG
www.nybrewery.co.uk

The brewery is housed in a former dairy at a moated country house hotel on the fringes of the North York Moors National Park. More than 20 organic beers are produced.

BREWING SECRET North Yorkshire uses natural spring water; that and the brewery's own yeast lends a distinctiveness to the beer.

OAKHAM

Maxwell Road, Woodston, Peterborough, Cambridgeshire, England PE2 7JB
www.oakhamales.com

Impressive growth from modest homebrew origins has led to the brewery now occupying its third site since 1993. The original owner sold the business in 1995 but the early vision and ambitions prevail.

BREWING SECRET American hop varieties with powerful floral characteristics are a feature of the range.

OKELL'S

Old Castletown Road, Kewaigue, Isle of Man, England IM2 1QG
www.okells.co.uk

Dr. William Okell's steam-powered brewery – which he designed himself in 1874 – was regarded as one of the most sophisticated in the world at the time. Okell's new plant, which it moved to in 1994, is the modern equivalent. It is controlled by computers rather than steam, but the passion and commitment to quality beer production remains unaltered.

MURPHY'S IRISH STOUT
STOUT 4% ABV
A beguiling aroma of roasted malt, coffee, and chocolate blends into a smooth, peaty sourness.

MURPHY'S IRISH RED
IRISH RED ALE 5.2% ABV
Nut, bread, and chocolate aromas develop creamy malt flavours and a degree of drying hoppiness.

FLYING HERBERT
STRONG BITTER 4.7% ABV
An assured full-flavoured bitter, with a grainy malt layer and fruit-influenced dry finish.

FOOL'S GOLD
STRONG BITTER 4.6% ABV
Premium, hoppy, and pale coloured, with bittersweet citrus notes throughout its well-defined flavour.

J.H.B. (JEFFREY HUDSON BITTER)
BITTER 4.2% ABV
Dominant citrus fruit hop aroma, which continues on the palate, blending into luscious malt flavours.

CITRA
GOLDEN ALE 4.2% ABV
A crisp, refreshing beer that oozes with grapefruit and even some peach flavours.

OKELL'S IPA
INDIA PALE ALE 4.5% ABV
Potential sweetness, offset by a high hopping regime for overall roundness, spiced by lemon notes.

OKELL'S BITTER
BITTER 3.7% ABV
Light coloured and complexly flavoured, with hints of honey and a long-lingering dry finish.

BREWERY

BEER

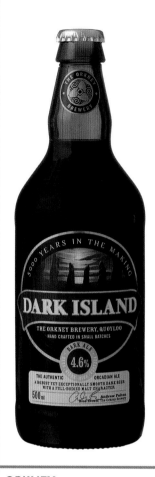

BREWERY

OLD LUXTERS

Henley-on-Thames, Oxfordshire,
England RG9 6JW
www.chilternvalley.co.uk

Part of Chiltern Valley Winery, Old
Luxters was set up in 1990 by David
Ealand, who was keen to revive
the tradition of farm-brewed ale.
The latest production technology
complements traditional practices.

BREWING SECRET This is the first
microbrewery with a royal warrant
of appointment to the Queen.

ORKNEY

Cawdor, Nairnshire,
Scotland IV12 5XP
www.sinclairbreweries.co.uk

Commendable ecological awareness
allows the brewery's waste water to
be filtered through two neighbouring
lochs that support fish and waterfowl.
It was first set up in 1988, and then
thoroughly modernized in 1994.
Recent expansions saw the addition
of a smart visitor centre and
shop, as well as the addition of
new brewing equipment.

OSSETT

Kings Yard, Low Mill Road, Ossett, West
Yorkshire, England WF5 8ND
www.ossett-brewery.co.uk

A lengthy career in some highly
respected breweries prepared owner
Bob Lawson perfectly for starting
his own business in 1997. Significant
expansion, driven by customer
demand for its light-coloured, florally
aromatic, and flavoursome ales, has
resulted in a new, purpose-built
brewery and expanding pub chain.

OTLEY

Unit 39, Albion Industrial Estate,
Pontypridd, Cilfynnydd, CF37 4NX,
Wales
www.otleybrewing.co.uk

Success has come quickly for this
brewery, which was founded in 2005,
and its beers have won many plaudits
for their use of spicy and aromatic
hops. Founder Nick Otley, a former
professional photographer, aims to
make Welsh ales with a difference.
He tries to locally source all his
beer ingredients.

BEER

BARN ALE

STRONG BITTER 5.4% ABV
Initially aromatic from its blend
of English hops, with a veneer of
savoury dried fruit.

WINTER ALE

WINTER ALE 5.4% ABV
Dark and flavoursome, it is a spicy
treat for a winter's evening.

DARK ISLAND

STRONG BITTER 4.6% ABV
Ruby-red and mysterious, with
blackcurrant fruit on the nose
and a full-roasted malt palate.

SKULL SPLITTER

BARLEY WINE 8.5% ABV
Forcefully malty nose; hints of
apple, spicy hop, and some nut
in the complex flavourings.

EXCELSIOR

STRONG BITTER 5.2% ABV
Fresh citrus floral aromas slip into
toffee mellowness, a full flavour,
and dry afterglow.

YORKSHIRE BLONDE

GOLDEN ALE 3.9% ABV
Low in bitterness, this full-bodied
beer is full of fruity hop flavours.

09 BLONDE

BLONDE ALE 4.8% ABV
A spicy, crystal clear wheat beer,
full of orange peel, coriander, and
clover flavours.

04 COLOMBO

GOLDEN ALE 4% ABV
American hops drive this beer,
which is favoured by serious
hopheads. Very bitter, it has
aromas of grass and herbs.

PALMERS

West Bay Road, Bridport, Dorset,
England DT6 4JA
www.palmersbrewery.com

Palmers is able to claim continuous
production on its original site over a
period of more than 200 years. From
the outside it has altered little, but this
is a contemporary brewing operation,
offering a diverse range of ales.

BREWING SECRET Maris Otter malted
barley and Golding hops combine
to give these beers their fruitiness.

RCH

Weston Super Mare, North Somerset,
England BS24 6RR
www.rchbrewery.com

Starting life in a hotel could never
have been easy, but the decision
was made to relocate when guests
started complaining about all the
water being used for brewing.
Now situated in a former cider mill,
continuous demand has prompted
brewhouse expansion and upgrading
to a 30-barrel (4,900-litre) plant.

RINGWOOD

Ringwood, Hampshire,
England BH24 3AP
www.ringwoodbrewery.co.uk

A brewery with the best of all birth
certificates – it was launched in 1978
by Peter Austin, the acknowledged
"father of British microbrewing".
Enthusiastic local support ensured it
outgrew its plant and premises, but
it remains unarguably the tidiest, most
efficient of operations. Marston's
acquired it in 2007, and continues to
develop its spirited potential further.

ROBINSON'S

Stockport, Cheshire,
England SK1 1JJ
www.robinsonsbrewery.com

One of the British Isles' largest regional
breweries, Robinson's began as the
Union Inn in 1838. Sixth-generation
family members are still in charge of its
development, overseeing huge advances
in brewing and bottling techniques.

BREWING SECRET Tradition continues
here, and the brewery still uses its
surviving 1920s yeast strain.

TALLY HO!

STRONG BITTER 5.5% ABV
Distinctly nutty and dark, with full-
bodied complexity emerging slowly,
then on to a lingering afterglow.

BEST BITTER

BEST BITTER 4.2% ABV
Styled on an India Pale Ale;
deliciously hoppy, with fruit
and malt undercurrents.

P.G. STEAM BITTER

BITTER 3.9% ABV
Complex and multi-layered, with
leafy hop aromas and a core flavour
of malt and fruit.

HEWISH IPA

INDIA PALE ALE 3.6% ABV
Lightly floral hopping, with a subtle
sweetness plus some malt and fruit
on the palate.

OLD THUMPER

STRONG BITTER 5.1% ABV
Peppered spice and apple aromas
develop rounded malt and caramel
flavours all the way to a fruity finish.

BEST BITTER

BEST BITTER 3.8% ABV
Tempting citrus aroma; slightly
tart, dry, and fruity flavours, with
an underlying malt sweetness.

OLD TOM

BARLEY WINE 8.5% ABV
Full bodied, with an aroma and
flavour alliance of malt, chocolate,
fruit, and port wine.

UNICORN

BEST BITTER 4.3% ABV
Golden, with some spicy hop and
malt on the nose, countered by a
bittersweet release.

BREWERY

ROOSTER'S

Wetherby Road, Knaresborough, North Yorkshire, England HG5 8LJ
www.roosters.co.uk

The rules are simple: unconditional care taken in the selection and preparation of raw materials is repaid in flavour. Beer is not an alcoholic commodity to master brewer Sean Franklin, but a serious sensory product, and inventive infusions of lychees, roses, coffee, grapefruit, and chocolate are teased from hop varieties.

RUDGATE

2 Centre Park, Marston Business Park, Tockwith, York, England YO26 7QF
www.rudgatebrewery.co.uk

More than 60 brewers' barrels (9,800 litres) are produced weekly from a former armoury building on the disused World War II Marston Moor airfield. "Special" ales are brewed each month, one on a Viking theme and another in the Brewer's Choice range, which encourages experimentation with hop flavours and idiosyncrasies.

ST. AUSTELL

63 Trevarthian Road, St. Austell, Cornwall, England PL25 4BY
www.staustellbrewery.co.uk

The enterprising spirit that drove Walter Hicks to mortgage his farm for £1,500 in 1851 and set up a brewery remains at the core of today's business. Many of his descendants are still with the company – in its estate of more than 170 pubs and in the brewery, which produces in excess of 86,500 barrels (118,000 hectolitres) annually.

ST. PETER'S

St. Peter South Elmham, Bungay, Suffolk, England NR35 1NQ
www.stpetersbrewery.co.uk

A custom-built brewery, St Peter's is laid out around a farm courtyard. Raw ingredients enter at one end; brewing proceeds along one side of the quadrangle, with fermentation, cask-filling, and bottling in neighbouring barns.

BREWING SECRET St. Peter's uses locally grown, floor-malted barley and water drawn from its own well.

BEER

YANKEE™
BITTER 4.3% ABV
Aromatic, softly bitter, with aromas of tropical fruit and Muscat grapes lingering alongside tangy malt.

WILD MULE
BITTER 3.9% ABV
New Zealand hops create a Sauvignon Blanc wine character in a remarkable and imposing beer.

BATTLE AXE
BITTER 4.2% ABV
A distinct hoppiness, with just-perceptible sweetness; complex fruit notes and significant aftertaste.

VIKING
BITTER 3.8% ABV
With a malt base, this is full and warming; then hop and fruit develop and linger in the finish.

PROPER JOB
INDIA PALE ALE 5.5% ABV
Full of flavour and packed with fresh hoppiness; the rounded palate arrives with veils of caramel.

TRIBUTE
BITTER 4.2% ABV
Specially grown Cornish Gold barley delivers a rich biscuit aroma, tempered by intense fruit flavours.

GOLDEN ALE
BITTER 4.7% ABV
Robust, with a strong hop bouquet and distinct, Czech lager-style malt and fruit balance.

BEST BITTER
BEST BITTER 3.7% ABV
Distinctly fruity, with caramel notes pushing its full-bodied complexity to a dry, hoppy finish.

SAMUEL SMITH

High Street, Tadcaster, North Yorkshire,
England LS24 9SB
www.samuelsmithsbrewery.co.uk

Tadcaster has three breweries, with
the enigmatic "Sam's" by far the
smallest – though it can rightly claim
to be Yorkshire's oldest. Its cask ales
are still served in pubs out of wooden
barrels and the brewery still brews
in traditional Yorkshire square
fermentation vessels made from
slate, which are said to give the beer
a distinctive edge. Brewing water is
supplied to the brewery from its
own wells. Sam's also owns Melbourn
Brothers brewery in Stamford,
Lincolnshire (www.allsaintsbrewery.
co.uk), a specialist in fruit beers that
are sold primarily to the US market.
The Stamford brewery was built
in 1825 and still uses steam power.
Much of the equipment dates back
to the Industrial Revolution of the
early 19th century.

SHARP'S

Rock, Cornwall,
England PL27 6NU
www.sharpsbrewery.co.uk

Becoming part of Molson Coors has
done nothing to diminish the creativity
or energy of Sharp's brewers, who
produce beers of great individuality.
Sharp's commendable approach to
sustainable energy and water recycling
is echoed by an energetic attitude,
which is inspiring for the future of
cask ale production.

SHEPHERD NEAME

17 Court Street, Faversham, Kent,
England ME13 7AX
www.shepherdneame.co.uk

It didn't take 12th-century monks
long to discover that Faversham's
pure spring water could be combined
with locally grown malting barley
to produce particularly fine ale.
When the town's mayor founded
a brewery in 1698 over an artesian
well, he launched the country's
longest-surviving brewery.
(Continues overleaf)

NUT BROWN ALE
BROWN ALE 5% ABV
A hazel-coloured speciality, with
a flavour profile of beech nuts,
almonds, and walnuts.

OLD BREWERY BITTER
BEST BITTER 4% ABV
A typical Northern malty bitter,
with a dash of hop and some fruit
on the palate.

ORGANIC STRAWBERRY
FRUIT BEER 5.1% ABV
A clean, fresh taste, with ripe fruit
flavours that quickly disappear into
a short, slightly tart finish.

ORGANIC APRICOT
FRUIT BEER 5.1% ABV
Deliciously dry, tartly fresh, with a
contrasting, well-balanced ripeness
lingering in the mouthfeel.

DOOM BAR
BITTER 4.3% ABV
Spicy resinous hop aromas and
sweet, delicate malts blend with
dried fruit and assertive bitterness.

ATLANTIC IPA
INDIA PALE ALE 4.8% ABV
Four hop varieties are added at
different stages to create candyfloss
aromas and crisp, delicate flavours.

SPITFIRE
PREMIUM BITTER 4.5% ABV
A underlying deep maltiness is
combined with a subtle hint of
toffee and boldly fruity citrus hops.

BISHOPS FINGER
STRONG BITTER 5.4% ABV
Generously fruity, with prominent
banana and pear flavours, a
biscuit-rich maltiness, and dried
fruit flavours.

BREWERY

(Continued) By 1864, through various partnerships, it was called Shepherd Neame. The community-focused company is still run by the Neame family, whose heritage and traditional values go hand-in-hand with contemporary standards of service and technological advances.

BREWING SECRET The brewery still makes use of mash tuns made from Russian teak, which were installed in 1914.

SLATER'S

St Alban's Road, Common Road Industrial Estate Stafford, England ST16 3DR
www.slatersales.co.uk

Expertise, enthusiasm, and 10 years' experience provided this family-run business with the confidence and ambition to open new premises in 2004, since when production has increased threefold. Numerous national and local awards were briefly eclipsed by an invitation to "guest" at the Strangers' Bar in the House of Commons in the UK Parliament.

SPRINGHEAD

Robin Hood Site, Main Street, Laneham, Retford, Notts, England DN22 0NA
www.springhead.co.uk

From being one of England's smallest microbreweries, Springhead has developed significantly through two massive expansions, highlighting how well the speciality ales sector is flourishing in the British Isles today. Now produced in a 50-barrel (8,300-litre) plant, Springhead beers are named with English Civil War themes in mind.

THEAKSTON

Masham, Ripon, North Yorkshire, England HG4 4YD
www.theakstons.co.uk

Ownership battles may have swept in numerous changes during its 180-year history but, fortunately today, tradition survives and thrives. Now returned to the Theakston family following Scottish & Newcastle's management, the company lives up to the name of its most famous beer – Old Peculier, a 12th-century word meaning "particular".

BEER

WHITSTABLE BAY ORGANIC ALE
BITTER 4.5% ABV
Organic barley and New Zealand hops orchestrate this elegant ale's bittersweet and floral flavours.

MASTER BREW BITTER
BITTER 4% ABV
Distinctly hoppy, well balanced, with a dusting of sweetness and a slight bitterness to the finish.

TOP TOTTY
BEST BITTER 4% ABV
A voluptuous aroma broadens into more complex hop notes, generous fruitiness, and rich malt infusions.

ORIGINAL
BITTER 4% ABV
A savoury malt aroma and ensuing succulent palate is countered by bitter, pepper-spiced hops.

MAID MARIAN
BLONDE ALE 4.5% ABV
A robust, full-flavoured beer. Pronounced citrus notes give way to a dry finish.

ROBIN HOOD BITTER
GOLDEN ALE 4.5% ABV
Easy drinking, with a long, dry finish, it's full of citrus and honey flavours.

OLD PECULIER
STRONG BITTER 5.6% ABV
Rich and deep, dark ruby in hue, with a mellow fruit aroma and a malty, full-bodied flavour.

BLACK BULL BITTER
BITTER 3.9% ABV
Bright amber coloured, with a crisp, dry palate weaving through citrus fruit flavours.

THORNBRIDGE

Riverside Brewery Buxton Road,
Bakewell, Derbyshire, England DE45 1GS
www.thornbridgebrewery.co.uk

Resounding success has followed from
the brewery's philosophy of being
"never ordinary". While brewing
heritage is of prime importance,
innovation, enthusiasm, experience,
and a commitment to creating
new and exciting recipes continue
to drive the business.

THWAITES

Daniel Thwaites PLC, Penny Street,
Blackburn, Lancashire, England BB1 6HL
www.thwaites.co.uk

Adaptation, modernization, and
progression have been watchwords
for more than two centuries. Dating
back to 1807, Thwaites remains
resolutely independent and family-
controlled – by descendants of its
founder, Daniel Thwaites. An estate
of more than 330 pubs reaches from
the Midlands to Cumbria.

TIMOTHY TAYLOR'S

Keighley, West Yorkshire,
England BD21 1AW
www.timothytaylor.co.uk

The Taylor family guides the
enterprise, as it has done since the
brewery's inception in 1858.

BREWING SECRET Pure Pennine water
from the brewery's own spring is a
natural companion to the Golden
Promise barley (also used extensively
for malt whisky); together, they
form the legendary "Taylor's taste".

TITANIC

Lingard Street, Burslem, Stoke-On-Trent,
Staffordshire, England ST6 1JL
www.titanicbrewery.co.uk

What began with brewing for
demonstration purposes on log-fired
Victorian equipment developed
into the production of in excess
of 2.3 million pints a year. Ecologically
friendly business practices – recycling
and conservation – are a priority. The
name is taken from the world's most
famous passenger ship, whose captain,
John Edward Smith, was born nearby.

JAIPUR
INDIA PALE ALE 5.9% ABV
Tantalizingly complex; emphasis
on citrus hoppiness; its powerful
length develops a bitter finish.

LORD MARPLES
BITTER 4% ABV
Easy-drinking bitter, with hints
of honey and caramel, and a long,
bitter afterglow.

LANCASTER BOMBER
BEST BITTER 4.4% ABV
Its inviting malty aroma is crossed
with floral hop and some fruit in
the flavour.

ORIGINAL
BITTER 3.6% ABV
A clean, dry-tasting, amber-glowing
bitter, with a citrus crispness and
firm malted base.

LANDLORD
PREMIUM BITTER 4.3% ABV
Complex hoppy aroma, well-
balanced spice and citrus fruit
flavours, tinged with biscuit malt.

BOLTMAKER
BEST BITTER 4% ABV
A full measure of maltiness
following citrus fruit, hoppy aromas
define an honest Yorkshire bitter.

STOUT
STOUT 4.5% ABV
Full roast, preserved fruit
aromas; the malt-influenced
palate accentuates more fruit
and liquorice tiers.

ICEBERG
WHEAT BEER 4.1% ABV
Golden in colour, soft floral flavours
give way to a long, hop citrus finish.

THE STORY OF...

Thornbridge

Thornbridge Hall, Ashford in the
Water, Derbyshire DE45 1NZ

For owner Jim Harrison, the idea of
founding a brewery in 2005 came shortly
after he and his wife Emma had bought
Thornbridge Hall, a stately home set in
100 acres of stunning parkland in the heart
of the Peak District in Derbyshire. "The
next step had to be to serve my own beer
in my own bar, reviving the tradition once
common of country house brewing."

But whereas many of Britain's new wave of
craft brewers are content with brewing
traditional English bitters, ordinary beer
isn't part of the Thornbridge mindset.
Unusually, an Italian head brewer, Stefano
Cossi, was appointed and an international
brewing team assembled, together drawing
on diverse brewing experiences and a wide
knowledge of ingredients – from herbs and
fruits to intriguing varieties of hops. An
example of this is the fruitily aromatic
Nelson Sauvin hop from New Zealand,
which is at the juicy heart of the Kipling
South Pacific Pale Ale.

In 2010, the state-of-the-art Riverside
Brewery was opened in nearby Bakewell.
It is here that most of the company's
production now happens. However,
the Hall brewery is still used for
exploring the boundaries of beer.

▲ **THORNBRIDGE HALL** The grand manor house
acts as an impressive beacon for the brewery, and also
houses the brewery's bar for hosting special events.

▶ **WORKSHOP** The brewery itself is located
in an old stonemason's and joiner's workshop,
in the grounds of the hall.

◀ **CONDITIONING ROOM**
The conditioning tanks – partly
reclaimed vessels that came
from Scottish & Newcastle –
are where the beers settle and
mature for between one and
two weeks. Thornbridge is
experimenting with far longer
maturation periods, and a barley
wine called Alliance has been
conditioning for 12 months.

▶ BREWING LABORATORY

Some of the UK's most innovative beers are created at Thornbridge. The brewing team is small, and made up mostly of qualified food technologists. This brings a more scientific approach to the methods of beer production. Plans are already underway to expand the brewing plant, while the current three-room brewery will become a brewing laboratory for trialling new beers.

▲ **HERB GARDEN** The philosophy of Thornbridge is to brew small batches of original beers using the finest raw materials. Sometimes this means the inclusion of local plants, fruits, and herbs, such as elderflower, sage, and nettle, to add new notes to the chorus of flavours. The hall has a walled garden where herbs and other plants are being grown specifically for this purpose.

▲ **CASK CONDITIONING** One of the latest Thornbridge ventures is to condition beers in wooden casks previously used to hold whisky. Saint Petersburg's Imperial Russian Stout was condition finished in whisky barrels from three distinct whisky regions, each lending its own characteristics to the beer. The Speyside Reserve has a dry, herbal edge, with an astringent finish; the Highland Reserve has a sweeter grassy palate; while the Islay Reserve has a bold peaty and marvellously smoky finish.

◀ **THE CRICKET INN** Thornbridge has the lease of a number of pubs locally, including The Cricket Inn in Totley, near Sheffield, which marries great food with a range of Thornbridge beers, including the award-winning Jaipur IPA, the even fruitier Kipling, the more bitter-edged Lord Marples, and Cricketers, a bitter brewed just for the pub.

BREWERY

TRADITIONAL SCOTTISH ALES

Bandeath, Stirling, Scotland FK7 7NP
www.traditionalscottishales.com

Possibly the only brewery in the world to occupy a former torpedo factory, TSA developed out of Bridge of Allan Brewery, which already had an impressive portfolio of ales.

BREWING SECRET King James IV of Scotland purchased beer for his coronation in 1488 from the old Tullibardine brewery (now a whisky distillery).

TRAQUAIR

Innerleithen, Peeblesshire, Scotland EH44 6PW
www.traquair.co.uk

The 18th-century brewing equipment in a house where Bonnie Prince Charlie once sought refuge remained untouched until their rediscovery in 1965. Since then, they have been put to use for brewing in authentic style.

BREWING SECRET Unusually in this day and age, Traquair's beers are fermented in oak over a seven-day period.

TRING

Tring, Hertfordshire, England HP23 6AF
www.tringbrewery.co.uk

Since the brewery was founded in 1992, Tring has earned increasing success through a commitment to quality. The beers' names are unusual – Side Pocket for a Toad is local parlance for something useless – and the pumpclip illustrations originate as watercolours.

BREWING SECRET Besides the core and seasonal ranges, Tring produces monthly "specials" to trial new recipes.

WADWORTH

Devizes, Wiltshire, England SN10 1JW
www.wadworth.co.uk

Established by Henry Wadworth, the brewery began producing beer in 1875 and was expanded 10 years later into an impressive, red-brick Victorian tower brewery. The original open cooper is still operational and wooden casks are used for local deliveries. A full-time cooper and a team of dray horses continue traditional customs.

BEER

BEN NEVIS
INDIA PALE ALE 4% ABV
A ruby-red, traditional Scottish 80-shilling ale, with succulent malt matched by light hop flavours.

1488 WHISKY ALE
SPECIALITY STRONG BITTER 7% ABV
Matured in malt whisky casks, it is peppery and slightly smoky, with a whisky-chased edge.

TRAQUAIR HOUSE ALE
BARLEY WINE 7.2% ABV
A dark and oaky winter brew, with ripe malt, fruit cake, and sweet sherry mystique.

TRAQUAIR JACOBITE ALE
BARLEY WINE 8% ABV
Herbal notes from the use of coriander warm the bittersweet chocolate and port wine flavours.

SIDE POCKET FOR A TOAD
BITTER 3.6% ABV
Distinct citrus notes appear through a floral aroma and crisp, dry, well-balanced palate.

DEATH OR GLORY
BARLEY WINE 7.2% ABV
A sipping beer, it is strong, dark, and full of dark fruit flavours.

6X
BEST BITTER 4.3% ABV
A malt and fruit nose, with restrained hop characteristics developing an intensity on the palate.

SWORDFISH
ALE 5% ABV
Pussers Rum adds to the intensity of this full-flavoured, copper-coloured ale.

WELLS & YOUNG'S

Bedford, Bedfordshire, England MK40 4LU
www.charleswells.co.uk
www.wellsandyoungs.co.uk

A major force in British brewing was created in 2006 from the partnership of London brewer Young's and Bedford-based Charles Wells, two of the most prodigiously accomplished operators in the industry. Charles Wells founded his brewery in 1876, and, five generations later, it remains family owned. When the companies merged, Young's left its London-based Ram Brewery, where brewing had been recorded on the site since 1551. Wells & Young's cask and bottled ale portfolio is one of the broadest in the brewing sector, particularly after Courage brands – Best Bitter and Directors Bitter – were added in 2007 under an agreement with Scottish & Newcastle.

BREWING SECRET Heavy on crystal malt, Well's Bombardier uses Challenger and Goldings hops for its fruity palate and spicy nose.

WENTWORTH

Wentworth, South Yorkshire, England S62 7TF
www.wentworthbrewery.co.uk

Water is drawn from the independent brewery's own spring and, indeed, part of the business is bottling this water in natural form. An extensive range of beer is offered, covering all the major styles, with strikingly labelled, monthly "seasonal" ales a speciality. A 2006 refurbishment has allowed production to increase dramatically.

WESTERHAM

Grange Farm, Pootings Road, Crockham Hill, Kent, England TN8 6SA
www.westerhambrewery.co.uk

When Robert Wicks founded the Westerham brewery in 2004, it brought brewing, which had ceased when the Black Eagle Brewery was closed in 1965, back to the town. The brewery uses many of the Black Eagle's original recipes, having tracked down its yeast at the National Collection of Yeast Cultures.

WELLS BOMBARDIER
PREMIUM BITTER 4.7% ABV
Powerful citrus hop aromas meet malt and dried fruit in a richly complex medley.

EAGLE IPA
INDIA PALE ALE 3.6% ABV
Preposterously flavour-packed, with malt and ripe apple sweetness, belying its relatively low strength.

YOUNG'S BITTER
BITTER 4.5% ABV
Well balanced, with citrus hop notes and enough malt for a flowery and bready finish.

YOUNG'S SPECIAL
BEST BITTER 4.5% ABV
Sweet hop aroma, but a robust malt and hop arrangement persists throughout layers of toffee.

WPA (WOPPA)
PALE ALE 4% ABV
An India Pale Ale-style beer, with teeming hoppiness and a bitterness that leans towards astringency.

OATMEAL STOUT
STOUT 4.8% ABV
Touted as "deeply delicious", this dark persuader revels in layers of roast malt, toffee, and chocolate.

FREEDOM ALE
PALE ALE 4.8% ABV
Emboldened by tropical fruit and barley sugar flavours, it has a full-bodied, biscuit malt finish.

SPIRIT OF KENT
GOLDEN ALE 4% ABV
Golden to the eye, a biscuit malty crispness partners some majestic citrus and floral notes.

BREWERY

WICKWAR

The Old Brewery, Station Road, Wickwar, Gloucester, GL12 8NB
www.wickwarbrewing.co.uk

A million-pound refurbishment has hoisted Wickwar from microbrewery status to regional heights, increasing its brewing capacity almost fourfold. Beers are matured in below-ground vaults at the former Arnold Perret & Co Brewery. The export market is an increasing area of interest, with encouraging European sales.

WILLIAM BROTHERS

New Alloa Brewery, Kelliebank, Alloa, Scotland FK10 1NU
www.williamsbrosbrew.com

Alloa was once second only to Burton upon Trent as a brewing centre, so it is encouraging to observe innovative beer styles still being developed there. Historic recipes and traditional folklore methods are skilfully applied.

BREWING SECRET In the Fraoch Ale, flowering heather is used instead of hops, reviving an ancient Celtic recipe.

WILLIAM WORTHINGTON'S

Horninglow Street Burton upon Trent, DE14 1NG, United Kingdom
www.worthingtonsale.com

Stefano Cossi, the creator of Thornbridge's Jaipur, has now taken on the mantle of brewing White Shield, a famed, historic bottle-conditioned beer, from the legendary Steve Wellington. The brewery, which dates to 1920, was reopened in 1995 as a museum in order to recreate discontinued Bass ales, and is now developing its own beers.

WOODFORDE'S

Woodbastwick, Norwich, Norfolk, England NR13 6SW
www.woodfordes.co.uk

Now on its third site, the brewery continues to increase production capacity and to broaden its ambitions. A tremendous local following has developed, and the country's top awards have been accrued – even for the beermats. Underpinning all this is high-quality water, which comes bubbling from an on-site borehole.

BEER

STATION PORTER
PORTER 6.1% ABV
Richly smooth, with roast coffee, chocolate, and dried fruits combining with complex spiced flavours.

BANKERS DRAFT
GOLDEN ALE 4% ABV
A distinctive citrus aroma partners with full-bodied biscuit malt flavour.

FRAOCH HEATHER ALE
SPECIALITY BITTER 5% ABV
Abundantly floral and aromatic, with a spicy mint piquancy, malty character, and whiff of peat.

KELPIE SEAWEED ALE
SPECIALITY BITTER 4.4% ABV
Organic barley from coastal farms and bladderwrack seaweed in the mash produce beguiling flavours.

WHITE SHIELD
INDIA PALE ALE 5.6% ABV
Enthusiasts appreciate its hop attack, its smokiness, treacle toffee sweetness, dusting of paprika, and serving of fried banana, stilton cheese, and sliced apple.

WHERRY
BITTER 3.8% ABV
Floral and citrus fruit aromas unlock a malt-infused middle, then a sustained finish.

NORFOLK NOG
OLD ALE 4.6% ABV
Deep red, with a roasted malt background developing through liquorice nuances and dried fruit.

WYCHWOOD

Eagle Maltings, The Crofts, Witney, Oxfordshire, England OX28 4DP
www.wychwood.co.uk

Striking beers and striking imagery quickly developed a huge fan base and younger market for traditional ales when Wychwood launched the celebrated Hobgoblin in bottles in 1996. The brewery is now part of Marston's, who has done nothing to inhibit the individuality of the Wychwood branding.

WYE VALLEY

Stoke Lacy, Herefordshire, England HR7 4HG,
www.wyevalleybrewery.co.uk

One of the first of a new wave of brewers in England, it was founded in 1985 by ex-Guinness brewer Peter Amor. It was hardly surprising that one of the first beers he brewed was a now much-acclaimed stout, Dorothy Goodbody's. Peter's son Vernon now runs the company.

WYLAM

Heddon-on-the-Wall, Newcastle upon Tyne, England NE15 0EZ
www.wylambrewery.co.uk

Production capacity was tripled in 2006 with a 20-barrel (3,200-litre) investment in the then six-year-old farm-based premises. An oil-fired steam generator proves that 19th-century technology can adapt to state-of-the-art beer production. Several industry awards have reinforced its reputation.

YORK

12 Toft Green, York, North Yorkshire, England YO1 6JT
www.york-brewery.co.uk

The phrase central to the company's philosophy is "professionally managed in a fun atmosphere" – and York manages to be an extremely well-run brewery and a tourist attraction at the same time. Visitor-friendly galleries overlook a much-expanded brewhouse with its 20-barrel capacity (3,200 litres), 10 conditioning tanks, and five fermenters.

KING GOBLIN
ALE 6.6% ABV
Rich and strong, it is reputedly only brewed when there's a full moon!

HOBGOBLIN
STRONG BITTER 5.2% ABV
Hefty in roasted chocolate and toffee malt flavours, with moderate hoppy bitterness and fruitness.

DOROTHY GOODBODY'S WHOLESOME STOUT
STOUT 4.6% ABV
Full of roasted and bitter flavours, it has a satisfying smooth, almost creamy, finish.

BUTTY BACH
GOLDEN ALE 4.5% ABV
Named after the Welsh word for "little friend", it's full of the swirling, fruity aromas of Herefordshire hops.

WYLAM ROCKET
STRONG BITTER 5% ABV
Copper-hued strong bitter with memorable malt fruitiness and pleasant hop bitterness that lingers.

WYLAM GOLD TANKARD
BITTER 4% ABV
Abundantly hoppy golden ale, with layers of malt and hints of citrus in the finish.

YORKSHIRE TERRIER
BITTER 4.2% ABV
An assertive bitterness is tempered by fruit and hop aromas, audacious flavours, and a hoppy finish.

CENTURION'S GHOST ALE
STRONG BITTER 5.4% ABV
Dark ruby, warming, and mellow, with a roasted malt complexion livened by autumn fruit flavours.

Worthington's White Shield, a cult beer for ale lovers, is a British bottle-conditioned pale ale.

Buggenhoot
Bosteels
De Landtsheer

Bosteels

Brugge
Halve Maan
Smisje

Halve Maan

Watou
Van Eecke
Sint Bernardus

Sint Bernardus

Oudenaarde
Liefmans
Roman

Liefmans

De Ko

Van Steenberge

Proefbrouwerij

Palm

Duvel Moortg

OOST-VLAANDEREN

De Dolle Brouwers   Urthel

De Struise

WEST-
VLAANDEREN

Westvleteren

Rodenbach

Vanhonsebrouck

Bavik

Alvinne

Bockor

Verhaeghe

Huyghe

Sint Canarus

Contreras

Cnudde

Glazen Toren

De Ryck

Van Den Bossche

Slaghmuylder

Affligem

Morte Subite

Girardin

De la Senr

Timmermans   Cantillon

BRUSSELS

Lindemans

De Cam

Drie Fonteinen

Boon

Hanssens Artisan

De Ranke

De Struise

Cazeau

Ellezelloise

Lefebvre

BRABA
WALL

Légendes   Silly/Mynsbrughen

Dubuisson/
Vapeur   Dupont

Brunehaut

HAINAUT

Ecaussinnes

Belgoo

La Binchoise

Abbaye Des Rocs

Brootcoorens

Silenrieux

Chimay

Westmalle

Achel

ANTWERPEN

Westmalle

Strubbe

LIMBURG

Loterbol

VLAAMS
BRABANT

Domus Huisbrouwerij

Kerkom

Hoegaarden

Grain D'orge
Val-dieu

LIÈGE

Bellevaux

Bocq

NAMUR

Fantôme

Caracole

Rochefort

Achouffe

LUXEMBOURG

Orval

Rulles

Orval

Sainte-Hélène

Orval

BELGIUM

Abbey ales, witbiers, lambics, gueuze, kriek –
Belgians have a staggering choice of beer styles for
the size of the country, and many more regional
variations are available to add subtlety to the
selection process of a connoisseur. And Belgians
certainly are connoisseurs when it comes to beer.
They choose it much as the French choose wine:
the right style and weight for the right occasion.

This map shows where some of the breweries
are based, with pullout boxes where a city or
town has more than one brewery.

Bellevaux

BREWERY

ABBAYE DES ROCS

37, Chaussée Brunehault, 7387
Montignies-sur-Roc, Belgium
www.abbaye-des-rocs.com

Jean-Pierre Eloir, a former exciseman,
took up brewing in 1979. The
business has since expanded, with
the beers gaining a good reputation,
particularly abroad, and some are now
being developed with export in mind.

BREWING SECRET Core beers are true to
the spiced and well-bodied Walloon
style; keg beers are often unfiltered.

ACHEL

Saint Benedictusabdij De Achelse Kluis
5556 VE Valkenswaard, Belgium
www.achelskluis.org

At a time when there were many
brewery closures, the Belgian beer
world had cause to celebrate in 1998.
That was when De Achelse Kluis –
a Trappist abbey on the Dutch border
– started brewing again after 84
unproductive years! It is run as a
pub-brewery, and draws in many
passing walkers and cyclists.

ACHOUFFE

Rue du Village, 32,
6666 Achouffe, Belgium
www.achouffe.be

One of the first new-wave micros,
Achouffe was set up in 1982 by two
Flemish and Walloon brothers-in-law.
In doing so, they started an unlikely
success story, finalized in the takeover
by Moortgat, the brewers of Duvel.
Prior to that, Achouffe had already
expanded into foreign markets in
Europe and elsewhere.

AFFLIGEM

Ringlaan 18, 1745 Opwijk, Belgium
www.affligembeer.be

Brouwerij De Smedt was a well-
established family brewery, especially
known for its Affligem abbey range,
when in 1999 mondial brewer
Heineken stepped in to streamline
the brews – and change its name.

BREWING SECRET Affligem Blond is
the staple, but specialists prefer the
Paters Vat Postel abbey range, formerly
made at defunct Campina Brewery.

BEER

BLANCHE DES HONNELLES
WITBIER 6% ABV
Not your usual wheat beer, this one
is made from malted barley, malted
wheat, and home-malted oats.

ABBAYE DES ROCS BRUNE
BELGIAN DARK STRONG ALE 9% ABV
Very spiced and sustaining, with
a nourishing touch. Well-liked
in Anglo-Saxon countries.

ACHEL BRUIN 8°
TRAPPIST BEER 8% ABV
More than the draft beers on tap,
this is a classic Trappist brew; heavy,
estery, and filling.

ACHEL EXTRA BRUIN
DARK TRAPPIST 9.5% ABV
The flagship of brewmaster Knops
– who refuses to drink anything
else; rich and rewarding.

MC CHOUFFE
SCOTCH ALE 8% ABV
Scotch ale is a tradition in Wallonia.
This is the Chouffe version, with
Belgian spicing and high strength.

LA CHOUFFE
BLONDE ALE 8% ABV
A bottle-conditioned staple beer:
sweet, bitterish, and spicy. A real
classic, and much praised.

POSTEL DOBBEL
ABBEY ALE 7% ABV
This estery brown "double"
abbey ale possesses chocolate
notes, and a dry finish.

POSTEL BLOND
ABBEY ALE 6.8% ABV
Alcohol warming, its flavours
are rounded, smooth, and
sweet, rather than bitter.

BELGIUM'S BEST-SELLING BEERS

For the enthusiast, Belgium is the country of unique and beguiling beers, but the vast majority of beer consumed there is bottom-fermented lager, locally known as "pils".

The brand of pils best-known abroad is Stella Artois, but in Belgium itself Jupiler is much more frequently seen. However, both hail from the same giant Anheuser-Busch InBev. The InBev part of the company was itself the result of the 2004 merger of Belgium's (largely family-owned) Interbrew and South American AmBev. Anheuser-Busch InBev owns different breweries all over the world, including several in Belgium, the two main ones being in Leuven and Jupille-sur-Meuse. Apart from the oceans of rather dull pils, they also offer an extensive range of other beer types, including the well-known Leffe range of abbey ales and the more-or-less "lambic-y" Belle-Vue beers (gueuze and different fruit concoctions). Thanks to their universal availability, they are often mistaken abroad – and indeed in Belgium itself – for being Belgium's best. The Alken-Maes brewing group owns the popular Grimbergen range.

JUPILER (PILS 5.2% ABV) *left*
STELLA ARTOIS (PILS 5.2% ABV)
LEFFE (ABBEY ALE 6.6% ABV) *centre*
BELLE-VUE KRIEK (CHERRY-LAMBIC 4.3% ABV) *right*
BELLE-VUE GUEUZE (FILTERED GUEUZE 5.5% ABV)
GRIMBERGEN BLOND (ABBEY ALE 6.7% ABV)
GRIMBERGEN DUBBEL (ABBEY ALE 6.5% ABV)

ALVINNE

Vaartstraat 4a 8552 Moen/Zwevegem
West Vlaanderen, Belgium
www.alvinne.be

Davy Spiessens and Glenn Castelein started as home-brewers, going professional in the smallest way possible – in a shed in the garden. Word got around about the quality of their beer, however, and in 2007 they moved to Heule. Their range of beers is constantly evolving, while others they produce have been specially commissioned.

GASPAR

WINTER ALE 8% ABV
A real connoisseurs' beer, Gaspar is a hoppy treat – and pretty strong!

BALTHAZAR

TRIPLE 11% ABV
Cardamom, ginger, and coriander all vie for attention in this dark, spicy beer.

HET ANKER

Guido Gezellelaan 49,
2800 Mechelen, Belgium
www.hetanker.be

Now here's a brewery with a history. The owners claim it began in 1369, but it was in 1873 that the family Van Breedam took over and began its modern brewing age. In the 1990s, the end for the classic Gouden Carolus seemed near, but a family buy-out from the ill-fated RIVA empire succeeded, and now the brewery is once more productive and innovative.

GOUDEN CAROLUS CLASSIC

STRONG DARK ALE 8.5% ABV
This malt bomb has a characteristic taste of raisins in portwine. An exemplarily strong, dark Belgian ale.

GOUDEN CAROLUS CHRISTMAS

STRONG DARK ALE 10.5% ABV
The raisins and molasses from the Carolus Classic are present, but with a greater alcohol kick.

BAVIK

Rijksweg 33, B-8531 Bavikhove –
Harelbeke, Belgium
www.bavik.be

With the fourth generation of the De Brabandere family, this brewery is run efficiently and encompasses a large number of tied pubs too.

BREWING SECRET Abbey ales and pilsners form an important role in the annual output (especially to supermarkets), but the most interesting brews are in the oud bruin tradition.

PETRUS OUD BRUIN (DARK)

OUD BRUIN 5.5% ABV
Recently, the brewery invested in giant wooden barrels for fermenting this vinous, quite traditional ale.

PETRUS AGED PALE

OUD BRUIN 7.3% ABV
In the new barrels, you'll find this: undiluted pale beer, ageing for years, gaining sourish, fruity notes.

BREWERY

BELLEVAUX
5, Bellevaux, 4960 Malmedy,
Belgium
www.brasseriedebellevaux.be

Though the name doesn't give anything away, this Walloon brewery is actually run by a Dutchman! In a true idyllic setting, this brand-new brewery has very modern equipment. Wil Schuwer doesn't like to do things half-heartedly, and his beers are the result of extensive and careful experimentation.

LA BINCHOISE
38, Faubourg Saint Paul,
7130 Binche, Belgium
www.brasserielabinchoise.be

Situated in the Hainaut province, this brewery was started in 1987 by André Graux. New management took over in 2001, and while they might have a more commercial agenda, La Binchoise is still worth a visit, both for the brewery tap and for the developing range of beers.

BOCKOR
Kwabrugstraat 5, B-8510
Bellegem, Belgium
www.bockor.be

This brewery is probably best known for its Jacobins (would-be lambics that use spontaneous fermentation). However, the brewery turns out a whole range of other beers, not in the least a traditional style oud bruin, created by former head brewer Omer Vander Ghinste. Founded in 1892, it is still family owned.

BOCQ
4, Rue de la Brasserie,
B-5530 Purnode, Belgium
www.bocq.be

One of the few breweries in the Namur province, Brasserie du Bocq is actually one of the larger Belgian regionals, not in the least because of the commission brewing side of the business. However, a few of Bocq's own brews are well known nationally, including the Gauloise range, the Saison 1858, and their witbier. All of its beers are top-fermented and

BEER

BELLEVAUX BLACK
OLD ALE 6.3% ABV
Nearly every taster would agree that the Black is Bellevaux's most interesting beer. Though fruity in character, it is simultaneously very dry.

BIÈRE DES OURS
FLAVOURED ALE 8.4% ABV
Bears know why: honey! Another traditional ingredient for Belgian speciality ales.

BELGO MAGUS
WITBIER 6.6% ABV
Bottle conditioned, it is a golden, sweet, spiced beer, full of dark fruit, orange, and yeast flavours.

VANDERGHINSTE OUD BRUIN
MIXED FERMENTATION BEER 5.5% ABV
Oud bruin relies both on wild and cultivated yeasts. The result, a beer in which flavours of berries, wood, and lactic sourness abound.

BLANCHE DE NAMUR
WITBIER 4.5% ABV
A cloudy, yellow, and very smooth wheat beer, with overtones of coriander and bitter orange.

SAISON 1858
SAISON 6.4% ABV
Unfiltered and cloudy, it's a classic marriage of citrus bitterness and refreshment.

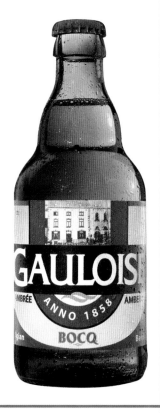

are living beers, meaning they still contain yeast when put into a bottle. In recent years, the brewery has won many prestigious awards for its beers.

BOON
Fonteinstraat 65, B1502
Lembeek, Belgium
www.boon.be

In 1975, when lambic-based beers and lambic brewers were dying out, Frank Boon took over the De Vits range. Deemed crazy, he still proves his detractors wrong by constantly growing and improving his business.

BREWING SECRET Most Boon beers are deemed "oud", meaning "in the old style" of unadulterated lambics.

BOSTEELS
Kerkstraat 96, 9255
Buggenhout, Belgium
www.bestbelgianspecialbeers.be

It is now the seventh generation of the Bosteels family that owns and runs this brewery. In recent times, they have shown a flair for flowing with fashion – not only in the beers but also in the spectacular glassware.

BREWING SECRET Tripel Karmeliet, one of the flagship beers, uses three grains in the mash: barley, wheat, and oats.

BRUNEHAUT
17, Rue des Panneries,
7623 Brunehaut, Belgium
www.brunehaut.com

In another part of Brunehaut village known as Guignies, Brasserie Allard & Groetembril had operated until 1990. That place closed, but, less than a year later, a new page was turned when the owners opened this brewery in Rogny. They have a broad range of regional beers, and are now producing a range of organic and gluten-free beers. (Continues on p196)

LA GAULOISE AMBRÉE
SPÉCIALE BELGE 5.5% ABV
The beer's liquorice and citrus peel flavours, together with the hops, clearly reveal it's Walloon character.

GEUZE MARIAGE PARFAIT
GUEUZE 8% ABV
"Perfect marriage", meaning the lambics, of course, resulting in the brewers' favourite dry gueuze.

BOON OUDE KRIEK
KRIEKEN 6.5% ABV
A fully unsweetened krieken (sour cherry) lambic, which makes it a delight for the tongue and eyes.

TRIPEL KARMELIET
ABBEY TRIPLE 8% ABV
Smoked and spicy nose announces a malt-dominated brew with a roasted character – unusual for a pale beer.

DEUS BRUT DES FLANDRES
BELGIAN STRONG ALE 11.5% ABV
The Dom Perignon lookalike bottle shows that this is aimed at upmarket drinkers; dry and spritzy.

ST. MARTIN ABBEY BLOND
BELGIAN ALE 8% ABV
Full mouthed with a malty sweetness, it is balanced by a florid, hoppy bitterness.

BRUNEHAUT BLANCHE
BELGIAN WITBIER 5% ABV
This gluten free beer has a fragrant nose, with hints of fresh flowers.

BEER STYLES

WILD BEERS

The Belgian brewery of Cantillon seems from another time, a world away from the gleaming stainless-steel brewing behemoths that pump out millions of hectolitres of mass-market lager. Here, beer is brewed using spontaneous fermentation, a process that harks back to the very dawn of brewing. After the wort has been produced, it is left overnight in massive cooling trays high up in the eaves of the brewery. During this time, wild yeasts drift in through holes in the roof and trigger the fermentation process. Once this is underway, the fermenting beer is transferred to oak and chestnut barrels, lined up in a dark and musty smelling room, to undergo a "long sleep". This ancient way of brewing has survived in the Payottenland region, close to Brussels in Belgium, and the beers produced here and in this way are known as lambics.

If the variety of beer styles is a family, then lambic and its other wild cousins must surely be the mad relations of the brood. Letting wild yeast, or *Brettanomyces* (Brett), infect the newly brewed wort is anathema to the majority of brewers; unpredictable and requiring great skill and experience to handle, it creates sour and challenging flavours. Yet the technique has not only continued and flourished in this corner of Belgium, it has gone on to influence brewers around the world in recent years.

LAMBIC This is one of the most challenging beers in the world. When young, it is sharp and acidic, somewhat reminiscent of a very dry English West Country cider. When aged, the effect is a more complex interplay of toasty, earthy, zesty, fruity flavours, and an assertive sourness. Some lambics have distinct grapefruit notes on the nose and palate.

GUEUZE Fresh lambics are blended with their more mellow elders, which have been ageing in wooden barrels for a year or more, to create Gueuze. This is the Champagne of the beer world – sprightly, elegant, sparkling.

AMERICAN WILD ALE Brewers in the USA have also begun brewing with wild yeasts, usually in conjunction with wooden barrels, producing ales even more quenchingly sour than their Belgian forefathers. Glacier Brewhouse in Alaska and Russian River in California are two of the keenest exponents.

The Delirium bar in Brussels stocks somewhere in the range of 2,000 different beers, 400 of which are from Belgium.

BREWERY

(*Continued from p193*) The brewery says its motto is "an alliance of modernity and tradition". It brews several historic beers in a state-of-the-art 21st-century brewery.

CANTILLON

Gheudestraat 56, 1070 Brussel, Belgium
www.cantillon.be

As early as 1900, the Cantillon family had beer-blending facilities here, in the old southern suburbs of Brussels. In 1970, Jean-Pierre Van Roy, who had married Claude Cantillon, took over the business, despite not being a brewer. Even though his background was not in beer, he turned into the staunchest defender of old-style brewing without compromises.

His son Jean, who now does most of the brewing, however, has shown that the brewery is not averse to experimentation, and recent years have seen the use of fresh hops, and even American C-hops – both anathema to the lambic tradition.

BREWING SECRET Cantillon's range of fruit beers uses whole fruit rather than being syrup based.

CARACOLE

86, Côte Marie-Thérèse, 5500 Falmignoul, Belgium
www.brasserie-caracole.be

Started in around 1990, Caracole moved after a few years from Namur to the present location. The brewery offers beers in two varieties: a "normal", and a "bio" (organic) version. Caracole means "snail", and production isn't rushed – but the beers are enjoying growing international recognition.

BEER

BRUNEHAUT BIO BLANCH
WITBIER 5% ABV
An organic wheat beer. A hop bitterness gives way to a short, dry finish.

GUEUZE
ORGANIC LAMBIC 5% ABV
Nose of citrus, horse blanket, wood, and hay; woody flavours, with green fruit and some sulphur; sour and tart in mouthfeel.

LOU PEPE FRAMBOISE
FRUIT BEER 5.5% ABV
A mix of lambic beer with a pure sugar solution. One of the most intense fruit beers on earth.

IRIS
SPÉCIALE BELGE 5% ABV
Lots of hops on the nose: cheesy, aged ones, and fresh, aromatic ones. Quite fruity, with a hoppy finish.

ST LAMVINUS
FRUIT BEER 5.5% ABV
Wet wood, sour fruit, sulphur, and horse-blanket aromas. The fruit is very prominent, but it is difficult to distinguish the grapes that are used.

TROUBLETTE BIO
WITBIER 5.5% ABV
A fully organic Belgian white, with no excess coriander, but a fine citrussy and refreshing finish.

NOSTRADAMUS
BELGIAN DARK ALE 9.5% ABV
Caracole's strong dark ale is a mix of roasted, fruity, malty, and higher alcohol notes.

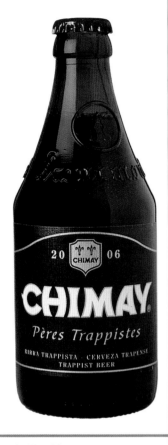

CHIMAY

8, Route Charlemagne,
6464 Baileux, Belgium
www.chimay.com

Though the bottling is done in Baileux, the brewery is still in the monastery at Forges-les-Chimay. Since 1861, monks have brewed here, but Chimay became the leading Trappist brewery through Père Theodore, who went to Leuven University to study brewing in a contemporary way. Chimay never stopped growing, and is vital to the economy of the region.

CONTRERAS

Molenstraat 110, B-9890
Gavere, Belgium
www.contreras.be

Contreras is an unlikely brewing survivor. When Willy Contreras retired, his daughter could not see her future in brewing, but in 2001 her husband, Frederik De Vrieze, took the business in hand. He set out on a straightforward modernizing path, and the first beer to benefit from the revamp was the breweries' top offering, Mars.

DE DOLLE BROUWERS

Roeselarestraat 12B,
8600 Esen, Belgium
www.dedollebrouwers.be

By buying and renewing the old Costenoble Brewery in the far west of Belgium in 1980, Kris Herteleer and his two brothers started, unknowingly, the country's microbrewery revolution. Fame soon reached international quarters – but then the "mad brewers" never searched for simplicity, a quiet life,

or easy money. "Quality does the trick" is the motto of Kris – the only remaining brewer of the original three. Adding to the complexity are the beer names, virtually all of which use Dutch wordplay of some sort.

BREWING SECRET Kris also makes specially oak-aged versions of some of his beers, dubbed "Réserva". They fetch vertiginous prices, are rare, and rather difficult to hunt down.

GRANDE RÉSERVE/CHIMAY BLEUE
BELGIAN STRONG ALE 9% ABV
Roasted malts, with some quite dominant bitterness, and dark, ripe fruit (plums, blue grapes), and pears.

CHIMAY TRIPEL
ABBEY ALE 8% ABV
Sweet, grapey taste, with bittering hops and herbal qualities; not entirely unlike a dry white wine.

CONTRERAS' ESPECIAL MARS
BELGIAN AMBER ALE 6.5% ABV
Mars is brewed with March water, which according to the lore of the brewery is "in bloom", and therefore creates a better beer. It used to be a dry, metallic oud bruin, but today is more of a classic Belgian amber ale – moderate acidity on top of crystal and amber malt sweetness. Creamy, but not full bodied.

ARABIER
BELGIAN PALE STRONG ALE 8% ABV
A dry-hopped, citrussy beer that can age beautifully to a potent brew.

STILLE NACHT
SEASONAL CHRISTMAS ALE 12% ABV
Overripe grapes, raisins, and other dried fruits. Some hoppy bitterness hiding behind lots of sweet malts; acidic lining for a great balance.

OERBIER
BELGIAN DARK ALE 9% ABV
Fruitiness throughout, from nose to finish. Very vinous character, grapey, and clearly strong in alcohol.

DULLE TEVE
TRIPLE 10% ABV
Lots of sweet malt, sugar, and a warming alcohol finish, with little bitterness.

ALL ABOUT...
GLASSES

We are what we drink from. A book-lined study on a winter's night demands Cognac in a voluminous balloon, a gourmet feast requires an array of different glasses especially suited to Champagne, Burgundy, Bordeaux, and so on. But what about beer? The best glassware for the best long drink in the world should be the priority. It's about showing a beer in the best possible light, and revealing its aroma, condition, appearance, and flavour. Nations, towns, and individual breweries have developed a wide range of different and distinguished glassware – some simple and straightforward, such as those for a kölsch or a British pint; others more ostentatious and theatrical, like the quirky Kwak glass. In the USA, Samuel Adams' Boston Lager has devised a glass, specially shaped to maintain the beer's temperature, and to maximize its aroma and flavour – yet another development in the ongoing refinement and reinvention of the beer glass.

SNIFTER For some of the strongest beers, a small, brandy-balloon-like glass, known as a snifter, is the best choice. The shape holds aromas well, and its scale lends itself to rich, powerful beers, such as the Austrian Samichlaus.

FLUTE In Germany, pilsners and wheat beers are commonly served in tall, thin, wasp-waisted flutes.

BALLOON Duvel is served in a balloon-shaped receptacle resting on a flat-bottomed stem. This allows the drinker to appreciate the beer and its soft foamy head at the same time while also savouring its fine aroma.

GOBLET Go to a Belgian bar and every beer gets a different glass. It has been known for drinkers to be refused their choice because no suitable glass is available. Trappist beers such as Orval and Westmalle should be served in goblets.

TUMBLER German wheat beer has an elegant, long-legged supermodel of a glass, while Belgian-style wheat beers have adopted a more robust, chunky tumbler, popularized by the Hoegaarden Brewery.

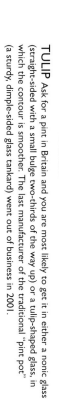

TEST TUBE Kwak has its very own glass – a vessel that looks rather like a test tube. Because it has a rounded bottom, it has to be served held in a wooden bracket, like a test-tube holder, to keep it from toppling over.

CYLINDER Kölsch is served in small, light, cylindrical glasses – little glass chimneys that show off the plume of the beer's flamboyant head.

TULIP Ask for a pint in Britain and you are most likely to get it in either a nonic glass (straight-sided with a small bulge two-thirds of the way up) or a tulip-shaped glass, in which the contour is smoother. The last manufacturer of the traditional "pint pot" (a sturdy, dimple-sided glass tankard) went out of business in 2001.

BREWERY

DE KONINCK

Mechelsesteenweg 291,
2018 Antwerpen, Belgium
www.dekoninck.be

De Koninck is an icon – as is its main beer. It embodies the town of Antwerp – whose inhabitants are a proud lot, and will say so. The amber "bolleke" (actually the glass) is still the staple diet in many bars.

BREWING SECRET The draught version is unpasteurized and should ideally be tasted at its source.

DE LANDTSHEER

Mandekensstraat 179,
9255 Buggenhout, Belgium
www.malheur.be

The brewery maintains the old family name, but the beers are better known under the brand name Malheur ("accident"). The company's steep rise might have shocked some of its competitors, but one of the men driving this venture was for many years a distributor for Westmalle, and so very well connected.

DE LA SENNE

Gentsesteenweg op 565,
1080 Brussels, Belgium
www.brasseriedelasenne.be

Yvan Debaets and Bernard Leboucq are two of the rising stars of the Belgian brewing scene. Committed to reviving old Belgian styles, they'd much prefer to sell their beers locally than export them. The owners say that they brew the beers they themselves want to drink. Several of their beers are lower in alcohol and easy drinking.

DE RANKE

1a, Rue du Petit Tourcoing,
B-7711 Dottignies, Belgium
www.deranke.be

A fully integrated Belgian brewery: the brewers are Flemish, the plant was set up in Wallonia in 2005, and a Brussels brewer was hired to help them out! They have a distinct keenness for lambics, for quality, and for outspoken taste profiles – as their beers amply testify.

BEER

DE KONINCK

AMBER "SPÉCIALE BELGE" 5.2% ABV
Amber malts, residual sugars, and hops give excellent balance to a fine ale, with a slight but distinct sulphury aroma and biscuit character. The draught version is particularly good – available in cask in the UK as well.

MALHEUR DARK BRUT

BELGIAN STRONG ALE 12% ABV
A dark version, but even more complex, with vinous, chocolate, fruity, and tannic notes.

MALHEUR BIÈRE BRUT RÉSERVE

BELGIAN STRONG ALE 11% ABV
Bottle fermented in the *méthode Champenoise* manner. Alcoholic, sweet brandy nose, then bitterish and fruity flavours.

TARAS BOULBA

SEASONAL BLOND ALE 4.5% ABV
A blond summer ale that's very easily drinkable, grassy, and malty, with a dry, bitter finish.

STOUTERIK

STOUT 4.5% ABV
The Senne stout is complex like none other, with American hops, parsley, tobacco, mushroom, and peppery flavours.

XX BITTER

BITTER 6.2% ABV
Inspired by English bitters, but at a very Belgian 6.2 per cent ABV, this is a wonderfully refreshing, hoppy brew.

KRIEK DE RANKE

FRUIT BEER 7% ABV
Mixed with lambic and cherries, this sourish fruit ale is close to fruit lambics – and yet quite different.

DE RYCK

Kerkstraat 24, 9550 Herzele, Belgium
www.brouwerijderyck.be

Female brewmaster Anne De Ryck has been driving a lot of the recent modernization at this family brewery, the roots of which go back to the 19th century. From keg-only production, the brewery now handles all kinds of bottling, often with beer on lees.

BREWING SECRET A 40 per cent ABV Bierschnaps is produced here too.

DE STRUISE

Kasteelstraat 50, 8640
Oostvleteren, Belgium
www.struise.com

Strictly speaking, the brewery here is Deca – an old established regional brewer – but De Struise Brouwers hire their facilities to such an extent that they claim 60 per cent of the overall output. Struise's Urbain Cotteau and Carlo Grootaers aim for the wild, complex, strong, flavour-packed beers so loved by new brew countries, such as the USA, Denmark, and Sweden.

DOMUS HUISBROUWERIJ

Tiensestraat 8, 3000 Leuven, Belgium
www.domusleuven.be

In the same town as mega-brewer Stella Artois, Belgium's first brewpub saw the light of day in 1985. But then Leuven is Belgium's foremost university town, and students do like a drink. The brewing may occur rather haphazardly, but the unfiltered pilsner is a peach – thanks to Mark Knops and Sam Croonen, huge hopheads that they are!

DRIE FONTEINEN

Hoogstraat 2A, 1650 Beersel, Belgium
www.3fonteinen.be

Armand Debelder, a blender and later brewer, rose to prominence in the beer world through the Drie Fonteinen ("3 Fountains") pub and restaurant. Debelder is the driving force behind this micro venture in brewing, though other gueuze blenders and enthusiasts of the beer style have helped him to keep going through some difficult years.

AREND WINTER
SPÉCIALE BELGE 6.3% ABV
Formerly known as "Christmas Pale-ale", this *Spéciale Belge* was often regarded as a real treat for the holiday season. A brown sugar aroma is matched by a herbal smell. Fairly sweet on the palate, with caramel notes; the hop flavouring varies from year to year.

PANNEPOT
DARK BELGIAN STRONG ALE 10% ABV
Fruity, vinous, and spiced; the complexity of this beer amazed everyone – an instant success.

AARDMONNIK – EARTH MONK
OUD BRUIN 8% ABV
Lighter than Pannepot, but it makes up for this in taste: lactic, earthy, vinous, and unfathomably complex.

CON DOMUS
PILSNER 5% ABV
An unfiltered, hazy pilsner, and very good on draught. A malty and grassy nose makes way for a herbal, peppery, and grassy taste, with plenty of bitterness. You can figure out the word play on the name yourself.

OUDE KRIEK
GUEUZE 5% ABV
Ruby red and very approachable, it has a tart aroma of cherries and musk.

OUDE GEUZE
GUEUZE 7% ABV
A top gueuze: horse blanket, leather grease, and lemon juice notes are all there, but so too is tarragon – the Belgian Chablis?

BREWERY

DUBUISSON

28, Chaussée de Mons,
7904 Pipaix, Belgium
www.br-dubuisson.com

Leuze is a town with three breweries, two of them in the Pipaix village. Dubuisson is probably the most dynamic, and its location, next to a major road, has made the brewery tap a very successful venture. The brewery excels in high-alcohol ales, so extreme caution is advised when drinking these beers.

DUPONT

5 Rue Basse, 7904 Tourpes, Belgium
www.brasserie-dupont.com

Western-Hainaut enjoys rich soil, and farmsteads here were huge – usually operating a brewery in the winter, making beer to be consumed on the land in summer (hence the style of beer known as *saison*). Brasserie Dupont became solely a brewery, but owner Olivier Dedeycker has re-engaged with the history of the land, by reintroducing farming and cheese making into this marvellous brewery – arguably one of Belgium's finest.

BREWING SECRET Most *saisons* of old carried a ferric tang because of the water, but Dupont was always an exception, as their well delivers very soft water. They are masters in restrained spicing.

DUVEL MOORTGAT

Breendonkdorp 58, 2870
Breendonk-Puurs, Belgium
www.duvelmoortgat.be

Started as a small family brewery, Moortgat continued producing top-fermented ale at a time when everywhere lager reigned. The Moortgat ale evolved into the iconoclastic Duvel, a beer that has become so popular that the brewery group renamed itself. Moortgat now owns breweries in Belgium and abroad.

BEER

BUSH AMBRÉE

BELGIAN STRONG ALE 12% ABV
In some markets known as "Scaldis", this is a treacherously drinkable alcohol-bomb.

BUSH PRESTIGE

BELGIAN STRONG ALE 13% ABV
This oak-aged version of the Ambrée is a true marvel in balance, despite its impressive strength.

BONS VŒUX

SEASONAL WINTER ALE 9.5% ABV
Once a complimentary winter ale, but so superb that it is now brewed year round. Barnyard and earthy aromas mingle with citrus zest. Grainy flavour: fresh white bread with nuts, spices, and walnut oil.

SAISON DUPONT

SAISON 6.5% ABV
Formerly brewed in winter with the hot summer months in mind – hence a dry, refreshingly light brew.

MOINETTE BLONDE

BELGIAN STRONG ALE 8.5% ABV
Related to the *saison* in style, but stronger and spiced – paradise seed especially takes up a major role.

DUVEL

BELGIAN STRONG ALE 8.5% ABV
Sometimes dubbed "red", to distinguish it from the filtered version, this ultra dry ale hides its potency as no other.

MAREDSOUS

BROWN ABBEY ALE 8% ABV
Arguably the best from the Maredsous Abbey range. Estery, fruity notes, and tobacco leaf.

ECAUSSINNES

Rue Restaumont, 118 B7190
Ecaussinnes, Belgium
www.belgianbeermoments.com

The Van Poucke couple arrived
on the brewing scene in 2000
with the Brasserie d'Ecaussinnes, a
microbrewery and tavern. Its rise has
been meteoric, and nobody would
call it a micro today. The lion's share
of the production is for export only,
and the brewery even makes a beer
exclusively for the Australian market.

FANTÔME

8, Rue Préal, 6997 Soy-Erezée, Belgium
www.fantome.be

Dany Prignon started this micro in
a shed in the Ardennes, and while
today he exports his beers to many
countries, the shed is still the
brewery's home – though it now
contains far more equipment.

BREWING SECRET More works of art
than products of brewing science;
many of the beers are never brewed
the same way twice.

GIRARDIN

Lindeberg 10, 1700 Sint-Ulriks-
Kapelle, Belgium

As rural as you can get, Girardin is
still very much a farm and brewery,
and this authentic lambic brewer
and gueuze blender has no time for
curious visitors. If, however, you
come simply to stock up on lambic
– as the locals and other blenders
do – the brewers will gladly take
you to their citrussy, spontaneously
fermented brews.

GRAIN D'ORGE

3 rue Laschet, 4852
Hombourg, Belgium
www.grain-dorge.com

Benoît Johnen started brewing
professionally in 2002 in his home
town, close to the "three countries"
border of Belgium, Germany, and the
Netherlands. His small but versatile
brewing plant enables him to vary
the output, following demand. Most
of the beer names are in reference to
the idyllic region in which his brewery
is located.

ULTRADÉLICE
BELGIAN STRONG DARK ALE 8% ABV
Ecaussinnes beers tend to be
sweet, and so is this one. But this
cinnamon-spiced beer has greater
complexity than most.

FORTISSIMI BELGAE
TRIPLE 10% ABV
Strong brown ale with hints of
liquorice, lots of bittering hops,
and a long, warming alcohol finish.

FANTÔME
SAISON 8% ABV
The brewery's staple blond beer:
fruity, lactic, variable, and in the
style of a *saison*.

BLACK GHOST
BELGIAN STRONG DARK ALE 8% ABV
One of the few regularly seen,
malty, with fruity depths, but also
flavours of cypress and pine.

FARO GIRARDIN
BLENDED LAMBIC 5% ABV
Caramel, meaty, and woody aromas;
slight sour edge around the caramel.
Filtered, as the yeast would wreak
havoc with sugars from the syrup.

GIRARDIN FOND GUEUZE
GUEUZE 5% ABV
This delectable unfiltered gueuze
has a marked grapefruit flavour.

BRICE
ABBEY BLOND-STYLE ALE 7.5% ABV
With a little spice edge, this dry
blond hides its strength very well.

TRIPLE AUBEL
TRIPLE 9% ABV
A golden lager with swathes of
hop bitterness, which is matched
by rich, sweet biscuit malt flavours.
It is very warming.

THE STORY OF...

Hoegaarden

Stoopkenstraat 46, 3320
Hoegaarden, Belgium

A village called Hoegaarden, near Tienen in Flanders, is the modern birthplace of Belgian white beer. Records of brewing in the village date back to 1445, when the local monks were enthusiastic brewers, but the tradition died out in the 1950s.

The beer's revival began in 1965, when milkman Pierre Celis decided to brew a beer in his hayloft that would be like the one he missed so much from his youth. With the help of a veteran brewer he founded the Cloister brewery – De Kluis in Flemish.

His brew soon gained cult status, especially among younger drinkers. In the 1980s, with demand for the beer continuing to grow, Celis bought a local soft drink factory that he rebuilt into a brewery. A fire at the brewery in 1985 led to Interbrew (now AB InBev) lending Celis money to rebuild. Over time, the loan became full ownership, and the relationship between the parties grew ill-tempered. Interbrew wanted a consistent, mass-market beer, while Celis continued to tinker with his recipe in the pursuit of brewing excellence. Eventually Celis left the company and set up in the USA. In Europe, the Hoegaarden brand went from strength to strength and, in the last few years, the beer has been rolled out worldwide, with sales in excess of 120 million litres per annum.

▲ **THE KEY INGREDIENTS** Celis used the traditional ingredients for a white beer: water, yeast, raw wheat, malted barley, hops, coriander seeds, and dried Curaçao orange peel.

▲ **HOEGAARDEN'S COPPERS** The brewing vessels at Hoegaarden are now used to brew more than the single style of witbier that Celis set out to recreate. The Spéciale is a stronger version of Hoegaarden, while the Grand Cru is brewed without wheat, and uses only barley; as a bottle-conditioned beer, it improves over a number of years. There is also a beer brewed to an old German recipe, and a beer called Forbidden Fruit – a full-bodied, sweet, and malty brew.

▲ **STAYING PUT** Tradition plays a big part in the story of top-fermented beers, and InBev came in for stinging criticism worldwide when it announced plans to close the Hoegaarden plant in 2005 and move production to Jupille. This sparked protests locally and worldwide, with beer lovers demonstrating their anger at the plan. Finally, in September 2007, InBev had a change of heart and, as part of a €60 million investment in its Belgian breweries, the Hoegaarden site will stay open.

◄**THE HOEGAARDEN BRAND** While Celis wanted to continually adjust his recipe for Hoegaarden, Interbrew (now AB InBev) wanted a consistent beer that they could market internationally.

BREWERY

DE HALVE MAAN

Walplein 26, B-8000 Bruges, Belgium
www.halvemaan.be

At the dawn of the 1980s – just as
the Maes family were reinventing their
old pilsner-brewing family brewery
as a speciality beer brewery – the
business ran into difficulty, and RIVA
took over. But heir Xavier Vanneste
had the brewing bug in his veins, and
managed to raise the funds for a buy
out. Since 2005, he has been brewing
here again with new appellations.

HANSSENS ARTISANAAL

Vroenenbosstraat 15/1,
B-1653 Dworp, Belgium

Not a brewery but a gueuze blender,
and yet another family business saved
by the son-in-law. Sidy Hanssens
married the right man in the right
place, and now blending has resumed
in the small town of Dworp – once
an important centre of lambic brewing
and gueuze blending. A strawberry
lambic is also produced.

HOEGAARDEN

Stoopkensstraat 46,
3320 Hoegaarden, Belgium
www.hoegaarden.com

Although this is now a brand in the
portfolio of brewing giant AB InBev,
it is the lifeblood and spirit of Pierre
Celis, Belgium's pre-eminent brewing
revolutionary, that still haunts this
brewery. Proof of this came in 2007,
when AB InBev's moguls wanted to
close the plant: fate, however, obliged
them to reverse their decision.

HUYGHE

Geraardsbergse Steenweg 14B,
9090 Melle, Belgium
www.delirium.be

Huyghe is a large regional, turning
out both top- and bottom-fermented
beers. In recent years, the brewery
has diversified by undertaking many
commissions, sometimes with very
specific demands, such as for gluten-
free beers, beers for fair trade sale,
and beers with unusual ingredients
(coconut, palm oil). Huyghe also brews
a range of low-alcohol fruit beers.

BEER

BRUGSE ZOT
GOLDEN ALE 6% ABV
Fruity and yeasty esters dominate
on the nose. Outspoken citrus
flavours make it fruity, even slightly
sour, yet quite dry.

OUDE GUEUZE
GUEUZE 6% ABV
All the necessary notes are here:
horse blanket, citrus, tannins, and
lactic. Tart, rather than sour.

OUDE KRIEK
KRIEK 6% ABV
Another tart one, yet this ruby
kriek (cherry beer) has a profound
sweetish background.

HOEGAARDEN WIT-BLANCHE
WITBIER 4.9% ABV
From as early as the 18th century,
the town of Hoegaarden was
importing blue Curaçao oranges.
The peel was mixed with coriander
seeds, and, as the rich soil of the
area yielded lots of wheat, a very
distinct, fruity, and spicy style of
beer evolved.

DELIRIUM TREMENS
BELGIAN STRONG ALE 8.5% ABV
Fruity-estery nose; fiery, alcoholic
taste. Flavours of pie crust, orange
zest, and apricots; quite sweet.

FLORIS KRIEK
FRUIT BEER 3.6% ABV
Deep red and slightly cloudy, there
is a balance of sweet and sour
with more than a touch of cherry,
hazelnuts, and marzipan.

KERKOM

Naamsesteenweg 469,
3800 Sint Truiden, Belgium
www.brouwerijkerkom.be

Jean Clerinckx used to work at the big Cristal Alken Brewery, but never forgot the ancestral one, which his father had closed. He restarted it, in the original location, in 1988. 11 years later, Marc Limet took over and, since then, the brewery has been in constant evolution. Currently, the brewing apparatus is being renewed – but always with tradition in mind.

LEFEBVRE

54, Chemin du Croly,
B-1430 Quenast, Belgium
www.brasserielefebvre.be

The first member of the Lefebvre family to be involved in brewing was Jules in 1876. The brewery is now in the hands of the sixth generation, with Paul Lefebvre.

BREWING SECRET For a family brewery, this one is very outward looking, and now 80 per cent of its beer production is exported.

LÉGENDES/
ELLEZELLOISE

19 Rue du Castel, B-7801 Irchonwelz; and 75 Street Guinaumont, B-7890 Ellezelles, Belgium
www.brasseriedeslegendes.be

When Philippe Gérard, brewer/owner of Ellezelloise, started to feel old age encroaching, he joined forces with microbrewery des Géants, run by Pierre Delcoigne and his wife, Vinciane. The companies merged at the end of 2006, though both sites have been kept active (hence the two addresses above).

Brasserie des Géants is situated in a grand farmhouse, and its brewing paraphernalia combines state-of-the art equipment with a mash tun from 1890 and a copper one from 1930. With the exception of the *saison*, the beers are classic strong Belgian ales. In 2012, Goliath Triple and Hercule Stout were both awarded medals in a competition to find the best beers in Wallonia.

BINK BLOND

BELGIAN BLOND ALE 5.5% ABV
Sweet and citrussy aromas, but seriously bitter in the taste, with both hop and citrus peel flavours.

KERCKOMSE TRIPEL

ABBEY-STYLE TRIPLE 9% ABV
Everybody needs a triple today – Marc Limet's is a very hoppy, ultra-dry version, with a respectable ABV.

FLOREFFE DOUBLE

BROWN ABBEY ALE 6.5% ABV
An ale of a chocolatey kind, which develops madeira and port notes with a little ageing.

SAISON 1900

SAISON 5.4% ABV
One of the few that refers to the brewery's past; delicate farmyard and rose-water aromas.

HERCULE STOUT

IMPERIAL STOUT 9% ABV
Proclaimed abroad as the first Belgian Imperial stout, this musty, inky brew is a fine, unspiced stout.

GOLIATH

BLONDE 6% ABV
A vivacious, fresh beer with a distinctive citrus nose. A good malt sweetness balances it.

SAISON VOISIN

SAISON 5% ABV
Referring to a former *saison* beer from neighbouring Flobecq, it has some farmyard and iron touches.

QUINTINE AMBRÉE

BELGIAN STRONG ALE 8% ABV
Under a huge head, this strong ale has an inviting medley of citrussy, spicy, and malt flavours.

BREWERY

LIEFMANS

Aalststraat 200, 9700
Oudenaarde, Belgium
www.liefmans.be

The brewery was founded in 1679
and moved to its present site in 1933.
It went into receivership in 2007, but
was rescued by Duvel Moortgat. The
beers are still fermented on site but
the mashing is done elsewhere.

BREWING SECRET Liefmans beers are
rare survivors from the once famous
Oudenaards bruin style.

LINDEMANS

Lenniksebaan 1479, 1602
Vlezenbeek, Belgium
www.lindemans.be

When considering lambic breweries,
we tend to think about small farm
brewers. Lindemans may seem to fit
this bill at first glance, yet it is also
on the margins of the 10 largest
breweries in Belgium. Its success is
owed to the rather sweetish fruit
concoctions it excels in, with nearly
half of the produce destined for
foreign markets.

LOTERBOL

Michel Theysstraat 58a,
B-3290 Diest, Belgium
www.loterbol.be

Brewing on this site started in
the 18th century, the name of the
brewery then being Duysters.
However, that brewery languished
in the 1970s and beer-making only
resumed here when the site became
a brewpub in 1995. The owner,
being a Trappist breweries agent,
has infinite wisdom in all things beery.

MORT SUBITE

Blarenberglaan 3C bus 2,
B-2800, Mechelen, Belgium
www.mort-subite.be

In 1970, De Keersmaeker Brewery
took over Brussels' famous Mort
Subite bar (named after a dice game),
where mainly gueuze and kriek were
consumed. From then on, "Mort
Subite" spontaneously fermenting
beers became the force of the
brewery. It has subsequently been
taken over by Alken-Maes, Scottish
& Newcastle, and now Heineken.

BEER

LIEFMANS GOUDENBAND
OUD BRUIN 8% ABV
A strong interpretation of the style,
its underlying acidity lends the beer
outstanding ageing possibilities.

LIEFMANS CUVÉE-BRUT
FLEMISH BROWN FRUIT 6% ABV
Aged brown beer is re-fermented
with sour cherries and, after 12
months, blended with Oud Bruin and
Goudenband. Sweet and tart flavours.

GUEUZE CUVÉE RENÉ
GUEUZE 5% ABV
Initially produced on demand for
export, now this caramel-and-sour-
apple gueuze is fairly common.

KRIEK CUVÉE RENÉ
KRIEK 5% ABV
Unfiltered kriek is rare and this
bottled beer is a dry notch above
the draught sweet version.

LOTERBOL 8 BLOND
PALE ALE 8% ABV
Highly attenuated, with most of
the sweet caramel sugars turned
into alcohol, it has a dry, bitter
finish and a red fruit aroma. Bottle
fermented, with good carbonation;
there are notes of spice.

MORT SUBITE GUEUZE ORIGINAL
GUEUZE 7.2% ABV
A woody gueuze with notes from
green apples and grapefruit. Lactic
acid dominates other acids, making
it fairly mellow, and with a marked
wheat character.

ORVAL

Abbaye d'Orval, Orval, n°1, B-6823
Villers-devant-Orval, Belgium
www.orval.be

The single Orval Trappist ale is a
symbol of the whole abbey: the best
in early 20th-century Art Nouveau
styling, blending with the medieval
ruins that surround it. The bottle,
glassware, and everything else is
designed with an eye for beauty and
peace. The ruins can be visited, but
alas, not the newly revamped brewery.

PALM

Steenhuffeldorp 3,
B-1840 Steenhuffel, Belgium
www.palm.be

Ranking among the largest of the
independently owned Belgian brewers,
it grew to fame in the 1920s when,
unable to afford to invest in the
refrigeration needed to make lager,
it started brewing a top-fermented
beer, stronger than a pilsen and with
more taste. It proved to be a big hit,
especially in the Netherlands, and
went to make the company's fortune.

PROEFBROUWERIJ

Doornzelestraat 20, 9080
Lochristi, Belgium
www.proefbrouwerij.com

The brewery hirer's dream: a
state-of-the-art brewery, capable of
caring for myriad brews at the same
time, with a vast array of ingredients
and yeasts to choose from. No
wonder it has been brewing not
only for Belgian clients but also
for many others from abroad. De
Proefbrouwerij is the brainchild
of Dirk Naudts, a tutor of brewing

sciences in Gent and Leuven. A group
of four brewing students known as
the Musketeers, decided to brew
their beers here, when they set up
the Troubadour brewery. Troubadour
Obscura was the first, but other
acclaimed beers have now followed.
Initially clients come and have trial
brews made before deciding which
composition and which strains of
yeast will work best for them – after
an intensive tasting session, of course.

ORVAL

AMBER ALE 6.2% ABV
An ultra dry ale that owes a
large part of its character to
Brettanomyces yeasts (not unlike
those that define lambic) and
to a high proportion of dry hops.

BRUGGE TRIPEL

ABBEY BLOND ALE 8.7% ABV
A style that originated in Brugge's
centre; the beer shows fierce
alcoholic and caramel notes.

DOBBEL PALM

SEASONAL ALE 5.7% ABV
The holiday offering – slightly darker,
slightly stronger than the usual Palm,
and a flavour of gingerbread.

VICARIS GENERAAL 8.5°

DARK ABBEY ALE 8.8% ABV
Brewed in the style of a dark abbey
ale, this one made an immediate
impression on beer festival-goers.

TROUBADOUR MAGMA

BELGIAN IPA 9% ABV
Amber in colour, this has the citrus
bitterness of an American IPA
married to the sweet fruitiness of a
Belgian ale. It is a well-balanced ale.

TROUBADOUR OBSCURA

BELGIAN DARK STRONG ALE 8.2% ABV
Obscura takes the middle ground
between a stout and a Belgian
strong ale.

TROUBADOUR BLOND

BLOND ALE 6.5% ABV
Spicy in the mouth, it has a
pleasant but not long, soft, bitter
finish. A nice marriage of fruit
and citrus hops.

BEER TRAIL

BRUSSELS

"B" is for Belgium, Brussels, and Beer. Today, Belgian beers can be drunk worldwide, but the very best place to embrace Belgian beer culture is in Brussels itself, with its unique cafés, bars, and brasseries.

JOURNEY STATS
2 hours, plus drinking time
10km (7 miles)

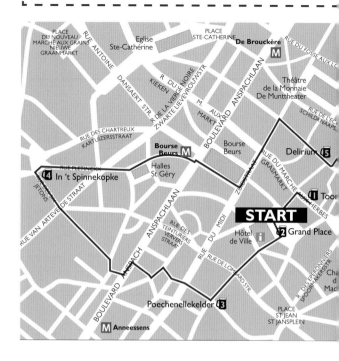

TOONE

The Beer Temple (*Rue du Marché aux Herbes 56*) is one of the world's best beer shops. It stocks most of Belgian's artisanal brewers. It is close to a narrow alleyway that forms the entrance to Toone, a puppet theatre with a bar. The walls of this hidden gem are adorned with staring marionettes and the atmosphere is as good as the Kwak beer served here – in the correct glass, of course. *Impasse Schuddevelde, off 21 Petit Ruedes Bouchers, Brussels (www.toone.be)*

POECHENELLEKELDER

Opposite one of the world's most improbable tourist attractions, the Manneken Pis, is the Poechenellekelder. Loved by the people of Brussels, the bar has a list of 90 fine beers – a perfect introduction to the world of Belgian beers. *5 Rue du Chêne, 1000 Brussels (www.poechenellekelder.be)*

GRAND PLACE

Brussels' famous Grand Place is home to the Belgian Brewers Association and Brewery Museum – both occupy the opulent Brewers House. Several bars surround the square, but there are even better places to drink nearby. In September, the square hosts an annual beer festival.

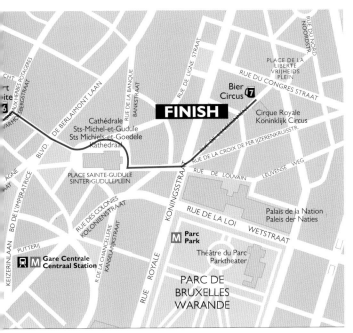

FINISH

4 IN 'T SPINNEKOPKE

Away from Grand Place, but not too far, can be found In 't Spinnekopke. "The Little Spiders Head" is a small, intimate two-bar restaurant and café. It is as Bruxellois as you can get and has to be one of the best places in Brussels to eat and drink beer. Chef Jean Rodriguez prides himself on pairing food and beer superbly. Who needs wine when you can pair a draught lambic with a plate of mussels? *1 Place du Jardin aux Fleurs, 1000 Brussels (www.spinnekopke.be)*

5 DELIRIUM

Ilot Sacré is a clamour of medieval lanes and fish restaurants with outrageous menu boards and energetic, and sometimes insistent, waiters trying to coerce people inside to dine. Down one such alley is Delirium. Don't wait at your table for service, go to the bar, which claims to stock more than 2,000 beers. *4 Impasse de la Fidélité, 1000 Brussels (www.deliriumcafe.be)*

6 MORT SUBITE

Along the road is Galeries Royales Saint-Hubert. Built in 1846, it was the world's largest covered shopping mall when it opened. It leads the way to Mort Subite – a magnificent Art Nouveau bar, which is said to be the best surviving fin-de-siecle long bar in the world. Here is the place to try wildly fermented lambic or gueuze beers – which are best ordered with a plate of marvelous *tête pressée* (brawn) or *kip kap* (pig cheeks). *7 Rue Montagne-aux-Herbes Potagères, 1000 Brussels (www.mort-subite.be)*

7 BIER CIRCUS

Up the hill from Central Station is Bier Circus. This friendly, bustling bar is the place to seek out beers from Belgium's growing band of artisanal brewers. It is the perfect place to experience the creative diversity of Belgian brewing. But take some friends with you – many of the beers are served only in 75cl (1¼ pints) bottles. But then, beer is always better drunk with a friend than alone. *57 Rue de l'Enseignement, 1000 Brussels (www.bier-circus.be)*

Morte Subite in Brussels
is celebrated for its Art
Nouveau interior and superb
range of Belgian beers.

BREWERY

ROCHEFORT

Abbaye Notre Dame de Saint-Remy,
B-5580 Rochefort, Belgium
www.abbaye-rochefort.be

Though brewing has been carried out here since 1900, it is only since 1998 that Rochefort has used labels on their bottled beer. Small may well be beautiful, but that does not preclude the search for innovation, and recently the smallest of the Walloon Trappist breweries decided to employ a lay brewmaster, Gumer Santos, to work on their beer

production. Since then, an amazing new lagering room has begun taking shape next to the abbey church, and the few visitors allowed into the abbey are now proudly shown the brand new tasting room.

BREWING SECRET All beers share one basic recipe, but are separately brewed and so may vary a little. As with most Trappist breweries, production is voluntarily limited.

RODENBACH

Spanjestraat 133-141,
8800 Roeselare, Belgium
www.rodenbach.be

The Rodenbach family started making beer in Roeselare in 1821. Now under the wing of Palm breweries, Rodenbach has turned resolutely modern, yet without doing away with its age-old traditions.

BREWING SECRET The "cathedral" of wooden fermenters is one of the most impressive sights in Belgian brewing.

ROMAN

Hauwaart 105, B-9700
Oudenaarde, Belgium
www.roman.be

Located just outside Oudenaarde town, Roman's commercial products are primarily mainstream lagers and pilsners. Even their relatively new Ename abbey ale range is a rather discreet interpretation of the style, and this also applies to the oud bruin-type beers, which are less bold than those of smaller producers.

BEER

ROCHEFORT 6 (RED)
ABBEY ALE 7.5% ABV
Six is a veiled reference to the beer's density (1060 OG) – and this lightest and rarest Rochefort enjoys a very fruity taste.

ROCHEFORT 10 (BLUE)
ABBEY ALE 11.3% ABV
A superior Trappist ale, with toffee, chocolate, raisins, and port flavours, and incomparable complexity.

ROCHEFORT 8 (GREEN)
ABBEY ALE 9.2% ABV
On top of the fruit flavours are the bready, dark, and roasted malts – a nourishing Trappist ale.

RODENBACH GRAND CRU
OUD BRUIN 6% ABV
A sour beer that is aged in barrels: very severe and dry; one for the connoisseur.

RODENBACH
OUD BRUIN 5.2% ABV
Bearing the signs of its mixed fermentation and wood ageing, it is vinous in character and refreshing.

ENAME DUBBEL
ABBEY ALE 6.5% ABV
The Ename abbey ales range includes this red-brown beer, which is wheaty and spicy.

ROMAN OUDENAARDS
OUD BRUIN 5% ABV
This beer is more bready, nutty, and malty than really lactic in the usual Oudenaards bruin style.

LA RULLES

Artisanale de Rulles, 36, Rue Maurice Grevisse, B-6724 Rulles, Belgium
www.larulles.be

Seldom does a brand new brewery (established only in 2000) meet with such immediate success. Grégory Verhelst's brews are mesmerizingly characterful, and the quality of the labels is equally amazing.

BREWING SECRET Grégory Verhelst enlisted the help of the Orval brewmaster to develop his beers.

SAINTE–HÉLÈNE

Rue de la Colinne, B6760
Ethe-Belmont, Belgium
www.sainte-helene.be

After a hectic start, this brewery really got going in 2005, when new brewing equipment was installed. The very southwest corner of Belgium seems to be particularly suited to brewing, as new breweries keep popping up there. Sainte-Hélène is enthusiastic about promoting its beers, and is a regular at Belgium's many beer festivals.

SILENRIEUX

Rue Noupré 1, 5630
Silenrieux, Belgium
www.brasseriedesilenrieux.be

One of the earlier Walloon micros, Silenrieux started in 1991. Where possible, the ECOCERT (organic certificate) has been obtained. Several commissioned beers are also produced.

BREWING SECRET From the beginning, the emphasis has been on the use of alternative grains, such as spelt (an ancient form of wheat) and buckwheat.

SILLY/MYNSBRUGHEN

2, Rue Ville Basse, 7830 Silly, Belgium
www.silly-beer.com

Established in the 19th century, this family brewery walks a fine line between maintaining traditions and employing technical developments geared towards satisfying changing market niches. A saison is still produced – bottled and, better yet, on draught – and they have recently launched a beer flavoured with rum and named after a regional rock band.

LA RULLES TRIPLE
BELGIAN PALE STRONG ALE 8.4% ABV
No lack of body here; herbal and dry bitterness on the palate, yet well-fermented and strong.

LA RULLES ESTIVALE
SEASONAL ALE 5.2% ABV
A refreshing, citrussy, blossom-laden summer ale – one of the best of its kind.

LA SAINTE HÉLÈNE AMBRÉE
BELGIAN AMBER STRONG ALE 8.5% ABV
Close in character to the triple, but with more caramel and tobacco notes; well balanced.

LA DJEAN TRIPLE
BELGIAN AMBER STRONG ALE 9% ABV
A beer with many flavours and impressions, from phenolic to fruity and dry to creamy.

SARA
BUCKWHEAT BEER 6% ABV
Brewed with organically grown buckwheat, the beer is slightly sour, with some solvent notes.

NOËL DE SILENRIEUX
SEASONAL BEER 9% ABV
A winter offering, with smoked red fruit and nutty overtones. Contains buckwheat too.

SAISON SILLY
SAISON 5% ABV
Fruity, madeira-like, thin bodied. Even when young, this is more like an oud bruin than a real saison.

SCOTCH SILLY
SCOTCH ALE 7.5% ABV
Scotch ales are a Walloon tradition. This very malty dark beer is full bodied and rich.

BREWERY

ST. BERNARDUS

Trappistenweg 23, 8978
Watou, Belgium
www.sintbernardus.be

This brewery really took off at the end of World War II, when St. Bernard(us) received the license for making the St. Sixtus ales from Westvleteren Brewery. That agreement ended in 1992, and now St. Bernardus produces abbey ales and other styles of beer, some broadly in the vein of the St. Sixtus ales. They have diversified, however, partly thanks to the influence of Pierre Celis, founder of Hoegaarden and grandfather of the Belgian brewing revival. The beers are particularly popular in Denmark, and several beers have been designed exlusively for the Danish market.

BREWING SECRET An original strain of yeast from the Trappist Westvleteren Brewery is still used at St. Bernardus.

SLAGHMUYLDER

Denderhoutembaan 2,
9400 Ninove, Belgium
www.witkap.be

This regional determined its future when gradually, in around 1980, the brewery obtained the rights to brew the Witkap Abbey ale range. It gave a dash to the company for several decades, and they carefully honed the recipes. With the Witkap fame now firmly established, the brewery has recently brought attention to their own range of lagers.

SMISJE

Driesleutelstraat 1, Oudenaarde,
East Flanders 9700, Belgium
www.smisje.be

Johan Brandt might currently be operating in rather cramped conditions, but then he needs space for his wine- and beer-making shop, as well as for his bee keeping. He is building up a new brewery in a different location, however, which is an indication of his ambition. His beers are very characterful, and sometimes entirely unique.

BEER

ST. BERNARDUS WIT
WITBIER 5.5% ABV
One of the best witbiers available, since Pierre Celis himself advised on this sweet and sourish recipe.

ST. BERNARDUS PATER 6
BOCK 6.7% ABV
This dark, top-fermented beer has notes of melon, banana, and honey, and finishes with an earthy bitterness.

ST. BERNARDUS TRIPEL
ABBEY ALE 8% ABV
Special malts, coriander, and lots of sweetness reign in this blond abbey ale.

ST. BERNARDUS ABT 12
ABBEY ALE 10% ABV
The flagship ale; imagine liquid Baba au Rum or the Sachertorte chocolate cake with added fruit, and you'll be close to the flavour.

WITKAP-PATER TRIPEL
ABBEY ALE 7.5% ABV
A triple with a very vinous character, like a dry white wine; easily drinkable for its strength.

WITKAP-PATER STIMULO
ABBEY ALE 6% ABV
Fruity and spicy, and made with local hops, this blond ale is quite floral. An excellent session ale.

SMISKE BRUIN
BELGIAN BROWN ALE 7% ABV
Well-carbonated. Red fruit flavours and sweet malt mingle in the glass; it finishes with a hint of sourness.

SMISKE NATURE-ALE
BELGIAN PALE ALE 7% ABV
This chestnut-coloured beer has an aroma of sweet caramel malt and a touch of bitter hops.

TIMMERMANS

Kerkstraat 11, B-1701 Itterbeek, Belgium
www.brtimmermans.be

Once a traditional lambic brewery, Timmermans was among the first to habitually mix top-fermented beer into its blends. The brewery has also been keen to produce all kinds of syrup-lambic concoctions, designed to appeal more to the younger generation. Timmermans products, including Tradition, are easily found in Belgian supermarkets.

URTHEL

Krommekeerstraat 21,
B8755 Ruiselede, Belgium
www.urthel.com

Though brewmaster Hildegard Van Ostaden lives in Belgium, production of her beer has been moved from Van Steenberge to the Dutch Trappist brewery La Trappe. The beers are widely available in Belgium, and the distinctive gnomes on the bottle labels – from illustrations by Hilde's husband Bas – have contributed much to Urthel's popularity.

VAL-DIEU

225, Val-Dieu, B-4480 Aubel, Belgium
www.val-dieu.com

Benoît Humblet set up this brewery in 1997 in the former agricultural section of the Cistercian monastery of Val-Dieu. Since then the brewery has produced a series of abbey ales that are executed with great respect for the local artisanal traditions of brewing. Here, the aim is for consistent quality rather than sudden and dramatic brilliance.

VAN DEN BOSSCHE

Sint Lievensplein 16, Plaats
9550 Sint-Lievens-Esse, Belgium
www.paterlieven.be

A long-standing family brewery in a brewery-rich part of Flanders. Long did it thrive on the local Buffalo ale, weaving colourful stories about its origins. Changes in the beer market have driven it to strengthen the Pater Lieven range – vaguely abbey-like in style – and, tentatively, to produce a beer expressly made for export.

TIMMERMANS KRIEK LAMBICUS

LAMBIC 4% ABV
It is full of cherry notes and is satisfyingly sweet, with hints of tartness and some acidity. A captivating blend of old and new beers, re-fermentation in the bottle adds a spark of mystery.

URTHEL SAMARANTH

BELGIAN BARLEY WINE 11.5% ABV
Barley wine in a Belgian style, with cake, fruit, and liqueur notes; a real after-dinner drink.

HOP-IT

BELGIAN ALE 9.5% ABV
Full of fruit and spice, it is a hoppy, tongue-tingling, warming ale, with a sweet finish.

VAL-DIEU BLONDE

BELGIAN BLOND ALE 6% ABV
A blond beer with a leafy, grainy flavour and an overall impression of wheat.

VAL-DIEU GRAND CRU

BELGAIN STRONG ALE 10.5% ABV
A chewy, dark ale, with flavours of roasted malts and spice; bitterish notes ride above the sweeter malts.

PATER LIEVEN BLOND

ABBEY ALE 6.5% ABV
Blossomy notes can be found in this abbey blond, while hops promised on the nose are delivered on the palate.

BUFFALO BELGIAN STOUT

STOUT 9% ABV
Not the legendary Buffalo Spéciale, but a high alcohol, roasted stout, geared for foreign markets.

THE STORY OF...

Orval

Abbaye d'Orval, Orval, n° 1,
B-6823 Villers-devant-Orval

In the world of beer there are many blessed brews, but the best must surely be those from the Trappist breweries. Today there are eight breweries that can use this appellation, meaning that their beers have been brewed within the enclosed community of a Trappist monastery. The magnificent eight abbeys where this brewing takes place are Achel, Chimay, Orval, Rochefort, Westmalle, and Westvleteren in Belgium, Koningshoeven in the Netherlands, and Stift Engelszell in Austria. Beer mythology has it that monks have been brewing continuously since medieval times. It's a good story, but one that omits the Reformation, when many monasteries were abandoned for years and were used as a source of building stone.

In 1926, the de Harenne family, who had acquired the Orval ruins and surrounding lands in 1887, donated them to the Cistercian order so that monastic life could be re-established at Orval.

In 1931, the monks decided to take up the tradition of brewing once again. Their goal is not profit but a "redevance" – that is, to generate enough funds for the upkeep of the abbey, to support the local community, and for charitable projects.

▲ **THE MONASTERY** Orval Abbey's lovely grounds are open to the public; unfortunately, the brewery is not. However, its beers, including Petit Orval (the beer that the monks can drink), can be bought from the adjacent Ange Gardien pub.

▲ **MOVING WITH THE TIMES** As part of its commitment to technological advancement, Orval is always looking to invest in modern equipment.

▲ **THE LONG VIEW** The abbeys share a common commitment to quality. As part of their philosophy, Trappist breweries not only use the finest ingredients but also invest in top-of-the-range brewing equipment. Orval director Francois de Harenne says, "The monks take a view of the long term, and want the very best equipment. The tradition of Trappist breweries is for the equipment to be sophisticated. We have a high level of quality and we must keep it".

▼ **BREW KETTLES** Orval maintains its equipment in splendid condition, as is evident by the glowing state of these 1930s kettles. As in all Trappist breweries, the beer is top-fermented. Other characteristics of Trappist beers are that they all tend to be strong, bottle-conditioned, aromatic, and full of yeasty and fruity flavours.

▲ **DRY-HOPPING** Sacks of dry Styrian Goldings hops are added to the beer while it is undergoing secondary fermentation. These add balance to the beer and give it a rich, round, earthy, sweet aroma.

▲ **THE ORVAL TROUT** Local legend has it that a widow called Matilda lost a golden ring in a lake and promised that, if it were found, she would thank God by building an abbey. The ring was brought to the surface by a trout, as depicted on the Orval label and bottle-tops, and in images at the abbey.

▲ **THE BEER** While some Trappist beers are dark and heavy, Orval is light and dry, and perfectly partners the cheeses that are made in the abbey's dairy. Three Belgian malts and white cane sugar produce a beer with a distinctive pale orange hue.

BREWERY

VAN EECKE
Douvieweg 2, 8978 Watou, Belgium
www.brouwerijvaneecke.be

The family that owns this brewery in rural Watou also owns another brewery, Leroy, in the vicinity. While Van Eecke specializes in abbey ales and posher brands, Leroy takes care of more mundane lagers and stouts.

BREWING SECRET The Kapittel range used to be in the oud bruin style, but in recent years the brewery has given it a more classic abbey ale profile.

VAN HONSEBROUCK
Oostrozebekestraat 43, 8770 Ingelmunster, Belgium
www.vanhonsebrouck.be

Defining a brewery as a "niche jumper" may hardly sound like praise, but Luc Van Honsebrouck describes his brewery this way himself, claiming that its strength lies in being flexible and more adaptable to market trends than the giants. Luc has a flair for PR, and his magnificent castle in the village acts as a signpost for the brewery.

VAN STEENBERGE
Lindenlaan 25, B-9940 Ertvelde, Belgium
www.vansteenberge.com

A very expansive regional brewer, Van Steenberge specializes in making tweakings and blendings for anybody interested in having their very own beer made. Yet, at the core, it has a range of very decent beers, both abbey ales and oud bruins.

BREWING SECRET Unusually, the abbey ales were formulated with the help of a Latvian brewmaster.

VAPEUR
1, Rue du Maréchal à
7904 Pipaix-Leuze, Belgium
www.vapeur.com

Jean-Louis Dits and his late wife, both school teachers by profession, saved this brewery from demolition in 1985. Jean-Louis now owns one of the world's last steam-operated breweries.

BREWING SECRET Voluntarily limiting the brewing to every last Saturday of the month, Jean-Louis also bows to his own, rather inflexible, ecological logic.

BEER

KAPITTEL PRIOR
ABBEY ALE 9% ABV
Strong and dark, and now with a bittersweet character. Rich fruitcake in fluid form.

KAPITTEL TRIPEL ABT
ABBEY ALE 10% ABV
A very strong blond ale, with a dry, spicy character, and sweet alcoholic overtones.

KASTEEL BLOND 7°
STRONG BELGIAN ALE 7% ABV
An unfiltered, strong blond beer, with sultana-like, alcoholic sweetness.

ST LOUIS FOND TRADITION GUEUZE LAMBIC
GUEUZE 4.5% ABV
Can west Flemish beer be real gueuze? This citrussy, unfiltered fresh beer certainly comes close.

AUGUSTIJN GRAND CRU
BELGIAN STRONG ALE 9% ABV
An amber ale, bottle conditioned, dry, and fairly sweet; but with a citrus note too, like orange zest.

AUGUSTIJN BLOND
BLOND ALE 7.5% ABV
Drunk young, it is hoppy and fruity; older beers have a more rounded, pronounced flavours.

SAISON DE PIPAIX
SAISON 6% ABV
Working from a long-kept recipe, Dits has cleaned it up to tart and citrussy flavours, with the metallic tang of old *saisons* all but gone.

VAPEUR EN FOLIE
SAISON 8% ABV
A lovely spicy, malty, and alcoholic interpretation of *saison* – with unexpected ageing potential.

VERHAEGHE

Vichte NV, Sint-Dierikserf 1,
B-8570 Vichte, Belgium
www.brouwerijverhaeghe.be

The outlook for a small family brewer locked in the clasp of supplying oud bruin and pilsner for local pubs may not appear especially bright, but in the case of Verhaeghe that summation would be wrong. The variety of oud bruins produced here is remarkable, and the "Duchesse de Bourgogne" in particular has attained cult beer status in new markets, especially the USA.

WESTMALLE

Antwerpsesteenweg 496,
2390 Westmalle, Belgium
www.trappistwestmalle.be

Monks started brewing here in 1836, selling beer at the gate 20 years later. Today, the abbey operates one of the world's most modern breweries, hidden behind the old brewhouse. Westmalle has come to define abbey ales through their "Dubbel" and "Tripel" styles. The "Extra" could be another world classic, if the monks were to commercialize it.

WESTVLETEREN

Donkerstraat 12, B-8640
Westvleteren, Belgium
www.sintsixtus.be

Does this brewery need introduction? The Abbey of St. Sixtus of Westvleteren is the reclusive star of the beer world. It sells its beer by telephone reservation only – unwillingly even – as if to emphasize that the operation is run by monks who brew in order to be able to pray, instead of pray in order to sell. Westvleteren voluntarily limits production. As Joris, the brother responsible for the brewery, says: "We refuse to go into an endless spiral of producing more, then having to sell more, and bring more brothers into the process, or even having to hire outside staff".

BREWING SECRET This is the only remaining Trappist brewery that still employs solely in-house monks.

VICHTENAAR
OUD BRUIN 5.1% ABV
Probably the most basic of the oud bruins, tart, refreshing, and with complex aromas.

ECHT KRIEKENBIER
OUD BRUIN 6.8% ABV
Sour cherries were often put on oud bruins. The cherries give an explosion of fruity, tart flavours.

WESTMALLE DUBBEL
ABBEY ALE 7% ABV
Dark and vinous, with sugar sweetness coming through; surprisingly hoppy. A classic.

WESTMALLE TRIPEL
ABBEY ALE 9.5% ABV
The dry Champenoise triple that made all triples blond. Sweetish and fruity, with a hoppy finish.

WESTVLETEREN BLOND
ABBEY ALE 5.8% ABV
A blond ale that starts with a big grain flavour, followed by very serious hops; best bitter like.

WESTVLETEREN 8
ABBEY ALE 8% ABV
Dark and strong, roasted, faint bitterish notes, with pears, plums, hazelnuts, and coffee.

WESTVLETEREN 12
ABBEY ALE 10.2% ABV
A truly massive dark Trappist ale, chewy like no other beer, and with a perfect balance of sweet and bitter notes.

MORE BEERS OF

BELGIUM

Characterful beers are made by a number of other microbreweries in Belgium, but distribution may be limited to a few small outlets at certain times of the year. These Belgian beers may be hard to track down, but they are worth the effort. Some have won awards.

BREWERY

BELGOO
38, Faubourg Saint Paul,
B7130 Binche, Belgium
www.belgoobeer.be

The founder, Jo Van Aert, likes to experiment with different malts and grains in his bottle-conditioned beers. Typically, he uses barley and wheat malt, as well as oats and spelt. He is also a fan of flavoursome hops and, in particular, dry hopping with aromatic hops. A fast-growing brewery, it exports to several countries including China.

BROOTCOORENS
197, Rue de Maubeuge,
6560 Erquelinnes, Belgium
www.brasserie-brootcoorens-
erquelinnes.be

Alain Brootcoorens started his microbrewery in the very last month of the 20th century. His staple beers, Angélus and La Sambresse, can be found at the brewery tap, but are also gradually finding wider distribution.

BREWING SECRET The brewery can also make individually commissioned beers.

CAZEAU
67 Rue de Cazeau,
7520 Templeuve, Belgium
www.brasseriedecazeau.be

Laurent Agache and Quentin Mariage resurrected Cazeau in 2004. It had operated since the mid-18th century, but in 1969, when Laurent's father Jean was in charge, brewing stopped.

BREWING SECRET The new saison is an indication that these brewers are keen to create styles of beer with more complex, less obvious flavours.

CNUDDE
Fabrieksstraat 8,
B9700 Eine, Belgium

When Louis Cnudde died in 1995, nobody would have wagered a penny on his brewery's future. But his three sons kept the brewery alive, even when brewing only sporadically. Though the beer is available elsewhere, admirers of this brew often like to drink it in the Casino under the brewery tower.

BEER

SAISONNEKE
SAISON 4.4% ABV
Wild yeast flavours gives the beer a nice edge along with some orange notes. The fruit lingers in the finish.

LUPPO
PALE ALE 6.5% ABV
The addition of extra hops as the beer conditions lends a citrussy aroma and taste. Barley, wheat, and spelt give it some pleasant, bready notes.

ANGÉLUS BLONDE
BELGIAN BLOND ALE 7% ABV
A flowery and seriously spicy beer, yet one that's also delicate and refreshing.

SAISON CAZEAU
SAISON 5% ABV
This is a truly light and refreshing saison. Elderflowers counterbalance the spicy touch.

TOURNAY NOIRE
BELGIAN STOUT 7.6% ABV
Bottle conditioned, it is dark and luscious and has a long, bitter, warming finish.

LOUIS V OUD BRUIN
OUD BRUIN 4.7% ABV
One of the very last beers of this sort, brewed in and around Oudenaarde town. Slight sourish flavour, lactic, and metallic, while balancing flavours of liquorice and sweet malts. Keg only.

BREWERY

DE CAM
Dorpstraat 67A, 1755 Gooik,
Belgium
www.decam.be

Karel Goddeau is brewmaster at Slaghmuylder Brewery, but in his free time he blends gueuze, selling it under the De Cam brand name. The lambic for the gueuze comes from different lambic brewers. Once blended, the beer is lagered in barrels that have a history of their own: they hail from the famous Czech Plzeňský Prazdroj Brewery, home of Pilsner Urquell.

GLAZEN TOREN
Glazen Torenweg 11,
9420 Erpe-Mere, Belgium
www.glazentoren.be

When three friends got together to make their hobby a profession, what transpired was a very modern microbrewery in which originality was the watchword.

BREWING SECRET Glazen Toren brews are very individualistic interpretations of well-known styles, such as saison, Abbey Triple, or Belgian witbier.

SINT CANARUS
Polderweg 2B, 9800 Deinze-Gottem,
Belgium
www.sintcanarus.be

Piet Meirhaeghe started brewing here in 2002, right in the shadow of the church in the delightful rural town of Gottem. However, demand for Piet's beer is such that part of the output is now outsourced and hails from the Proefbrouwerij. The Sint Canarus Brewery is open to visitors on weekends.

STRUBBE
Markt 1, 8480 Itegem, Belgium
www.brouwerij-strubbe.be

Marc Strubbe inherited the family brewery, and made it a point to incorporate advanced laboratory techniques into the traditional brewing methods. Brewing commissioned beers and foreign beers under license helps things tick over.

BREWING SECRET The barrels and fermentation tanks allow Marc to work with variable blending.

BEER

DE CAM OUDE GEUZE
GUEUZE 6.5% ABV
Tart, with yogurt, wood, grapefruit, and horse-blanket notes – a classic gueuze from the newest blender.

DE CAM OUDE KRIEK
FRUIT LAMBIC 5% ABV
Overwhelming fruit flavours, as well as notes from the cherry stones; a headless and spritzy fruit lambic.

ONDINEKE OILSJTERSEN TRIPEL
ABBEY BLOND ALE 8.5% ABV
The name is only pronounceable by Aalst town inhabitants. Fruity, very balanced, and dangerously drinkable.

JAN DE LICHTE
WITBIER 7% ABV
A sweet-sour balance, with the unmistakable spice of coriander.

POTTELOEREKE
BELGIAN STRONG DARK ALE 8% ABV
Semi-sweet, richly bodied, with notes of gingerbread, caramel, and pear drops.

ICHTEGEM'S GRAND CRU
OUD BRUIN 6.5% ABV
The newest in the range, and an interesting, stronger variation of an Oudenaarde bruin, resulting in a velvety, yet woody dark ale.

BEER STYLES
FRUIT BEER

The addition of fruit to beer is not a recent invention. Over many centuries, raspberries, blackberries, peaches, apricots, damsons, lemons, bananas, and even coconuts have been used to create unusual and distinctive flavours. In the county of Kent, in England, surplus cherries were traditionally used to produce the local favourite cherry ale. Sadly, the last few decades have seen most of the cherry orchards disappear, and the beer along with them. In Belgium, however, fruit beer retains a strong presence. In the Brussels region, lambic brewers have been adding cherries to their beer for hundreds of years. While some fruits may be added in the form of a purée, syrup, or flavouring, the use of whole cherries does more than affect the flavour of the beer – wild yeast on the fruit's skin helps to spark off a secondary fermentation.

LAMBIC Authentic Belgian lambic fruit beer is both fermented and flavoured with whole cherries, and known as kriek, or raspberries (frambozen or framboise). Eminent examples of this style of beer include Cantillon's Kriek Lambic and Oud Beersel Oude Kriek.

FLEMISH Another classic Belgian fruit beer is Flemish brown ale, which is also flavoured with cherries or raspberries. The stylishly tissue-wrapped Liefmans' Kriek and Frambozen are good examples.

AMERICAN Craft brewers in the USA are now raiding the fruit bowl for their beers. New Glarus's Raspberry Tart remains faithful to the Belgian framboise style while using berries from Oregon. Other notable American fruit beers are Samuel Adams' Cherry Wheat and New Belgium's seasonal Frambozen.

BRITISH Although less in evidence now than in the past, British fruit beers do exist. Melbourn Brothers specialize in such brews, with cherry, strawberry, and apricot beers, and Old Luxters produces a tasty Damson Ale using Cumbrian fruits.

Liefmans, in the Flemish city of Oudenaarde, Belgium, brews a local style of ale called oud bruin.

Plzeň

Gambrinus

Pilsner Urquell

Prague

Staropramen

U Medvídků

U Fleků

U Medvídků

Gambrinus

České Budějovice

Budweiser Budvar

Pivovar Samson

Pivovar Samson

Zlatopramen

Svijany

Klášter

Žatec

Dětenice

Krušovice

Nymburk

Chodovar

Kutná Ho

Purkmistr

Kozel

Ferdinand

Lobkowicz

Herold

Poutník

Platan

Regent

Eggenberg

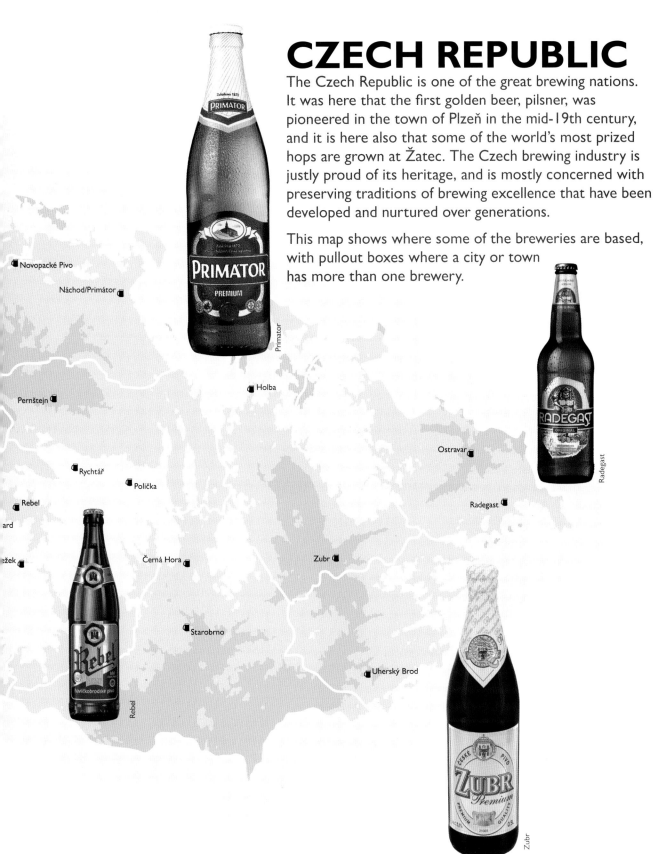

CZECH REPUBLIC

The Czech Republic is one of the great brewing nations. It was here that the first golden beer, pilsner, was pioneered in the town of Plzeň in the mid-19th century, and it is here also that some of the world's most prized hops are grown at Žatec. The Czech brewing industry is justly proud of its heritage, and is mostly concerned with preserving traditions of brewing excellence that have been developed and nurtured over generations.

This map shows where some of the breweries are based, with pullout boxes where a city or town has more than one brewery.

Novopacké Pivo

Náchod/Primátor

Pernštejn

Rychtář

Polička

Rebel

ard

ežek

Černá Hora

Starobrno

Holba

Ostravar

Radegast

Zubr

Uherský Brod

Primator

Radegast

Rebel

Zubr

BREWERY

BERNARD

5 Května 1, 396 01 Humpolec,
Czech Republic
www.bernard.cz

While reviving 16th-century Humpolec brewery in 1991, Stanislav Bernard and two partners took the daring decision to produce traditional unpasteurized beers using microfiltration. Since then, awards and an expanding export market have followed.

BREWING SECRET Bernard has its own floor maltings and uses spring water.

BUDWEISER BUDVAR

Karolíny Světle 512/4, České Budějovice 3, 37004, Czech Republic
www.original-budweiser.cz

The town of České Budějovice (Budweis) has been a home of brewing since 1265. Today, the Budějovický (Budweiser) Budvar product name has Protected Geographical Indicator status within the EU (like Cognac and Parma ham), but in the USA, where Anheuser-Busch's Budweiser is trademarked, it is called Czechvar.

ČERNÁ HORA

Černá Hora 3, 679 21 Černá Hora, Czech Republic
www.pivovarcernahora.cz

The nearby Black Hill (Černá Hora) – one of the Czech Republic's finest skiing areas – gives this brewery its name. The town's first written brewing record is dated to 1530, but brewing here is believed to predate that considerably. The brewery's traditional techniques and high quality ensure frequent competition successes.

CHODOVAR

Pivovarská 107, 348 13 Chodová Planá, Czech Republic
www.chodovar.cz

Albi, a dog said to have discovered the bountiful spring that provided water for brewing here in the Middle Ages, was symbolically reinstated by the brewery in 2000, and he now stands proudly on the company emblem.

BREWING SECRET The brewery has an on-site beer spa, complete with a dark beer bath and herbal remedies.

BEER

CELEBRATION/SVÁTEČNÍ LEŽÁK

PREMIUM LAGER 5% ABV
Delicate herb-like hop and yeast aromas overlay a peppery bitterness for a grassy finish.

DARK ČERNÉ PIVO

LAGER 5.1% ABV
Winner of a World Beer Award, it is a strong, malty sweet black beer, with a light, bitter finish.

BUDWEISER BUDVAR/CZECHVAR

PREMIUM LAGER 5% ABV
Spritzy, with an attractive head, floral and grapefruit fruitiness on the nose, and a dry, biscuit malt palate.

CZECH DARK LAGER

DARK BEER 4.7% ABV
Its distinct malty flavour develops a cinnamon spiciness before rolling into biscuit undertones.

SKLEPNÍ

PREMIUM LAGER 4% ABV
Unfiltered, with a light body and lingering biscuit malt finish.

GRANÁT

DARK BEER 4.5% ABV
A reddish brown, award-winning lager, with a distinct caramel palate complementing a plummy aroma.

PREZIDENT PREMIUM

BLENDED PILSNER 5% ABV
Southern Bohemian malt lager and refined pilsner blend for a full body and bitter finish.

ZLATÁ JEDENÁCTKA

PREMIUM LAGER 4.5% ABV
Brilliantly golden, with unmistakable hop aromas and velvety malt fullness. Soft, bitter finish.

DĚTENICE

507 24 Dětenice, Czech Republic
www.detenice.cz/en

This castle-based brewery – once owned by the Prague chapter of the Knights of Malta – closed in 1955 after several years of nationalization, and reopened only in 2000.

BREWING SECRET Beers are brewed in direct-fired vessels and are filtered through straw, fermented in wooden vats, then lagered in oak barrels.

EGGENBERG

Latrán 27, Český Krumlov,
Czech Republic
www.eggenberg.cz

Nowhere but in Bohemia could two towns merge over brewing disputes. Years of arguing about wheat beer privileges were resolved simply by uniting neighbours Latrán and Krumlov, and establishing a single brewery. Over time, the brewery passed from the Eggenberg family to the Schwarzenbergs and down the centuries to its present owners, Dionex.

GAMBRINUS

U Prazdroje 7, 304 97 Plzeň,
Czech Republic
www.gambrinus.cz

There are several versions of the origin of the name Gambrinus, but all trace their origins back to beer in some way, be it brewing, cellars, or hops.

BREWING SECRET The brewery shares its malthouse, filtration facilities, and filling lines with Pilsner Urquell. The brewhouses, however, are separate.

HEROLD

Zámecký obvod 31, Březnice u Příbrami, PSČ: 262 72, Czech Republic
www.pivovar-herold.cz

Attached to the town's Baroque castle, the brewery produces traditional, hand-crafted, pilsner-style beers based on a "small is beautiful" philosophy. The range includes wheat beers and Bohemian Black Lager.

BREWING SECRET Open fermenters, home-drawn water, and resident maltings accentuate its heritage.

SVETLÉ DETENICKÉ PIVO 12°
PREMIUM LAGER 4% ABV
Aromatically floral, finely structured body; sweet malt and honey influences, and a hoppy afterglow.

TMAVÉ DETENICKE PIVO 13°
DARK BEER 4% ABV
A typically full-bodied dark lager; malty, some spice, and faintly bitter towards the finish.

EGGENBERG SVĚTLÝ LEŽÁK
PREMIUM LAGER 5% ABV
Powerfully floral with sweet, butterscotch notes; zesty, firm, and delightfully balanced to a bitter finish.

EGGENBERG TMAVÝ LEŽÁK
DARK BEER 4.2% ABV
Deep and dark, with a hop pungency, then a malty caramel and toffee bittersweet palate.

GAMBRINUS PREMIUM
PREMIUM PILSNER 5% ABV
A fresh, grassy, and lemon aroma, with hints of butter throughout a full malt flavour.

GAMBRINUS SVĚTLÝ
PILSNER 5% ABV
A malt and vanilla palate follows a honeyed, grassy nose to a spicy, bitter finale.

BOHEMIAN BLACK LAGER
DARK LAGER 5.3% ABV
A schwarzbier-type lager; bitter chocolate flavours, plus a little malty sweetness, and a long, dry, slightly smoky finish.

TRADITIONAL CZECH LAGER
LAGER 4.1% ABV
Crisp tasting, yet softly textured, with a classic creamy malt veil and a late hop dryness.

BREWERY

HOLBA

Pivovarská 261, 788 33 Hanušovice,
Czech Republic
www.holba.cz

Among the largest and best equipped breweries in the country, Holba – based in the Jeseníky Mountains – is intensely proud of its regional heritage and independence as a traditional beer producer. It describes its portfolio as "genuine beer from the mountains" and reinvests much of its profits in quality control.

JEŽEK

Vrchlického 2, 586 01 Jihlava,
Czech Republic
www.pivovar-jihlava.cz

From its earliest days, Ježek beer was exported to Austria – the Viennese monarchy showed particular interest. Wholesale reconstruction in the mid-1990s saw environmentally friendly production methods put in place and improvements made to the quality, taste, and stability of the beer. Ježek also has an on-site restaurant.

KOZEL

Ringhofferova 1, 251 69 Velké Popovice,
Czech Republic
www.kozel.cz

The famous goat emblem was created by a travelling French artist in return for hospitality. The town's new brewery opened in 1874 and, by 1912, German innkeepers would boast they kept Kozel's beer. Since 2002, it has been part of Plzeňský Prazdroj – owned by SABMiller – with massive investment driving development.

KRUŠOVICE

270 53 Krušovice 1,
Czech Republic
www.krusovice.cz

According to the town's historical records, brewing first began here in 1581. A couple of years later the Austrian Emperor and Czech King Rudolph II bought the brewery from Jiří Birka, and began brewing for the residents of Prague Castle. From 1731 to 1945, the brewery was owned by the Furstenberg family, when it was nationalized and came

BEER

HOLBA ŠERÁK
PILSNER 4.7% ABV
Bitterly hoppy, with a surprising malt richness. The brewery's advice is to drink "at least one a day".

HOLBA CLASSIC 10°
PREMIUM LAGER 4.2% ABV
A thirst quencher with a mild, slightly bitter flavour, some malt, and an earthy hop aroma.

JIHLAVSKÝ GRAND
EXTRA PREMIUM LAGER 8.1% ABV
An extraordinary honey-gold beer, with malt and bread aromas, and a rich malt palate.

ŠENKOVNÍ 10°
LAGER 4.4% ABV
Golden in colour, with a nice bitterness and a crisp malt finish.

KOZEL PREMIUM
PREMIUM LAGER 4.8% ABV
Florally hoppy, with a biscuit malt palate and engaging bitterness.

KOZEL ČERNÝ
DARK BEER 3.8% ABV
Aromatic hops dominate, and dark malts give spicy caramel flavours.

KRUŠOVICE IMPERIAL
PREMIUM LAGER 5% ABV
A dry straw aroma heightens a bitter palate, with a floral hop and malt finish.

MUŠKETÝR
LAGER 4.5% ABV
Zatec hops add a soft, floral note to this golden, sweet-tasting beer.

under state control. Privatized in 1994, it has had several owners but, in 2007, it became part of international brewer Heineken. It is now the largest producer of beer in the Czech Republic.

LOBKOWICZ

Vysoký Chlumec 29, 262 52 Vysoký Chlumec, Czech Republic
www.lobkowicz-premium.cz/en

The noble Lobkowicz family has owned the brewery since 1466 and are proud that it is a relatively small operation. Some of the beer is exported as Premium Czech Lager.

BREWING SECRET The brewery promotes ecologically-sensitive production methods and uses water from an artesian well.

NÁCHOD/PRIMÁTOR

Dobrošouská 130, 547 40 Náchod, Czech Republic
www.primator.cz

One of the most technically advanced breweries in the country, Náchod draws its water from the Ardšpach-Teplice protected landscape region. The brewery's origins lie in 1872, with enlargement following in 1925 and 1930. More recent improvements include a new brewhouse, and better storage and filling facilities.

NOVOPACKÉ PIVO

Pivovarská 400, 509 01 Nová Paka, Czech Republic
www.novopackepivo.cz

The advantages of brewing and malting houses sharing the same site was recognized in Nová Paka almost 500 years ago, and its significance persists today through passionately traditional practices. Emphasis on tourism at the Art Nouveau-style complex keeps its profile high at home, while 40 per cent of production is exported.

KRUŠOVICE ČERNÉ

BLACK LAGER 3.5% ABV
Sweet and easy drinking, it has notes of dark chocolate, molasses, and coffee.

KRUŠOVICE SVĚTLÉ

LAGER 3.8% ABV
Sunlight yellow, it is an easy-drinking, refreshing beer.

LOBKOWICZ PREMIUM

LAGER 4.7% ABV
Golden and clear, it has notes of malty bread and a good hop bitter finish.

LOBKOWICZ BARON 12°

DARK BEER 4.7% ABV
A dark lager, with flavour notes of chewy caramel and chocolate emerging from sweet malt.

PRIMÁTOR PREMIUM

PREMIUM LAGER 5% ABV
Soft vegetable hop aroma, a distinct bitterness on the palate, lapping in full malt richness.

PRIMÁTOR DOUBLE 24°

DARK LAGER 10.5% ABV
A spirited kick detectable from its sweet malt aroma, then spice and dried fruit lusciousness.

KUMBURÁK

PREMIUM LAGER 5.3% ABV
A rich malt palate follows some citrus fruit aromas through to a memorable hop aftertaste.

PODKRKONOŠSKÝ SPECIÁL DARK

DARK BEER 6.3% ABV
An intriguing dark colour and deep flavours that unearth chocolate and coffee notes.

Prague's Old Town Square is thronged with visitors throughout the year, enjoying its many pavement bar-cafés.

BREWERY

NYMBURK

Pražská 581, 288 25 Nymburk,
Czech Republic
www.postriziny.cz

In the mid-19th century a monopoly was broken up in Nymburk when beers from other towns could be offered for sale on one condition – that they must be tasty! The present brewery's first beer flowed in 1898. The acclaimed writer Bohumil Hrabel was raised in the town and now features on most of the bottle labels.

PERNŠTEJN

Palackého 250, 530 33 Pardubice,
Czech Republic
www.pernstejn.cz

In the late 19th century, the brewery's porter was renowned throughout Europe for its flavour and strength, winning international medals almost at will. This rare example is still produced today, alongside fruit drinks and non-alcoholic beverages (similarly with several of the country's breweries) in an impressive portfolio.

PILSNER URQUELL

U Prazdroje 7, 30497 Plzeň,
Czech Republic
www.pilsner-urquell.cz

The Czechs have blessed us with the microwave oven, soft contact lenses, and beer that changed the world. It was, however, a Bavarian who was the key player in the Pilsner Urquell story. As a young brewer, Josef Groll presented the nation with its first pilsner on 4 October 1842. This sensational clear golden beer spread across Europe like wildfire from its "original source".

PIVOVAR SAMSON

Lidická 458/51, 370 54,
České Budějovice, Czech Republic
www.samson.cz

Pivovar Samson is the new name for the Budweiser Burgerbrau (BB), after the brewery's trademark rights to its use of the Budweiser name were bought by AB InBev in 2011. The purchase only includes BB rights to its Budweiser trademarks, which were used on two of its brands. Pivovar Samson retains the ownership of the brewery and all other non-Budweiser trademarks.

BEER

TMAVÝ LEŽÁK
Dark Beer 4.3% ABV
Dark amber in colour, with a rich coffee and caramel palate and chocolate-coated finish.

POSTŘIŽINSKÉ ZLATOVAR
Premium Lager 4.7% ABV
Hrabel is indeed depicted on the label of this fully malty and mildly bitter charmer.

PERNŠTEJN SVĚTLÝ LEŽÁK
Lager 5% ABV
Invitingly deep gold in colour, with high malt levels counterbalancing a final hop bitterness perfectly.

PARDUBICKÝ PORTER
Porter 8% ABV
Spice and coffee notes get intimate with sweet malt – an accomplished bottom-fermented stunner.

PILSNER URQUELL
Classic Pilsner 4.4% ABV
The ideal 35mm (1½in) tight head leaves a lacing down the glass with every sip of spiced leaf and preserved fruit flavours, developing a sweet malt piquancy and a long, enveloping finish.

SAMSON BUDWEISER BIER
Premium Lager 4.7% ABV
Some butterscotch and citrus aromas and a honeyed, sweet, malty palate. The finish is peppery and dry.

BB BUDWEISER BIER ORIGINAL
Pilsner 5% ABV
Vanilla and herb hop aromas, a bittersweet, malt-veiled mouthfeel, with final traces of tobacco.

RADEGAST

739 51 Nošovice, Czech Republic
www.radegast.cz

Radegast, roughly meaning "dear guest", was the Slavic God of fertility and crops, and consequently became proclaimed God of hospitality too. Despite its nominal connections with the dawn of time, the brewery began operating only in 1970. It continues to be one of the country's most technologically advanced and best-equipped beer producers.

REBEL

Dobrovského 2027,
Havlíčkův Brod, Czech Republic
www.hbrebel.cz

In 1995, ownership returned to the descendants of the original 1843 brewery owners with a renewed reconstruction impetus. Havlíčkův Brod's brewing tradition has survived centuries of disruption – destruction by Hussites, a town-razing fire, two wars, and political upheaval. The Rebel name honours Czech nationalist and dissident Karel Havlíček Borovský.

REGENT

Trocnovské náměstí 124, 379 01 Třeboň,
Czech Republic
www.pivovar-regent.cz

The brewery's name was inspired by an accountant who became a knight, then regent and uncrowned king of the entire Bohemia kingdom. Today's brewery was created in the mid-19th century, and delivery trains exporting Regent beer soon traversed Europe. Owners have included the ubiquitous Schwarzenbergs and, from 2000, brothers Ferdinand and Václav Stasek.

STAROBRNO

Hlinky 160/12, 661 47 Brno,
Czech Republic
www.starobrno.cz

Brewing around Brno began in monasteries and convents, notably those of the Augustinian Brothers and Cistercian Sisters. The highest production and technical standards – features of its Mandell and Huzak family ownership since 1872 – have earned Starobrno a coveted "Czech Made" quality certificate. It is now owned by Dutch firm Heineken.

RADEGAST ORIGINÁL
PILSNER 4% ABV
A light malt and spiced hop nose, malt-sweet flavours and a crisp, grainy bitterness.

RADEGAST PREMIUM
PREMIUM LAGER 5% ABV
A characteristic herbal, hoppy aroma and medium-sweet malt intensity dwell on cereal notes.

REBEL ORIGINAL PREMIUM
PREMIUM LAGER 4.8% ABV
Fragrantly aromatic and fully malty in the classic Czech style, then a dry hop finish.

DARK REBEL
LAGER 4.7% ABV
A dark ruby-coloured lager with hints of butterscotch and sweet sugars. The finish is mild, but bitter.

BOHEMIA REGENT PREZIDENT
PREMIUM LAGER 6% ABV
Flamboyant hop aromas prepare the palate for a well-rounded malt sweetness of flavour.

BOHEMIA REGENT PALE LAGER
PILSNER 5% ABV
The floral aroma leaves traces of cinnamon, then a toffee palate with hints of honey.

STAROBRNO MEDIUM
PREMIUM LAGER 4.7% ABV
Unpasteurized light lager with a malty and subtle floral hop aroma.

STAROBRNO TRADIČNÍ
LIGHT BEER 4% ABV
Unpasteurized light beer with a golden-yellow colour, pleasant bitterness, and malt aroma.

THE STORY OF...

Pilsner Urquell

U Prazdroje 64/7,
301 00 Plzeň, Czech Republic

Pilsener, pilsner, or pils are the names often given to the most famous lager style in the world. And the birthplace of the world's first bright golden beer is the city of Plzeň in Bohemia, in the Czech Republic. Czech beers were brown in colour and probably cloudy until 1842, when Josef Groll from Bavaria was contracted by the town of Plzeň to brew a beer for the new citizens' brewery (the Plzeňský Prazdroj) which could rival a new style of copper-coloured beers emerging from Vienna. He created a fresh, clear, gold beer, topped with a wispy, snow-white head. The lightness of the beer was made possible by advances in malting, in which direct heat from hot coals was replaced by a more controllable heat in the form of warm air, which enabled paler shades of malt to be produced.

It was given the name Pilsner Urquell (meaning from Plzeň, the original source) and the style has been mimicked, but rarely bettered, all over the world. A true pilsner, at 4.4 per cent ABV, has a moderate amount of alcohol; typically most beers from continental Europe have an alcoholic strength of 5 per cent ABV. The unfermented sugar in the beer contributes to its assertive richness. Today the Pilsner Urquell Brewery produces one in five of the Czech Republic's beers and is its biggest exporter.

▲ **THE BREWERY** Built on the bank of the Radbuza River, as this 19th-century panorama shows, the brewery stands on sandstone foundations that were carved out to create tunnels for cold storage, or lagering, of the beer. A maze of underground galleries contains more than 3,500 large pitch-lined oak casks, where very slowly in the cold, damp conditions the beer is matured from a precocious brew into one with a majestic fullness.

▲ **STEEL FERMENTERS** The beer was originally fermented in open vessels made of Bohemian oak. Today, steel fermenters are used, and Pilsner Urquell's master brewer Václav Berkais is convinced that his predecessor Josef Groll would have used steel rather than wood had it been available.

▲ **COLD FERMENTATION** Because it is cold fermented, the beer maintains more of its flavours from the spicy Žatec hops and sweet Bohemian or Moravian barley malt. The hops impart an especially fresh, herbal aroma, and contribute to a certain and classy finish.

◀ **CONFIDENCE AND PRIDE** The grandiose entrance to the brewery exudes a pride and confident swagger in the work that takes place inside. The cylindrical water tower holds supplies from the brewery's own springs. This low sulphite, low carbonate water is ideal for making pilsner.

▼ THE BREWING HALL Large, graceful, copper-coloured vessels dominate the brewing hall. Pilsner Urquell uses a triple decoction mash in its brewing. Portions of the mash are drawn off at three different times, and each portion, or decoction, is heated, boiled briefly, then returned to the main mash. The process helps break down the complex carbohydrate in the malt into simpler fermentable sugars.

◀ THE MUSEUM AND VISITOR CENTRE The brewery is much more than a workplace. It also welcomes people to its visitor centre, and offers a sensory exhibition of raw materials and an insight into how beer was brewed over 100 years ago in the on-site museum.

▲ STONE CELLARS The highlight for any visitor has to be a walk into one of the dimly lit, ice-cool sandstone cellars, where unfiltered and non-pasteurized Pilsner Urquell can be sampled straight from the barrel.

BREWERY

STAROPRAMEN

Nádražni 84, 150 54 Prague 5,
Czech Republic
www.staropramen.com; and
Hornopolní 57, Ostrava 1,
Czech Republic
www.ostravar.cz

Far-sighted developers situated
the Smíchov Brewery in Prague's
future industrial area, where
demand for beer was assured.
From the start, Staropramen –
Prague's largest brewer – was
perceived as a Czech beer for

Czech people, which gave it an
advantage amongst nationalist leaning
consumers. Today it is owned by
Molson Coors, which also operates
the Czech Republic's Ostrovar
Brewery in the city of Ostrova.
A popular feature of both the sites
are the well-known brewery tours,
museums, and visitor centres.

SVIJANY

Svijany 25, 463 46 Příšovice,
Czech Republic
www.pivovarsvijany.cz

Beer was crucial to the region's
economy long before this brewery's
foundation in 1564, and family
dynasties have marked Svijany's long
history. That stopped in the mid-20th
century with nationalization, but
further changes of ownership followed
the brewery's privatization in 1998,
and, under the current ownership,
Svijany is seeing a revival in fortunes.

UHERSKÝ BROD

Neradice 369, 688 16 Uherský Brod,
Czech Republic
www.pivovar-uherskybrod.cz

Weary of leasing the Kaunic family
brewery, František Janáček built
his own in 1894, and it was soon
regarded as the best in southeast
Europe. His son Jaromír turned it
into one of the most modern, then
his nephew guided it through a period
of considerable reconstruction. The
company is part of the Lobkowicz
brewery group.

BEER

STAROPRAMEN DARK BEER
DARK BEER 4.5% ABV
Its light body loops around malty
caramel, liquorice, and aniseed
notes to a floral finale.

STAROPRAMEN PREMIUM LAGER
PREMIUM LAGER 5% ABV
A rich floral bite unveils a
full-bodied satisfier with a *riz*
("just right") finish.

OSTRAVAR PREMIUM
PREMIUM LAGER 5.1% ABV
A rich head promoting malt and
hop aromas straddle a full-bodied,
strong, bitter bite.

VELVET
LAGER 5.3% ABV
A Czech take on an English ale,
it has a bittersweet malt finish.

SVIJANSKÝ RYTÍŘ 12%
PILSNER 5% ABV
Pilsner-style with a yeast-rich,
sweet malt aroma and high levels
of fruit vitality.

SVIJANSKÝ KNÍŽE 13%
PILSNER 5.6% ABV
Fragrantly hoppy "special light"
lager with a full, sweet, malt body
and bitter finale.

PIVO PATRIOT 11
LAGER 4.6% ABV
A full malt biscuit taste is
augmented by a hop bitter finish;
nutty flavours give way to a soft,
bitter finish.

KOUNIC YEAST
LAGER 4.6% ABV
Unpasteurized version of an amber
Viennese beer; a dry, nutty undertone
gives way to a spicy, crisp finish.

U MEDVÍDKŮ

Na Perštýně 7, 100 01 Prague 1,
Czech Republic
www.umedvidku.cz

The restaurant and brewhouse date back to 1466, though the brewery has been completely modernized – along with extensions and additions to the *pension*, which retains its original Gothic rafters and Renaissance painted ceilings. This is one of the biggest beer halls in Prague, and it hosted the city's first cabaret.

ŽATEC

Žižkovo náměstí 81, 438 01 Žatec,
Czech Republic
www.zatec-brewery.com

There is no escaping it in Czech beer production – every brewery uses the town's succulent hops and, as far back as 1585, Žatec beer was praised for "its essence, strengths, and virtues".

BREWING SECRET Significant recent investment has upgraded its yeast plant, restored open fermenters, and introduced state-of-the-art kegging.

ZLATOPRAMEN

Drážďanská 80, 400 07 Ústí nad Labem,
Czech Republic
www.zlatopramen.cz

Modernization may have accelerated in recent years, but this brewery's history is as long as the existence of brewing privileges. The use of Austrian Emperor Franz Joseph II's eagle for its emblem was granted in the early 20th century, while the Zlatopramen trademark was adopted in 1967. It is now owned by Heineken.

ZUBR

Komenského č. 35, Přerov, PSČ 751 51,
Czech Republic
www.zubr.cz

The Zubr (buffalo) label is a well-regarded one, with more than 20 national and international brewing awards to its name. It also has a "mark of quality" certificate for best food product. It is one of the country's largest volume producers, with 12 per cent of its output going for export throughout Europe.

OLDGOTT BARIQUE
PILSNER 5.2% ABV
Earthy and melon-fruity aromas. Yeasty characteristics develop into a roasted malt, caramel infusion.

X-BEER 33
SPECIALITY BEER 12.6% ABV (VARIABLE)
Matured for 28 weeks in oak vessels for an elaborate, sweet flavour, and indulgent complexity.

ŽATEC BLUE LABEL
PREMIUM LAGER 4.6% ABV
Hints of grassy hop and sweet malt, then banana with biscuit malt on the palate.

ŽATEC DARK
LAGER 5.7% ABV
Heavily hopped, it is a rich, dark beer with a sweet, lingering finish.

ZLATOPRAMEN 11°
PILSNER 4.9% ABV
A faint, earthy hop aroma unfolds into a full biscuit flavour with a potent bitterness.

ZLATOPRAMEN 11° UNFILTERED
PILSNER 4.7% ABV
An unfiltered, tanked version of the brewery's bottled pilsner. Drunk fresh, it's a heady, zesty affair.

ZUBR PREMIUM 12°
PREMIUM LAGER 5.1% ABV
Golden, with a glass-embracing froth throughout its rounded mouthfeel and a medium bitterness.

ZUBR CLASSIC 10° LIGHT
PILSNER 4.1% ABV
A good-quality hop aroma and sweetly malty, driving its medium body to a flinty bitterness.

MORE BEERS OF

THE CZECH REPUBLIC

The Czech Republic has a long and proud brewing heritage. Unlike the new wave of brewing that has swept through the USA and parts of Europe in recent years, most of these Czech breweries have been around much longer, largely supplying a local market.

BREWERY

FERDINAND

Táborská 306, 256 01 Benešov, Czech Republic
www.pivovarferdinand.cz

Brewing is entrenched in Benešov, as is evident by street names such as Na Chmelnici ("At The Hop Garden"). The core of today's brewery dates to 1897, while extensive 1970s reconstruction stimulated steady growth. The trademark Ferdinand, adopted in 1992, triggered a series of national awards for the range.

KLÁŠTER

294 15 Klášter Hradiště nad Jizerou, Czech Republic
www.pivovarklaster.cz

Unpasteurized beers are fermented and aged here in caves hewn out of solid rock deep beneath the handsome brewery in 1570. Traditional brewery methods and maturation processes have elevated Klášter's award-winning beers to connoisseur status.

BREWING SECRET Medieval recipes are used for some of the beers.

PLATAN

Pivovarská 168, 398 61 Protivín, Czech Republic
www.pivovar-protivin.cz

The avenue leading to the brewery is explanation enough that Platan means "plane tree". Brewing has taken place here since 1598, and for several hundred years it was in the hands of Schwarzenberg in family – however in 2008, it was purchased by Lobkowicz brewery. The brewery is growing its production by exporting.

POLIČKA

Pivovarská 151, 572 14 Polička, Czech Republic
www.pivovar-policka.cz

The small-walled town of Polička began brewing in the 16th century and has never stopped. Some of the equipment still in use at the brewery today dates back to a 1865 rebuild.

BREWING SECRET Beer is bottled unpasteurized, as is some cask production – well worth seeking out in its wide-ranging sales territory.

BEER

LEŽÁK SVĚTLÝ 12%
PREMIUM LAGER 5% ABV
Medium bodied, vigorous, and fragrantly hoppy, with a finely balanced malt and bitter integrity.

LEŽÁK TMAVÝ 11%
DARK BEER 4.5% ABV
Dark amber in colour, with a sweet and slightly spiced flavour and a lengthy, sweet finish.

KLÁŠTER LEŽÁK 11°
PREMIUM LAGER 4.6% ABV
A fine, grainy, generous malt texture performs effectively with a faint hoppiness and bittersweet finale.

KLÁŠTER LEAK
PILSNER 4.6% ABV
Light golden with a nice head, a beady aroma gives way to a full malt taste. The finish is nicely bitter.

PLATAN 11%
LAGER 4.8% ABV
Golden-orange, with a good malty nose, this lager ends with a pleasant hoppy bitterness.

PRÁCHEŇSKÁ PERLA
LAGER 6% ABV
Full bodied and a hearty mixture of malt and fruit, it has a lingering bitter finish.

10° HRADEBNÍ SVĚTLÉ VÝČEPNÍ
PILSNER 4% ABV
A bready aroma, thin body, but surprising level of caramel malt.

11° OTAKAR SVĚTLÝ LEŽÁK
PREMIUM LAGER 4.5% ABV
Microbiologically filtered to retain natural flavours of floral-to-fruity hop and bittersweet malt.

BREWERY

POUTNÍK

Pivovarská 856, 393 17 Pelhřimov, Czech Republic
www.pivovarpoutnik.cz

Centuries of brewing in Pelhřimov have earned this brewery a reputation for quality through progress, but it wasn't until 2003 that the new owners – the DUP Coop, adopted Poutník (Pilgrim) as the brewery's brand name. New methods, strategies, and recipe alterations were also introduced to concentrate output on unpasteurized beers in distinctive styles.

PURKMISTR

Selská náves 2, 32600 Plzeň – Černice, Czech Republic
www.purkmistr.cz

One of the new waves of Czech brewers, it opened in 2007. Not only is there a beer spa on site, but each September it plays host to one of the best craft beer festivals in the world. The brewer often adds unusual flavours to his beers, which are foraged from nearby fields and woods.

RYCHTÁŘ

Resslova 260, 539 01 Hlinsko v Čechách, Czech Republic
www.rychtar.cz

Beginning life in 1913 as the "Social Brewery", Rychtar has undergone impressive modernization at the hands of its current Czech investment group owners.

BREWING SECRET A new fermenting cellar and microfiltration plant have improved levels of production quality, particularly for unpasteurized beers.

U FLEKŮ

Křemencová 11, 110 01 Prague 1, Czech Republic
www.ufleku.cz

A brewpub of wide renown, its restoration has remained true to its 1499 origins. The atmosphere is heightened by stained glass, stylish furniture, a picturesque courtyard, and Gothic vaulted beer halls.

BREWING SECRET Traditional oak fermenters and stacked cooling vats are among the unusual brewery features.

BEER

POUTNÍK PRÉMIUM 12°
PREMIUM LAGER 4.8% ABV
Unmistakably malty, but well balanced with earthy notes, then a bittersweet aftertaste.

POUTNÍK SPECIÁL 14°
PREMIUM LAGER 5% ABV
Fully rounded with plum-like aromas complementing a superbly malty body and bitter finish.

SVETLÝ LEŽÁK
LAGER 4.8% ABV
A classic Czech pale lager, which has great depth of flavour.

PIVO WASABI
SPICE LAGER 4.8% ABV
A slight green hue hints at the beer's hot character from its spicy addition. The heat is balanced by a good malt sweetness.

KLASIK 10°
PILSNER 4% ABV
Often described as the brewery's "daily drinker", it is typically pale but malty and bittersweet.

PREMIUM 12°
PREMIUM LAGER 5% ABV
Distinctly malty, with a light natural carbonation and a developing, sharply defined hop finish.

FLEKOVSKÝ TMAVÝ LEŽÁK
DARK BEER 4.5% ABV
A classic dark lager – and one of the world's greats – unfiltered and complex, with roasted coffee and cream aromas meeting a bitter palate via spiced hop, then liquorice and coffee influences.

Folk musicians frequently entertain drinkers in the traditional bar-restaurants of Prague's Old Town.

BEER TRAIL

PRAGUE

The city of Prague is one of the world's greatest beer destinations. And where better to start a beer trail than in the Old Town Square (Staroměstské náměstí), location of the famous 15th-century Astronomical Clock – one of the world's oldest clocks still in working order. Many bars edge the square, each spilling out onto the pavements with seating and canopies.

A short walk away is the dramatic Powder Tower, built in 1475 on the site of one of Prague's 13 city gates. Nearby is the impressive 14th-century Charles Bridge. Walk over it and see Na Kampe, where Hollywood actor Tom Cruise, as Special Agent Ethan Hunt, blew up a car in the film *Mission Impossible 3*. Less frenetic than the Old Town side of the bridge, Na Kampe is home to several new bars that have recently opened in the area.

JOURNEY STATS

1 hour, plus drinking time
5km (3 miles)

OLD TOWN SQUARE
Here it is possible to sit outside and savour a beer, while watching the thousands of visitors who now flock to the Czech capital. Displays of folk dancing and music can often be enjoyed here too.

FINISH

U ZLATÉHO TYGRA
One of the Old Town's most atmospheric and oldest bars, U Zlatého Tygra is crowded with small tables, which always seem to be full with locals deep in energetic conversations – so be prepared to stand. It's a favourite of the writer and former Czech President Václav Havel; President Clinton has also drunk here. The unfiltered Pilsner Urquell is said to be the best in Prague. *Husova 228/17, Prague (www.uzlatehotygra.cz)*

U PINKASŮ
In 1843, U Pinkasů was the first bar in Prague to serve Pilsner Urquell, and it is still available today. The bar was saved from extinction in 2000, when it was extensively refurbished. A more recent refurbishment has opened up more of the building. *Jungmannovo náměstí, 15/16, Prague (www.upinkasu.cz)*

4 NOVOMĚSTSKÝ PIVOVAR

An Art Deco-style entrance leads visitors down an alleyway of shops to this wood-panelled brewery, pub, and restaurant. Unfiltered light and dark beers are available. The food is unashamedly Czech, with specialities such as goulash, tripe soup, and roast knuckle of pork. *Vodičkova 682/20, Prague (www.npivovar.cz/en)*

5 PIVODUM

The Pivodum restaurant and bar is dominated by gleaming coppers. Traditional Czech beers are served, as well as other interesting brews, including a sour cherry beer, a coffee beer, and Šamp – a beer champagne. Groups can order eight beers for the price of seven, and they are served in a large Giraffe-like container. A sample tray of eight beers is also available. *Ječná/Lípová 15, Prague (www. pivovarskydum.com)*

6 U FLEKŮ

Crowded it may be, a haunt of many tourists it certainly is, but U Fleků should not be missed. Brewing began here in 1499, and it is said to be the world's oldest brewpub. It comprises many large rooms, including one for a booming oompah band. It has a small museum and daily brewery tours. The superb house beer is Flekorský tmavý ležák, which comes in dark and light versions. *Křemencova 11, Prague 1 (en.ufleku.cz)*

BEERS TO TRAVEL FOR

REST OF THE WORLD

EUROPE • THE AMERICAS • ASIA • AUSTRALASIA • AFRICA

Wolf, Canada

■ CANADA

Quilmes, Argentina

Hue, Vietnam

Cerveceria Bucanero, Cuba

■ MEXICO

■ CUBA

■ TRINIDAD & TOBAGO

■ PERU

■ BRAZIL

■ ARGENTINA

Beba, Italy

Stiegl, Austria

REST OF THE WORLD

The world of beer is expanding. Markets are growing in territories less associated with brewing, but of more interest are the nations where craft brewing is burgeoning. Italy is one of the most interesting of these: not only are its brewers producing flavour-rich, experimental beers, but they are also showing how to market beer in elegantly designed bottles. This is true, to some extent, in Denmark and Scandinavia too, while over in East Asia, Japan is developing great variants of European beers, with their own, quirky take on classic design.

Herslev Bryghus, Denmark

SWEDEN
NORWAY
FINLAND
ESTONIA
LATVIA
LITHUANIA
DENMARK
NETHERLANDS
POLAND
EMBOURG
SLOVAKIA
AUSTRIA
UKRAINE
FRANCE
HUNGARY
SWIZERLAND
SLOVENIA
ROMANIA
CROATIA
SERBIA
SPAIN
ITALY
GREECE
TUGAL
MALTA
CYPRUS

RUSSIA

Ochakovo, Russia

MONGOLIA

CHINA

SOUTH KOREA

JAPAN

Hideji, Japan

INDIA
LAOS
THAILAND
VIETNAM
SRI LANKA
SINGAPORE
INDONESIA

AUSTRALIA

NEW ZEALAND

Mac's, New Zealand

Thaibev, Thailand

Little Creatures, Australia

SOUTH AFRICA

BREWERY

32 VIA DEI BIRRAI
Via Cal Lusent 41, 31040 Pederobba
Treviso, Italy
www.32viadeibirrai.com

Born into a brewing family, Belgian-Italian Fabiano Toffoli founded his microbrewery in 2006 after working as a brewer and a brewing consultant.

BREWING SECRET Toffoli brews with pure water from several sources to lend distinct characteristics to different beers; the hops are from Poperinge.

ALMOND 22
Via Dietro le Mura 36/38,
65010 Spoltore (PE), Italy
www.birraalmond.com

This microbrewery was founded in 2003 in the seaside town of Pescara by Swedish-Italian Jurij Ferri. He brews highly praised ales inspired by British and Belgian styles, as well as some original, experimental beers that use local ingredients.

BALADIN
Piazza V Luglio 15,
12060 Piozzo (CN), Italy
www.birreria.com

Charismatic, pioneering Teo Musso is internationally known as one of the most creative brewers in the world. He has turned beer into a type of wine and created beer truffles – not even he knows what he will do next.

BREWING SECRET Musso plays music to his yeasts during the fermentation process, believing that they respond.

BARLEY
Via Colombo, 09047 Maracalagonis
Cagliari, Italy
www.barley.it

Skilful home-brewer Nicola Perra established this microbrewery in 2006 in southern Sardinia, challenging the mass-market lagers so popular in the region (consumption here is the highest in Italy).

BREWING SECRET Local ingredients such as Sardinian wine wort and organic honey are used in the ales.

BEER

OPPALE
BELGIAN BLOND ALE 5.5% ABV
Refreshing, easy-to-drink, cloudy ale, with a very pleasant dry, bitter finish of chives.

AUDACE
BELGIAN GOLDEN STRONG ALE
8.4% ABV
Strong golden ale, rich in ester flavours. Warming, spicy, and dry, with a long, bitter, citrussy finish.

TORBATA
BARLEY WINE 8.5% ABV
Peated ale with a smoky flavour similar to a Scotch whisky. Easy to drink despite its strength.

FARROTTA
SPELT WHEAT ALE 5.7% ABV
Cloudy golden ale brewed using barley and locally grown spelt; easy drinking and thirst-quenching.

NORA
SPICED ALE 6.8% ABV
Inspired by ancient Egypt, using kamut grains, ginger, and myrrh. A balsamic bitterness comes from Ethiopian resins.

XYAUYÙ
BARLEY WINE 14% ABV
Radical oxidization gives "solera" sherry-like favours. A flat, warming, velvety nightcap. A masterpiece.

TOCCADIBÒ
GOLDEN STRONG ALE 8.4% ABV
A warming ale; spicy, hoppy, and dry, with intriguing bitter-almond notes of amaretto.

BB 10
BARLEY WINE 10% ABV
A unique brew made with *sapa*, the boiled wort of local Cannonau grapes. A highly distinctive nightcap.

THE BEST-KNOWN ITALIAN BEERS

Despite the booming micro market, Italy's most popular beers are still mass-market, multinational lagers from foreign-owned groups.

Heineken Italia owns the Dreher, Von Wunster, and Prinz brands, as well as Birra Moretti from Udine, with its classic Moretti, pure malt Baffo d'Oro, and deep amber La Rossa. SABMiller controls Whürer and, most importantly, the renowned Peroni brewery in Rome, home to the iconic Birra Peroni, Nastro Azzurro, the most famous Italian beer, and the acclaimed pure malt Peroni Gran Riserva.

Carlsberg Italia has Splügen and Birra Poretti, brewing Poretti Premium and both Blonde and Red Bock 1877.

The only large independent Italian producer is Forst, a family company that brews straightforward lagers as well as quality beers such as VIP Pils and the doppelbock Sixtus. Forst also controls the renowned Menabrea brand, with its flagship Menabrea 150° Anniversario.

Unionbirrai, the Italian union of small craft brewers, was formed in 1998 to help small brewers survive as independents.

BIRRA PERONI (LAGER 4.7% ABV) *left*
PERONI NASTRO AZZURRO (PREMIUM PILSENER 5.1% ABV) *centre*
BIRRA MORETTI (LAGER 4.6% ABV) *right*
MORETTI LA ROSSA (AMBER STRONG LAGER 7.2% ABV)
MENABREA 150° ANNIVERSARIO (PREMIUM LAGER 4.8% ABV)

BEBA

Viale Italia 11,
10069 Villar Perosa (TO), Italy
www.birrabeba.it

Pioneering brothers Alessandro and Enrico Borio brew a wide range of regular and seasonal lagers at their microbrewery, founded in 1996 near Turin. The adjoining taproom serves all the house beers on draught along with excellent food. The local speciality is *gofri*, a crisp unleavened bread stuffed with cheeses, cured meats, or preserves.

MOTOR OIL
STRONG DARK LAGER 6.8% ABV
Ebony coloured, with strong notes of liquorice and roasted coffee beans, and a long bitter finish. As viscous as its namesake.

TALCO
RYE LAGER 4.5% ABV
Seasonal "rye weizen-lager" is a thirst-quenching treat on a hot summer afternoon.

BIRRA DEL BORGO

Via del Colle Rosso,
02021 Borgorose (RI), Italy
www.birradelborgo.it

Birra del Borgo was founded in 2005 by former home-brewer Leonardo Di Vincenzo. Having learnt his trade at a brewpub in Rome, he established his own in a small village around 100km (60 miles) from the capital. Here, he brews fine ales, often inspired by British styles, and also experiments with unusual ingredients such as tobacco, tea leaves, and gentian roots.

KETO REPORTER
TOBACCO PORTER 5.5% ABV
Kentucky Toscano tobacco leaves are infused in this smoky, peppery porter. Surprisingly easy to drink.

REALE EXTRA
INDIA PALE ALE 6.4% ABV
Generously hopped with Amarillo and Warrior; well balanced, with sweet caramel and fruity notes.

BIRRIFICIO ITALIANO

Via Monviso, 1, 22070 - Limido
Comasco, Como, Italy
www.birrificio.it

Agostino Arioli founded his renowned brewpub in 1994 with his brother Stefano and other friends. His pils and bock soon became cult favourites. He brews a large range of seasonal beers, such as a sparkling blackcurrant lager and a cask-conditioned ale spiced with cinnamon and ginger. The restaurant serves great regional food and has live music.

SCIRES®
CHERRY ALE 7.5% ABV
Whole black Vignola cherries, lactic bacteria, wild yeast, and wood chips create this fantastic sour beer.

FLEURETTE®
FLAVOURED LIGHT ALE 3.8% ABV
Made with barley, wheat, and rye, and flavoured with rose and violet petals, elderberry juice, black pepper, and citrus honey.

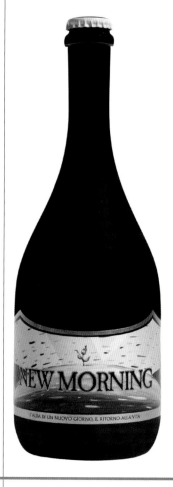

BREWERY

BRÙTON
Via Lodovica 5135, 55100 San Cassiano di Moriano (LU), Italy
www.bruton.it

Named, they say, after the beer made by the Minoans of ancient Crete, this stylish Tuscan brewpub offers good regional food and interesting ales, bearing a logo of the minotaur, created by young, former home-brewer Alessio Gatti.

CITABIUNDA
Via Moniprandi1/a Fraz. Bricco di Neive, 12052 Neive (CN), Italy
www.birrificiocitabiunda.it

Brewpub Citabiunda ("blonde girl" in the local dialect) is set in a charming former village schoolhouse in high Piedmont. It offers original, intriguing beers and home-cooked food.

BREWING SECRET Marco Marengo, who was taught the art of brewing by Teo Musso of Baladin, uses Champagne yeasts to create his distinctive brews.

CITTAVECCHIA
Z.A. Stazione di Prosecco 29/E, 34010 Sgonico (TS), Italy
www.cittavecchia.com

Cittavecchia was founded in 1999 in this wine-producing village between Trieste and the Slovenian border. Former home-brewer Michele Barro was compelled by his passion for good beer to leave his job as designer and take up brewing full time. Now his lagers and ales are sold in the region's best restaurants and bars.

DUCATO
Via Strepponi 50/A, 4301 Roncole Verdi di Busseto (PR), Italy
www.birrificiodelducato.net

Young brewer Giovanni Campari set up his microbrewery in 2007 near Giuseppe Verdi's birthplace, not far from Parma. He proved his skills from the outset, brewing four beers full of character. Further new lines are confirming Ducato as one of the most promising Italian craft breweries.

BEER

MOMUS
STRONG AMBER ALE 7.5% ABV
Inspired by Belgian abbey ales, it has an intense aroma of soft toffee, honey, and cocoa, with hints of toasted malt.

LILITH
AMERICAN PALE ALE 5.5% ABV
Well balanced, rich in caramel notes, with grapefruit flavours from a generous amount of Cascade hops.

BIANCANEIVE
BELGIAN WITBIER 4.8% ABV
Strongly spiced wheat beer, easy to drink, refreshing, and thirst-quenching, with flowery notes from the Champagne yeasts.

SENSUALE
BELGIAN ABBEY AMBER ALE 7% ABV
Well-balanced strong ale, rich in vinous and citrus fruit notes; sweet right through to the aftertaste.

FORMIDABLE
STRONG DARK ALE 8% ABV
Strong, fruity, Belgian-style ale with liquorice notes. George Simenon's sleuth Maigret drank his beer from a formidable litre (two-pint) tankard.

SAN NICOLÒ
SPICED ALE 6% ABV
Amber ale, generously spiced with cardamom, brewed once a year for Saint Nicholas' Day.

NEW MORNING
SAISON 5.8% ABV
Amazing *saison*, flavoured with chamomile flowers. Easy drinking and thirst-quenching, with lovely earthy notes.

AFO
AMERICAN PALE ALE 5.4% ABV
AFO means "Ale For the Obsessed" and is dedicated to hop lovers. Nice citrus fruit aromas, caramel notes.

GRADO PLATO

Viale Fasano 36/bis,
10023 Chieri (TO), Italy
www.gradoplato.it

This brewpub near Turin was founded in 2003 by former home-brewer Sergio Ormea. His son Gabriele helps him run the pub, which is well known for its food – notably snails cooked in over 20 different ways!

BREWING SECRET Regional produce, such as chestnuts and barley, feature strongly in these inventive, eclectic ales.

LAMBRATE

Via Adelchi 5, 20131 Milano, Italy
www.birrificiolambrate.com

The first (and still the best) brewpub in Milan, founded in 1996 by brothers Davide and Giampaolo Sangiorgi and their friend Fabio Brocca after a visit to 't IJ Brewery in Amsterdam. They have recently expanded production, adding some new interesting ales. The menu features some creative beer-influenced dishes, such as pork cooked in beer mash.

L'OLMAIA

Via delle Robinie 15 (zona artigianale) 53045 Sant'Albino, Montepulciano, Siena, Italy
www.birrificioolmaia.com

A tiny pretty microbrewery founded in 2005 near Siena, in the green and leafy Val d'Orcia. Young enthusiastic brewer Moreno Ercolani creates intriguing natural ales with passion, often using local produce, such as honey from the elms that grow profusely here (olmaia means elm).

MALTUS FABER

Via Fegino 3/U, 16161
Genova-Rivarolo, Italy
www.maltusfaber.com

This stylish and creative microbrewery is located on the site of a former brewery in Genoa. It was founded by two friends, Fausto Marenco, a former home-brewer, and Massimo Versaci, a well-known collector of "breweriana". Inspired by a love of Belgium, they brew clean, interesting, and promising ales.

CHOCARRUBICA

COFFEE-CHOCOLATE STOUT 7% ABV
An original brew, featuring cocoa and carob beans from Sicily. Soft and velvety on the palate.

STRADA SAN FELICE

CHESTNUT STRONG LAGER 8% ABV
Dark, strong lager made with local nuts, giving a gentle smoked aroma and a marked taste of chestnuts, with a slightly bitter finish.

GHISA

SMOKED ALE 5% ABV
Ebony in colour with a "cappuccino" foam; lighty smoked, easy to drink, and balanced, with plum notes and a long, hoppy finish.

MONTESTELLA

BLOND ALE 5% ABV
Their flagship ale; pale, with fresh aromas of hay and hops with a long, dry finish cleansing the palate.

PVK

BELGIAN WITBIER 4.5% ABV
Easy-drinking blond ale brewed with durum wheat, barley, oats, red pepper, coriander, and orange rind.

CHRISTMAS DUCK

BELGIAN STRONG DARK ALE 8.5% ABV
Remarkable seasonal winter warmer using local elm-tree honey that gives bittersweet and fruity notes.

IMPERIAL

IMPERIAL STOUT 7.8% ABV
Full of coffee and dark chocolate flavours followed by an intense, lingering hop bitterness.

AMBRATA

BELGIAN AMBER ALE 7% ABV
Rich in caramel and nutty notes, well balanced, with a long, dry, and bitter finish.

BREWERY

MONTEGIOCO

Frazione Fabbrica 1, 15050
Montegioco (AL), Italy
www.birrificiomontegioco.com

Riccardo Franzosi, who left a secure
job in the family building firm to
assemble his own beers, is one of
the most eclectic brewers in Italy.
He brews a wide range of regular
and seasonal ales, using local products
– cherries, peaches, and blueberries.

BREWING SECRET The coriander he uses
comes from his neighbour's garden.

PANIL (TORRECHIARA)

Strada Pilastro 35/a, 43010
Torrechiara (PR), Italy

Renzo Losi, a biology graduate, got
his brewing break in 2000, when his
winemaker father gave him permission
to make beer at the family's vineyard
estate, south of Parma.

BREWING SECRET The links with the
family winemaking tradition are
retained in the use of oak barrels
and *spumante* yeasts.

PICCOLO BIRRIFICIO

Via Riva 10A, 21013 Gallarate (VA), Italy
www.piccololab.it

This microbrewery, founded in 2005,
is housed in a former olive oil mill in
the lovely medieval village of Apricale,
near the French border. Brewer
Lorenzo Bottoni produces a range
of fine ales under the brand name
of Nüa ("naked"), including some
amazing brews using unusual local
fruits and plants.

SCARAMPOLA

Località Monastero 9, 17017
Millesimo (SV), Italy
www.birrificioscarampola.it

Founded in 2004 in the cellars of
an old mansion, this brewpub has
now moved to a charming nearby
abbey. Brewer Maurizio Ghidetti
likes to use local ingredients, such
as chestnuts and chinotto fruits.
Beers are available on draught
in the taproom Osteria del Vino
Cattivo in nearby Cairo Montenotte.

BEER

DOLII RAPTOR

STRONG ALE 8.5% ABV
Matured in Barbera wine barrels for
over six months, then re-fermented
with white wine yeasts.

QUARTA RUNA

SOUR PEACH ALE 7% ABV
Volpedo peaches are heated in an
oven before fermentation for extra
"peachiness". The sourness comes
from wild yeasts on the peach skins.

PANIL BARRIQUÉE SOUR

FLEMISH SOUR RED ALE 8% ABV
The flagship ale, barrel aged
for three months. Sour, vinous,
and uncompromising.

DIVINA

WILD BEER 5.5% ABV
Spontaneously fermented by being
left, uncovered, on the back of a
truck in a field overnight. Sweet-
sour, yeasty, and citrussy.

SESON

BELGIAN SAISON 6% ABV
Matured in Chardonnay barrels
with spices and local chinotto peel
(from a small, bitter, citrus fruit).

CHIOSTRO

SPICED ALE 5% ABV
Spiced with *Artemisia absinthium*
(wormwood), then fermented with
Trappist yeasts, giving complex and
unique aromas and flavours.

IPA

FRUIT BEER 7% ABV
In this case IPA doesn't mean India
Pale Ale but Italian Pompelmo
(grapefruit) Ale. Grapefruit peel
and Cascade hops are used.

NIVURA

CHESTNUT ALE 6.5% ABV
A new style, very popular in Italy.
Smoked notes from chestnuts dried
in traditional stoves called *tecci*.

MORE BEERS OF

ITALY

Italy has a growing band of small-batch craft producers, who are experimenting with many ingredients and methods.

BI-DU

Via Torino, 50-22077
Olgiate Comasco (CO), Italy
www.bi-du.it

This brewpub was founded in 2002 in the tiny village of Rodero, close to the Swiss border. It takes its name from a Sumerian beer used to pay workers. The owner Beppe Vento is one of the best, and most awarded, brewers in Italy.

BREWING SECRET Vento brews beers only in styles that he personally loves.

MOSTO DOLCE

Via Frà Bartolomeo 211,
59100 Prato, Italy
www.mostodolce.it

This microbrewery was founded in 2003 by Francesca Torri and Elio Dall'Era. Torri is the brewer, creating her successful range of lagers and ales with passion. There are two beautiful taprooms in which to sample her brews, one in Prato (Via dell'Arco 6) and the other in Florence (Via Nazionale 114 R).

RODERSCH
KÖLSCH 5% ABV
A cloudy, fresh digestif with a lovely touch of bitterness; typical of the brewer's philosophy.

ARTIGIANALE
BITTER ALE 6.2% ABV
A celebrated strong bitter ale, with a good balance between malts and hops, and a long bitter finish.

ELIO'S 50
INDIA PALE ALE 6% ABV
Inspired by British brewing traditions, it has a pronounced hop bitterness and a citrus aroma.

MARTELLINA
CHESTNUT HONEY ALE 7.4% ABV
Uncompromising, strong, but very drinkable amber ale with a great punch coming from the flavour of local chestnut honey.

TROLL

Via valle Grande 15, 12019
Vernante (CN), Italy
www.birratroll.it

Beer enthusiast Alberto Canavese transformed his bar, set in a charming alpine village, into a brewpub in 2002. Brewer Daniele Meinero is well known for the unusual herbs and spices he adds to his ales.

BREWING SECRET Meinero was trained by radical brewer Teo Musso of Le Balandin in Piozzo.

ZAHRE

Frazione Sauris di Sopra, 3, 33020
Udine, Italy
www.zahrebeer.com

Sauris, a mountain village in the Friuli region close to the Austrian and Slovenian borders, was known as Zahre in ancient times. Sandro Petris, who founded his microbrewery in 1999, is able to use the purest, freshest mountain spring water for his highly appreciated lagers.

TENUTE COLLESI

Pian della Serra, Apecchio, Italy 61042
www.tenutecollesi.it

Joseph Collesi and Roberto Bini's passion is to make great beers using the very best ingredients the local fertile soil can grow. The brewery is located in the quaint medieval village in the Marche, along the ancient Via Flaminia, the traditional trading route from Rome to Rimmini. Their beers are exported to discerning drinkers worldwide.

VECCHIO BIRRAIO

Via Caselle 87, 35010 Campo San
Martino Padova, Italy

Beer enthusiast and pioneer Stefano Sausa founded his family brewery in 1995 not far from Padua, with the goal to brew tasty, natural, and genuine craft beers without any adjunct. Good food alongside fine lagers and ales seem to be the secret of this successful brewpub.

PALANFRINA
CHESTNUT ALE 9% ABV
Intense flavour from local chestnuts used in several different ways, such as dried, smoked, and in the form of chestnut honey.

SHANGRILA
SPICED ALE 8.5% ABV
A deep amber ale enlived with a Himalayan blend of spices, giving exotic aromas and flavours.

AFFUMICATA
SMOKED LAGER 6% ABV
A deep red, well-rounded lager full of smoked barley malt aroma. Perfect with the acclaimed local crudo ham.

CANAPA
FLAVOURED LAGER 5% ABV
A surprisingly elegant, delicate, easy-drinking lager flavoured with local Carmagnola hemp flowers.

AMBRATA
BELGIAN ALE 7.5% ABV
Unfiltered, it has intense flavours of orange, cherries, and soft red fruits, with a lingering caramel finish.

BIONDA
BLOND ALE 6% ABV
The use of pilsen malts give this unfiltered beer a light touch, which balances with the aromatic hops.

SAUSA PILS
PILSNER 5% ABV
Flagship of the brewery, awarded pils from Bohemian inspiration, with a dry and long hoppy finish.

BLACK HORSE
FOREIGN EXTRA STOUT 6.5% ABV
Full-bodied strong stout with pleasant notes of coffee, chocolate, and dried fruit.

BREWERY

BEER

BREWERY

BEER

ALL ABOUT...

FLAVOURINGS

The *Reinheitsgebot* (German Beer Purity Law) dictated that German brewers use only malt, hops, yeast, and water for their beers. But cross the border into Belgium and the shelves of a native brewhouse will groan under the weight of jars of spices and herbs. Crushed coriander seeds and dried orange peel add spicy and rich citrus notes to a witbier, such as Hoegaarden, while ginger, aniseed, cumin, and star anise also find their way into various brews. Eclectic brewer Dany Prignon at Fantôme plays around with oregano – no doubt that his beer is great with pizza. There are even Belgian beers brewed with tea, honey, and mustard.

Herbal flavourings have a long history in brewing: before hops, brewers in the British Isles experimented with sweet gale, wild rosemary, ground ivy, and bog myrtle. In northern Europe, the mixture of herbs used for flavouring beer was called "gruit". And, as European countries colonized the world, all sorts of spices were brought back, and it was only natural that some, such as ginger, ended up in the brewing kettle.

Contemporary use of flavourings is on the increase and is no longer confined to Belgian mavericks like Prignon. For example, Scottish brewmaster Bruce Williams has brought back to life heather ale – an ancient style of beer that was brewed by the Picts, while Italian brewers are experimenting with chestnuts, myrrh, and tobacco.

HEATHER
Scottish heather flowers are used in the boil alongside a minimum of hops to create the Williams Brothers' Fraoch. The ale has an almost peaty, floral nose and dry, astringent finish.

GINGER, MYRRH, AND HONEY
Brewers in Italy are getting somewhat spicy with the fruits of their labours. Baladin's Nora contains ginger root and myrrh, while heather honey goes into the brewery's Erika. Honey is also a traditional ingredient of some Belgian beers, such as Binchoise's Bière des Ours.

CHESTNUTS AND TOBACCO
Strada San Felice from Grado has chestnuts in their brew, while Birra del Borgo's Keto Reporter uses Kentucky Toscano tobacco leaves to help give their porter a peppery character.

COFFEE AND CHOCOLATE
The ever-inventive Meantime Brewery of London has produced beers with Fairtrade coffee beans in the mix. In the USA, Rogue Ales Chocolate Stout is a chocoholic's delight. Both coffee and chocolate harmonize beautifully with similar notes in the malts of these dark beers.

GOOSEBERRIES, PINE, AND SEAWEED
Williams Brothers of Scotland brews beers made with gooseberries and bog myrtle, scots pine and spruce shoots, and bladderwrack seaweed.

NOUGAT
France's Bourganel Brewery produces artisan beers using regional ingredients, such as chestnuts and bilberries, and nougat from Montélimar, which lends an almond flavour to the beer.

BREWERY

AU BARON

2 rue du Bourlard,
59570 Gussignies, France
www.brasserieaubaron.com

Set on a riverbank in a charming valley, this microbrewery and restaurant has been owned by the Bailleux family since the 1970s. It is a delightful place, where you can take a tour of the brewery, dine on grilled meat or fish, and sample beers such as the Cuvée des Jonquilles – a brew as golden as the daffodils after which it is named.

BOURGANEL

7 avenue Claude Expilly,
07600 Vals les Bains, France
www.bieres-bourganel.com

In 1997, Christian Bourganel, a drinks distributor in the Ardèche, decided to develop a range of blonde artisan beers flavoured with regional produce.

BREWING SECRET Unusual ingredients include chestnuts (*marrons*), bilberries (*myrtilles*), nougat from Montélimar, and Verveine du Velay liqueur, which is flavoured with verbena.

CASTELAIN

13 rue Pasteur,
62410 Bénifontaine, France
www.chti.com

Founded in 1926, this family brewery was passed into the hands of Yves and Annick Castelain from their parents in 1978. Under the name of Ch'ti (local patois for a northerner), they have developed a range of strong, mellow lager beers with a long, cold secondary fermentation period.

LA CHOULETTE

16 rue des Écoles,
59111 Hordain, France
www.lachoulette.com

Founded in 1885, this farmhouse brewery is a rare survivor among the thousands of breweries that existed in the region in the late 19th century. Alain Dhaussy, the current brewer, has succeeded in creating artisan beers of real quality, faithful to the traditions of northern France, but with a real sense of innovation too.

BEER

CUVÉE DES JONQUILLES

Ale 7% ABV
Strong but thirst-quenching, this ale is packed with delicious flavours of citrus and exotic fruits.

BOURGANEL AU NOUGAT

Flavoured Lager 5% ABV
An amazing nougat bouquet and, in the mouth, the flavour of grilled almonds.

BOURGANEL AUX MARRONS

Flavoured Lager 5% ABV
An amber beer; elegant, very fruity, and refreshing, with a hint of vanilla as well as chestnut.

MALTESSE

Premium Lager 7.7% ABV
Blonde, rich, and strong, with a taste of barley, and an appealing hint of bitterness in the finish.

CH'TI BLONDE

Lager 6.4% ABV
Full bodied, with just enough bitterness to be very refreshing. Mellow and tasty.

LA CHOULETTE FRAMBOISE

Fruit Beer 6% ABV
Refreshing, with a slight sourness. The note of ripe raspberries is present, but not too intrusive.

LES PORTE DU HAINAUT AMBRÉE

Amber Ale 7% ABV
Medium-bodied fruity beer, with flavours of cooked apples, pears, and caramel; slight bitterness.

DEUX RIVIÉRES

2 place de la Gare,
29270 Carhaix, France
www.coreff.com

This Breton brewery's foundation, in
Morlaix in 1985, pioneered the revival
of artisan breweries in France. Now in
Carhaix, in central Brittany, it produces
British-style real ales (stout and
porter are in the range), but wheat
and blonde beers are also made here.

BREWING SECRET All of Deux Rivieres's
beers are unpasteurized and unfiltered.

COREFF AMBRÉE

AMBER ALE 5% ABV
Deep, appealing ale with notes of
brown sugar, toasted malt, and
caramel, and a good bitterness in
the finish. A classic since 1985.

DUYCK

113 route Nationale, 59144 Jenlain, France
www.duyck.com

Originally a farmhouse brewery, Duyck
was established in 1922, producing
beers in the northern *bière de garde*
style – brewed and bottled in the
winter for laying down and drinking in
the summer. In the 1950s, the family
began bottling their beers in recycled
champagne bottles. Mathiew Duyck,
the present manager, is the fourth
generation of this family of brewers.

JENLAIN AMBRÉE

AMBER ALE 7.5% ABV
Full bodied, with a hint of bitterness,
the mellowness of roasted malt,
and aromas of stewed prunes and
caramel. A perfect accompaniment
to food, but also an ingredient
in rustic local dishes, such as
carbonnade flamande (beef cooked
in beer).

GAYANT

BP20089, 59500 Douai, Cedex France
www.brasseurs-gayant.com

Established in 1919, this independent
family-owned brewery has always
embraced and pioneered new styles
of brewing, from ales made using the
top-fermentation technique to Celta,
the first non-alcoholic beer.

BREWING SECRET Brasseurs de Gayant
brews the strongest beer in France,
called Bière du Démon (12% ABV).

LA GOUDALE

ALE 7.2% ABV
Golden, dense, and full of malty
aromas, with a slight bitterness
imbued by the Flemish hops.

ST LADELIN MYTHIQUE

WHEAT BEER 7.5% ABV
Cloudy and pale yellow, this is
a light and refreshing beer, with
aromas of citrus fruit and coriander.

KRONENBOURG

67 route d'Oberhausbergen,
67037 Strasbourg, France
www.brasseries-kronenbourg.com

A tiny Strasbourg brewpub, opened
in 1664, grew to become France's
largest brewery in the 20th century,
a feat achieved by selling refreshing
lager beer at low prices all over
the world. Nowadays, its sales have
declined somewhat, and it is owned
by the Danish Carlsberg group.

1664

SPECIAL LAGER 5.5% ABV
A smooth, golden, and refreshing
lager, slightly bitter on the palate
and with hints of malt.

1664 BLANC

WHEAT BEER 5% ABV
Fresh and fruity notes and a touch
of coriander make for a crisp and
refreshing beer.

<table>
<tr><td rowspan="2" style="writing-mode: vertical-lr;">BREWERY</td></tr>
</table>

BREWERY

LANCELOT
La Mine d'Or, 56460 Le Roc
Saint-André, France
www.brasserie-lancelot.com

Established in 1990, and now housed in the buildings of a 19th-century gold mine, Lancelot creates beers that are – in their names and imagery on the labels at least – linked to Breton and Celtic traditions, and Arthurian legends. Lancelot's production methods, however, are very much in the mould of Belgian beer-making.

LEPERS
199 Bis, Rue Marle 59930 La Chapelle D'armentières, France
www.langelus.fr

Established in 1901, this tiny brewery is run by the Lepers family, brewers for five generations. Their most well-known beer features a reproduction of Jean-François Millet's masterpiece *L'Angelus* (1857) on its label. It is a jewel of the northern French style of long-matured beers known as *bière de garde* (beer for keeping).

BRASSEURS DE LORRAINE
3 rue du Bois le Prêtre,
54700 Pont à Mousson, France
www.brasseurs-lorraine.com

In 2003, three dynamic young partners opened a new brewery in the heart of the Lorraine region, in northeast France. Their aim was to revive a regional tradition of beer-making that had almost entirely died out there. The brewery now produces six main brands, all of them in distinct styles.

METEOR
6 rue du Général Lebocq,
67270 Hochfelden, France
www.brasserie-meteor.fr

Brewing on the same site since 1640, Meteor is now the longest-established independent family brewery in France. Alsace traditions are in evidence, but Meteor also develops new beer styles.

BREWING SECRET Meteor was the first French brewery to be granted the rights to use the term "Pils" by the Czech authorities in 1927.

BEER

MORGANE
ALE 5.5% ABV
This organic beer is pleasantly refreshing and light in style.

CERVOISE LANCELOT
ALE 6% ABV
The colour is amber, the flavour fruity and malty, with hints of honey and spices.

L'ANGELUS
WHEAT BEER 7% ABV
Rich, smooth, and wonderfully aromatic, with hints of coriander and a syrup sweetness.

ABBAYE DES PRÉMONTRÉS
ABBEY ALE 6% ABV
Amber, malty in taste, but with a delicate bitterness. Stewed fruits and caramel in the finish.

DUCHESSE DE LORRAINE
RED BEER 5.5% ABV
Malty, spicy, and with a hint of dried fruits, this beer is made using an 18th-century recipe.

METEOR GRAND MALT
PILS LAGER 6.1% ABV
Sweet and malty, it has a short but warming alcohol finish.

MICHARD

6 place Denis Dussoubs,
87000 Limoges, France
www.bieres-michard.com

Jean Michard was a pioneer in the revival of artisan brewing in France, opening his first brewpub in 1987 in Limoges. Using Bavarian styles, he and his daughter Julie develop fine beers in traditional ways, by hand, and with no use of electronics. Rare and hard to acquire, these beers are sold only at the brewpub.

PIETRA

Route de la Marana,
20600 Furiani, France
www.brasseriepietra.com

The first Corsican brewery in history opened in 1996. Brewers Armelle and Dominique Sialelli use raw materials native to the island, such as *maquis* herbs and chestnut flour, which forms an ingredient rather than just a flavouring in their Pietra beer. *Biera Corsa* has been a great success both in Corsica and overseas.

LA ROUGET DE LISLE

Rue des Vernes,
39140 Bletterans, France
www.brasserie-rouget-lisle.com

Opened in 2002 and named after the locally born composer of *The Marseillaise*, La Rouget de Lisle develops up to 15 new beers each year, some of them using local ingredients instead of hops for their bitter notes.

The brewery's motto is to allow its customers to discover, enjoy, and share its passion for brewing craft beers using high quality ingredients.

BREWING SECRET Among the ingredients used to replace hops are wormwood, dandelion, blackcurrant, and gentian.

AMBRÉE
BAVARIAN 5.5% ABV
Brillant copper colour; very smooth on the palate, with a light sourness and bitterness in the finish.

COLOMBA
WHEAT BEER 5% ABV
Very fresh and sharp, with unusual aromas of arbutus, myrtle, and juniper. A refreshing summer beer.

PIETRA
AMBER LAGER 6% ABV
Elegant flavours of toasted malts, nuttiness, and a slight bitterness.

MILLEFLEUR
LAGER 6.4% ABV
Gold and effervescent, a honey sweetness and floral notes linger till the end.

LE BIÈRE BLANCHE
WHEAT BEER 5% ABV
Unfiltered, it's a cloudy refresher, with a tart, thirst-quenching, spicy yeast finish.

FOURCHE DU DIABLE
LAGER 5.4% ABV
Amber-coloured beer, with aromas of spring flowers and an unusual bitter note from gentian roots.

MONTBÉLIARDE
LAGER 7.5%
Powerful and strong, it has a warming finish with a hint of honey. It's a marvellous partner to Comté cheese.

BREWERY

ST GERMAIN

26 route d'Arras,
62160 Aix-Noulette, France
www.page24.fr

Three young but experienced brewers opened this brewery in 2003, with top-fermentation beers in the *bière de garde* style. One takes its name from Saint Hildegard, a German abbess of the 11th century, who is often (though incorrectly) credited with the introduction of hops into the beer-making process. In 2008, the owners decided to only use locally grown hops from a French Flanders farmers' cooperative, thereby maintaining the long history of hop growing in the area. All of its beers are unpasteurized and undergo a secondary fermentation in the bottle.

ST SYLVESTRE

121 rue de la Chapelle,
59114 St-Sylvestre-Cappel, France
www.brasserie-st-sylvestre.com

There has been a brewery in this small Flemish village since 1789. The Ricour family has brewed traditional beers, using barley malts and hops, for many generations.

BREWING SECRET Three different strains of yeast are used to develop strong and rich aromas in the beers.

THEILLIER

11 rue de la Grande Chaussée,
59570 Bavay, France

In this small town near Valenciennes, the Theilliers have been brewing since 1832. Very little has changed since then, in fact – from the equipment used to the art of brewing one of the most splendid French beers.

BEWING SECRETS A very long cooking time, in old copper kettles, is one of the secrets of Michel Theillier, the current brewer.

BEER

HILDEGARDE AMBRÉE
ALE 6.9% ABV
Golden, with a rich nose of cereals, spices, and honey. Very smooth, with a good bitterness and a long finish.

CHICORÉE
FLAVOURED ALE 5.9% ABV
Clear and golden, flavours of chicory shine through the notes of fruit and spices.

RHUBARBE
ALE 5.9% ABV
Gold in colour, with floral aromas. Very refreshing, with a special acidity contributed by rhubarb.

BLANCHE
WHEAT ALE 4.9% ABV
Light gold and naturally cloudy, it is full of refreshing citrus zest flavours.

3 MONTS
ALE 8.5% ABV
Brilliant gold, with a rich and malty nose. Very fruity, it has good bitterness and a long finish.

GAVROCHE
AMBER ALE 8.5% ABV
Deep amber, with aromas of toasted malts and stewed red fruits; a little bitterness and a long finish.

LA BAVAISIENNE
AMBER ALE 7% ABV
A hue of amber, and with cereal aromas on the nose, this is a complex, deep, and malty beer, with notes of brown sugar and caramel, and a rich bitterness. Wonderful.

THIRIEZ

22 rue de Wormhout,
59470 Esquelbecq, France
www.brasseriethiriez.com

From working as a manager in a food distribution company, Daniel Thiriez changed his life to become an artisan brewer. He established his brewery on an old farm in Flanders in 1996, and uses traditional brewing methods.

BREWING SECRET Thiriez's unfiltered beers have a second fermentation in the bottle, on their lees.

ETOILE DU NORD

BLOND ALE 4.5% ABV
The moment the bottle is opened, an extraordinary smell of fresh hops comes to the nose. The beer's refreshing bitterness is in perfect harmony with its fine malt aromas.

1516 BREWING COMPANY

Schwarzenbergstraße 2,
A-1010 Vienna, Austria
www.1516brewingcompany.com

Not all the beers of this American-style brewpub are brewed in accordance with the German Purity Law passed in 1516 – the date that lends this establishment its name – but then the brewpub was only founded in 1998.

BREWING SECRET 1516 specializes in extremely hoppy brews, most of which are extremely strong.

1516 WEISE

BAVARIAN WHEAT BEER 5.2% ABV
Unfiltered and cloudy, it is full of banana and clove flavours, with citrus notes from the Cascade hops.

AMERIKANSKY

INDIA PALE ALE 5.8% ABV
Caramelized sugar candy and orange vie with citrus aromas from Slovenian hops for attention.

EGGENBERG

Eggenberg 1, 4655 Vorchdorf, Austria
www.schloss-eggenberg.at

Schloss Eggenberg is a small castle in Upper Austria that has been brewing for more than 500 years. A broad range of lagers (including a non-alcoholic one) is produced for the local market, and some fine bock beers are brewed for export; these include an urbock and even a blond version of the traditionally dark Samichlaus beer.

HOPFENKÖNIG

PILSNER 5.1% ABV
Very pale, with a firm head and hay-like spicy hop aromas. Light body followed by some dry bitterness.

SAMICHLAUS

DOPPELBOCK 14% ABV
Intense malt aroma, with noticeable alcohol. Sweet and fruity (dried cherries, figs, and plums); very little hop character present.

FORSTNER

Dorfstraße 52, A-8401 Kalsdorf bei Graz, Austria
www.forstner-biere.at

One of the more adventurous new brewers, Gerhard Forstner has recently made inroads into brewing Belgian and American-style ales. His brewery is in an old farmhouse building that has also served as a school. Some of his beers are endorsed by the Slow Food movement and are sold at Slow Food festivals.

STYRIAN ALE

BITTER ALE 6.2% ABV
Very dark burgundy; roasty and fruity (grapefruit?) aromas; slightly tart and very refreshing, with a medium bitterness.

TRIPLE 22

BELGIAN-STYLE TRIPLE 9.5% ABV
Copper, with a firm head and aroma of pawpaw and mango. Sweet and full bodied; spicy and bitter finish.

BREWERY

FREISTÄDTER

Brauhausstraße 2, A-4240
Freistadt, Austria
www.freistaedter-bier.at

The town of Freistadt lies close to Austria's border with the Czech Republic, and its brewery is owned by the townspeople. Since 1777, every owner of a building inside the old city walls automatically owns a certain number of shares of the brewery; those shares can be sold only along with the building itself.

GÖSSER

Brauhausgasse 1,
A-8707 Leoben-Göss, Austria
www.goesser.at

Part of the Heineken group, Gösser is one of the most popular and most valuable brands in Austria, and its bestselling beer is a *märzen*.

BREWING SECRET Head brewer Andreas Werner uses locally grown Fuggles hops, known as Styrian Goldings, for the Reininghaus Jahrgangspils.

GUSSWERK

Römerstraße 3, 5322
Hof bei Salzburg, Austria
www.brauhaus-gusswerk.at

Established in 2007 in a former bell foundry, Brauhaus Gusswerk is a very small operation. It has a stylish brewery tap, but its bottled beers can be found in organic shops across the nation. The brewery is proud of its green credentials, not just for the ingredients it uses, but because all of its electricity is sustainably generated using environmentally sensitive sources.

BREWING SECRET Brewer Reinhold Barta adheres strictly to the standards of organic beer production issued by the international Demeter organization.

BEER

RATSHERRN PREMIUM

EXPORT 5.2% ABV
A firm head and a full body. Low hop bitterness, with a hint of grass in the aftertaste.

DUNK'L

DUNKEL 4.8% ABV
Dark brown with swirls of red, it is full of cocoa, coffee, and dark malt flavours.

MÄRZEN

AUSTRIAN MÄRZEN LAGER 5.2% ABV
Malty nose, with notes of hay and hops; sweet, malty, well-balanced flavour, with a robust bitterness.

REININGHAUS JAHRGANGSPILS

PILSNER 4.9% ABV
Herbal and hay-like aromas; dry and hoppy, with some fruity (ripe red apples?) aromas in the aftertaste.

EDELGUSS

BLONDE ALE 5.1% ABV
Golden and crystal clear. Some grainy aromas and a hint of sponge cake. Herbal notes in the aftertaste.

WEIZENGUSS

WHEAT BEER 5.4% ABV
Organic and unfiltered, with clove notes, it is a refreshing beer for a hot summer's day.

AUSTRIAN AMBER ALE

PALE ALE 5.6% ABV
American hops bring lots of citrus grapefruit flavours to this refreshing beer.

BLACK BETTY

DARK ALE 5.4% ABV
Locally foraged herbs add mysterious layers of medicinal flavours to this black as night beer.

HIRTER

Hirt 9, 9322 Micheldorf, Austria
www.hirterbier.at

This old brewery, founded in 1270 in the southern province of Carinthia, offers a broad variety of beer styles. The fame it has won, however, is focused on the pilsner beers – these are widely available nationwide and through export. Hirter's *weizen* and *märzen* beers, on the other hand, are much harder to find.

KALTENHAUSEN

Salzburgerstraße 67, 5400 Hallein, Austria
www.kaltenhausen.at

Its history might go back to 1475, but Kaltenhausen is a modern, forward-looking brewery. Its best known beer, Edelweiss, which was developed here in the 1980s, is now brewed at its brewery in Zipf. Today, the brewery produces small batch of speciality beers, including ones flavoured with coffee, chestnuts, and cherries.

MOHRENBRÄU

Dr Waibel Straße 2,
A-6850 Dornbirn, Austria
www.mohrenbrauerei.at

Austria's westernmost brewery has won fame for brewing strong beers. The brewery building is also home to a small museum, which showcases the brewing traditions of the province of Vorarlberg.

BREWING SECRET The soft palate of the Mohrenbräu's Kellerbier is due to a small amount of wheat in the mash bill.

SCHWECHATER

Mautner Markhof-Straße 11, A-2320 Schwechat, Austria
www.schwechater.at

A large brewery that claims to have brewed the first lager beer in 1840, though, to be precise, it was the Vienna lager that was invented here by Anton Dreher. Production of that beer was discontinued in the early 20th century. Nowadays, the brewery is part of Heineken and produces golden lagers.

HIRTER PRIVAT PILS
BOHEMIAN-STYLE PILSNER 5.2% ABV
Pale golden, with a faint floral hop aroma and an overall mild bitterness that is embedded in an almost sweetish, malty body.

HIRTER MÄRZEN
LAGER 5% ABV
Aromatic hops dominate this well-rounded, fully matured, and well-attenuated lager.

EDELWEISS HOFBRÄU
BAVARIAN-STYLE HEFEWEIZEN 4.5% ABV
Spicy, clove-like aromas, with a little hint of banana. Very spritzy and refreshing, with a rather slight body.

KALTENHAUSER WEISSE
WHEAT BEER 5% ABV
Top-fermented, it is a refreshing, bubbly balance of banana, clove, and ginger flavours.

MOHREN KELLERBIER
LAGER 5.7% ABV
Very fruity and yeasty on the nose; soft on the palate and with hardly any bitterness.

MOHREN BOCKBIER
BOCK 7% ABV
Intense hay-like hop aromas. Full bodied and well balanced, with not too much sweetness or bitterness.

SCHWECHATER ZWICKL
UNFILTERED PILSNER 5.4% ABV
Herbal hop aromas and a hint of lemon zest. A lot of wheat in the mash bill. Dry and hoppy finish.

SCHWECHATER BIER
PALE LAGER 5% ABV
Golden colour, malty aromas. Full bodied, with hops being noticeable from the start to the finish.

ALL ABOUT...

BEER AND FOOD

Even though beer is great on its own, it is also a perfect companion at the dining table. In the past, wine has garnered all the culinary kudos, while beer has been dismissed as of little consequence when it comes to fine dining. Yet beer is a natural friend of food, as an increasing number of chefs, brewers, and drinkers are discovering.

European beer nations such as Belgium, Germany, Austria, and Hungary have been in on this great secret for centuries, and their bars and restaurants have never had qualms about cooking with beer or serving it alongside their dishes. In Belgium, *cuisine à la bière* includes the likes of rabbit cooked in cherry beer, and Flemish beef stew. Visit the Czech Republic and a glass of Budvar or Bernard is an essential accompaniment to Bohemian staples such as potato pancake stuffed with spicy pork. The same goes for Bavaria, where pork dishes share table space with a dark and delicious dunkel or doppelbock.

This approach is now spreading throughout the rest of the world, as chefs and brewers catch on to the pleasures of matching beer with food. For example, American brewpubs take great delight in pairing up adventurous beer styles with creative modern cuisine, as well as splashing their brews about in the kitchen. In both dining room and kitchen, beer is at last beginning to vie for space with wine, and has earned the right to be regarded with equal respect.

BEER AND OYSTERS
In the British Isles, an affinity between stout and oysters has long been appreciated, and brown ale traditionally plays a part in steak-and-kidney pudding.

ACIDITY Sour beers such as lambics and Flemish reds can hold their own in partnership with pickled dishes; perhaps surprisingly, they also work superbly with big-flavoured, ripe, pungent cheeses.

MALT FLAVOURS
The sweet flavours of malt harmonize with the natural sweetness of a meat, such as pork, making this a winning combination. Roast malts deliver smoky, roasted notes, so beers made with them are ideal partners for grilled meats and barbecues.

HOP FLAVOURS
Beers that have a spicy, peppery finish chime exquisitely with aromatic Asian dishes, while the citrus and orange-marmalade notes in a hoppy beer elevate the great cheeses of the world to another plateau. Hop bitterness also cuts through fat and cleanses the palate for the next mouthful.

"DIFFICULT" FLAVOURS
Beer wins the day when it comes to those foods that experts consider difficult to pair with a suitable wine: chocolate and asparagus are notable examples. A sticky chocolate dessert and a Belgian kriek are divine together, while a Bavarian-style weissbier, with its trademark custard-and-cream aroma and palate, is perfect with steamed asparagus. A smoky rauchbier sits well with a Bavarian dish like sausages and asparagus.

TASTING BOARDS
In Sydney, Australia, the stylish Redoak Boutique Beer Café serves tasting boards that offer small plates of inventive culinary delights, each one accompanied by a different, complementing beer.

BREWERY

SIEBENSTERNBRÄU

Siebensterngasse 19,
A-1070 Vienna, Austria
www.7stern.at

Siebensternbräu was the first brewpub in Austria to brew speciality beers – IPA, chilli, and fruit flavoured. Owner Sigi Flitter also helped re-introduce many of Austria's indigenous but forgotten beer styles.

BREWING SECRET The range varies with each season, but expect a wheat beer in summer and a smoked one in winter.

STIEGL

Kendlerstrasse 1,
A-5017 Salzburg, Austria
www.stiegl.at

Austria's largest independent brewery produces Austria's single most successful beer, Goldbräu. The brewery itself dates back to 1492 and, over time, has built up a splendid collection of beer-related exhibits for the "Brauwelt" – the largest museum on the continent entirely devoted to brewing.

STIFTSBRAUEREI SCHLÄGL

Schlägl 1, 4160 Schlägl, Austria
www.stift-schlaegl.at

The small village of Schlägl, close to the Czech and Bavarian borders, is home to the only Austrian brewery wholly owned by a monastery – in this case the Premonstratensian order. In recent years, the product range has grown considerably and now includes several ales.

VILLACHER

Brauhausgasse 6, A-9500 Villach, Austria
www.villacher.com

Austria's southernmost brewery was founded in 1858. It began as a strictly regional brewery, but has become a national one in the last 25 years and has even developed an export market in Italy. The beers are branded as Villacher, though the brewery's official name is Vereinigte Kärntner Brauereien. It now owns Schleppe (a speciality brewer) and Piestinger near Vienna.

BEER

PRAGER DUNKLES

DARK LAGER 4.5% ABV

While most dark beers in Austria are terribly sweet, this one is dry. Intense toasty notes, very little hop aroma. Roasty finish.

RAUCHBIER

SMOKED BEER 5.1% ABV

The beers of Bamberg, Germany inspired this full-bodied, beechwood-flavoured smoky brew.

GOLDBRÄU

AUSTRIAN MÄRZEN-TYPE LAGER 4.9% ABV

Relatively low bitterness and a hint of malty sweetness in the aroma and on the palate.

PARACELSUS ZWICKL

ORGANIC LAGER 5% ABV

Unfiltered, so hazy orange in hue; aromas of malt and yeast; medium body and very low bitterness.

STIFTER BIER

RED ALE 5.7% ABV

Malty sweetness with a refreshing fruit (peach and melon) undertone. Just a faint hint of hops.

DOPPELBOCK

DOPPELBOCK 8.3% ABV

A big, malty nose. Fruity (pears and apples) and sweet from the start, but very well-balanced finish.

VILLACHER MÄRZEN

LAGER 5% ABV

Golden to the eye, malt rather than hops dominate. Sweet without being sickly, it is easy drinking.

VILLACHER DUNKEL

DUNKEL 4.9% ABV

Chestnut brown in colour, it's full of breaded malt flavours with some chocolate and sweet caramel notes.

DIE WEISSE
5020 Salzburg, Rupertgasse 10, Austria
www.dieweisse.at

Founded in 1901, Die Weisse could be considered Austria's oldest brewpub. Until the early 1990s, its modest output was sold exclusively in the two-room pub, but, since then, it has become fashionable, and its beers are now served in bars and restaurants across the country. The range has broadened too, and now includes seasonal bocks and a *märzen*.

WEITRA BRÄU
Sparkassaplatz 160,
3970 Weitra, Austria
www.bierwerkstatt.at

Weitra claims to hold Austria's oldest brewing privilege, issued in 1321. In medieval times most of the buildings around the town square exercised their right to brew, now there is only one brewpub and this brewery left.

BREWING SECRET This organic speciality brewery, bought by Zwettler in 2002, still brews using open fermenters.

ZILLERTAL BIER
Umfahrungsstrasse 3,
A-6280 Zell am Ziller, Austria
www.zillertal-bier.at

This brewery in the small Zillertal valley in Tyrol has been around for more than 500 years. Each May it celebrates the Gauderfest, a festival that dates back to 1428, with a beerfest that lasts for four days.

BREWING SECRET A special bock beer is brewed for the festival, and is available only on that weekend.

ZIPFER
A-4871 Zipf, Austria
www.zipfer.at

A mass-production brewery, now owned by Heineken, Zipfer creates beers that tend to be extremely pale and show a distinct hop aroma due to the use of whole hops. The flagship beer is the crisp Urtyp, introduced in 1967, which should not be confused with the Pils. Head brewer Günther Seeleitner finds time to occasionally brew one-off beers.

DIE WEISSE ORIGINAL
BAVARIAN HEFEWEIZEN 5.2% ABV
Gold and cloudy, with a large pillowy head, intense spicy aromas, and a surprisingly dry, bitter finish.

HADMAR
ORGANIC VIENNA LAGER 5.2% ABV
Sweet and malty on the nose and palate; hints of roastiness, bitterness; variable from batch to batch.

WEITRA HELL
LAGER 5% ABV
Straw coloured, with estery aroma and very little carbonation. Soft on the palate, with a mild hoppiness.

GAUDER BOCK
MAIBOCK 7.8% ABV
Aromas of vanilla and alpine herbs. Unusually intense bitterness helps balance the malt to give a dry finish.

ZILLERTAL WEISSBIER
HEFEWEIZEN 5% ABV
Aromas of citrus and banana. Refreshing and prickly, light and aromatic (cloves), rather than sweet.

PILS
PILSNER 5.2% ABV
Pale, with a stable white head. Intense floral hop aromas (Tettnanger); extremely dry and hoppy.

STEFANIBOCK
BOCK 7.1% ABV
Citric and hay-like aromas dominate. Malty, but hardly sweet on the palate; lighter and more easy drinking than other bock beers.

BREWERY

ZWETTLER

Syrnauer Strasse 22-25,
A-3910 Zwettl, Austria
www.zwettler.at

A large, family-owned brewery,
Zwettler grew to its present size
over the last 40 years when owner
Karl Schwarz decided first to mass-
produce relatively cheap lager and
then, subsequently, to establish more
prestigious brands of speciality beers.

BREWING SECRET Zwettler introduced the
first unfiltered Zwickl in the late 1970s.

CALANDA

Kasernenstr 36, CH-7007 Chur,
Switzerland
www.calanda.com

Heineken has turned Calanda into
the largest brewery in eastern
Switzerland. Apart from brewing
ubiquitous international brands
for the Swiss market, the brewery
still produces five traditional local
beers, as well as Ittinger, originally
created by Actienbrauerei
Frauenfeld. This was sold off
in 1994. Altogether, Heineken

Switzerland, of which Calanda is
the largest part, now accounts
for about 25 per cent of the total
Swiss beer production.

EICHHOF

Obergrundstrasse 110, 6002 Luzern,
Switzerland
www.eichhof.ch

Founded in 1834, it was once one
of Switzerland's largest independent
breweries. In 2008, it was taken over
by Heineken. Swiss fears that the
company will lose its local identity
have thus far proved unfounded.

BREWING SECRET This brewery uses
water from the Pilatus, a landmark
mountain in the central Swiss alps.

BEER

ZWETTLER ORIGINAL
PILSNER 5.1% ABV
Malty and quite full bodied; balanced
with a mild bitterness from locally
grown Perle and Select hops.

ZWICKL
UNFILTERED LAGER 5.5% ABV
Yeast and lemon in the nose.
Refreshing, smooth, and balanced,
with a moderate hop bitterness.

CALANDA
LAGER 4.8% ABV
Sweetish estery nose; an almost
fruity and refreshing first impression
that gives way to a mild bitterness.

CALANDA EDELBRÄU
LAGER 4.8% ABV
A sweetish malty, easy-tasting
beer with a light bitterness, which
is an ideal refresher after skiing or
walking in the hills and mountains.

ITTINGER AMBER
AMBER LAGER 5.6% ABV
Malty, slightly roasted aroma.
The flavour is sweet with hints
of grains, caramel, and bitter
hops. Short, dry finish.

DAS BÜGELBRÄU
LAGER 4.9% ABV
Pale golden, with a somewhat
yeasty nose. Full bodied, with hints
of vanilla, and very mildly hopped.

DAS BARBARA
LAGER 6.5% ABV
Slightly sweetish, toffee-like nose
and very balanced on the palate.
Fruity (red apple) notes in the finish.

FALKEN

Brauereistrasse 1, Postfach 186 8201
Schaffhausen, Switzerland
www.falken.ch

The Falken Brewery is located in
Schaffhausen, where the river Rhine
forms the border with Germany.
Founded in 1799, it is one of the
larger independent breweries in
Switzerland. Although slightly hoppier
than most other Swiss beers, the
"falcon" beers give a very smooth
overall impression that resembles
traditional Czech lagers.

PRINZ
LAGER 5.5% ABV
Butterscotch and herbal aromas;
full body, with lots of carbonation,
sweet and spicy (perhaps ginger)
notes, and butterscotch in the finish.

FIRST COOL
LAGER 4.5% ABV
Very little aroma. Sweet and soft
on the palate due to a generous
portion of maize on the mash bill.

LOCHER

Brauereiplatz CH-9050
Appenzell, Switzerland
www.appenzellerbier.ch

Appenzell is Switzerland's smallest
province (kanton), but the beer
produced by the local brewery has
won it a lot of fame.

BREWING SECRET In the 1990s, the
Locher family found out that beers
brewed on the full moon ferment
more easily; they have, therefore,
created a line of "Vollmond-brews".

VOLLMOND BIER NATURTRÜB
ORGANIC LAGER 5.2% ABV
An aroma of hops and lemon zest;
medium body – chewy. Hoppy, but
not excessively bitter.

HOLZFASS-BIER
LAGER 5.2% ABV
Aromas of sweetcorn, very little
carbonation, and a distinctive note
from the oak in which it is matured.

BIERVISION MONSTEIN

Monstein, 7278 Davos Monstein,
Switzerland
www.biervision-monstein.ch

Andreas Aegerter and Christian Ochs
started this village brewery high up in
the mountains near Davos in 2001,
together with 756 small investors
(each of them a devoted customer).
They all shared the vision that there
is a market for unusual beers, as well
as beer-related products, such as
cheese crusted with malt and spirits
distilled from beer.

MONSTEINER WÄTERGUOGE BIER
DUNKEL 5% ABV
Named after an Alpine lizard, it is
unfiltered, dark, with a pronounced
smoky flavour.

MUNGGA
KÖLSCH 3.5% ABV
Brewed from organic Swiss
ingredients, Mungga ("groundhog")
has aromas of violets, a dry taste,
and an elegant bitterness.

RUGENBRÄU

Wagnerenstrasse 40, CH-3800
Interlaken, Switzerland
www.rugenbraeu.ch

This family-run brewery is located in
the tourist resort of Interlaken, close
to the Eiger and Jungfrau mountains
– landmarks of Berner Oberland.
Owner-president Bruno Hofweber
promotes beer and gourmet cuisine
in cooperation with the chefs of
the larger hotels in the vicinity,
most notably the Victoria-Jungfrau.

ALPENPERLE
LAGER 4.8% ABV
Pale golden, with a sweetish nose
and a light body. Some sweetness
but very little hops in the aftertaste.

ZWICKEL
UNFILTERED LAGER 4.8% ABV
Straw coloured and slightly hazy; a
faint aroma of lemon zest; dry and
balanced, with a herbal bitterness
in the finish.

BREWERY

SONNENBRÄU

Alte Landstrasse 36, Postfach 144 9445 Rebstein, Switzerland
www.sonnenbraeu.ch

This is the only surviving brewery of 34 that once existed in the Rhine valley on Switzerland's eastern border. It has been quick to introduce new beers to the market – including Switzerland's first "Light" beer in 1978.

BREWING SECRET It focuses on local produce, and uses corn from the region in the brewing process.

BEIERHAASCHT

240, Avenue de Luxembourg, L-4940 Bascharage, Luxembourg
www.beierhaascht.lu

Tradition and 21st century combine in this hotel and brewpub, where gleaming kettles are central to the design of the bright airy bar. The menu features traditional regional specialities as well as dishes made with beer.

BREWING SECRET The beers adhere to German brewing purity rules (the *Reinheitsgebot*).

CORNELYSHAFF

83 Haaptstrooss, Heinerscheid L-9753, Luxembourg
www.cornelyshaff.lu

Situated in a nature park, Cornelyshaff comprises a popular bar, restaurant, and hotel, as well as a brewery that is open to visitors. It is modern, gleaming, and energy efficient – the cooperative that owns it prides itself on minimizing its environmental impact. The bar and restaurant showcase the beers and much farm produce from the area.

SIMON

14 rue Joseph Simon, L-9550 Wiltz, Luxembourg
www.brasseriesimon.lu

Situated in the very hilly and heavily forested Ardennes countryside, the brewery has operated within sight of the church in the lower town of Wiltz since 1824, and used to provide beer to the Grand Duke in its early years.

BREWING SECRET Open fermenters and copper kettles, visible through the brewery windows, are still used here.

BEER

RHEINTALER MAISBIER
LAGER 5% ABV
Grassy hops hide the maize aromas. Very smooth mouthfeel and late, not very intense, hop bitterness.

CRAFT 1
LAGER 5.1% ABV
Californian, Simcoe hops bring a marvellous, zesty citrus aroma to this unfiltered classic.

AMBRÉE
DUNKEL 5.2% ABV
A bold balance of hops and malt, its bitterness and sweetness runs in harmony.

HELLES
LAGER 5.1% ABV
Soft on the palate with nice carbonation, the malt is bready and satisfying without being too sweet.

WËLLEN OURDALLER
BUCKWHEAT BEER 6.5% ABV
Amber in colour, spicy and caramel notes dominate the taste of this beer made with buckwheat.

OURDALLER WAÏSSEN TARWEBIER
WITBIER 4.6% ABV
An unfiltered, cloudy wheat beer; assertive in character, it is full of spice.

SIMON DINKEL
SPELT WITBIER 4.5% ABV
Brewed from 70 per cent barley, 30 per cent unmalted spelt – an ancient form of wheat grown in the area – the beer is pale and has a soft, fruity aroma.

OKULT NO 1
WITBIER 5.4% ABV
Cloudy to the eye, it is tart and refreshing, with a zesty aftertaste.

Stiegl is Austria's largest independent brewer, and its Goldbräu lager is one of the country's biggest-selling beers.

BREWERY

DE 3 HORNE

Marktstraat 40-A, Kaatsheuvel,
Noord-Brabant 5171 GP, Netherlands
www.de3horne.nl

Founded in his garage by home-brewer
Sjef Groothuis in 1991, De 3 Horne
was transferred to the larger
premises of a former shoe factory
in 1993. The building also houses a
tasting room and a shop. Most of the
beers are Belgian- inspired, and some
are produced for third parties, such
as Kandinsky Bier, which is made for
a Tilburg beer café.

ALFA

Thull 15-19, 6365 AC Schinnen,
Netherlands
www.alfabier.nl

One of the few independent, family-run
breweries left in the Netherlands,
Alpha has been controlled by the
Meens family since its foundation in
1870. The beers are brewed from
spring water, each bottle numbered
to keep tabs on the amount used.

BREWING SECRET One of the few Dutch
brewers to adhere to the *Reinheitsgebot*.

BRAND

Brouwerijstraat 2, 6321 BG Wijlre,
Netherlands
www.brand.nl

Despite being incorporated into the
Heineken empire in 1989, Brand has
managed to maintain its reputation
and identity. Dating back to 1340,
it is easily the oldest Dutch brewery.

BREWING SECRET It brews a highly varied
range of bottom-fermented beers:
pilsners, a dubbelbock, an amber bock,
Imperator, and the pale Meibock.

BROUWERIJ 'T IJ

Funenkade 7, 1018 AL Amsterdam,
Netherlands
www.brouwerijhetij.nl

Amsterdam's favourite micro is now
the city's oldest brewery, even though
it was founded only in 1985. Strong
Belgian-style ales form the backbone
of the output, though there's also
a pils and a witbier. Set in an old
windmill, the taproom is thronged on
warm summer afternoons; its outdoor
seating taken up by drinkers enjoying
the lowest beer prices in Amsterdam.

BEER

TRIPPELAER

ABBEY-STYLE TRIPLE 8.5% ABV
A biscuity, bready aroma is followed
by lots of sweet malt and a touch
of bitter orange.

DOBBELAER

ABBEY-STYLE DOUBLE 6.5% ABV
Malty, sweetish beer, with a nutty
finish. Clean, flavourful, and as good
as most Belgian dubbels.

ALFA EDEL PILS

PILS 5% ABV
Tobacco and citrus hop aromas
overlay a buttery maltiness. One
of the most distinctive Dutch pils.

ALFA SUPER DORTMUNDER

DORTMUNDER EXPORT 7.5% ABV
A bitter Export that combines
grassy hops, honey, and vanilla with
the trademark Alfa butteriness.

BRAND IMPERATOR

AMBER LAGER 6.5% ABV
Dried fruit, toffee, and spicy
hops fight for supremacy in this
beautifully balanced amber beer.

BRAND UP

PILS 5% ABV
Aromatically hoppy; lemon, pepper,
and pine notes predominate. First
brewed in 1952 and still one of
Holland's best pils beers.

IJWIT

BELGIAN WHITE 6.5% ABV
A cloudy, golden-yellow fresh-
tasting beer; coriander and lemon
make it a real thirst quencher.

COLUMBUS

STRONG ALE 9% ABV
A balance of biscuity malt,
coriander, lemon, and resinous,
minty hops. Assertive, but not
overpowering.

THE BEST-KNOWN DUTCH BEERS

The vast majority of beer drunk in Holland is pils put out by one of four large brewing groups: Heineken, Bavaria, Grolsch, and Anheuser-Busch InBev.

Between them, these brewing companies control about 95 per cent of the Dutch beer market – Heineken leading the way with 50 per cent, and its three competitors following with around 15 per cent each. Heineken's main offerings are their ubiquitous Pils, Amstel Pils, the better-quality Amstel 1870 (another pils) and witbier Wieckse Witte. During the autumn bock season, sweet Heineken Tarwebock and the surprisingly good Amstel Bock are available. Bavaria, now the largest wholly Dutch-owned brewer, concentrates on the cheaper end of the market. In addition to their branded Bavaria Pils, they also produce several own-label beers for supermarket chains. Anheuser-Busch InBev closed their largest Dutch brewery, Oranjeboom, in Breda, in 2002. Dommelsch, their largest remaining plant, is much smaller, and large quantities of Jupiler Pils are imported from Belgium. Dommelsch Pils, strong lager Dommelsch Dominator, and autumn seasonal Dommelsch Bokbier Primeur are the main Dutch-brewed brands.

HEINEKEN PILS (PILS 5% ABV) *left*
HEINEKEN TARWEBOCK
  (BOCK 6.5% ABV)
AMSTEL PILS (PILS 5% ABV) *centre*
AMSTEL 1870 (PILS 5% ABV)
AMSTEL BOCK (BOCK 7% ABV)
BAVARIA PILS (PILS 5% ABV) *right*

BUDELS

Nieuwstraat 9, 6021 HP Budel, Netherlands
www.budels.nl

Budels is among the few established, predominantly bottom-fermenting Dutch breweries. Started in 1870, the business is currently run by the fourth generation of the founding Aerts family.

BREWING SECRET In recent years, Budels has diversified into top-fermenting beers, such as kölsch, altbier, and an abbey-style dubbel.

GROLSCH

Brouwerslaan 1, Boekelo, 7548 XA Enschede, Netherlands
www.grolsch.nl

Now owned by SABMiller, Grolsch used to operate two breweries: one in Groenlo (from which the name derives) and one in Enschede. In 2004, a new hypermodern plant was opened in Boeklo, just outside Enschede, and the two older breweries were closed. The bulk of Grolsch's sales are pils, though it has tried, with varied success, to diversify its product range.

GRUNN

Bornholmstraat 40, 9723 AX Groningen, Netherlands
www.grunn-speciaalbier.nl

The brewery was established by Jaap van der Weide and Egbert Timmerman in 2000, with their beers being brewed under contract in Belgium and Germany. However, a small brewery has now been installed and some of its beers are brewed in-house. Tasting sessions are regularly run at the brewery.

BUDELS CAPUCIJN
ABBEY-STYLE DUBBEL 6.5% ABV
Sweet, toasted malt aromas are complemented by bitterness, dates, and the merest hint of smoke.

BUDELS ORGANIC BEER
LAGER 5% ABV
Fresh tasting, it is a good balance of understated sweet malt and aromatic hops.

GROLSCH PREMIUM LAGER
PILS 5% ABV
Good aroma of Noble hops and a pleasant spiciness in the finish; a little too much sweetness perhaps.

GROLSCH WEIZEN
HEFEWEIZEN 5.5% ABV
Hazy golden, with the orange, cloves, and basil aromas typical of a German-style wheat beer.

DOMINIKANER HEFE WEISS
GERMAN WHEAT BEER 5% ABV
Unfiltered, it has an orange hue and aromas of banana and clove.

GRUNN DREI DUBBEL
TRIPLE 8.5% ABV
Dubbel by name but triple by strength. The sweetness of the malt is offset by a bitter finish and warming alcohol.

BREWERY

GULPENER
Rijksweg 16, 6271 AE Gulpen, Netherlands
www.gulpener.nl

Like the majority of the country's older brewers, Gulpener is located in the south of the country. A wide range of both top- and bottom-fermented beers are produced.

BREWING SECRET Gulpener's Mestreechs Aajt is a blend of sour beer that has been aged for at least a year in wood and freshly-brewed beer.

HERTOG JAN
Calvary 44, 5944 AND Arcen, Netherlands
www.hertogjan.nl

A management buyout in 1981 saved this old brewery from closure when it was part of the Oranjeboom group. A clause in the agreement prohibited brewing bottom-fermented beers, however, and so a range of Belgian-style ales was developed. Oranjeboom bought back the brewery to get hold of its speciality brands, before selling it on to Interbrew (now AB InBev) in 1995.

JOPEN
Gedempte Voldersgracht 2, 2011 WD Haarlem Netherlands
www.jopen.nl

Jopen was founded in 1995 with the intention of recreating old beer styles specifically from the Haarlem locale – once an important brewing centre. This is Holland's first brewery to concentrate on local recipes, and no other in the world produces beer in these styles. The brewery is open daily for visitors.

KLEIN DUIMPJE
Hyacintenlaan 2A, 2182 DE Hillegom Netherlands
www.kleinduimpje.nl

This is the brewery of a prize-winning amateur brewer Erik Bouman, whose porter was chosen as the best of more than 400 entries at the Dutch Home-brewing Championship of 1997. Bouman's competition success prompted him to start brewing professionally. His extensive range of top-fermenting ales includes his celebrated porter.

BEER

GULPENER PILSNER
PILSNER 5% ABV
Easy drinking, the soft malt character is matched by the subdued hop nose.

GULPENER KORENWOLF
WITBIER 5% ABV
A Belgian-style white beer packed with orange, ginger, wheat, and coriander flavours. It is brewed from barley, wheat, spelt, and rye.

HERTOG JAN GRAND PRESTIGE
STRONG DARK ALE 10% ABV
A big, fruity, strong ale, overflowing with caramel, liquorice, toffee, and apple flavours topped off with hops.

HERTOG JAN PILSENER
LAGER 5% ABV
English and Belgian malts give this beer an easy mouthfeel and a short, sweet finish.

JOPEN KOYT
GRUIT BEER 8.5% ABV
A recreation of a pre-hop beer brewed from three grains and herbs. Fruity, spicy, and delicious.

JOPEN HOPPENBIER
AMBER ALE 6.8% ABV
Based on a recipe from 1501 using barley, wheat, and oats; hints of coriander, ginger, and cloves complement spicy hops.

HILLEGOMS TARWE BIER
WITBIER 5.5% ABV
Flavoured with coriander and orange peel, this wheat beer is spicy, citric, and just ever so slightly sweet.

PORTER
PORTER 5.5% ABV
Espresso-like roast malt combines with a chocolate sweetness, backed up with liquorice and toast.

LINDEBOOM

Engelmanstraat 54, 6086 BD Neer,
Netherlands
www.lindeboom.nl

Established by farmer Willem Geenen
in 1870, Lindeboom is the country's
smallest surviving lager brewery. Still
owned by members of the Geenen
family, it is a modest producer of
mostly pils. It does also produce
altbier, and further diversification
into top-fermentation came with
the development of the Gouverneur
family of ales in the late 1990s.

DE MOLEN

Overtocht 43, 2411 BT Bodegraven,
Netherlands
www.brouwerijdemolen.nl

Since starting Molen in 2004, brewer
Menno Olivier has quickly gained an
enviable reputation. This is one of only
a handful of Dutch micros to export;
its cask-conditioned beer, Engel, is
designed especially for the UK market.

BREWING SECRET Aficionados regard
Tsarina Esra, an Imperial porter, as
one of Europe's very finest beers.

MOMMERIETE

De Oostermaat 66, 7783 BX
Gramsbergen, Netherlands
www.mommeriete.nl

Home-brewers Gert and Karina Kelder
were delighted when they discovered
that a local restaurant had a spare,
unused room. It was the perfect
location to finally brew professionally
after 15 years as amateurs, and they
set to work in 2004. Mommeriete
beers are available on tap in De
Ganzenhoeve restaurant and in bottles
through specialist Dutch beer shops.

DE PRAEL

Oudezijds Voorburgwal 30, 1012 GD
Amsterdam, Netherlands
www.deprael.nl

Set up with the help of government
grants, Amsterdam's smallest brewery
has a workforce made up of recovering
psychiatric patients. The first choice
of name – De Parel ("The Pearl") – had
to be changed when Budels complained
that it infringed on the copyright
of their Parel beer. The solution
was simply to shuffle the letters
of the name around.

VENLOOSCH ALT
ALTBIER 5% ABV
The sugary fruit aroma is deceptive
as the taste is dry and hoppy. A
reasonable try at the altbier style.

LINDEBOOM OUD BRUIN
OUD BRUIN 3.8% ABV
A fruity and very sweet low-alcohol
dark lager, in a style that is unique
to the Netherlands.

HEL & VERDOEMENIS
IMPERIAL STOUT 10% ABV
Big, bold, and very black, it is full
bodied, sweet, and full of chocolate
and coffee notes.

PALE ALE CITRA
INDIA PALE ALE 4.8% ABV
Blond in colour and light-bodied,
it is a refreshing glass of citrus fruit
and grassy flavours.

SCHEERSE TRIPEL
TRIPLE 9.5% ABV
Biscuit and yeast aroma, honey on
the tongue, and a spicy hop finish
with notes of tobacco and pepper.

VROUWE VAN GRAMSBERGH
STRONG DARK ALE 10% ABV
Black toffee, bread, and plum
aromas, and a honey sweetness slip
into a resiny, roasty, bitter finish.

HEINTJE
WITBIER 5.4% ABV
Unspiced, but with prominent
citrus aromas, a touch of fruit,
and an unexpectedly hoppy finish.

MARY
BARLEY WINE 9.7% ABV
Neither malt nor hops dominate
this fruity strong ale, laced with
pepper, toffee, and caramel.

BREWERY

DE SCHANS

Schans, 17–21, 1421 BA Uithoorn, Netherlands
www.schansbier.nl

Guus Rooijen started up De Schans when he began brewing professionally in 1998. The brewery has the reputation for brewing imaginative new beers and recreating old ones, though these days it is concentrating on its distilling business.

BREWING SECRET More adventurous than most Dutch micros, the range of beers is constantly changing.

SCHELDEBROUWERIJ

Wenenstraat 7, Meer (Hoogstraten), Belgium 2321, Netherlands
www.scheldebrouwerij.nl

One of the oldest and largest Dutch micros, Scheldebrouwerij has been through many changes since opening in 1994. The current owners, brothers Frans and Jan Ooms, are keen to expand the business further; with that in mind, they have moved the beer production over the border into neighbouring Belgium.

ST CHRISTOFFEL

Metaalweg 10, 6045 JB Roermond, Netherlands
www.christoffelbieren.com

Operating since 1986, St Christoffel is one of the oldest Dutch micros, founded (but no longer run) by Leo Brand, a member of the Brand brewing dynasty. It produces the very best lagers brewed in the Netherlands.

BREWING SECRET The Robertus beer is a rare example of a Münchner dark lager that is true to the Bavarian style.

LA TRAPPE

Eindhovenseweg 3, Berkel-Enschot, Netherlands
www.latrappe.nl

There are just eight genuine Trappist breweries in the world; Koningshoeven (better known as La Trappe) is the only one outside Belgium. The monastery had problems recruiting new monks, and that was one of the factors that prompted the sale of the brewery to Bavaria. Brewing still takes place within the monastery grounds under the supervision of the monks.

BEER

VAN VOLLENHOVEN'S STOUT
STOUT 7% ABV
A complex yet light-bodied stout, combining espresso roastiness with dark fruit and chocolate flavours.

SCHANS BOK
BOK 7% ABV
Masses of Munich malt make this a big, bold beer; dry rather than sweet, with a bitter finish.

STRANDGAPER
BLOND ALE 6.2% ABV
Named after a freshwater crustacean, it has a full-bodied malt biscuit taste and a soft, bitter, floral finish.

HOP RUITER
TRIPLE 8% ABV
Full bodied and alcohol warming, the beer is dry hopped, which unleashes swathes of citrus flavours.

CHRISTOFFEL BLOND
PILS 6% ABV
Spicy hop flavours burst from the glass – basil, mint, ginger, grapefruit, and cloves are all there.

CHRISTOFFEL WIJS
WHEAT BEER 6% ABV
Amber in colour with caramel notes, the beer moves from initial sweetness to a light, refreshing bitterness.

LA TRAPPE WITTE TRAPPIST
WITBIER 5.5% ABV
Unspiced, but a subtle use of aromatic hops more than compensates, providing delicious citrus and pepper flavours.

LA TRAPPE TRIPEL
STRONG ALE 8% ABV
Sweetness and fruit give way to coriander, orange, and hop bitterness in this supremely balanced beer.

The Dutch city of Amsterdam is said to have a bar for every 500 citizens – 1,200 in total.

BREWERY

BØGEDAL BRYGHUS

Høllundvej 9, DK-7100 Vejle, Denmark
www.boegedal.com

This farmhouse is the world's only commercial brewery producing the old Danish style of "Goodbeer", a strong, rich beer dating back to before the industrial age. The same recipes are usually followed, yet no two beers are alike, hence, like vintage wines, they are numbered rather than named.

BREWING SECRET Most of the processes are done by hand, not machinery.

BREWPUB

Vestergade 29, 1456 København K, Denmark
www.brewpub.dk

This successful microbrewery with restaurant is located in the heart of Copenhagen in a beautiful 17th-century building. The pub brews seven beers, all of which are served unfiltered from tanks in its cellars. The chefs also feature beer as an ingredient in the seasonal menus. Advice on pairing beer with food is also provided.

CARLSBERG

100 Ny Carlsberg Vej,
1799 Copenhagen V, Denmark
www.carlsberg.com

Denmark's leading brewing company was founded in 1847 by the visionary brewer JC Jacobsen. Carlsberg is a pioneer of steam-brewing, refrigeration techniques, and the propagation of a single yeast strain. The company has a wide portfolio of beers and sells to more than 150 countries. It has recently moved all of its production, with the exception of speciality beers

and the Jacobsen brand, from its original brewery in Copenhagen to Fredericia, located 200km (125 miles) from its former home. In its place, a new city district is being developed, which will conserve the historic brewery buildings, and be the site of the Carlsberg Visitors Center.

BEER

NO 321

STOUT 6.1% ABV
Vanilla, dark chocolate, and coffee flavours give way to a sweet, citrus bitterness from the New World hops.

NO 288

PALE ALE 6% ABV
Sweet, with hints of almond and citrus; the bitterness is understated.

AMARILLO

RED ALE 5.5% ABV
Fresh aroma and flavours of plum and citrus. Balanced bitterness from caramel and red ale malt.

PACIFIC

INDIA PALE ALE 6% ABV
The addition of Cascade and Centennial hops gives this beer a distinctive hop floral and citrus nose.

CARLSBERG ELEPHANT

STRONG PILSNER 7.2% ABV
High-alcohol lager, with high hop and malt content, resulting in a rich and bitter character.

CARLSBERG PILSNER

PILSNER 5% ABV
Another bottom-fermented lager with flavours of hops, grains, pine needles, sorrel, and Danish apples.

SEMPER ARDENS ABBEY ALE

BELGIAN ABBEY ALE 7.3% ABV
Unfiltered; brewed with Münchener and chocolate malt, and featuring burnt undertones and a hint of blackcurrant on the palate.

TUBORG PILSNER

PILSNER 4.6% ABV
Denmark's favourite beer. Bottom-fermented lager, lightly roasted, with aroma of flowers and grain.

GOURMETBRYGGERIET

Bytoften 10-12,
DK-4000 Roskilde, Denmark
www.gourmetbryggeriet.dk

Owned by Harboe Bryggeri A/S, the Gourmet Brewery was founded in 2008 and the mission was to create speciality beers that are designed to be paired with food. Today Gourmetbryggeriet products are delivered in cans and you can also enjoy Gourmet Bryggeriet draught beer at many restaurants and cafes in Denmark.

HERSLEV BRYGHUS

Kattingevej 16 , Herslev,
4000 Roskilde, Denmark
www.herslevbryghus.dk

This small microbrewery, established in 2004 by Tore Jørgensen, is part of a family farmhouse located in Herslev, a small village outside Roskilde. The beer here is unfiltered, unpasteurized, and naturally carbonated.

BREWING SECRET Four kinds of grain are the foundation of the brewing process, creating beers with unique character.

HORNBEER

Hornsherredvej 463, 4070 Kirke Hylinge, 40311580 Denmark
www.hornbeer.dk

According to brewer Jorgen Rasmussen, beer should have no boundaries as it is a drink for everyone and not just young males. His beers are creativity in a bottle; they are a testament to the brewer's skill and artistry in understanding the contribution each ingredient makes to a beer. The range of beers spans Imperial stouts to sour raspberry ales.

JACOBSEN BREWHOUSE

Gamle Carlsberg Vej 11, DK-1799 Copenhagen V, Denmark
www.jacobsenbeer.com

Named after Carlsberg's founder, Jacobsen was established in 2005 to produce high-quality speciality beers with a Scandinavian touch. The brewhouse remains in the original 1847 Carlsberg brewery complex.

BREWING SECRET Jacobsen also brews an exclusive Vintage series, matured in oak barrels.

GOURMETBRYGGERIET BOCK2

DOPPLEBOCK 7.2% ABV
Deep reddish in colour, with a heavy aroma of malt and caramel backing up the strong body.

FINALE

AMERICAN PALE ALE 6.5% ABV
Golden red and masses of carbonation, its bold spice malt base partners with aromatic hops, adding grapefruit and elderflower.

HVEDE

WHEAT BEER 5% ABV
Southern-German inspired, with Bamberg wheat and buck malt. Sweet, with fruity nuances, balanced with bitterness.

PALE ALE

PALE ALE 5.9% ABV
Combines English barley and oats, and Amarillo hops. Golden colour, fresh and fruity aroma and flavour.

DRYHOP

ALE 5% ABV
Amarillo hops are the star of this dry beer, bringing bitterness and floral aromatic notes.

FUNKY MONK

BELGIAN ALE 8.8% ABV
A big, bold beer with lashings of caramel flavours. Unfiltered; it evolves in the bottle the longer it is kept.

JACOBSEN SAAZ BLONDE

PALE ALE 7.1% ABV
Extract of angelica adds a juniper-like flavour that complements the fruity taste of the yeast.

JACOBSEN EXTRA PILSNER

PILSNER 5.5% ABV
A premium lager using Nordic ingredients, such as Danish organic pilsner malt and Swedish sea buckthorn juice.

ALL ABOUT...
BOTTLE SHAPES

Brewing folklore has it that we have a little-known 16th-century Tudor clergyman to thank for the advent of bottled beer. It is said that Alexander Newell, dean of St. Paul's Cathedral in London, liked to fish, taking with him some home-brewed beer in an old medicine bottle. At the end of one trip, he left the bottle behind. On his return to the river bank, some time later, he found the bottle and opened it. There was a satisfying pop and hiss, and he realized that the beer had remained in good condition. Although glass bottles were probably used for storing beer before Newell's time, this piscatorial (and quite possibly apocryphal) anecdote has survived to mark the beginnings of bottled beer.

Due to the high cost of its labour-intensive production, bottled beer remained a luxury for the next couple of centuries. Matters changed for the better in the British Isles in 1845, when the abolition of a Glass Tax helped to boost the availability of glass bottles. To make sure that the beer didn't escape, they were stoppered with corks, then screw tops, and finally the crown corks (more commonly known as just bottle-tops), that are still in use today.

COMMON SHAPES
Most bottle profiles favour either a slender design with a long, tapering neck or a fatter form with a short neck and rounded, slumped shoulders, like that of Sierra Nevada ale from the USA.

OVAL-SHAPED
England's St Peter's Brewery uses bottles that hark back to an oval-shaped design of the late 18th century.

PAPER-WRAPPED Bottles wrapped in paper, such as those of Belgium's Corsendonk Agnus from Bocq Brewery, and Italy's Birrificio Montegioco beers, add a touch of mystique to the beer's presentation.

ELEGANT Recent years have seen some brewers reconfigure the aesthetics of beer bottles by looking to the world of wine and Champagne for inspiration. Italian craft brewers, such as Baladin and 32 Via dei Birrai, are at the cutting edge with stylish and graceful bottles that owe more to wine than beer.

ARTISAN Some artisanal brewers are keen on corks, especially for their stronger beers. After all, these are beers that have been hand-crafted and are the beer equivalent of wine – why not make them special? The use of corks has been prevalent in northern France and Belgium for a long time, but new-wave brewers such as the Danish Bogedal Brewery are also embracing this technique.

BØGEDAL № 321

Type: Mørk muscovado   Opskrift: Mørk #1
Humle mv: Cascade, Columbus, Perle, Muskovado
Alkohol: 6,1 %
Brygget: 30/10 2012
Tappet: 12/11 2012

STUBBY Several Belgian brewers use a distinctive stubby bottle. Strong and heavy, it can withstand the high pressure created by secondary fermentation in the bottle, a crucial element of beers like Duvel and Steenberg's Augustijn Grand Cru.

Grand   Cru

Augustijn

ANNO 1295

Oosterbier ~ Bière de ...

SWING TOP On the European mainland, many bottles are sealed with swing tops rather than with crowns. They are famously used for Grolsch in the Netherlands and by German breweries such as Berg. They are also popular with home-brewers.

32

OPPALE

Berg Brauerei
ULRICH ZIMMERMANN
Ulrichsbier

BREWERY

MIDTFYNS BRYGHUS

Industrivej 11-13, 5792 Årslev,
Denmark
www.midtfyns-bryghus.dk

This microbrewery is on the island of
Fyn off the eastern Danish mainland.
Founded in 2005, it was bought by
American entrepreneur Eddie Szweda
in 2007. It has since found success
with its quality hand-crafted brews.

BREWING SECRET It first gained much
appreciative attention for the
now-discontinued Braveheart beer.

MIKKELLER

Vesterbrogade 20, I.TH., DK-1620
Copenhagen V, Denmark
www.mikkeller.dk

An innovative brewery producing
an eclectic range of beer. Mikkeller
adopts an American rule-breaking
approach to brewing and has achieved
significant international recognition
with several of its brews.

BREWING SECRET A brewing troubadour,
Mikkeller doesn't own a brewery, but
uses other people's.

NØRREBRO BRYGHUS

Ryesgade 3, 2200 Copenhagen N,
Denmark
www.noerrebrobryghus.dk

Opened in 2003, this brewpub serves
up to 10 hand-crafted beers. The
ambition of the company's first
brewer, Anders Kissmeyer, to make
the best and most varied beers in
Denmark, continues even though he
has now left the company. The beers
are also an integral part of the whole
dining experience in the restaurant.

REFSVINDINGE BREWERY

Nyborgvej 80,
5853 Ørbæk, Denmark
www.bryggerietrefsvindinge.dk

Since 1885, four generations have run
this farmhouse brewery. It was among
the first to brew ales in Denmark and
is credited with developing Danish
white beer (*hvidtøl*) and the old-style
smoked "ship's beer" (*skibsøl*), as well
as two varieties of beer for children
(not entirely alcohol free!).

BEER

CHILI TRIPEL
TRIPEL 9.2% ABV
A spiced beer; chilli and alcohol
add to the warming finish of this
Belgian-inspired ale.

GUNNERS ALE
ALE 7.3% ABV
Brewed as a tribute to the brewer's
favourite football team, Arsenal, it
is a fine balance of malt and hops.

BEER GEEK BREAKFAST
OATMEAL STOUT 7.5% ABV
An award-winning stout with a rich
nose, smooth and balanced taste,
and coffee and chocolate notes.

BLACK
IMPERIAL STOUT 17.5% ABV
Exceptional body of sugars, roasted
coffee beans, and black chocolate;
a complex and lingering aftertaste.

BOMBAY PALE ALE
INDIA PALE ALE 6.5% ABV
English Marris Otter malt gives
a deeply intense malt character.
Fruity aromas, high bitterness, and
some sweetness.

NEW YORK LAGER
LAGER 5.2% ABV
A powerful, rich, bottom-fermented,
malty beer with a long, tingling
bitter finish.

ALE NO 16
BROWN ALE 5.7% ABV
Well-rounded, typical dark ale using
original English yeast to produce a
sweet, fresh taste.

MORS STOUT
PORTER 5.7% ABV
Dark, smooth porter brewed using
malt that has been roasted with
cocoa beans.

ROYAL UNIBREW

Faxe Allé 1, DK-4640 Faxe, Denmark
www.royalunibrew.com

Formerly The Danish Brewery Group, Royal Unibrew is Denmark's second largest brewery and Scandinavia's largest exporter. The company owns two regional breweries, Faxe and Albani, Danish brands such as Ceres, Thor, and Maribo, and a number of international breweries. The Royal brand is its most popular in Denmark.

SVANEKE BRYGHUS

Svanevang 10, 3740 Svaneke, Bornholme, Denmark
www.svanekebryghus.dk

A small-town brewery on Bornholm Island, which is big on taste. Its core beers are brewed in both lager and ale styles. It produces an interesting range of specials, which are pushing brewing ideas to new boundaries.

THISTED BRYGHUS

Bryggerivej 10, DK-7700 Thisted, Denmark
www.thisted-bryghus.dk

Located in a town with the same name, the brewery is owned by the town's current and former residents. It has been making traditional lagers since 1899 and is famous for its all-malt organic brews.

BREWING SECRET Thisted's malt mill was first used at the Carlsberg brewery as early as 1902.

AASS BRYGGERI

P.O.Box 1530 Bedriftssenteret, N-3007 Drammen, Norway
www.aass.no

Norway's oldest brewery dates back to 1834. Named after Poul Lauritz Aass (pronounced "ouse"), it is a family-owned business run by five generations since 1860.

BREWING SECRET Aass brews according to the strict 1516 Bavarian Law of Purity, drawing its water from the nearby lake of Glitre.

ROYAL EXPORT
PREMIUM LAGER 5.6% ABV
The best-selling beer in the range, it has mild, aromatic, and balanced taste. It uses a special yeast to give a smooth, vinous character.

CERES JULEHVIDTØL
WHITE BEER 1.9% ABV
A classic low-alcohol Christmas brew with dark malts and sugar giving a sweet, full-bodied taste.

MØRK GULD
LAGER 5.7% ABV
Copper coloured, it is full of soft, bitter hops and chestnut flavours, with a caramel finish.

SVANEKE CLASSIC
LAGER 4.6% ABV
A deep golden lager, dominated by biscuit and grain flavours. It has a spicy, ginger finish.

LIMFJORDS PORTER
BALTIC PORTER 7.9% ABV
Almost black in colour; rich and complex. Bottom-fermented and brewed with smoked malt and liquorice for rich flavour and aroma.

PORSE GULD
PALE LAGER 5.8% ABV
A classic Thisted brew. Fruity and sweet golden lager flavoured with locally gathered bog myrtle.

AASS BOCK
DUNKLER BOCK 6.5% ABV
Smooth and creamy; brewed using Munich malt and Hallertau hops. Lagered for at least three months.

AASS JULEØL
DUNKLER BOCK 6.5% ABV
The most sought-after Christmas beer in Scandinavia. Thick and malty, with a smooth, rich flavour.

BREWERY

BERENTSENS BRYGGHUS

PO Box 53 N-4379 Egersund, Norway
www.berentsens.no

This regional brewery uses fresh and natural raw materials to produce high-quality ales, as well as cider, spirits, and soft drinks. Managing director Harald Berentsen is the fourth generation to run the company, which was founded by his great grandfather, Captain Wilhelm Berentsen in 1895.

HAAND BRYGGERIET

Skogliveien 4, Bygg H, Sundland 3047 Drammen, Norway
www.haandbryggeriet.net

This small brewery is known for its handmade brews and for keeping Norwegian brewing traditions alive. Housed in a 200-year-old wooden building, it is run by volunteers, and experimentation is encouraged.

BREWING SECRET As well as using old oak wine barrels, they are now ageing beer in former Akevitt spirit casks.

HANSA BORG BRYGGERIER

Kokstaddalen 3, Pb. 24, Kokstad, 5863 Bergen, Norway
www.hansa.no

Norway's second-largest brewing company also runs as a brewpub (Kalfaret Brygghus) in Bergen. Founded in 1891, Hansa merged with Borg Breweries in 1997. Its original name reflects Bergen's history as a member of the Hanseatic League, a historic Baltic regional trading alliance.

LERVIG AKTIEBRYGGERI

Vierveien I, Hillevåg,
4016 Stavanger, Norway
www.lervig.no

Established by an enthusiastic group of brewers in 2003, the brewery began as a protest against the closure of the region's local brewery, Tou. Today, it is an established independent and industrial craft brewery, which supplies to local beer-lovers, as well as bars and restaurants, with quality brews and non-alcoholic beverages.

BEER

ROGALANDS PILS
LAGER 4.7% ABV
Made with Czech hops and Scottish malt. Rich and deeply flavourful with well-balanced bitterness.

RAV AMBER ALE
AMBER ALE 4.7% ABV
This over-yeasted ale features a generous amount of American Cascade hops, giving a clear bitterness and complex character.

DARK FORCE
WHEAT STOUT 9% ABV
Uses wheat and dark roasted malts and house wheat yeast. High hop aroma and ample bitterness.

NORWEGIAN WOOD
TRADITIONAL ALE 6.5% ABV
Made from naturally smoked Munich, Crystal, and chocolate malts; spiced with locally gathered juniper twigs and berries.

PILSNER
PILSNER 4.5% ABV
The brewery's most popular beer, this is a crisp, light lager with a citrussy finish.

BAYER
DARK LAGER 4.5% ABV
Semi-dark Munich-style beer. Dark malts give it a toffee-like finish.

HOPPY JOE
AMERICAN AMBER ALE 4.7% ABV
Chocolate and caramel flavours are balanced by pine and tropical fruit notes from three New World hops.

LUCKY JACK
AMERICAN PALE ALE 4.7% ABV
Amarillo, Chinook, and Citra hops give this easy-drinking beer a flourish of grapefruit and tropical fruit flavours.

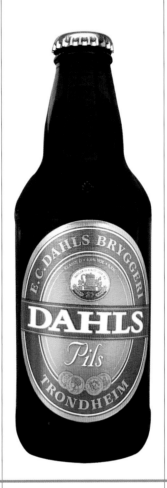

MACK'S BREWERY

Storgata 4, N-9291 Tromsø, Norway
www.mack.no

This brewery and soft drinks company, founded by Ludwig Markus Mack in 1877, is best known for its highly popular pilsner, originally introduced in 1891. It produces beers to honour special occasions and has a "Party" and a "Seasonal" series. Despite claims, it is not the world's northernmost brewery, since a microbrewery was set up in Honningsvag in 2000.

NØGNE Ø

Gamle Rykene Kraftstasjon,
Lunde 8, 4885 Grimstad, Norway
www.nogne-o.com

Kjetil Jikiun launched Nøgne Ø ("naked island") in 2003 after learning home-brewing in the USA. Now his brewery is Norway's largest supplier of bottle-conditioned ale.

BREWING SECRET Nøgne Ø mixes British Marris Otter malt with American C-hops, including Cascade, Centenneal, Chinook, and Columbus.

RINGNES

Thorvald Meyersgate 2,
N-0555 Oslo, Norway
www.ringnes.no

Norway's largest brewery was founded by brothers Amund and Ellef Ringes in 1876. Through a long succession of mergers, this historic brewery is now owned by the Carlsberg Group. As well as Carlsberg and Ringnes, its brands include Tuborg Lysholmer, Dahls, and Frydenlund.

CARLSBERG SWEDEN AB

Bryggerivägen 10
SE-161 86 Stockholm, Sweden
www.carlsberg.se

Sweden's largest brewing company, and the fifth largest worldwide, brews beer in Stockholm, Goteborg, and Falkenberg. It was established in 2001 through a merger of the Falcon and Pripps breweries. Its main beer brands in Sweden include Pripps, Falcon, Eriksberg, Carlsberg, and Tuborg.

ARCTIC BEER
PALE LAGER 4.5% ABV
A pale golden beer, with a hint of hops on the nose and a dry finish.

MACK HAAKON
LAGER 4.75% ABV
A commemorative beer launched to celebrate the 1994 Winter Olympics in Lillehammer. Rich-tasting and amber in colour.

SAISON
SAISON 6.5% ABV
East Kent Goldings and Crystal hops and Belgian ale yeast produce a light and refreshing brew, available all year but ideal in summer.

IMPERIAL STOUT
IMPERIAL STOUT 9% ABV
A dark, rich ale with a generous sweetness and bitterness coming from the roasted malts.

DAHLS PILS
PILSNER 4.5% ABV
Golden, smooth, aromatic lager with a rich taste, malty and fruity flavour, and lingering bitterness.

RINGNES PILS
PILSNER 4.5% ABV
Fresh and pure, with a slightly dry character, light sweetness, low fruitiness, and a well-balanced hop bitterness.

CARNEGIE STARKPORTER
PORTER 5.5% ABV
The oldest active brand, dating back to1836. Fruity flavour with elements of caramelized sugar, coffee, and chocolate.

FALCON EXPORT
LAGER 5.2% ABV
Brewed since 1896; it has a rich and malty taste with a well-balanced bitterness.

BREWERY

ÅBRO BRYGGERI

598 86 Vimmerby, Sweden
www.abro.se

Sweden's oldest family-run brewery is located in the southern Småland region. Lieutenant Per W Luthander founded Åbro in 1856. Axel Herman Johansson purchased the brewery in 1898, and it is still owned and operated by his descendents today.

BREWING SECRET The brewery is located beside the source of fresh spring water that it uses in its brewing.

DUGGES ALE & PORTERBRYGGERI

Östra Björrödsvägen 12438 93 Landvetter, Sweden
www.dugges.se

The brewery was founded in 2005 by Mikael Dugge Engström. His series of beers include Gothenburg, marrying old Swedish traditions with British and American inspiration, and Express Yourself, a collection of speciality brews with names like Holy Cow (an IPA) and Fuggedaboudit! (a brown ale).

GOTLANDS BRYGGERI

St Hansgatan 47,
621 56 Visby, Sweden
www.gotlandsbryggeri.se

Gotland is the largest island in the Baltic sea. This experimental microbrewery, owned by Spendrups, is in the old Hanseatic town of Visby, housed in a brewery and church dating from the 1700s. It is known for its speciality and seasonal beers.

BREWING SECRET The range includes an authentic Maclay's Scotch Ale.

JÄMTLANDS

AB Bangårdsgatan 31 831 45 Östersund, Sweden
www.jamtlandsbryggeri.se

This innovative small microbrewery was established in 1996 in the capital of the Jämtland region of central Sweden. It brews a wide variety of beers, including a strong English ale, Baltic Porter, and Vienna lager and consistently wins awards at the Stockholm Beer Festival.

BREWING SECRETS It draws from British, German, and Alsace beer styles.

BEER

SMÅLAND
PILSNER 5.2% ABV
Brewed with Czech yeast. Full bodied, moderately bitter taste, with elements of hops and apricot.

ÅBRO ORIGINAL
PREMIUM LAGER 5.2% ABV
A full-bodied, light lager; rounded bitterness and sweetness, and an aromatic hoppy character.

DUGGES AVENYN ALE
AMERICAN PALE ALE 5% ABV
Aromas of hops, flowers, and citrus fruits; flavours of grapes, pine, and a hint of caramel.

HIGH FIVE!
INDIAN PALE ALE 7.5% ABV
Dark amber. Intense hop aroma; notes of strawberry jam, pine, and chocolate, and a dry bitterness.

WISBY WEISSE
WEISSBIER 5.2% ABV
A Bavarian-style wheat beer containing 60 per cent wheat and caramel malt. Unfiltered and unpasteurized.

WISBY KLOSTERÖL
ALE 5% ABV
Scottish yeast plus Pilsner, Munich, and wheat malts give an orangey fruitiness and a honeyed flavour.

PRESIDENT
PORTER 5.2% ABV
This bottom-fermented beer has a medium bitterness and the soft aroma of Czech Saaz hops.

OATMEAL PORTER
PORTER 4.8% ABV
An unfiltered and top-fermented porter with a ruby-black colour. Espresso in a glass!

NYNÄSHAMNS ÅNGBRYGGERI

Box 186, Lövlundsvägen 4,
SE-149 22 Nynäshamn, Sweden
www.nyab.se

Nynäshamns Ångbryggeri, meaning "steam brewery", produces mainly ales, stouts, and porters using British and American methods. Founded in 1997 by four enthusiasts, all of its beers are named after places in the archipelago and the harbour town of Nynäshamn.

BEDARÖ BITTER
PREMIUM BITTER 4.5% ABV
A well-balanced, hoppy ale with a fruity taste and a bitter, dry finish.

SMÖRPUNDET
PORTER 5% ABV
A full-bodied porter with chocolate notes and a mild bitterness.

NILS OSCAR

Fruängsgatan 2, 611 31 Nyköping, Sweden
www.nilsoscar.se

This microbrewery and distillery was established in 1996 and makes well-balanced beers that go well with food. It has won many awards, including four medals in the World Beer Cup.

BREWING SECRET Nils Oscar has its own maltings, and a farm where barley and other cereals for malting are grown.

IMPERIAL STOUT
IMPERIAL STOUT 7% ABV
Well balanced and rich from ageing. Chocolate aromas with caramel giving way to a bittersweet finish.

INDIA ALE
INDIA PALE ALE 5.3% ABV
Heavily hopped with Amarillo, giving an aroma of tropical fruits; the fruitiness is balanced by the crystal malt sweetness.

SPENDRUPS

Box 3006, 143 03 Vårby, Sweden
www.spendrups.se

The largest Swedish-owned brewing company, it was founded in 1897. It owns three breweries in Grängesberg, Vårby, and Gotlands. Its CEO and brewmaster, Johan Spendrup, is the fourth generation of his family to run the brewery.

BREWING SECRET This is the only brewery in Sweden to produce beer according to the 1516 Bavarian Purity Law.

PISTONHEAD KUSTOM LAGER
LAGER 4.9% ABV
Milder than the imagery suggests, it's grainy with a dry finish, with hints of flowery hops and pear drops.

SPENDRUPS OLD GOLD
PILSNER 5% ABV
German-style pilsner made with Czech Saazer hops. Citrus notes, a dry bitter finish, and long aftertaste.

FINLANDIA

Palomäentie 342, Sastamala,
38510 Finland
www.finlandiasahti.fi

Finlandia is a specialist brewer of *sahti*, a traditional Finnish home-brew made with rye and other grains, flavoured with juniper twigs and berries. Beer enthusiasts can sample Finlandia Sahti in Helsinki at St Urho's Pub and the Restaurant Savotta. The best time to do so is during Helsinki's Sahti Week, which takes place in May each year.

SAHTI STRONG
SAHTI 10% ABV
Sweet and somewhat oily on the palate; the juniper nose gives way to a bubble-gum aftertaste.

TAVALLINEN
SAHTI 8% ABV
A deep chestnut colour, with a heavy juniper nose and a hint of blackcurrant.

BREWERY

HARTWALL

Atomitie 2a, FI-00371 Helsinki, Finland
www.hartwall.fi/en

Hartwall was bought by Royal Unibrew from Heineken in August 2013. Brands include Hartwall Jaffa, Hartwall Novelle, Upcider, Lapin Kulta, and Karjala beers. Victor Harwall founded it in 1836 as the first mineral water supplier in Scandinavia. Brewing began in 1966 with Karjala beer – its Karelian name and logo defied the Soviet Union, then occupying much of the region.

LAITILAN

Limonaadikuja 4, LAITILA 23800, Finland
www.laitilan.com/english

This is one of the fastest-growing breweries in Finland. Founded in 1995, it brews a range of full malt beers under the Kukko (rooster) name, Oiva Scandinavian cider, and old-fashioned lemonades.

BREWING SECRET The brewery uses wind power for all its energy needs, and was the first in the world to develop a gluten-free, full malt beer.

MALMGÅRDIN PANIMO

Malmgård 47, 07720 Malmgård, Finland
www.malmgard.fi

Located in south-eastern Finland, most of the brewery's ingredients come from the organic farm where it is based. Formerly known as the Huvila brewery, until it was taken over by Malmgård in 2009, all its beers are unfiltered and made without the use of additives. The Huvila brand is still used for more experimental beers.

NOKIAN PANIMO

Nuijamiestentie 17, 37120 Nokia, Finland
www.nokianpanimo.fi

Nokian Panimo was founded in 1991 and specializes in unfiltered lagers sold under the Året Runt, Kommodori, and Jouluolut brands. It also brews filtered lagers including Keisari Pils and Keisari Strong. It produces approximately 2.5 million litres (660,000 gallons) of beverages per year, including beer, mineral water, and juice-based soft drinks.

BEER

KARJALA IVB

STRONG LAGER 8% ABV
Golden, strong lager with a generous head; smooth malts and hops give a robust character.

LAPIN KULTA PREMIUM

LAGER 4.5% ABV
Crisp and smooth; now brewed to a new recipe using only natural ingredients, and with more malts and hops in the mix.

KUKKO PILS

PILSNER 4.5% ABV
A German-style pilsner with the strong bite of aromatic hops. It has won the best beer award in Finland three times.

KUKKO LAGER

LAGER 4.7% ABV
Light golden in colour, the aromatic hops are dominated by a malt sweetness.

MALMGÅRD DINKEL

ALE 4.5% ABV
Unfiltered, with a slight haze; wheat and spelt add biscuit texture to this malt-driven beer.

HUVILA X-PORTER

PORTER 7% ABV
Top-fermented and unfiltered, black in colour, it is creamy with hints of hazelnut and a chocolate, and caramel finish.

ÅRET RUNT IV

STRONG LAGER 5.7% ABV
Deep brown, unfiltered lager. Fruity, slightly sweet, and mildly roasted, with a strong hops flavour.

KEISARI 66

AMERICAN PALE ALE 4.2% ABV
Unfiltered and slightly cloudy, the Cascade hops bring a touch of citrus sophistication to the beer.

OLVI

Olvitie I–IV, FI-74100 Iisalmi, Finland
www.olvi.fi

Finland's third largest brewer, Olvi is also the only Finnish-owned brewery with national operations. A publicly traded company, founded in 1878, Olvi has subsidiaries in Estonia (A. Le Coq), Lithuania (Ragutis), and Latvia (Cesu Alus). It is a regular sponsor of Oluset, Finland's largest and oldest annual summer beer festival.

PLEVNA BREWERY

Itäinenkatu 8, FI-33210 Tampere, Finlayson Finland
www.plevna.fi

This brewpub and restaurant was established in 1994 and is situated in the historic Finlayson cotton mills of Tampere, Finland's third largest city. The brewery produces a variety of beers, including dark and pale lager, stout, and wheat beer. Following tradition, all beers conform to the *Reinheitsgebot* purity laws.

SINEBRYCHOFF

Oy Sinebrychoff Ab, Sinebrychoffinaukio 1 PL 87, FL-04201 Kerava, Finland
www.sinebrychoff.fi

Sinebrychoff is part of the Carlsberg Group, and its abbreviated name and main brand range, Koff, is one of the most popular in Finland. It is the oldest Nordic brewery, founded by Russian Nikolai Sinebrychoff in 1819.

BREWING SECRET Karhupanimo, their new microbrewery, is producing a range of hand-crafted lagers.

TEERENPELI

Liimaajankatu 9, 15520 Lahti, Finland
www.teerenpeli.com

Teerenpeli operates a brewery and whisky distillery at Taivaanranta, one of its two restaurants in Lahti. Here diners can watch the brewers at work, as the brewery is the centrepiece of the smart restaurant. The company also has restaurants in Tampere, Helsinki, Turku, and Lappeenranta. Teerenpeli's beers have won medals at the Helsinki Beer Festival on a number of occasions.

OLVI III

LAGER 4.5% ABV
Olvi's most popular beer, a Pilsner-type full-bodied lager with a sweet and malty flavour.

OLVI TUPLAPUKKI

PALE DOPPELBOCK 8.5% ABV
Finland's best-selling strong beer, rich in malt and hops. A spicier version is produced for Christmas.

SIPERIA STOUT

IMPERIAL STOUT 8% ABV
A strong, rich stout with a typical tar-like flavour combined with a roasted fruitiness.

SAVUOLUT JAMES

SMOKED BEER 5.2% ABV
This dark copper-coloured beer has a slightly roasted, tarry flavour. It is full bodied, with a bite of bitter in the aftertaste.

SINEBRYCHOFF PORTER

IMPERIAL STOUT 7.2% ABV
Robust and brimming with coffee flavours, this beer has a long, warming finish.

KARHU III

LAGER 4.6% ABV
Described by the brewer as "untamed". Full bodied, with stronger flavours of hops and malt than are usual for a lager.

ONNENPEKKA PILS

PILSNER 4.7% ABV
Golden and refreshing. Made with Pilsner barley malt from the Lahti region, and pure water from the Salpausselkä area.

LAISKAJAAKKO

DARK LAGER 4.5% ABV
This full-bodied, malty dark lager is brewed with Crystal 50 and black malt, and Hallertau hops.

BEER STYLES
WHEAT BEER

Little more than a generation ago, Bavarian *weissbier*, or *weizen*, was in sharp decline. Once the privilege of kings and princes, this historic brew had come to be regarded as an old person's drink in comparison to the youthful gloss of lager. In the early 1980s, all this changed. Hip drinkers rediscovered it, and word spread from Bavaria to intrigue and inspire beer-lovers and brewers all over the world. At about the same time, Belgium's spicy *witbiers* (white beers) also appeared on the beer-drinkers' radar, beginning with Hoegaarden, the creation of former milkman Pierre Celis.

The international appeal of these beers has been picked up on by brewers from Britain, the USA, and many other nations. Some are now producing wheat beers in the Bavarian *weissbier* tradition; others favour spicy and zesty brews in the style of Belgian *witbiers*.

MALT Wheat beers are a mixture of pale and wheat malt, with the latter making up a sizeable percentage of the grist. This gives the beer a tart and refreshing flavour. Subtle hopping adds a lemony, spritzy fruitiness.

YEAST Bavarian *weissbiers* from breweries such as Schneider and Maisels feature banana, clove, and vanilla notes from the yeast, and may be cloudy (*hefeweizen*) with suspended yeast, or clear (*kristall*). Darker wheat beers are called *dunkel*, and stronger ones *weizenbock*.

SPICES Belgium *witbiers* tend to be spicy, almost peppery, due to the use of spices, such as coriander seeds and rare African grains of paradise, as well as bitter Curaçao orange peel. Some, such as St Bernardus Wit, have a luscious silkiness.

AMBER

ul. Gregorkiewicza 1, Bielkówko,
83-050 Kolbudy, Poland
www.browar-amber.pl

Owned by the Przybylo family, this medium-sized brewery is one of the most modern in Poland. Situated close to Gdansk in Pomerania, an area with a rich brewing tradition, the brewery is a supporter of the Slow Food movement, and organizes the Kozlaki Bielkowskie food and drink festival every September. According to a consumer poll of Polish drinkers, the brewery's Grand Imperial Porter is one of the best beers made in Poland. A chilli-flavoured version of the porter has recently been introduced.

BROWARMIA

ul. Królewska 1, Warszawa 00-065, Poland
www.browarmia.pl

Opened in 2005, this fine brewpub has a vibrant atmosphere – busy, convivial, and loud on music nights. Polish food with a modern twist is a speciality to match the beers on tap. Eleven beers are currently brewed in the smart cellar brewery, with more planned for the future.

KOMPANIA PIWOWARSKA SA

ul. Szwajcarska 11, 61-285
Poznán, Poland
www.kp.pl/eng

This company has won many brewing awards and has a reputation for quality. Owned by SABMiller, it is expanding quickly. Also the owner of the Browar Belgia Brewery in Kielce, it is aggressively marketing its brands in home and world markets. (*Continues overleaf*)

BREWERY

KOŹLAK
DUNKEL BOCK 6.5% ABV
A ruby-red beer, it is rich in malt and yeasty flavours, with a warming aftertaste.

GRAND IMPERIAL PORTER
PORTER 8% ABV
Dark ebony coloured, with a ruby edge. Rich liquorice and roasted malt taste, with hints of sweet chocolate and fresh black fruits.

ZYWE
PILSNER 6.2% ABV
Pale in colour, it has lemon flavours and uses hops and barley from the Lubin region.

PSZENICZNIAK
WHEAT ALE 5.2% ABV
An ale-style wheat beer, it has a light, hazy colour, with notes of spice and banana.

PSZENICZNE
PALE ALE 4.8% ABV
Not quite a Burton ale, it is strongly hopped in the kettle before being dry-hopped in the lagering tank.

RASPBERRY SUMMER WHEAT
WHEAT BEER 5% ABV
The house wheat beer is in the Bavarian style, with the addition of fresh raspberries. The fruit adds a refreshing, zesty tartness.

TYSKIE GRONIE
LAGER 5.5% ABV
Crisp, clean-tasting beer with a clear yellow hue. Poland's favourite beer, it is sold worldwide.

DEBOWE MOCNE
DARK LAGER 7% ABV
A strong, German-style *doppelbock*, its rich taste is the result of being matured in oak barrels.

BEER

BREWERY

(*Continued*) All its beers are bottom-fermented brews. Currently, one of every six beers sold in Poland is a Tyskie, making it the country's favourite brand, and Zubr is not far behind with 13% of the market share. Sales of Lech are growing too.

KOSZALIN

ul. Spółdzielcza 8, 75-202 Koszalin, Poland
www.vanpur.com.pl

The brewery has had a long and chequered history since it was opened in 1874. Post World War II, it became Soviet controlled. In 1990, it was one of the first companies in the country to be privatized. In 2005, it was bought by Danish company Royal Unibrew. In 2009, it was bought by Polish company Van Pur.

OKOCIM

ul. Browarna 14, 32-8-Brzesko, Poland
www.okocim.com.pl

Built in 1845, the Okocim brewery is one of the finest buildings in Bresko. Much of the original site is well preserved, and it is one of the few remaining breweries left from this period. Now owned by Carlsberg, there has been considerable investment in recent years.

BREWING SECRET Closed conical fermenters are a modern addition.

WARKA

Gośniewska 65, 05-660 Warka, Poland
www.warka.com.pl

The town of Warka is celebrated as the birthplace of Kazimierz Pulaski (1745–1779), a Polish nobleman who became a hero of the American Revolution. Brewing has taken place here since the Middle Ages, and, in 1478, Warka brewers were granted the exclusive rights to supply beer to the Warsaw royal court. Today, the Warka brewery is owned by Heineken.

BEER

LECH PREMIUM
LAGER 5% ABV
Golden in colour, it has a subtle bitterness and some malty corn notes. It is a summer refresher.

ZUBR
LAGER 6% ABV
A pale yellow; hints of floral hops give way to a caramel sweetness.

BROK SAMBOR
PILSNER 6% ABV
Golden in colour, with a thin, white head. Sweetcorn and candy flavours predominate, with little hop aroma.

BROK EXPORT
LAGER 5.2% ABV
Golden in colour, its malty nose exudes a hint of sweetness. There's a subtle hop presence.

OKOCIM MOCNE
LAGER 7% ABV
A full-bodied, strong beer with intense flavours of sweet malt, it's known as the jewel in Carlsberg Polska's crown.

OKOCIM PORTER
PORTER 9% ABV
A porter in the Baltic tradition, with a soothing, almost medicinal, taste and hints of cinnamon.

WARKA STRONG
LAGER 7% ABV
Copper coloured, it is light in malt and with a hint of hops. A complex, dry bitterness, but a sweet finish.

WARKA
LAGER 5.7% ABV
A deep, rich golden colour, topped with a bold, white head. An easy-drinking, if strong, beer.

ŻYWIEC

ul. Browarna 88, 34-310 Żywiec,
Poland
www.zywiec.com.pl

Established in 1852 by the Hapsburg family, this brewery fell into state ownership after World War II, and was acquired by Heineken in the mid-1990s. It is home to a lively brewing museum that takes visitors right through the brewing process.

BREWING SECRET The Żywiec Porter uses a recipe from 1881.

HEINEKEN SLOVENSKO

Novozámocká 2 947 01 Hurbanovo,
Slovakia
www.heinekenslovensko.sk

Once Heineken had three breweries in Slovakia, but only the Hurbanovo plant is now left. Heineken leads the Slovak beer market with a share of 45 per cent (nearest rival SABMiller has 38 per cent). Heineken has close relations with the region's farmers as it operates the largest malt-producing plant in the area.

TOPVAR

a.s. Pivovarská 9082 21, Veľký Šariš,
Slovakia
www.topvar.sk

The brewery operates at two sites in Slovakia: Topolcany and Velký Šariš. In 2000, the brewery launched a beer called Brigita, named after the Slovak finance minister Brigita Schmögnerovà. A popular beer, it remained on sale for some time after her resignation in 2002. The company is now owned by SABMiller.

BORSODI SÖRGYÁR

Rákóczi út 81, Bocs,
Hungary
www.borsodi.hu

One of the largest breweries in Hungary, Borsodi Sörgyár was privatized in 1991 after the fall of communism. It has had several owners since then and is now part of Molson Coors. Typically, one of the characteristics of state ownership is a lack of investment in quality control, and that's something that has been rectified in recent years.

ŻYWIEC

LAGER 5.6% ABV
Crisp, bright gold, and easy drinking, with flowery, hoppy aromas. It is now being exported worldwide.

PORTER

BALTIC PORTER 9.5% ABV
A dark, strong beer, brewed with Munich and other special malts for sweetness and colour. Aromatic hops provide a rich aroma.

ZLATÝ BAŽANT/
GOLDEN PHEASANT

LAGER 4.2% ABV
Clear and golden, with a hint of straw, this is an easy-drinking beer without any complexities. Beers of this type were like "liquid bread" to factory workers. It is also available in a non-alcoholic version.

TOPVAR SVETLÉ 10

LAGER 4.7% ABV
A sunburst of yellow tones, with a thin, wispy, white head. The beer has an attractive, subtle aromatic nose of citrus flavours.

BORSODI BIVALY

LAGER 6.5% ABV
A bold, golden yellow, this is a strong, grainy beer with an overt sweetness on the palate.

BORSODI SÖR

LAGER 4.6% ABV
A golden-coloured, light beer, with a wispy head, it is sweet and easy to drink. A working man's beer.

BREWERY

BLONDER SÖRGYAR

H-8314 Vonyarcvashegy Fö út 9, Hungary
www.blonder.hu

One of a handful of microbreweries to have emerged in recent years in Hungary, Blonder Sörgyar is situated close to Lake Balaton, the largest lake in central Europe. As well as beer brewed on the premises, this roadside inn offers accommodation and has a restaurant. The food is very Hungarian – wholesome, and a fine accompaniment to the beer.

DREHER

Jászberényi street 7-11, 1106 Budapest, Hungary
www.dreherrt.hu

For many years this brewery was run by Anton Dreher, one of the great beer innovators. In the mid-19th century, he developed the technology to ferment beer at low temperatures and created a new kind of malty amber beer, called Vienna lager. For his achievements, Dreher was dubbed "The King of Beer". The company is now owned by SABMiller.

HEINEKEN HUNGÁRIA

9400 Sopron, Vándor Sándor utca 1, Hungary
www.heinekenhungaria.hu

Sopron might be at the heart of Hungary's wine region, but it has also had a brewery for over 100 years. Founded by Gyula Lenck in 1895, Heineken Hungária (as it is now known) is one of the largest brewers in the country. It also has a production plant at Martfü.

PÉCSI SÖRFÖZDE

Alkotmány utca 94, Pécs, H-7624, Hungary
www.pecsisor.hu

Pécsi Sörfözde is the oldest brewery operating in Hungary. It was founded in 1848 by Hirschfeld Lipó. It is now Hungary's fourth-largest brewery and the largest not owned by a multinational (although most of the equity is owned by the Austrian company Ottakringer). The main brand is Szalon, which was first brewed in 1907.

BEER

VILÁGOS

LAGER 5.6% ABV
Yellow in colour, this is a strong, grainy beer with an overt sweetness. Somewhat rough at the edges, but it works well with Hungarian cuisine.

DREHER CLASSIC

PILSNER 5.5% ABV
With a crisp, fresh aroma, this is a bitter, golden-yellow beer with an aroma of hops and a hint of malt.

DREHER BAK

DUNKLER BOCK 7.3% ABV
A rich, full-bodied, dark beer, with notes of caramel and malt that are reminiscent of bittersweet chocolate.

SOPRONI ÁSZOK

LAGER 4.5% ABV
Light to taste, this beer is crisp on the palate. Not a complex beer, but very refreshing.

STEFFL

PILSNER 5.3% ABV
A clear, clean, sparkling golden pilsner. A nice level of hops and a sweet aroma.

SZALON BARNA

DUNKEL 5.8% ABV
Hungarian hops and Bavarian malt combine in this malty sweet, aromatic brew.

SZALON SÖR

PILSNER 4.6% ABV
Brewed for over 100 years, this is the company's flagship beer. Golden yellow with a thick, long-lasting head and barley aromas.

URSUS BREWERIES

2-6 Manastur St., 340 Cluj-Napoca,
Cluj county, Romania
www.ursus-breweries.ro

Now a subsidiary of SABMiller, this
brewery first opened in 1878. Its main
brand, Ursus, is advertised under the
slogan "The King of Romanian Beers".
Each September the town of Cluj
Napoca, in the heart of Transylvania,
hosts a beer festival.

BREWING SECRET These beers are
fermented using Bavarian yeast.

APATINSKA PIVARA

Trg oslobodjenja 5 25260, Apatin,
Serbia
www.jelenpivo.com

The biggest brewer in Serbia and the
largest in the Balkans, the brewery
is now owned by Molson Coors
who aims to take the beer to a
wider audience. The town of Apatini,
which is on the Danube, is in a fertile
barley-growing area called Vojvodina.
Records show that brewing has taken
place in the town since 1756.

KARLOVAČKO

Dubovac 22, 47000 Karlovač, Croatia
www.karlovacko.hr

Karlovačka is Croatia's second-largest
brewery, with about 22 per cent of
the domestic beer market. Founded
in 1854, it is in the very heart of
Croatia, on the delta of four rivers –
the Korana, Kupa, Mrenica, and
Dobra. Heineken bought the brewery
in 2003. The town of Karlovač
organizes a beer festival at the end
of August in its city square.

ZAGREBACKA

Ilica 224, 10000 Zagreb, Hrvastka, Croatia
www.ozujsko.com

Zagrebacka Pivovara, Croatia's largest
brewery, was established in 1893 and
is now owned by Molson Coors.
After years of falling beer consumption,
the market is now growing again,
with domestic lager brands being the
most popular segment of the market.

BREWING SECRET Double-malted dark
chocolate barley gives the dark lager
its prized aromas, flavours, and colour.

URSUS PREMIUM PILS
PILSNER 5.2% ABV
Lively carbonation, a malty aroma,
hints of fresh hops and bread, and
lemony notes in the finish.

TIMISOREANA
LAGER 5% ABV
A light-yellow, easy-drinking beer
that doesn't challenge the senses.
Made to a recipe from 1718.

JELEN PIVO
LAGER 5% ABV
Light yellow in colour, with a white,
wispy head. It has hints of grass and
grain and aromas of hops and malt.
Jelen means "deer".

APATINSKO PIVO
LAGER 5% ABV
A fresh-tasting beer with floral
notes and a citrus aroma.

KARLOVAČKO SVIJETLO PIVO
LAGER 5.4% ABV
Golden-yellow beer, with yeasty
and toasted malt aromas, and a
refreshing bitterness; the favourite
beer of visitors to Croatia.

OŽUJSKO PIVO
LAGER 5% ABV
A golden lager, with a deep, white
head. A sweetcorn and malt nose
gives way to a fruity finish.

TOMISLAV PIVO
DARK LAGER 7.3% ABV
This deep ruby-red lager has
aromas of roasted malt and
coffee, and a dry finish.

Ožujsko Pivo, the medium-strength lager produced by Zagrebacka, is one of Croatia's most popular beers.

UNION

Pivovarniška ulica 2, 1000 Ljubljana, Slovenia
www.pivo-union.si

This brewery was founded in 1864 by the Kozler family, but state-of-the-art technology makes it one of the most modern in Slovenia. A fascinating museum takes visitors through the brewing process. However, you have to be there on the first Tuesday morning of the month to enjoy it.

RIDNA MARKA

71 Mikgorod str. Radomyshl, Ukraine 12200
www.ridnamarka.com.ua

Beer-making in Radomyshl dates to 1886, when this brewery was founded by the Czech Albrechtam brothers who found the soft water ideal for brewing. The modern brewery has adapted Bavarian technology to Ukrainian ingredients.

BREWING SECRET The brewhouse has been specifically designed to produce unfiltered, genuine wheat beers.

OBOLON

3 Bogatyrska Str. Kiev, Ukraine
www.obolon.com

Obolon was built in 1980 by the Soviets, who wanted a world-class brewery. Czech brewers acted as consultants. In 1992, the company was the first in Ukraine to be privatized. Ukraine is the largest beer market in the CIS, the former Soviet Union. Obolon has a 26 per cent share of the market, and is also the country's biggest beer exporter.

BALTIKA

6 Verkhny per., d. 3, 194292
St Petersburg, Russia
www.eng.baltika.ru

The Russian beer market has been going through a period of rapid change as it continues to adjust to a capitalist economy. Baltika's rise has been swift, and it is now one of the country's largest brewers. It brews the top two brands – Baltika and Arsenalnoye. The company is now owned by Carlsberg.

BREWERY

UNION STOUT
STOUT 5.2% ABV
A light-tasting, slightly sweet stout with a pronounced roasted malt flavour. It is easy drinking.

UNION LAGER
LAGER 5% ABV
A Slovenian favourite. A sweet, golden beer, it has corn overtones.

ETALON WEISSBIER
WHEAT BEER 5% ABV
Spicy, with a rich, creamy malt note and a long, quenching flavour and finish. Hints of bananas and vanilla.

OBOLON PREMIUM
LAGER 5% ABV
Light gold in colour, with a sweet malt taste. The use of rice in the grist gives the beer a softness.

OBOLON LIGHT
LAGER 4.5% ABV
Light on the palate, it has a mild malt sweetness and a gentle hop bitterness in the finish.

BALTIKA NO 6 PORTER
PORTER 7% ABV
A well-balanced beer. Dark roasted malts, chocolate, and molasses flavours fill the glass, overlayed by a good hop finish.

BALTIKA NO 3 CLASSIC
LAGER 4.8% ABV
A malty nose gives way to a bitter finish. Widely available across Russia.

BEER

BREWERY

HEINEKEN RUSSIA
193230, St. Petersburg, ul. Telman 24 A, Russia
www.heinekenrussia.ru

Bochkarev started life as a soft drinks manufacturer in 1988 and began brewing in 1999. Owned by Heineken since 2002, it is now the sixth-largest single-site brewery in Europe. St. Petersburg is known as Russia's beer capital and has a fast-evolving beer culture. Bochkarev has 17 per cent of the St Petersburg market, and a seven per cent market share in Moscow.

OCHAKOVO
44, Riabinivaya, 121471 Moscow, Russia
www.ochakovo.ru

Ochakovo is the largest independent brewery in Russia and is trying to remain so. It has four production plants across the country. Ochakovo's original brewhouse in Moscow has been transformed into a successful interactive museum, which takes visitors, step-by-step, through the brewing process and features many exhibits from the 19th century.

BREWING SECRET In 2005, the brewery launched an unpasteurized, unfiltered "live" beer, aimed at the health market.

SUN INBEV RUSSIA
17 Building A Business Park "Krylatsky Hills", 121614 Moscow, Russia
www.suninbev.ru

Founded in 1999, as an amalgamation of two important players in the Russian and Ukraine beer markets – InterBrew and SUN brewing. The company now owns many breweries across the region and is the second largest brewer in the area. It is now part of AB InBev. The Brazilian beer Brahma is now being brewed in Klin, and it is proving to be very popular.

BEER

BOCHKOVOE
LAGER 4.3% ABV
Its name means "barrelled". Thin, clear yellow, light in body, the nose is light and malty with corn flavours.

KREPKOE OSOBOE
LAGER 8% ABV
Full of malt flavours, this strong beer has a warming finish but could do with more balance.

OCHAKOVO CLASSIC
LAGER 5% ABV
Corn yellow in colour, with intense malt overtones and a hoppy finish.

ALTSTEIN
LAGER 5% ABV
Low in carbonation, it is full of malt, grain, and corn flavours. The finish is sweet.

STOLICHNOE
LAGER 5% ABV
Light and fresh tasting, with a sweet malt taste and some bitterness from the hops.

KLINSKOYE SVETLOE
LAGER 4.5% ABV
Straw coloured, the mild flavour is achieved by the use of maize or rice in brewing. It has a soft, hoppy aroma.

TOLSTIAK DOBROYE
LAGER 5% ABV
A pale beer with a rich, sweet taste and a pleasant, hoppy bitterness.

ŠVYTURYS-UTENOS

Kūliu Vartų g. 7, Klaipėda, Lithuania
www.svyturys.lt/en

Brewing began here in 1784, making this the oldest brewery in Lithuania. The company has a reputation for the quality of its beers and has won several international brewing awards. It is open to the public for tours twice a week for groups of five to 25 (via the tourist office at www.klaipedainfo.lt).

BREWING SECRET All the employees give their feedback on each new brew.

GUBERNIJA

Dvaro str. 179, LT-76176
Siauliai, Lithuania
www.gubernija.lt/en

Lithuania has a long and proud brewing tradition, and records show that beer was being made in Siauliai in the 14th century. The first record of the Gubernija Brewery on its current site dates from 1786. Over the years, the brewery has been rebuilt many times, most recently in 2000 when the modern plant was installed.

KALNAPILIS

Taikos Avenue 1,
LT-35147 Panevėžys, Lithuania
www.kalnapilis.lt/en

Over 100 years old, the brewery was founded by German Albert Foight, who named it Bergschlösschen ("little castle on the hill"); later the name was changed to the Lithuanian Kalnapilis. Now owned by Danish Royal Unibrew, the company prides itself on its innovation – it was the first brewer in Lithuania to use twist caps on bottles and the first to market beer in cans.

ALDARIS

Tvaika iela 44, Rīga, Latvia
www.aldaris.lv/en

Founded in 1865, the brewery became part of Carlsberg in 2008. In 2014, the company invested in a new brewhouse to produce small runs of speciality beers. The brewery is located on the site of the famed Waldschlosschen, which in 1906 was one of the most modern breweries in the world. A brewery museum and visitor centre (*Continues overleaf*)

ŠVYTURYS EKSTRA
DORTMUND LAGER 5.2% ABV
Clear and golden, it has a firm, white head, an intense aroma of hops, and a slight bitterness.

ŠVYTURIO
LAGER 5% ABV
Translucent gold in colour, it has a good balance of rich malt and bitter hops. In Lithuania it is known simply as "Red", due to its label colour.

GUBERNIJOS EKSTRA
LAGER 5.5% ABV
Medium gold in colour. Strong, rich, and warming with caramel and sweetcorn overtones. A dry finish with citrus and hop flavours lingering on the palate.

ORIGINAL
LAGER 5% ABV
A pale, golden-yellow beer, with a good, foamy head. It has a sweetcorn aroma with a hint of Saaz hops.

BROWN
LAGER 4.8% ABV
Sweet tasting, with malty, caramel overtones; it has a short finish.

ALDARIS GAIŠAIS
LAGER 5% ABV
This light beer has a fresh, hoppy aroma and a softly bitter taste. Not too challenging, it is a refreshing drink.

DIŽAIS GAMBRINUS
LAGER 5% ABV
Named after the patron saint of brewing, it is sweet to taste with a floral nose.

BREWERY

(*Continued*) has also been opened. The brewery is also going back to using Latvian malt now that a malting has re-opened in the country.

A. LE COQ

Tähtvere 56/62, 50050 Tartu, Estonia
www.alecoq.ee/eng

This brewery was founded in 1826, and purchased in 1913 by A. Le Coq, a London-based company. At the time, it was looking for a brewery in the Russian Empire where it could produce its Imperial Stout rather than export it from England. Production was halted in the 1960s but revived in 1999. A small museum is housed in the former maltings.

SAKU

Tallinna mnt 2, Saku, Harju County 75501, Estonia
www.saku.ee/english.php

First documented in October 1820, the brewery was built by Count Karl Friedrich Rehbinder, on his Saku estate. Now owned by Carlsberg, it is the largest brewer in Estonia. Saku's Originaal, launched in 1993, was one of the first beers that came out in the post-Soviet period in Estonia and quickly became a hit with consumers.

In 2008, the company was bought by Carlsberg. In 2010, it launched a series of beers called the Saku Gourmet Collection that was designed to be paired with food.

BEER

ALDARA LUKSUS
LAGER 5.2% ABV
Saaz hops impart a delicate floral aroma to this drinkable beer.

ZELTA
LAGER 5.2% ABV
A malty sweetness dominates this golden beer.

DOUBLE BOCK
BOCK 8% ABV
A strong and warming light bock, it has a surprisingly mellow finish for a beer of this strength.

LE COQ PORTER
PORTER 6.5% ABV
A strong, dark beer – a worthy successor to the famous Imperial Extra Double Stout.

ORIGINAAL
LAGER 4.6% ABV
A mild-flavoured beer, the colour of pale straw, with pleasant hints of sweetcorn in the aroma.

HOMEBREW
LAGER 4.8% ABV
Styled as a farmhouse beer, this full-bodied beer has a sweet taste.

HELE
LAGER 5.2% ABV
A strong, hoppy flavour and hints of grass and hops on the nose. Thin in colour, it lacks the body to be a star.

PORTER
PORTER 6.9% ABV
Dark, with hints of toffee and coffee. It is sweet and warming.

The cool crispness of pilsner-type lager is well-suited to the Spanish climate, and this is the most popular style of beer, however wine tends to dominate cultural tastes in Spain, as elsewhere in southern Europe.

BREWERY

ALHAMBRA

Avenida de Murcia 1, 18012 Granada, Spain
www.cervezasalhambra.es

The Alhambra Group, which was founded in 1925 and named after Granada's famed Moorish palace, is now owned by San-Miguel-Carlsberg. Water from the Sierra Nevada mountain range, claimed to be Spain's purest, is used to brew Alhambra's beers.

BREWING SECRET The brewery uses traditional techniques that include fermentation lasting up to 39 days.

HEINEKEN ESPAÑA

Carretera Córdoba, 23005 Jaén, Spain
www.heineken.es

Heineken España (formerly El Alcázar), in its current form, was created in 1999 when acquisitive Heineken bought the five breweries of the Cruzcampo group to add to the two El Águila breweries it already owned. It was then forced by the competition authorities to sell two breweries in Madrid and Valencia to Damm.

DAMM

Rosselló 515, 08025 Barcelona, Spain
www.damm.es

Auguste Kuentzmann Damm brought Alsace-style lager brewing to Barcelona in the 19th century. The original brewery operated until 1992, when the production plant was moved to the town of El Prat de Llobregat in order to increase beer production capacity and modernize processes.

DAMM PORTUGAL

Quinta da Mafarra, 2009-003 Várzea, Santarém, Portugal
www.sumolcompal.pt

Damm Portugal was originally set up after the revolution of 1974, when the Portuguese brewing industry was nationalized. It went into private ownership in the 1990s. It distributes Damm's Spanish brewed brands across Portugal. The brand Tagus, traded as Sumol Compal, has been part of the Spanish brewing group Damm since 2012.

BEER

MEZQUITA
WHEAT BEER 7.2% ABV
A full-bodied, assertive red wheat beer with caramel notes and hints of pepper in the aroma.

ALHAMBRA PREMIUM LAGER
LAGER 4.6% ABV
A soft gold in colour, its nose is lemony and fresh with a hint of malt. A well-balanced quaffable beer.

CRUZCAMPO
LAGER 5% ABV
Pale gold in colour, light tasting, with a fine balance of malt and hops, and a floral, aromatic aroma. One of Spain's most popular beers.

BOCK DAMM
STOUT 5.4% ABV
A Munich-style stout, rich with toasty flavours and a warming sweetness on the finish.

ESTRELLA DAMM
PILSNER 5.4% ABV
A light, refreshing beer with a creamy head, and a rather dry and bitter taste.

TAGUS
LAGER 4.8% ABV
A clear golden colour with shimmers of amber, the beer has a sprightly, bubbly carbonated character, which is topped with a white, foaming head. Light and refreshing, it has hints of corn sweetness and is best drunk well chilled.

SOCIEDADE CENTRAL DE CERVEJAS

Estrada da Alfarrobeira, 2625-244 Vialonga, Portugal
www.centralcervejas.pt

Now part of Heineken, the brewery's portfolio has had influences from several countries. It produces a wide range of dark and light beers using a spectrum of coloured malts. From a crisp Pilsen to its fruity Bohemian, these are beers of some distinction.

SIMONDS FARSONS CISK

The Brewery, Mdina Road, Mriehel, BKR 3000, Malta
www.farsons.com

Wherever the British army went, beer was soon to follow, and this brewery, founded in 1928, was built in lavish Art Deco style at the end of World War II in 1946. The site is being redeveloped, with the old brewing vessels at the heart of a visitor centre.

BREWING SECRET It brews the potent XS (9 per cent ABV) for the export market.

KEO

Franklin Roosevelt Ave, Limassol, 3602 Cyprus
www.keobeer.com.cy

Limassol is the main port and the fastest-growing city on the island of Cyprus. It is also home to the Keo Brewery, and no trip to Limassol is complete without visiting the plant, which lies just beyond the Old Port. During the week there is a daily tour around the brewery – finishing, of course, in the tasting room.

MYTHOS

570 22 Sindos Thessaloniki, Greece
www.mythosbrewery.gr

One of Greece's best known breweries, especially by holiday-makers, Mythos is now owned by Carlsberg. The biggest selling beer is Mythos itself. It is the leading Greek lager brand, and its sales are increasing at an average of 10 per cent each year. Mythos also brews the Greek lager Golden and German beers Henninger and Kaiser.

SAGRES PRETA (DARK)

LAGER 4.1% ABV
A Munich-style dark lager with a mahogany hue, a creamy head, and a nutty aroma. It tastes slightly chocolatey, with hints of toffee and caramel, but balanced with plenty of bitterness from hops.

CISK LAGER

LAGER 4.28% ABV
A refreshing, golden-coloured beer, with loads of malt and fruit flavours.

FARSONS STRONG ALE

ALE 6.7% ABV
Swathes of old-style English hop aromas and toffee malt flavours are key to the appeal of this characterful and surprising beer.

KEO

LAGER 4.5% ABV
A pale lager with a thick head and a sweet malt taste, it is easy on the palate and very drinkable.

MYTHOS

LAGER 5% ABV
An easy-drinking beer, with a bright blond colour and a thick, white head. Light caramel aftertaste. A touch of maize is added to the beer, which sweetens the taste and lightens its colour.

Portugal's Sociedad Central de Cervejas produces the Sagres brand, which comprises a range of beers based largely on German lager styles.

BREWERY

AMSTERDAM BREWERY

45 Esandar Drive, Toronto,
Ontario, M4G 4C5, Canada
www.amsterdambeer.com

Purity, passion, and revelry are
the watchwords for Toronto's
first brewpub. Founded in 1986
on John Street in the entertainment
area, it was an immediate success.
Business was brisk, and it soon
moved to another site before
finding its current home in 2005.
A large retail shop is part of the
site, and tours are organized twice

a day throughout most of the year.
The brewery stands opposite the Fort
York, a National Historic site and the
1793 birthplace of modern Toronto.
In 2003, when the Kawartha Lakes
Brewing Company closed, its brands
were sold to Amsterdam Brewing,
who continue to brew a range of
Kawartha Lakes' (KLB) beers,
including a raspberry wheat beer
and the KLB Nut Brown Ale.

BIG ROCK

5555–76th Avenue SE, Calgary,
Alberta T2C 4L8, Canada
www.bigrockbeer.com

Alberta's warm days and cool nights
produce the finest two-row malting
barley in the world. The most popular
variety, Harrington, is the only malt
used in Big Rock beers. There are
regular brewery tours for visitors.

BREWING SECRET The brewery shuns the
use of adjuncts and other processing
aids in its beer-making.

CHURCH-KEY BREWING

1678 County Road 38, Campbellford,
Ontario, K0L 1L0, Canada
www.churchkeybrewing.com

Located in a former Methodist
church where it was founded in
2000, Church-Key Brewing is the
brainchild of John Graham. John
has put environmental principles
into action here: solar hot water,
biodiesel, radiant floor heating, and
heat recovery units are all employed
to lower the carbon output of this
award-winning brewery.

BEER

KLB NUT BROWN ALE
BROWN ALE 5% ABV
The unmistakable tang of East Kent
Golding hops. Sweet to taste, it has
hints of honey and chocolate.

URBAN WHEAT
WHEAT BEER 4.16% ABV
Golden amber, it has citrus notes
and some subtle fruity flavours.
The finish is dry.

AMSTERDAM NATURAL BLONDE
LAGER 5% ABV
Crisp and clean, with hints of citrus.
Canadian malt combines with
aromatic Czech and German hops.

SPRING BOCK
LAGER 7.2% ABV
Mahogany hued with a rich,
mouth-warming body; the
three malts provide wonderful
fruit flavours.

GRASSHOPPER
WHEAT BEER 5% ABV
Crisp, refreshing, and only lightly
hopped. Locals drink it with a slice
of lemon, which adds assertiveness.

MCNALLY'S EXTRA
IRISH-STYLE RED ALE 7% ABV
A strong, full-bodied Irish ale.
It has a flowery aroma and
a rich fruity maltiness.

HOLY SMOKE SCOTCH ALE
SCOTCH ALE 6.25% ABV
A dark and malty ale, the use of
whisky malt gives it an intense
smoky aroma and peaty taste.

NORTHUMBERLAND ALE
ALE 5% ABV
Also known as Church Key, this
is a crisp and light brew, with
a dry, citrus finish.

CREEMORE SPRINGS

139 Mill Street, Creemore, Ontario, L0M 1G0, Canada
www.creemoresprings.com

Ownership by Molsons since 2005 has done little to lessen the independence of this 100-year-old brewery. The town of Creemore nestles between the curiously named Mad and Noisy rivers. Every August the brewery is a sponsor of a town-centre party called the Copper Kettle Festival. Regular brewery tours are run.

PREMIUM LAGER
LAGER 5% ABV
Soft malt and fruit flavours give way to nutty overtones and a dry hoppy finish.

URBOCK
BOCK 6% ABV
Dark brown, with a sweet, nutty texture; fruit aromas can be found as the beer warms in the glass.

GRANVILLE ISLAND BREWING

1441 Cartwright Street, Vancouver, BC V6H 3R7, Canada
www.gib.ca

When the brewery opened in 1984, the owners of Granville Island had an inkling that the British Columbian public was ready for a natural, pilsner-style beer. Sales of the first release, Island Lager, confirmed their thoughts. In 2009, the brewery was bought by Creemore Springs, a subsidiary of Molson Coors.

ENGLISH BAY PALE ALE
PALE ALE 5% ABV
Copper hued and in the tradition of classic English ales. Smooth and mild, with a caramel malt aroma.

CYPRESS HONEY LAGER
LAGER 4.7% ABV
Honey from Fraser Valley gives crispness and a hint of sweetness in the finish. Lightly hopped.

GREAT LAKES BREWERY

30 Queen Elizabeth Boulevard, Etobicoke, Toronto, Ontario M8Z 1L8, Canada
www.greatlakesbeer.com

Great Lakes Brewery restored craft beer to Toronto in 1997, when it opened. It was bought by Peter Bulut in 1991. It had a solid, but unremarkable reputation until 2006 when it launched Devil's Pale Ale. This lead to a range of seasonal and one-off brews which captured the imagination of the region's discerning beer drinkers.

PUMPKIN ALE
SPECIALITY ALE 5.4% ABV
Amber coloured, this autumn brew is made with pumpkin, cinnamon, clove, nutmeg, and allspice. The flavour is spicy, warming, and bittersweet.

DEVIL'S PALE ALE
AMERICAN PALE ALE 6.6% ABV
Amber in colour, it has a prominent citrussy character balanced by malty grain.

CANADA'S BEST-KNOWN BEERS

In Canada today, the major brewers are either foreign-owned or have been forced to merge with international drinks corporations.

The most recent of these mergers affected Molson, which joined with US rival Coors in 2005. Anheuser-Busch InBev owns Labatt Breweries, and Japan's Sapporo owns Sleeman Breweries, which is currently Canada's third largest beer producer. The market in Canada for domestic beer is dominated by two brands, Labatt Blue and Molson Canadian, both of which are marketed using strong Canadian imagery of mountains, the great outdoors, and ice hockey. The big two have a long history in Canada. John Molson founded a brewery in Montreal in 1786 and John Kinder Labatt started in London, Ontario, in 1847. Both Molson and Labatt have a wide range of niche brands. Canada has many fine craft brewers and brewpubs, many operated using environmentally responsible brewing methods. The Cheval Blanc exemplifies this spirit. It is one of Canada's best-known brewpubs and was the first to open in Montreal. A good time neighbourhood tavern, it has been wowing locals and beer lovers from around the globe since 1986.

LABATT BLUE (PILSNER 5% ABV) *left*
MOLSON CANADIAN
   (LAGER 5% ABV) *centre*
SLEEMAN CREAM ALE
   (ALE 5% ABV) *right*

BREWERY

MAGNOTTA BREWERY

271 Chrislea Road, Vaughan, Ontario, L4L 8N6, Canada
www.magnotta.com/brewery

Magnotta opened in 1996 and focusses on producing classy lagers and ales, marrying traditional processes with modern craft brewing equipment. All its beers are made without the use of corn or rice adjuncts, preservatives, or pasteurization. The company also shuns high gravity brewing that requires dilution and blending.

MCAUSLAN

5080 St-Ambroise, Montréal, Québec, H4C 2G1, Canada
www.mcauslan.com

McAuslan Brewing began in January of 1989 when its founder Peter McAuslan decided to turn his home-brewing hobby into a business. It quickly established itself as one of the area's best microbreweries and was one of the first in Canada to bottle its products. It produces a challenging range of seasonal beers.

MOOSEHEAD

89 Main Street West, Saint John, New Brunswick, E2M 3H2, Canada
www.moosehead.ca

Canada's oldest independent brewery can trace its roots back to 1867, when Susannah Oland first started brewing in her Dartmouth, Nova Scotia backyard. Today, the company is still owned and operated by the Oland family. Moosehead has stakes in McAuslan and wholly owns the Niagara Falls Brewing Company.

PUMP HOUSE BREWERY

131 Mill Road, Moncton, New Brunswick, E1A 6R1, Canada
www.pumphousebrewery.ca

Today, the Pump House Brewery is a group of brewing and bar catering businesses. It was opened as a brewpub in downtown Moncton in 1999 by owners Shaun Fraser, a local fire department chief, and his wife Lilia. The couple have won many awards for their beers and for their business skills, and the brewpub's popularity grew so quickly

BEER

TRUE NORTH INDIA PALE ALE
INDIA PALE ALE 6.5% ABV
Spicy, grassy, and fruity hop flavours are combined with an assertive bitterness. Very fruity.

TRUE NORTH WUNDER WEISSE
WHEAT BEER 5% ABV
Yellow coloured, with a slight, natural wheat beer haze. Subtle aromas of yeast and delicate ripe banana.

ST-AMBROISE APRICOT WHEAT ALE
FRUITY WHEAT BEER 5% ABV
Apricot essence and malted wheat combine to create an original tasting beer with a clean, fruit nose.

ST-AMBROISE OATMEAL STOUT
STOUT 5% ABV
Brewed from dark malts and roasted barley, this stout carries strong espresso and chocolate notes.

MOOSEHEAD LAGER
LAGER 5% ABV
Pale straw-coloured, clean-tasting session beer; best drunk cold.

CLANCY'S AMBER ALE
ALE 5% ABV
Top-fermented, Clancy's is a reddish beer, with a distinct malt aroma and overlays of caramel.

BLUEBERRY ALE
FRUIT BEER 5% ABV
Blond, with a blueberry aroma. Sweet flavours of blueberry and malt, with a hint of pepper.

FIRE CHIEF'S RED ALE
RED ALE 5.5% ABV
Reddish brown, with toffee and nut flavours, followed by light chocolate notes and a bitter aftertaste.

that expansion was soon necessary. In July 2002, a brewing and bottling plant was built outside the city centre, and production began in the same year. A restaurant called the Barn Yard BBQ was also established on the same site.

BREWING SECRET In autumn, the brewery hosts an "Oktoberfest" and creates a special lager in its honour.

SLEEMAN

551 Clair Road West, Guelph, Ontario, N1L 1E9, Canada
www.sleeman.com

The Sleeman family started brewing in Canada in 1834, the year John Sleeman, an ambitious young brewer from England, arrived in Ontario. In 1851 he started the first Guelph-based Sleeman Brewery, making small, 100-barrel batches with local well water, prized for its purity and hardness. The company is now owned by Sapporo.

STEAMWORKS

3845 William Street, Gastown, Burnaby, British Columbia, V5C 3J1 Canada
www.steamworks.com

A popular pub and brewery located in the historic Gastown area of Vancouver, Steamworks offers fabulous views of the harbour.

BREWING SECRET Steamworks produces a wide range of seasonal brews using a potpourri of ingredients, including fresh cherries, pumpkin, cinnamon, nutmeg, ginger, and cloves.

UNIBROUE

80 Des Carrières Street, Chambly, Québec, J3L 2H6, Canada
www.unibroue.com

In the spring of 1992, André Dion launched his first unfiltered, bottled *sur lees* beer. The yeast remains living in the bottle, changing the characteristics of the beer as it ages. The beers are very popular, and the company was bought by Sleeman in 2004. As with Sleeman, it is now owned by Japanese brewer Sapporo.

SCOTCH ALE
ALE 5% ABV
Deep amber, with a smoky aroma. Flavours of caramel are followed by chocolate, then a slight bitter aftertaste of roasted malt.

HONEY BROWN LAGER
LAGER 5.2% ABV
A refreshingly smooth, full-bodied lager, with a subtle touch of honey, which creates a slightly sweet finish.

CREAM ALE
ALE 5% ABV
Designed to combine the refreshing quality of German lager with the distinctive taste of English Ale.

OATMEAL STOUT
STOUT 5% ABV
Rolled oats and black roasted barley give this beer a warm, roasted nose and distinct dryness.

PALE ALE
ALE 5.2% ABV
British crystal malt gives the beer a rich colour, caramel maltiness, and adds a whiff of toffee to the nose.

MAUDITE
RED ALE 8% ABV
Deep amber red, with a rocky foam head and an appealing aroma of wild spices and floral hop notes.

BLANCHE DE CHAMBLY
WHITE BEER 5% ABV
Pale golden in colour, with an effervescent foam and a subtle bouquet of spice and citrus notes.

BREWERY

VANCOUVER ISLAND

2330 Government St, Victoria, British Colombia, V8T 5G5, Canada
www.vanislandbrewery.com

The inspiration for this company's formation in 1984 was the absence of locally made beers on Vancouver Island. The brewery believes that brewing should be a perfect blend of art and science, with no short cuts.

BREWING SECRET Though the hops and yeast are imported, only the finest Canadian barley is used.

WELLINGTON BREWERY

950 Woodlawn Road West, Guelph, Ontario, N1K 1B8, Canada
www.wellingtonbrewery.ca

The brewery is dedicated to Arthur Wellesley, the 1st Duke of Wellington, the British commander who defeated Napoleon's French army at Waterloo in 1815. The building is known for its distinctive conical rooftop, which replicates that of an oast house – a structure traditionally used for drying hops in the English county of Kent.

WOLF BREWING

940 Old Victoria Road, Nanaimo, British Colombia V9R 6Z8, Canada
www.wolfbrewingcompany.com

Class and quality exude from this microbrewery, which was founded in 2000. Wolf Brewing is part of a new wave of thinking that says that beer is fun and fashionable, and should be made by hands-on brewers who have an affinity with the environment. The beers are distinctive, idiosyncratic, and very well made.

YUKON BREWING

102 Copper Road, Whitehorse, Yukon, Y1A 2Z6, Canada
www.yukonbeer.com

Clean water makes clean beer. Yukon beers start with North America's cleanest water. Named by some as the Wilderness City, Whitehorse nestles on the banks of the famous Yukon River, surrounded by mountains and clear mountain lakes. Yukon makes eight beers, including one flavoured with coffee beans.

BEER

HERMANNATOR ICE BOCK

EISBOCK 9.5% ABV
Brewed and then frozen, it is a symphony of complex chestnut colours and spicy flavours.

HERMANN'S DARK LAGER

BAVARIAN LAGER 5.5% ABV
A toasty malt nose with similar flavours on the palate; takes on a somewhat nutty character.

SPECIAL PALE ALE

ALE 4.5% ABV
An amber-coloured, English-style ale. It is easy drinking, has a full malt base, some gentle aromatic hops, and a nice bitter finish.

IMPERIAL RUSSIAN STOUT

STOUT 8% ABV
A rich, exceptionally complex beer, with an almost coffee-like flavour.

RANNOCH

SCOTCH ALE 6% ABV
A deep, dark amber, the taste is rich and fruity, with lots of warming caramel and maple syrup flavours.

WOLF GOLDEN HONEY ALE

GOLDEN ALE 6% ABV
Organic honey gives the beer a gentle and refreshing sweetness, which shines through the graininess of the malt.

LEAD DOG ALE

ALE 7% ABV
Intricate malt flavours predominate. Reminiscent of a porter, it has a slightly darkened creamy head.

DISCOVERY-HONEY E.S.B

PALE ALE 5% ABV
Brewed using honey made from Fireweed, the official flower of the Yukon. It finishes dry on the tongue.

MORE BEERS OF
CANADA

Canada has a small, stable core of brewpubs and craft breweries, many of which have a loyal following in the vicinity of their home towns. Some of these brewers do produce bottled beers that travel further afield, but many do not, and sell only draught beer locally.

BRICK BREWING

400 Bingemans Centre Drive, Kitchener, Ontario, N2B 3X9, Canada
www.brickbeer.com

Founder Jim Brickman travelled to no fewer than 29 countries and visited 68 breweries for research before achieving his ambition of setting up his own brewery in 1984. At the time, it was the first brewery to open in Eastern Canada for 37 years. The brewery's home town, Waterloo, hosts a Bavarian beer festival every October.

DIEU DU CIEL

259 rue de Villemure, Saint-Jérôme, Québec J7Z 5J4, Canada
www.dieuduciel.com

A small brewpub that opened in 1998, Dieu du Ciel is owned by Jean-François Gravel, who turned his passion for making beer into a business. Gravel is constantly pushing the boundaries of brewing and loves to create new beers. He believes that beer is a wonderful adventure, which brings together both art and science.

FERME BRASSERIE SCHOUNE

2075 Chemin Sainte Catherine, St-Polycarpe, Québec, J0P 1X0, Canada
www.schoune.com

All the beers draw on the Schoune family's Belgian links. All use pure barley malt, and the white uses a proportion of local wheat.

BREWING SECRET The beers are unfiltered, so the yeast remains in the bottle to help produce deep, rich fruit flavours to complement the spiciness.

GRANITE

6054 Stairs Street, Halifax, Nova Scotia, B3K 2E5 Canada
www.granitebreweryhalifax.ca

The Granite Brewery uses wholly natural ingredients in its brewing. They include Canadian two-row barley malt from western Canada, caramel malt, which provides flavour and colour, and English black malt for a deeper colour.

BREWING SECRET Crushed Canadian wheat flour is employed to enable good head retention on the beers.

BREWERY

WATERLOO DARK
LAGER 5% ABV
Roasted malts give this beer a dark ebony colour and an espresso nose. It is surprisingly light to taste.

LAKER LAGER
LAGER 5% ABV
Light to the eye, with little aroma, it is an easy-drinking, unassuming, refreshing beer.

CHAMAN
IMPERIAL PALE ALE 9% ABV
Strong amber hues and dominating hop flavours; very complex and bitter, but always well balanced.

ROUTES DES ÉPICES
RYE BEER 5.3% ABV
A rye beer to which pepper has been added during brewing to give a wonderful peppery flavour.

LA REB'ALE
STRONG ALE 7.5% ABV
The rock 'n' roll of the range: copper red, deeply malty, and a powerful caramel mouthfeel.

LA BLANCHE DE QUÉBEC
WHITE BEER 4.1% ABV
With a spicy character, it refreshes the palate with a citrus caress; an ideal partner with goat's cheese.

PECULIAR
ALE 5.6% ABV
A dark red ale with a slightly sweet but dry palate.

GIN LANE ALE
BARLEY WINE 9% ABV
Dry hopped, with an assertive, almost winey character; the bitterness derives from Kent Golding and Fuggles hops.

BEER

LE CHEVAL BLANC

809 Rue Ontario Est, Montreal, Quebec, H2L 1P1, Canada
www.lechevalblanc.ca

Montreal's first brewpub – a good time neighbourhood tavern that has been wowing locals and beer lovers from all over the world since 1986. Its small kitchen produces some fine Hungarian hot dogs too. Long regarded as one of the coolest bars in the city, it keeps its decor simple and hosts exhibitions and music evenings.

RUSSELL

202-13018 80th Avenue, Surrey, British Columbia, V3W 2B2, Canada
www.russellbeer.com

When Russell Brewery was founded in 1995, its owners had a single goal in mind: to brew the best pure natural beer, with no pasteurization and no short cuts taken. Currently the beers are available on draught in the Vancouver area, though there are plans to put the brewery's output into bottles and cans in the near future.

SPINNAKERS

308 Catherine Street, Victoria, British Colombia, V9A 3S8, Canada
www.spinnakers.com

A must-visit brewpub, and, as it has accommodation, the perfect base to explore other creative craft brewers in the area. Its beers are eclectic, drawing on styles from all over the world. There is also a malt vinegar brewery on the premises, which uses traditional oak barrel ageing methods for its naturally brewed malt vinegars.

STORM BREWING

310 Commercial Drive, Vancouver, BC, V5L 3V6, Canada
www.stormbrewing.org

The brewery was named Storm to reflect the harsh marine environment of Newfoundland. The brewery recently took part in a zero emissions experiment that saw oyster and shiitake mushrooms and earthworm cultivation on the brewers' spent grains. The beers are unpasteurized and contain no preservatives or additives.

BREWERY

AMBER
RED ALE 7.5% ABV
A classic caramelized red ale, with a clean, refreshing bitterness. A well-balanced, drinkable beer.

MINI IPA
INDIA PALE ALE 3.7% ABV
Light and blond, it lacks the alcoholic bite of stronger IPAs. It is easy drinking.

RUSSELL PALE ALE
PALE ALE 5% ABV
Amber in colour, the malts come from Scotland, the hops from Yakima. It has soft citrus overtones.

RUSSELL CREAM ALE
ENGLISH ALE 5% ABV
Made with English malts, it is dark gold and smooth, with Canadian barley married to American hops.

BLUE BRIDGE DOUBLE PALE ALE
INDIA PALE ALE 8.2% ABV
Old and new world hops create a complex floral aroma, which is well balanced by sweet malt.

ÜBER BLONDE
BELGIAN TRIPLE 8.2% ABV
Glorious fruit esters are balanced by a bold, blond, malty body.

HURRICANE I.P.A.
INDIA PALE ALE 7% ABV
A golden, complex, intense beer, which marries a handful of bitter and aromatic hops with an assertive malt character.

IMPERIAL FLANDERS RED ALE
BELGIAN SOUR 11% ABV
Aged in wood, it is a complex cocktail of dry and sour flavours.

BEER

rst Stops He

OPENING HOURS
MON - SAT
630 am - 900 pm

CARIB

Carib

Lager

BEER

The Carib brand launched in
1950 on the island of Trinidad soon
enjoyed international success.

BREWERY

CERVECERIA BUCANERO

Circunvalación Sur Km 3.5,
Holguin, Cuba
www.cerveceriabucanero.com

A surprisingly modern and
sophisticated brewery, which is
increasingly gearing production
towards the burgeoning tourist trade
and exports. You can see the Cristal
logo everywhere in Cuba, especially
on the popular Cristal Bici-taxis, the
drivers of which are always ready to
take you to the nearest bar.

CARIB

Eastern Main Road,
Champs Fleurs, Trinidad
www.caribbrewery.com

The sole brewery on Trinidad since
1960, Carib has formed business
links with AB InBev, Carlsberg, and
Diageo – the owner of Guinness.
The company also has breweries in
St. Kitts and Nevis, and Grenada. The
British brought commercial brewing
to Trinidad just after World War I;
the local taste favours sweet lagers
and strong stouts.

CUAUHTÉMOC MOCTEZUMA

Monterrey/Veracruz-Llave, Mexico
www.cuamoc.com

Mexico's most innovative brewery, it
is now owned by international group
Heineken, which plans to increase
exports of the beers worldwide. It has
a powerful brand portfolio including
Tecate, Dos Equis, Sol, Indio, Bohemia,
and Carta Blanc, many of which are
sold in style bars worldwide. Its beers
tend to be smooth, with a spritzy finish.

GRUPO MODELO

Lago Alberto 156 Colonia Anáhuac,
Mexico DF, 11320, Mexico
www.gmodelo.mx

Founded in 1925, Grupo Modelo is
the leader in Mexico, with more than
60 per cent of the local beer market
and seven brewing plants throughout
the country. In 2013, AB InBev, after
clearance by the US competition
authorities, completed its $20.1 billion
purchase of Grupo Modelo. As part
of the deal, Constellation Brands
acquired the (*Continues overleaf*)

BEER

CRISTAL

LAGER 4.9% ABV
Lightly hopped and full of cane
sugar sweetness. A drink best
suited to a hot day.

CARIB LAGER

LAGER 5.1–5.4% ABV
Pale, but full bodied, with a rich
head formation. Slightly aromatic,
balanced between sweet and bitter.

STAG

LAGER 5.4–5.9% ABV
European-style lager. It is has a pale
golden straw colour with a rich
head formation. Very sweet.

SOL

LAGER 4.5% ABV
A crisp, light-bodied lager with
a corn syrup aroma.

DOS EQUIS AMBAR

VIENNA LAGER 4.7% ABV
Rich and dark red, with chocolate
and orange flavours; its warming
sweetness gives way to a long finish.

CORONA EXTRA

LAGER 4.6% ABV
Light straw in colour, it's a refresher
on a hot day. Best drunk with lime
for taste.

LEON NEGRA

VIENNA LAGER 6% ABV
Caramel in colour, with malt hints
and a toasty caramel edge. A
satisfying sweetnesss when chilled.

BREWERY

(Continued) Corona and Modelo license for the US and Modelo's state-of-the-art brewery in Piedras Negras. AB InBev chief executive officer Carlos Brito said: "The AB InBev and Grupo Modelo transaction has always been about Mexico and making Corona more global in all markets other than the US, where the brands will be owned and managed by Constellation".

CERVESUR

Arequipa, Peru
www.cusquena.com

Based in southern Peru in the Andes, the company, which is of German origin, has been brewing since 1898 and is now part of SABMiller. It is currently being merged with SABMiller's other Peruvian company Backus & Johnson. Its main brand, Cusqueña, is Peru's best-selling lager.

BREWING SECRET The water for brewing comes from a source high in the Andes.

ANTARES

7749 Mar del Plata, Pcia.
Bs As, Argentina
www.cervezaantares.com.ar

Antares is the brightest star in the Scorpius constellation, and the brewpub that shares its name sparkles too. Stylish and smart, it offers a lively alternative to beers from international brewers. Brews include a kölsch, a Scotch ale, a honey beer, a cream stout, a barley wine, and an imperial stout, with some variations in style.

BARBA ROJA

Ruta 25 N° 2567, Escobar, 1625
Buenos Aires, Argentina
www.cerveceriabarbaroja.com.ar

Part of a leisure park complex in Escobar, Barba Roja is a pirate-themed brewpub. The heritage of the range of beers is unashamedly German, but with a local twist. The beers are pushing Argentinian brewing to new heights and show that good beer can be served in the family atmosphere of a leisure park. Local soft fruits find their way into

BEER

PACIFICO CLARA
LAGER 4.5% ABV
Pale yellow, it has a nose of lemon and sweetcorn. Easy drinking, it's described as a "lawn-mower" beer.

VICTORIA
VIENNA-STYLE LAGER 4% ABV
Well bittered, it has a strong biscuit malt flavour. It is a sweet beer from the first sip to the last.

CUSQUEÑA
LAGER 5% ABV
Pronounced "Cus-Ken-Ya", the beer is crisp and refreshing, with a lingering lemon aroma.

KÖLSCH
KÖLSCH 5% ABV
A well-hopped and highly drinkable ale. Good fruity overtones make it an ideal partner to food.

IMPERIAL STOUT
IMPERIAL STOUT 8.5% ABV
Intense liquorice and toasted flavours give way to roasted coffee and caramelized orange intensities.

WINNER
DOPPELBOCK 4.8% ABV
Hints of chocolate and liquorice in this double bock. Sweet, with a warming finish.

TIPO
DOPPLEBOCK 4.8% ABV
Dark chestnut, it has a smoky, sweetish nose with hints of toast, coffee, and chocolate.

MORE BEERS OF
SOUTH AMERICA

Argentina and Brazil have a smattering of excellent craft brewers, mixing styles from Europe and the Americas. Here are a few more.

BULLER BREWING COMPANY

RM Ortiz 1827, Buenos Aires, Argentina
www.bullerpub.com

Buenos Aires can have few better pub gardens, and this one has the added bonus that at least six beers are brewed on site. Inspiration is drawn from the old and new worlds.

BREWING SECRET Argentinean honey, German malts, and American hops vie for attention in a fine array of beers.

HONEY BEER
FLAVOURED BEER 8.5% ABV
Together with the malts used, the Argentinean honey gives the beer an assertive character.

OKTOBERFEST
GERMAN ALE 5.5% ABV
Vienna and Munich malts impart a strong flavour profile; with little hop bitterness, the malt dominates.

EISENBAHN

Cervejaria Sudbrack Ltda, Rua Bahia, 5181 – Salto Weissbach, 89032-001 Blumenau SC, Brazil
www.eisenbahn.com.br

Owners Jarbas and Juliano Mendes established this brewery in 2002 and brew without the use of adjuncts or preservatives. They create a wide range of beers, from German-style weizenbier to special Belgian-style ales. Eisenbahn beers are exported to France and the United States.

EISENBAHN KÖLSCH
KÖLSCH 4.8% ABV
Four malts, including wheat, combine in this malty, golden beer; slight fruity aroma and low bitterness.

EISENBAHN PILSNER NATURAL
PILSNER 4.8% ABV
Brazil's first organic beer. Light and golden, and low in bitterness. The nose is malty biscuit.

---

some of the brews and experiments are being made with barrel ageing some beers. For those who are less adventurous, there is a range of pale lagers, some of which feature herbs, or lemon and lime juice.

BREWING SECRET The area is renowned for its flowers and fruit – all of which feature in some of the brewery's seasonal beers.

QUILMES

Tte. Gral. Juan D. Peron 667 103, Buenos Aires, Argentina
www.quilmes.com.ar

The dominant beer in Argentina, Quilmes is now part of the AB InBev embrace. Like many breweries in South America, it was begun by a German, the brewery and malt plant being founded in the 1880s by Otto Bemberg. "Quilmes" derives from an indigenous name for the place where the brewery is located.

SUL BRASILEIRA

BR 392, Km 05, Santa Maria – RS, 97000, Brazil
www.xingubeer.com

Local folklore says that Sul Brasileira's Xingu beer is the daughter of a beer brewed in ancient times by pioneering Amazonian brewsters. The river Xingu (pronounced "shin-goo") is a tributary of the Amazon River, which is home to the few surviving cultures and species of native Amazonian life.

SZOT

20210 Balmaceda, Talagante, Región Metropolitana, Chile
www.szot.cl

The brewery was established in 2006 by Californian Kevin Szot who draws upon his American roots for inspiration for his beers. In a country dominated by large international brands, his bottle-conditioned beers are something of a rarity. However, locals are now developing a taste for his well-hopped India pale ales, strong ales, double IPAs, and barley wine.

STRONG RED ALE
WOOD-AGED ALE 9% ABV
Chestnut amber in colour, it has aromas of smoke, roasted barley, caramel, spice, and coffee.

RUBIA
LAGER 4.5% ABV
Golden yellow, the bouquet is soft and delicate, with a hint of vanilla. Well conditioned, the finish is dry and crisp.

QUILMES CRISTAL
LAGER 4.9% ABV
Thin, pale, and without any aromatic distractions. Surprisingly drinkable, though, with refreshing sweetness.

QUILMES STOUT
STOUT 4.8% ABV
Three malts clamour for attention – but the expected coffee flavours are overwhelmed by sweetness.

XINGU BLACK BEER
SCHWARZBIER 4.6% ABV
Dark in colour, but light and sweet to taste. Still in the glass, its head soon disappears.

PALE ALE
AMERICAN PALE ALE 5.8% ABV
Aromas of papaya and passion fruit, and a sweetness from the malt can be found in this blond, slightly cloudy beer.

DIIPA
DOUBLE IMPERIAL IPA 10% ABV
Long-matured, intense flavours of malt sweetness and hop bitterness dominate this impressive beer.

BREWERY

BEER

BREWERY

BEER

Asahi Super Dry, underpinned by huge promotional campaigns, has been a Japanese favourite since the 1980s.

BAIRD BREWING

T410-0843, 9-3, Tadehara-cho,
Numazu, Shizouka, Japan
www.bairdbeer.com

Founded by Ohio native Bryan Baird
and his wife Sayuri in January 2001,
Baird has come to be considered
Japan's best brewery. Baird now
has 10 regular beers and brews
50–60 limited release beers each
year. It runs four taprooms, three
of which are in the Tokyo Yokohama
area. Its original Numazu brewpub
has expanded several times as news
spread about the quality of its beers.
The Bairds now have three other
bars in the Tokyo area, where its
complex beers can be tasted.

RISING SUN PALE ALE
PALE ALE 5.5% ABV
A brilliant American-style pale ale
made with British Maris Otter
malt and with a unique American
hop signature.

KUROFUNE PORTER
PORTER 6% ABV
A dark and luscious beer, it's full
of mocha and liquorice flavours.

ANGRY BOY BROWN ALE
BROWN ALE 7% ABV
Exciting and complex, this strong
brown ale has a complex flavour
profile and a richly satisfying finish.

WHEAT KING ALE
WHEAT ALE 4% ABV
Brewed with an ale yeast, the
focus is on the wheat. It's a
bready, refreshing, beer.

COEDO

385-10 Kamitome, Miyoshi-machi,
Iruma-gun, Saitama-ken Kawagoe-shi,
354-0045, Japan
www.coedobrewery.com

The brewery opened in 1996 and
now there is a restaurant on the
site, too. A local speciality is sweet
potato which, as well as being used as
a vegetable, is used to flavour coffee
and ice cream. Now it is being used
by the brewer in one of the Coedo
beers, Beniaka. Wheat, pilsner, and
dark beers also feature.

SHIKKOKU
BLACK LAGER 5% ABV
Smoky barbecue notes exude from
this beer; its finish is silky smooth
with a nice, gentle hop bitterness.

BENIAKA
SPECIALITY BEER 7% ABV
Reddish brown in colour, its taste
is reminiscent of a pumpkin ale,
with chestnut, caramel, and sweet
potato notes.

JAPAN'S BEST-KNOWN BEERS

On the international
market, several Japanese
beer names stand out:
Asahi, Kirin, Orion,
and Sapporo.

Asahi, a major Japanese brewer,
came strongly forward in the
market with the release of
enduringly popular Asahi Super
Dry back in the 1980s. Asahi
beers are noted for their subdued
hop aroma profiles and clean,
crisp taste; they are brewed in
many locations, nationally and
internationally. Asahi Stout is
a rare exception to the signature
Asahi flavour profile. Kirin
once maintained as much as
two-thirds of the Japanese beer
market thanks to its classic Kirin
Lager. That changed, however,
with Asahi's introduction of Super
Dry. Orion is based on the island
of Okinawa and has more than
50 per cent of the market there,
as well as a sizeable export
market. Sapporo has dropped
to fourth place among the major
breweries in sales terms, but
many fans love its soft mouthfeel
and pleasant drinkability. Founded
on the northern island of
Hokkaido in the 1870s, it soon
became a popular national, then
international brand. It is, however,
the brewery's Edel Pils that stands
out in terms of quality and flavour.

ASAHI KURONAMA (BLACK LAGER
5% ABV) *left*
KIRIN (LAGER 5% ABV) *centre*
SAPPORO (PREMIUM LAGER
4.7% ABV) *right*

BREWERY

ECHIGO

3970 Fukui, Nishiura-ku, Niigata City,
Niigata 953-0076, Japan
www.echigo-beer.jp

The brewers of the venerable
Tsurukame saké of Niigata opened
Japan's first microbrewery in February
of 1995 to great fanfare. Operations
have expanded from the original
brewpub to a large-scale brewery with
canning line today. While the canned
products are well regarded, the more
expensive small-production bottled
products are even more highly prized.

HIDEJI

747-56 Mukabaki, Nobeoka
882-0090, Japan
www.hideji-beer.jp

Interest in this sleepy little micro
was enlivened after the election
of maverick prefectural governor
Higashikokubaru, whose corruption-
fighting efforts have won him
immense public support. Interestingly,
Hideji beer has also improved
recently, together with the fortunes
of Miyazaki prefecture.

The brewery's beer range includes
a US-influenced pale ale, a Germanic
pilsner, and a Belgian wheat beer.
Every month a one-off special beer
is produced.

HITACHINO NEST

1257 Konosu, Naka City,
Ibaraki 311-0133, Japan
www.hitachinonest.com

The parent company is an old regional
saké brewery that also produces
shochu spirits and even wine. Beer
was added to the range in 1996,
followed by exports to the USA.
In fact, half of the production is now
exported, primarily to the US market.
The best beers are Belgian in style.
Beer fans visiting the brewery not
only learn about the brewing process,

BEER

PILSNER

PILSNER 5% ABV

This reasonably priced craft beer
has a rich malty flavour, moderate
bitterness, and a clean, quick finish.

STOUT

STOUT 7% ABV

Higher gravity and more care in
the brewing of this beer results
in a brilliant interplay of rich,
roasty flavours.

HIDEJI STOUT

STOUT 6.8–7.2% ABV

Dry, with a fair measure of tartness,
the beer develops a roastiness and
soft texture as it warms.

GOLDEN FOX

PILSNER 4.7% ABV

Golden in colour, it has a soft,
floral, hoppy nose and a biscuit
malt finish.

SHINKAN

AMERICAN PALE ALE 5% ABV

Bright amber gold, with a tangy, rich
malt flavour, accented by plummy
fruit notes. The hops are subdued
in a more British interpretation.

DARK BOAR

WHEAT BEER 5.2% ABV

Complex and invigorating, it's a
mixture of fruit and spice, with
a pleasant bready aroma.

WHITE ALE

WITBIER 5.5% ABV

Modelled on a Belgian wit, but with
a pronounced orange flavour due
to the use of real juice.

ESPRESSO STOUT

STOUT 7.5% ABV

Dark brown, with a dense, white
head, it is dominated by rich,
roasted grains, figs, caramel, and
coffee notes.

but they can make their own beer too. Participants can either brew one of the distinctive Hitachino Nest beers or they can, with the help of one of the company's brewers, create their own recipe.

ISE KADOYA
6-428 Jingu, Ise City,
Mie 516-0017, Japan

Said to date back to the 16th century as an enterprise producing miso (fermented soya bean paste) and soy sauce, Ise kadoya branched out into brewing in the 19th century for a brief time, supplying foreign ships with ale provisions. They resurrected their beer business in 1997, keeping to the same 19th-century label designs.

IWATE KURA
5-42 Tamuramachi, Ichinoseki City,
Iwate 021-0885, Japan
www.sekinoichi.co.jp

Located in a rather remote area of Northern Japan, Iwate kura has been distinguishing itself in recent years with a range of creative beers. They include a flavoured ale with a striking caramel taste.

BREWING SECRET Local oyster beds renowned for their quality are harvested for the oyster stout.

KINSHACHI
1-7-34 Sakae, Naka-ku, Nagoya City,
Aichi 460-0008, Japan
www.kinshachi.jp

Old line saké brewer Morita Shuzo produced beer briefly some 100 years ago for sale primarily to US whaling ships. One of the most internationally famous members of the family was Akio Morita, one of the founders of electronics giant Sony. In 1996, the company reopened a disused soft-drink bottling plant as a small brewery, under the old Kinshachi brand name.

RED RICE ALE
ALE 7% ABV
A Belgian Ale with a complex Japanese rice twist and a hint of strawberries. Good bitter finish.

SWEET STOUT
STOUT 7.5% ABV
A powerful nose of coffee leads to vanilla, figs, chocolate, and a finish of roasted bitterness.

ISE KADOYA PALE ALE
PALE ALE 5% ABV
Initially produced in a more English style, recent versions have featured more assertive hopping, common to American pale ales. Still, it retains rather subdued characteristics.

WEIZEN
WHEAT BEER 5.5% ABV
A Japanese take on a German favourite. Fragrant and fruity, it is a refresher.

OYSTER STOUT
STOUT 7% ABV
The brewery revives this classic English-style, with a rich yet dry interpretation, minimal hopping, and only a faint hint of oyster flavour.

NAGOYA RED MISO LAGER
FLAVOURED BEER 6% ABV
Miso is a speciality of the Nagoya region, where Kinshachi is located. Only a small amount is used, giving the beer a faintly meaty flavour.

HATCHO BLACK MISO LAGER
DARK LAGER 6% ABV
This newer version is made with very dark "hatcho" miso, and has an even richer, almost nutty taste.

BREWERY

MINOH BEER

3-19-11 Makiochi, Minoh City,
Osaka 562-0004, Japan
www.minoh-beer.jp

Established by liquor store owner
Masaji Oshita, and run by his
daughters Kaori and Mayuko, the
brewery makes a variety of beers
drawing on American and European
brewing traditions for inspiration.
In recent years its beers have been
recognized beyond Japan as the
company has picked up awards in
international brewing competitions.

NASU KOHGEN

3986 Oaza Takakukoh, Nasu-cho,
Nasu-gun, Tochigi 325-0001, Japan
www.nasukohgenbeer.co.jp

Set in a picturesque forest just off the
primary motorway leading north from
Tokyo, this brewery is known for its
superior quality, with prices to match,
and an emphasis on traditional English
styles. The brewery is in the vicinity
of the Japanese royal family's summer
villa, and a beer named after Princess
Ai upon her birth has become one
of Nasu Kohgen's best sellers.

SANKT GALLEN

1137-1 Kaneda, Atsugi City,
Kanagawa 243-0807, Japan
www.sanktgallenbrewery.com

This enterprise snuck under the
radar before the liberalization of
microbreweries with their less-than-
one per cent-alcohol brews back in
the early 1990s. Now, however, Sankt
Gallen seems to be specializing in
high-gravity "sweet beers" aimed at
women, though its golden, amber,
and pale ales remain popular too.

SHIGA KOGEN

1163 Hirao, Yamanouchi-machi, Shimo
Takai-gun Nagano 381-0401, Japan
www.tamamura-honten.co.jp

In September 2004, saké brewer
Tamamura Honten broke a little of
their 200-year tradition and began
brewing beer. Within three years,
Shiga Kogen had become one of
the most respected Japanese craft
beer brands. Clear product identity
and superior label designs have
contributed to the beer's popularity.

BEER

MINOH IMPERIAL STOUT
IMPERIAL STOUT 8.5% ABV
Chocolate and coffee flavours
exude from this full-bodied beer.
The finish is bittersweet.

MINOH W-IPA
STRONG IPA 9% ABV
Bold, strong, and exciting, this
former seasonal brew is now
available all year round.

NINE-TAILED FOX BARLEY WINE
BARLEY WINE 11% ABV
Remarkably subdued flavour profile
for a beer with such high alcohol.
In 2007, the brewery released a
10-year vertical set, containing years
1998 to 2007 in 330ml (11fl oz)
bottles, which sold out quickly.
These same years are still available
separately in large 500ml (16fl oz)
ceramic crocks.

IMPERIAL CHOCOLATE STOUT
IMPERIAL STOUT 8.6% ABV
The most popular of the "sweet
beers", this limited edition bottling
is released in time for St. Valentine's
Day and quickly sells out. Lots of
rich chocolate and caramel flavours
are tempered by a touch of acidity
and very low hopping.

HOUSE DPA/DRAFT PALE ALE
PALE ALE 8% ABV
American in style, with a brilliant
orange-gold hue, complex floral
hop aroma, and lingering sweetness.

MIYAMA BLONDE
SAISON-LIKE BEER 7% ABV
Made using the Miyama Nishiki
strain of saké rice, along with
European hops and barley. Rich and
interesting, but with a brisk finish.

MORE BEERS OF

JAPAN

Suntory may be famous for its whisky, but its beer is also worth trying among these other Japanese brewers.

HELIOS

405 Kyoda, Nago City,
Okinawa 905-0024, Japan
www.helios-syuzo.co.jp

Originally a distiller of rum from Okinawa's abundant fields of sugar cane, Helios branched out into craft beer in 1996. Their flagship product is a rich weizenbier, which goes well in Okinawa's sub-tropical climate, while their Goya Dry is their most "local" and distinctive brew.

OTARU BEER

3-263-19 Zenibako, Otaru City,
Hokkaido 047-0261, Japan
www.otarubeer.com

Japanese owners, a German brewer, and an American manager combine to make Otaru Beer an international endeavour. The bottom line here is quality. No beer is shipped beyond a 100-km (70-mile) radius of Otaru. The brewery's high production values are a match for those of most German brewers.

GOYA DRY

FLAVOURED BEER 5% ABV
Bitter melon, the "national vegetable" of Okinawa, is used alongside hops to bitter this curiously refreshing beer. Naturally, it is ideal with pork-predominant Okinawan cuisine.

OTARU PILSNER

PILSNER 4.9% ABV
A stellar interpretation of the world's most popular beer style. Otaru's version is perfectly balanced.

SHONAN

7-10-7 Kagawa, Chigasaki City,
Kanagawa 253-0082, Japan
www.kumazawa.jp

A saké brewing enterprise since 1872, Kumazawa Shuzo began brewing beer in 1996, naming the brand after the Shonan coastal region where the brewery is located. Quality has always been high, and Shonan has garnered many international awards over the past decade.

YOHO

1119-1 Otai, Saku City,
Nagano 385-0009, Japan
www.yonasato.com

Yona Yona Ale is perhaps the most popular craft beer in Japan, available in brightly coloured cans and on draught all over Japan. While the recipe predates head brewer Toshi Ishii (who previously worked at Stone Brewing in San Diego, USA), he is responsible for their second big success, Tokyo Black, a tasty porter with remarkable flavour and smooth balance.

OZENO YUKIDOKE

7-3 Nishi Honmachi, Tatebayashi City,
Gunma 374-0065, Japan

Quality and product stability was a bit uneven in the first few years of this brewery, which was founded in 1997. However, from around 2004 onwards, Ozeno Yukidoke's beer began to improve dramatically and it now produces several tasty brews. The parent company is an old established saké brewer.

SUNTORY

Daiba 2-3-3, Minato-ku,
Tokyo 135-8631, Japan
www.suntory.com

A long-standing whisky enterprise with recent awards to their credit, Suntory is a relative newcomer to the world of beer. Established in the early 1960s to take advantage of their large distribution network, the brewery has only recently developed a repuation for quality lager.

LIEBE

SCHWARZBIER 5% ABV
Surprisingly dry and drinkable for such a dark, richly flavoured beer, Liebe is an award-winning lager of superior depth and complexity.

WEIZEN BOCK

STRONG WEIZENBIER 7% ABV
Superb body, aroma, and balance for a high-alcohol beer, though it could be considered a bit staid by some.

YONA YONA ALE

PALE ALE 5.5% ABV
Square in the American Pale Ale category. Brisk and citrussy, with Cascade hops giving a sharp finish.

TOKYO BLACK

PORTER 5% ABV
This tasty roasty beer can best be described as a session porter, with a unique twist. Brewer Ishii has brewed a batch in England.

BROWN WEIZEN

HEFEWEIZEN 5% ABV
Unusual cloudy brown appearance, with a subtle lactic note. Richness suddenly comes in at mid-palate, leaving a long and satisfying finish.

INDIA PALE ALE

IPA 6% ABV
Patterned on the US West Coast style of IPA, it is boldly bitter with a quick, hoppy finish.

THE PREMIUM MALT'S

LAGER 5.5% ABV
Having taken three Monde Selection awards in a row, this superior 100 per cent malt lager is one of the best in Japan.

A man walks past an illuminated sign at the Tsingtao International Beer Festival in Shandong, China.

GUANGZHOU ZHUJIANG

118 Modiesha Avenue, East Xingang
Road, Guangzhou PR, China 510308
www.zhujiangbeer.com

Zhu Jiang is brewed in Guangzhou, in
the South of China. Guangzhou is the
third largest city in Mainland China
with a population of 14 million. AB
InBev has had a 24 per cent stake
in the brewery since 2002. Beers
from the brewery are widely exported
around the world.

ZHUJIANG GOLDEN LAGER
LAGER 5.3% ABV
The beer has a pale yellow,
straw-like appearance, with a
subtle malt flavour highlighted
by a delicate hop balance that
finishes crisp and clean. Czech
hops, German yeast, Chinese
rice, and Canadian barley malt
are used.

SUN LIK

22 Wang Lee Street,
New Territories, Hong Kong, China
www.sunlikbeer.co.uk

Sun Lik is Cantonese for San Miguel,
one of the most famous beer brands
worldwide. San Miguel Brewery,
Hong Kong is a non-wholly owned
subsidiary of San Miguel Corporation.
The brewery holds the franchise to
produce and sell San Miguel's beer
brands in Hong Kong, Macao, and
Hainan province in Mainland China.

SUN LIK
LAGER 5% ABV
Rice is used in the beer grist,
which gives the beer a crisp, if
somewhat sugary, finish. The beer
is pale yellow in colour and has
a sweetcorn nose.

TSINGTAO

Hong Kong Road, Central,
Qinqdao, China 266071
www.tsingtaobeer.com

The Tsingtao Brewery was founded in
1903 by German settlers in Qingdoa.
Until recently, AB InBev had a large
shareholding in the brewery, which
is China's second biggest, but most
of these shares were sold to Japanese
brewer Asahi. However, it is
rumoured that another international
brewer, Carlsberg, would like to buy
the brewery.

TSINGTAO
LAGER 4.8% ABV
Crisp, slightly malty flavour, and a
nutty sweet taste. The colour is
bright yellow; aroma grainy, with
a hint of sweetness. A high level
of carbonation makes it very fizzy.

HITE JINRO

640, Yeongdeungpo-Dong,
Yeongdeungpo, Seoul, South Korea
www.hitejinro.com

Founded in 1933 as Chosun
Breweries, Hite is one of Korea's
leading brewers with around 50 per
cent of local sales. The company
makes beer under various brand
names, such as Hite, Hite Pitcher,
Max, Stout, and S. The company is
now targeting exports and is looking
at increasing its sales in Europe,
China, and the USA.

HITE
LAGER 4.5% ABV
Golden in colour, Hite is a light,
easy-drinking beer – with an aroma
of bubble-gum.

PRIME MAX
LAGER 4.5% ABV
Pale orange in colour; with a
sweetcorn aroma, it has hints
of biscuit and citrus fruits.

BREWERY

BEER

BREWERY

ORIENTAL BREWERY

Hanwon Bldg, 1449-12 Seocho-dong, Seocho-gu, 137-070 Seoul, South Korea
www.ob.co.kr

Founded by the Doosan Group in 1952, Oriental vies with Hite to be the number one brewer in Korea. The international giant AB InBev had bought shares of the company in 2003. In 2006, it took full control of them, but sold the shares in 2008 to reduce its debt. In 2014, the company once again became a part of AB InBev.

KHAN BRÄU

Ulaanbaatar-44, Sukbaattar District, 3rd Khoroo, Ulaanbaatar, Mongolia
www.khanbrau.net

The microbrewery was opened in 1996 as a joint Mongolian and German venture. The company's pub, the Khan Lonkh, offers draft pilsner in a western-style environment. The company says it is brewing beer to comply with the German purity rules.

BREWING SECRET Khan Bräu takes its water from the crystal pure Tull River.

BOON RAWD

999 Samsen Road, Bangkok 10300, Thailand
www.boonrawd.co.th

Boon Rawd was founded in 1933 by Phraya Bhirom Bhakdi, who had toured Germany and Denmark to learn about brewing. The brewery is still owned by the Bhirom Bhakdi family. The company operates three breweries in Thailand.

THAIBEV

14 Vibhavadi Rangsit Road, Chomphon Sub-District, Chatuchak District, Bangkok, 10900 Thailand
www.thaibev.com

Thailand's other major beer producer is in fierce competition with Boon Rawd. Its Chang brand is the best-selling beer within the country and is widely exported. The company also makes the famous Mekhong rice whisky.

BEER

OB GOLDEN LAGER

LAGER 4.4% ABV
Originally brewed in 1948. When AB InBev purchased the company, the recipe was altered to include rice.

CASS

LAGER 4.5% ABV
Pale and golden, Cass was once South Korea's biggest selling beer; it now ranks number three.

BAADOG

VIENNA LAGER 4.8% ABV
Reddish brown in colour, it has sweet overtones with hints of caramel and burnt sugar.

KHAN BRÄU

PILSNER 4.8% ABV
A crisp beer that uses German malt and hops. The Bavarian hops provide a spicy flavour.

SINGHA

LAGER 5% ABV
A full-bodied barley malt beer with a strong hop character. Clean to taste, it complements spicy food.

SINGHA LIGHT

LAGER 3.5% ABV
Lacks the complexity and vitality of its stronger stablemate. It is pale yellow of hue and thin to taste.

CHANG

LAGER 5% ABV
The export version is golden and light, aimed at an international palate. The domestic version is stronger (6.4% ABV), slightly darker, and brewed with rice as well as malt and hops.

LAO BREWERY

Km 12 Thadeua Road, Hatsayfong District, Vientiane, Lao PDR
www.beerlao.la

The Lao Brewery began production in 1973 and was originally known as Brasseries et Glaci è res du Laos. Two years later, in 1975, it became state owned. In 2002, Carlsberg and TCC, a Thai company, each agreed to acquire a 25 per cent stake in Lao Brewery; the remaining shares are still held by the Laos government.

HUE

243 Nguyen Sinh Cung
Hue City, Vietnam
www.huda.com.vn

The Hue Brewery is based in Hue City, the old capital of Vietnam, on the banks of the famous Perfume River in central Vietnam. Carlsberg – which entered Vietnam in 1993 with the acquisition of a 60 per cent stake in South East Asia Brewery, based in the north of the country – took over the brewery in 2011, making Hue its wholly owned subsidiary.

ASIA PACIFIC BREWERIES

459 Jalan Ahmad Ibrahim,
Singapore 639934
www.tigerbeer.com

The company's origin can be traced back to a single brewery in Singapore over 80 years ago – a joint venture between Heineken and Fraser & Neave which formed Malayan Breweries and brewed Tiger beer – AP's most famous beer. Tiger was first produced in the 1930s, when the "Time for a Tiger" slogan was first used. Anthony Burgess named the first novel in his "The Long Day Wanes" trilogy *Time for a Tiger*.

All of the brewer's beers are widely available across Asia, and are now brewed in seven different countries. Today the iconic Tiger Brewery forms the heart of a vibrant visitor centre.

BEERLAO LAGER
Lager 5% ABV
Described as Asia's best beer, Beerlao has a pleasant sweetness. Lightly bitter, with hints of honey.

BEERLAO DARK
Lager 6.5% ABV
Reddish brown, it is full of sweet toffee and toast flavours. A short but warming finish.

HUE BEER
Lager 4.8% ABV
A corn yellow colour with a thin, white head, and the body seems somewhat thin too. It is an easy-drinking beer, without surprises and a nose with hints of toast. Not much complexity, but a refresher nonetheless.

TIGER
Lager 5% ABV
A golden-coloured, refreshing lager. It is normally served so chilled that its taste and aromas are masked.

BARONS STRONG BREW
Lager 8.8% ABV
A well balanced, not too sweet beer, with a warming finish.

ABC EXTRA STOUT
Stout 8% ABV
A strong, but easy-drinking beer. The nose is robust, with roasted coffee and chocolate flavours.

TIGER CRYSTAL
Lager 4.1% ABV
Pale sweetish beer, best drunk well chilled.

BREWERY

MULTI BINTANG

Jl. Daan Mogot Km 19, Jakarta,
Indonesia 10032
www.multibintang.co.id

Indonesia's largest brewery produces
and markets a range of drinks, including
Bir Bintang, Heineken, Guinness Stout,
and the low alcohol Green Sands. It was
founded in 1929, with Heineken taking
a share of the company in the 1930s.
Though taken over by the Indonesian
government in 1957, Heineken became
involved again in 1967, and today the
brewery is largely owned by them.

MYSORE BREWERIES

Jalahalli Camp Rd, Yeshwanthpur,
Bangalore, India 560022
www.sabmiller.in

One of the world's biggest brewers,
SABMiller is bringing some spice
to the Indian beer market under
the Indus Pride brand. Designed for
the Indian palate, its range of beers
includes coriander-, cardamom-,
fennel-, and cinnamon-flavoured
brews. The company also brews one
of India's best known strong beers,
Haywards 5000.

UNITED BREWERIES

Level 12-16, UB Tower, UB City
24, Vittal Mallya Road, Bangalore,
560001 India
www.theubgroup.com

It is said the company's logo –
a Pegasus – once carried a cask of
beer between its wings as a gift to the
gods. Its Kingfisher brand is the flying
leader in India's soaring beer market,
and what once was a company that
supplied beer to the troops of the
British Empire has now acquired
a worldwide reputation.

LION BREWERY

254 Colombo Road,
Biyagama, Sri Lanka
www.lionbeer.com

The Carlsberg owned company's best
known beer is Lion Stout. The beer
is brewed from British, Czech, and
Danish malts, with Styrian hops
and an English yeast strain. All the
ingredients are transported along
precarious roads to the brewery,
located 1,000m (3,500ft) above sea
level in the midst of tea plantations.

BEER

BINTANG PILSENER

LAGER 4.7% ABV
The beer is a crystal-clear yellow,
with a light, malty aroma and a
hint of corn, which gives way to
a dry, hoppy finish. Best served
well chilled, it has a nice level
of carbonation. The beer clearly
draws on its Dutch ancestry.

INDUS PRIDE CITRUSY CARDAMOM

SPICED BEER 5% ABV
Cardamom, the queen of spices,
adds delicate aromatic notes to
this citrus hop-flavoured beer.

HAYWARDS 5000

LAGER 7.5% ABV
Well-rounded, full-bodied beer,
caramel malt sweet with corn on
the nose. Good and warming finish.

KINGFISHER PREMIUM LAGER

LAGER 5% ABV
Brewed under licence in many
countries. It has a crisp taste with
a sweetish overtone.

KINGFISHER ULTRA

LAGER 4.6% ABV
Golden yellow, with good
carbonation; it is crisp, with
a subdued hop finish.

LION STOUT

STOUT 7.5% ABV
A world-class beer, with pruney,
mocha aromas and flavours. It
has a tar-like oiliness of body and
a peppery, bitter-chocolate finish.
The alcohol gives it a long,
warming finish.

CASTLE/SAB

65 Park Lane, Sandown,
Sandton, South Africa
www.sablimited.co.za

SAB – South African Breweries – was founded in 1895 and began producing its Castle Lager brand in the mining town of Johannesburg. The company soon became the biggest brewer in southern Africa. In 2002, SAB bought Miller Brewing in the USA, and as SABMiller it has become one of the biggest global drinks companies.

MITCHELL'S

3 Arend Street, Knysna Industrial,
Knysna, South Africa
www.mitchellsbrewing.com

Founded in 1983 by Lex Mitchell, this microbrewery handcrafts a characterful range of unfiltered draught beers that are predominantly British in style, combined with a German influence. Some of Mitchell's ales are bottled and widely available in the Cape region, but the beers are not exported.

SHONGWENI/ROBSON'S

Estate B13 Kassier Rd, Shongweni Valley, KwaZulu-Natal, South Africa
www.shongwenibrewery.com

Shongweni mainly produces bottle-conditioned beers, using the infusion mash technique and fermentation in open-top vessels. All its beers are unfiltered and unpasteurized. Since 2012, the brewery is owned by former home-brewer Brian Stewart and his two sons, who are continuing with the company's innovative brewing programme.

TRIGGERFISH

Intersection De Beers Avenue & Broadway Rd, Somerset West, Western Cape, South Africa
www.triggerfishbrewing.co.za

Triggerfish has made an explosive entry into South Africa's craft beer scene. Opened in 2011, it is housed in a former dynamite factory and its beers have certainly come with a bang. Brewer Eric Van Heerden is a former home-brewer who honed his talents in the United States. His creative beers are a volatile mix of hops and malt.

CASTLE LAGER
Lager 5% ABV
Award-winning lager made from African Gold Barley and Southern Star hops. It is brewed in nine countries and sold in 40.

CASTLE MILK STOUT
Milk Stout 6% ABV
Dark, highly hopped, strong stout with a complex taste of roasted black malts, coffee, and caramel.

90 SHILLING ALE
Scottish-style Amber Ale 5% ABV
Aromatic with pale, crystal, and black malts, bark cinnamon, and caramel. The name refers to an old Scottish tax on a barrel of ale.

RAVEN STOUT
Milk Stout 5% ABV
Pale and black malts with lactose and some caramel. Full bodied and smooth, with a distinct hop aroma.

DURBAN PALE ALE
India Pale Ale 5.7% ABV
Brewed with pale malt, and Cascade and Challenger hops. Crisp, fruity, and well balanced.

EAST COAST ALE
Golden Ale 4% ABV
A smooth and refreshing golden ale, made with a single malt variety along with Brewers Gold and Challenger hops.

ROMAN RED
American Amber Ale 5.2% ABV
Full in flavour, American hops bring some glorious pine and citrus aromas to this balanced malt brew.

HAMMERHEAD IPA
India Pale Ale 6.2% ABV
Citrus and pine notes are underpinned by a bold, malt base and some dried fruit flavours. It is a beer for hopheads.

BREWERY

JAMES BOAG'S

39 William Street, Launceston, Tasmania 7250, Australia
www.boags.com.au

From a once-moribund regional brewery, Boag's has ridden a wave of popularity since the launch of James Boag's Premium Lager in 1994. Lagers comprise the bulk of production, but Boag's has rolled out some fine limited-edition ales in recent years. The brewery was acquired by the Lion Nathan group in late 2007.

BOOTLEG

Corner Johnson & Pusey Roads, Wilyabrup, Western Australia 6280
www.bootlegbrewery.com.au

"An oasis of beer in a desert of wine" is the mangled metaphor Bootleg use to state that they were the first craft brewery in the Margaret River wine region. Since opening in 1994, four other micros have joined them. Bootleg is housed in a sprawling homestead, with a tasting room, restaurant (lunches only), and beer garden.

BRIDGE ROAD BREWERS

Old Coach House Brewers Lane, 50 Ford Street Beechworth, Victoria 3747, Australia
www.bridgeroadbrewers.com.au

Winemaker-turned-brewer Ben Kraus operates from his home town in regional Victoria – where renegade bushranger Ned Kelly was sentenced to death. Kraus has a wide range of beers on tap at his brewery door bar.

BREWING SECRET Ben is one of the few Australian brewers to produce styles such as *saison* and *bière de garde*.

BRIGHT

Great Alpine Road, Bright, Victoria 3741, Australia
www.brightbrewery.com.au

A relative newcomer, Bright is situated in the regional Victorian town of the same name. The brewery door bar (open Fri–Sun) has a decidedly alpine feel, and is indeed close to ski fields. Flavour and balance have been at the forefront of each new style.

BREWING SECRET Bright's seasonal beers are available only at the brewery door.

BEER

WIZARD SMITH'S ALE

ENGLISH ALE 5% ABV
A solid malt backbone, with toffee and spicy hop notes, is rounded out by a significant bitterness.

TOM'S AMBER ALE

AUSTRALIAN AMBER ALE 4% ABV
Deep garnet-brown; roasty and bitter initially, with treacle notes. Dry finish.

RAGING BULL

STRONG DARK ALE 7.1% ABV
Dark mahogany, complex coffee, treacle, and bitter chocolate notes; bristling late bitterness.

CHESTNUT PILSNER

SPECIALITY 5% ABV
Locally grown chestnuts add a nutty character, which works harmoniously with the aromatic Galaxy hops.

CHEVALIER SAISON

SAISON 6% ABV
Lively carbonation, complex palate, with hints of sherbet, wine, fennel, and yeast; a tingling, dryish finish.

HELLFIRE AMBER ALE

BRITISH PALE ALE 5% ABV
Amber-gold; toffee and spice notes, dash of roasted malt; balanced, with a satisfying bitterness.

THE BEST-KNOWN BEERS IN AUSTRALIA

Australia's biggest-seller is Victoria Bitter (now owned by SABMiller), which accounts for roughly one in every five beers consumed.

No one can really explain the phenomenal rise of "VB" over the past two decades, although it did coincide with changes in brewery ownership and an erosion of traditional loyalty to individual state brands. Somewhat ironically, Foster's Lager is one of the largest-selling brands globally and yet accounts for only around one per cent of the domestic beer market. Carlton Draught (another Foster's group brand) remains strong in its Victorian home market, as do Toohey's in New South Wales and Castlemaine XXXX in Queensland. But the latter has been eclipsed recently by XXXX Gold, a "mid-strength" (lower alcohol) version; such mid-strength beers enjoy widespread popularity in the sun-belt states of Queensland and Western Australia, but have yet to make their mark elsewhere. Increasingly, Aussie drinkers are turning to local premium and imported lagers, and to craft beers. The fastest-growing brand in the past couple of years has been Carlton Pure Blonde – a lower-carbohydrate beer that has already attracted a host of copycat brands.

VB (LAGER 4.9% ABV) *left*
CARLTON DRAUGHT
  (LAGER 4.6% ABV) *centre*
TOOHEYS (LAGER 5% ABV)
XXXX GOLD (LAGER 3.5% ABV)
  right
CARLTON PURE BLONDE
  (LAGER 4.6% ABV)

CASCADE

131 Cascade Road, South Hobart, Tasmania 7004
www.cascadebrewery.com.au

Australia's oldest operating brewery, complete with on-site maltings, is also the most striking, with the castellated sandstone building nestled in the foothills of the sometimes snow-capped Mount Wellington. Now part of the SABMiller empire, Cascade attracts tens of thousands of beer lovers annually to its visitor centre.

COOPERS

461 South Road, Regency Park, Adelaide, South Australia 5010
www.coopers.com.au

While most Australian breweries were progressively "lagerized" during the 20th century, this family-run Adelaide brewing dynasty kept knocking out cloudy, bottle-conditioned ales and stouts. Since opening a new expanded brewery in 2001, surging demand for their beers has driven them to become the country's third-largest beer-maker.

The beers are direct descendants of the brash, hoppy ales that founder Thomas Cooper made for his sick wife in 1862, hoping they would be restorative. Coopers is now experimenting with storing its stronger ales to see how the vintages will change over time.

CASCADE STOUT

MEDIUM STOUT 5.8% ABV
Coffee notes up front, with milk chocolate on the palate, followed by a moderately bitter finish.

CASCADE BLONDE

SUMMER ALE 4.8% ABV
Clean and crisp, with a hint of citrus hop flavour.

COOPERS SPARKLING ALE

AUSTRALIAN PALE ALE 5.8% ABV
Cloudy; fruity aromatics with a hint of peach; rounded, dry, yeasty finish.

COOPERS BEST EXTRA STOUT

DRY STOUT 6.3% ABV
Espresso and bitter chocolate notes, with banana hints too; robustly bitter finish.

EXTRA STRONG VINTAGE ALE

STRONG ALE 7.5% ABV
Notes of coffee, fudge, orange, and vinous grape can be found in this extraordinary beer. An aged beer, it is constantly evolving.

ORIGINAL PALE ALE

GOLDEN ALE 4.5% ABV
Carbon bubbles dance on the tongue of this sprightly ale. Hints of citrus give way to a dry finish.

BREWERY

FERAL

152 Haddrill Road, Baskerville,
Western Australia, 6056, Swan Valley
www.feralbrewing.com.au

The Swan Valley wine region
outside Perth boasts a handful of
microbreweries, including Feral. The
company's logo features a feral pig
– many of which roam the Aussie
bush and are keenly sought after
by hunters. Unusually, the flagship
brew is a Belgian witbier, which,
fortunately, is free of any feral yeasts.

HOLGATE BREWHOUSE

79 High Street, Woodend,
Victoria 3442, Australia
www.holgatebrewhouse.com

Brewpubs serving hand-pumped real
ale are rare in Australia, and Holgate
is well worth seeking out. Paul and
Natasha Holgate took over the lease
of the stately Keatings Hotel in 2002,
relocating their microbrewery there
four years later (it had previously been
in a large shed beside their home).
They produce English-inspired ales.

KNAPPSTEIN

2 Pioneer Avenue, Clare,
South Australia, 5453
www.knappstein.com.au

Microbreweries in wine regions are
increasingly common in Australia. This
one operates out of a gorgeous stone
building that housed the Enterprise
Brewery until 1916 and, more
recently, has been the headquarters
for Knappstein winery. Their sole
brand is a full-bodied lager, which
is the beer equivalent of a good
Clare Valley Riesling.

LITTLE CREATURES

40 Mews Road, Fremantle,
Western Australia
www.littlecreatures.com.au

Based in an enormous hangar-like
building on the water's edge at
Fremantle (close to where erstwhile
beer baron Alan Bond lost the
America's Cup yachting challenge in
1987), Little Creatures combines
a bar/restaurant within a busy
microbrewery. The flagship Pale Ale is
inspired by the likes of the US-based

BEER

FERAL WHITE
Belgian Witbier 4.6% ABV
Hazy, pale lemon; juggles delicate
citrus and clove characters, with
a crisp, tart finish.

HOLGATE ESB
English Bitter 5% ABV
Biscuity malt notes intertwined
with leafy hop flavours, rounded
off with a satisfying bitterness.

HOLGATE WINTER ALE
Robust Porter 6% ABV
Espresso and treacle aromatics;
palate shows coffee and cream, dark
chocolate, and blackcurrant hints.

KNAPPSTEIN RESERVE LAGER
Bavarian Lager 5.6% ABV
Lifted fruity aromas; passion fruit
and melon notes married to rich
malt; fulsome bitterness.

LITTLE CREATURES PALE ALE
American Pale Ale 5.2% ABV
Citrus/grapefruit hop aromas;
chewy malt and citrus-tinged,
robust bitterness.

LITTLE CREATURES BRIGHT ALE
Pale Ale 4.5% ABV
Bags of floral hops; juicy sweet
malt balanced with tropical
fruit-laced hop flavours.

Sierra Nevada, and, along with the venue, has been a runaway success. In 2012, the company was taken over by Japanese-owned Lion Nathan. Kirin's latest acquisition follows on less than 12 months after SABMiller's takeover of Australia's biggest beer brewer, Foster's.

BREWING SECRET Little Creatures uses impressive quantities of fresh hop flowers to flavour the beer.

LORD NELSON

19 Kent Street, The Rocks, Sydney, New South Wales 2000, Australia
www.lordnelsonbrewery.com

Still going strong after 20-plus years, Sydney's original modern brewpub attracts ale lovers to this historic hotel, which claims to be the city's "oldest continuously licensed pub". The early brews were basic malt extract-based beers, but have evolved into tasty and complex ales, worthy of this gem of a watering hole.

MALT SHOVEL

99 Pyrmont Bridge Road, Camperdown, Sydney, New South Wales 2050, Australia
www.maltshovel.com.au

Positioned as Lion Nathan's craft brewing arm, the Malt Shovel Brewery has grown an impressive portfolio of beer styles under US-born brewmaster Dr Charles "Chuck" Hahn. The brewery's first release in 1998 was Amber Ale, which found ready acceptance with traditional lager drinkers. Their James Squire

brands are named after a former convict and highwayman, who became the colony's first successful hop grower and brewer. Malt Shovel consistently rolls out ground-breaking and true-to-style beers from within the Lion Nathan fold.

BREWING SECRET Adventurous limited edition releases have included a porter that was matured in rum barrels and a raspberry wheat beer.

ROGERS' BEER
AMBER ALE 3.8% ABV
Biscuity malt notes; caramel-laced mid-palate and spicy, citrus hoppiness; short finish.

LITTLE CREATURES PILSNER
PILSNER 4.6% ABV
Using Czech Saaz hops, Little Creatures Pilsner is classically European – crisp, clean, and fresh.

OLD ADMIRAL
STRONG ALE 6.1% ABV
Dense, malty palate, with plummy notes, lively bitterness, and a warming afterglow.

THREE SHEETS
PALE ALE 4.9% ABV
Malty, fruity aromatics; malt-accented, with citrus and apricot hints; well-rounded bitterness.

FOUR 'WIVES' PILSNER
CZECH PILSNER 5% ABV
Faintly spicy aromas; rich, malty palate, with honey notes and fulsome bitterness.

STOWAWAY IPA
INDIA PALE ALE 5.6% ABV
Chewy, caramel-tinged maltiness balanced by robust (dry-hopped) hop flavour and lingering bitterness.

THE CHANCER GOLDEN ALE
GOLDEN ALE 4.5% ABV
Easy-drinking summer ale, with passion fruit/citrus hop flavours; crisp, moderately bitter finish.

JACK OF SPADES PORTER
PORTER 5% ABV
Hints of coffee, dark chocolate, and dark fruit (plums); a sumptuous beer, with a smooth finish.

BREWERY

MATILDA BAY

89 Bertie Street, Port Melbourne, Victoria 3207, Australia
www.matildabay.com.au

Australia's first modern craft brewery, which kicked off in Fremantle in 1984, was acquired by Foster's (now part of SABMiller) six years later, and has been revitalized in recent times. Original brews such as Redback (a hefeweizen) and Dogbolter (a dark lager) have been supplemented with a wide range of beer styles. Much of the new direction occurred under

the watch of the head brewer Brad Rogers, who after 15 years decided that he wanted the challenge of a new brewing venture.

BREWING SECRET The Matilda Bay output includes an experimental "out there" series, which features a *saison* (named Barking Duck) and Crema, which is a coffee-infused pale ale.

MOO BREW

655 Main Road, Berriedale, Hobart, Tasmania 7011, Australia
www.moobrew.com.au

A stunningly appointed microbrewery, with commanding views of Derwent River and Mount Wellington from the second-storey, glass-fronted brewhouse. An offshoot of Moorilla Estate winery, Moo Brew has set a new benchmark among Australian craft producers, with slick packaging, uncompromising beers, and premium pricing.

MOUNTAIN GOAT

Corner North and Clarke Streets, Richmond, Melbourne, Victoria 3121, Australia
www.goatbeer.com.au

Self-styled "goat guys" Cam Hines and Dave Bonighton have clocked up a decade in craft brewing and generously mentored dozens of aspiring players over the years. Open nights are staged every Friday at the brewery, and attract a mixed crowd of ale lovers and funky Melbourne types, with brewery tours on offer.

BEER

ALPHA PALE ALE

AMERICAN PALE ALE 5.2% ABV
Rich, caramel-toffee malt character; resinous hop flavour; and, finally, a bold, bitter finish.

DOGBOLTER

DARK LAGER 5.2% ABV
Roasty, dark chocolate notes; complex mid-palate; smooth, coffee-like finish.

BOHEMIAN PILSNER

CZECH PILSNER 5% ABV
A solid maltiness to the pilsner is well balanced with a generous hop bitterness.

REDBACK

KRISTALL WEIZEN 4.7% ABV
Pale straw; banana, vanilla, and clove hints; delicate complexity; crisp, refreshing finish.

MOO BREW PILSNER

CZECH PILSNER 5% ABV
Bright golden, with finely beaded bubbles; honey-ish malt character balanced by herbal hop bitterness.

MOO BREW PALE ALE

AMERICAN PALE ALE 4.9% ABV
Citrus aromatics; grapefruit notes dominate mid-palate, rounded out with a substantial, tingling bitter finish.

HIGHTAIL ALE

ENGLISH PALE ALE 4.5% ABV
Cloudy amber; chewy malt, with bristling hop flavour and an after bitterness.

SUREFOOT STOUT

MEDIUM STOUT 5% ABV
Attractive mocha aromatics; dusty, roasty characters with treacle hints; restrained bitterness.

MURRAY'S

3443 Nelson Bay Road, Bobs Farm (Port Stephens) New South Wales 2316, Australia
www.murraysbrewingco.au

The ironically named Pub With No Beer takes its name from a popular song by late country singer Slim Dusty and is the rather unlikely base for an exciting new craft brewery.

BREWING SECRET Murray's has pushed the boundaries of traditional beer styles and rolled out a handful of flavour-packed, limited edition brews.

REDOAK

201 Clarence Street, Sydney, New South Wales 2000, Australia
www.redoak.com.au

The Redoak Boutique Beer Café is the showcase for a staggering array of beer styles from David Hollyoak, one of Australia's most awarded brewers, despite the fact that he only launched his beer range in mid-2004. A fruit-infused ale, a Baltic porter, a hand-pumped English bitter, and a wood-aged barley wine are just a few on offer.

WIG & PEN

Canberra House Arcade, Civic, Canberra, Australian Capital Territory 2601, Australia
www.wigandpen.com.au

Real ale diehards come for the hand-pumped house beers, but there's a beer style for every taste at this busy brewpub, situated in the centre of the nation's capital. Seasonal brews might include an annual imperial stout, Berliner Weisse, and whatever takes brewer Richard Watkins' fancy. A haven of characterful beers.

DUX DE LUX

Cnr Hereford & Montreal Streets, Christchurch, New Zealand
www.duxbrew.co.nz

One of South Island's most revered craft brewers, The Dux has brewpubs in Christchurch and Queenstown. A broad range of styles is produced under the watchful eye of brewmaster, winemaker, and chef Richard Fife.

BREWING SECRET Visitors to The Dux are likely to be rewarded with limited release seasonal specialities.

ANGRY MAN
PALE ALE 5% ABV
Complex biscuit and toffee flavours are balanced by citrus and lychee aromas from the New Zealand hops.

SASSY BELGIAN BLONDE
BELGIAN ALE 4.5% ABV
Distinctly Belgian character with robust yeast notes, and a hint of fennel; dry, yeasty finish.

LAMBIC BLACKBERRY WHEAT BEER
SOUR ALE 5% ABV
Tart and refreshing, the locally grown blackberries add a new dimension to Lambic-style beer.

SPECIAL RESERVE
WOOD-AGED ALE 12% ABV
Fermented and conditioned for many months in oak barrels, the beers have a symphony of complex tastes and textures.

BULLDOG BEST BITTER
ENGLISH BITTER 4% ABV
Soft, fruity nose; biscuity malt notes balanced by zingy hop flavours and a firm bitterness.

CREAMY STOUT
DRY STOUT 6% ABV
Silky body, with chocolate and caramel notes; distinctly smooth, satisfying finish.

NOR'WESTER
ENGLISH PALE ALE 6.5% ABV
Early grainy sweetness, then hints of nuts and smoke, fruity esters and a deep, lingering, hoppy finish.

GINGER TOM
SPECIALITY ALE 4% ABV
Golden in colour, it is an easy-drinking, ginger-flavoured beer, with a citrus nose.

BREWERY

EMERSON'S BREWERY
14 Wickliffe Street, Dunedin,
New Zealand
www.emersons.co.nz

New Zealand's most awarded microbrewery offers an enviable portfolio of year-round beers, as well as seasonal specialities such as Taieri George, a spiced dark ale, and an NZ clam stout. Its delightful session beer called Bookbinder is available both on tap and in a bottle.

GALBRAITH'S
2 Mt Eden Road, Grafton,
Auckland, New Zealand
www.alehouse.co.nz

Located in a former library, New Zealand's first real ale brewpub is best known for its home-brewed English-style ales – all served by hand pump. Visitors can also enjoy an excellent Abbey-style ale and a couple of flavoursome lagers, as well as a fine range of imports and craft beers from other New Zealand brewers.

MAC'S
27 Napier Street, Freeman's Bay,
Auckland, New Zealand
www.macs.co.nz

Eighteen years after opening the country's first microbrewery in an old cider factory in Nelson, former All Black rugby player Terry McCashin sold the Mac's brand to Lion Breweries in 1999. Since then the beer range has been extended and production split between Nelson and the Shed 22 brewery, on the Wellington waterfront.

MOA
Jacksons Rd, RD3 Blenheim, New Zealand
www.moabeer.co.nz

Nestled among vines in Marlborough's wine country is Moa's brewery and tasting room – the brainchild of winemaker Josh Scott, who wanted to make super premium beers with the winemaking techniques used for Champagne-style sparkling wines.

BREWING SECRET Moa's larger 750ml (1¼ pints) bottles undergo the full *méthode traditionelle* production regime.

BEER

PILSNER
PILSNER 4.9% ABV
Citrus and passion fruit bursts out of the malty sweet beer. Crisp, dry finish.

LONDON PORTER
PORTER 5% ABV
A roasted barley nose is balanced by hints of sweetness and some coffee notes. The finish is creamy smooth.

BELLRINGERS BITTER
ENGLISH BEST BITTER 4.5% ABV
Copper-coloured ale with a biscuity, toffee-like palate, plenty of earthy hops, and an appetizingly dry finish.

BOB HUDSON'S BITTER
ENGLISH BITTER 4% ABV
A full-flavoured session bitter very much in the vein of the English pale ale Timothy Taylor's Landlord.

SASSY RED
NEW WORLD BEST BITTER 4.5% ABV
A sweetish amber brew with a leafy, hopsack aroma and suggestions of toffee, nuts, chocolate, and toast.

BLACK MAC
DRY STOUT 4.8% ABV
A full-bodied, flavoursome, stout-like dark lager, with roasted malt, dark chocolate, caramel, and liquorice.

MOA ORIGINAL
BOTTLE-CONDITIONED PILS 5% ABV
Extended yeast contact rewards this delightful dry, crisp pilsner with a savoury toastiness.

MOA BLANC
BOTTLE-CONDITIONED
WHEAT BEER 5% ABV
Dry, crisp, hints of banana and vanilla; soft natural carbonation.

NEW ZEALAND'S BEST-KNOWN BEERS

New Zealand's best known domestic beers are all made with a high proportion of sugar and are warm-fermented with lager yeasts.

As a result of this process, the beers tend to be sweet, light-bodied, and, by European lager standards, somewhat estery. The market leaders, Speight's, Tui, and Export Gold are made by the country's two dominant brewers, Lion, now owned by Japanese brewer Kirin, and DB. There are three basic Kiwi beer styles. A bronze or amber-coloured brew is confusingly termed "draught" — even when packaged in bottles and cans! Anything paler is usually identified as "lager" (the brand name often suffixed with the word "gold"). A deeper coloured beer is simply known as "dark". In the case of New Zealand's "draughts" and "darks", the term ale is often erroneously appended. In the last decade, there has been a strong swing away from traditional Kiwi styles in favour of paler, crisper, so-called premium lagers. These days, New Zealand's most famous international beer, Steinlager (which is now available in both Classic and Pure versions), competes with locally brewed-under-license lagers, such as Heineken, Stella Artois, and Carlsberg, as well as a plethora of imported brands from Europe, America, Asia, and Australia.

SPEIGHT'S GOLD MEDAL ALE
(LAGER 4% ABV)
TUI (LAGER 4% ABV) *left*
EXPORT GOLD (LAGER 4% ABV)
centre
STEINLAGER (LAGER
5% ABV) *right*

MONTEITH'S

Corner of Turamaha & Herbert Streets, Greymouth, New Zealand
www.monteiths.co.nz

Now one of four breweries operated by the DB group (which itself is indirectly overseen by Heineken), Monteith's can trace its roots back to 1868. Although many of Monteith's beers are produced elsewhere, the Greymouth brewery — with its rare coal-fired boilers and open fermenters — is well worth a visit.

THE MUSSEL INN

Onekaka, Takaka, Golden Bay, New Zealand
www.musselinn.co.nz

Quirky, rustic, and ecologically aware, The Mussel Inn brewpub-cum-café is located in one of the country's most remote and unspoilt regions. The famous Captain Cooker Manuka Beer is affectionately known as "The Pig", a reference to New Zealand's wild pigs, which were first released by Cook. It is also brewed under license by Belgium's Proefbrouwerij.

SHAKESPEARE HOTEL

61 Albert Street, Corner of Wyndham & Albert Streets, Auckland, New Zealand
www.shakespearehotel.co.nz

The Shakespeare has been open as a bar and hotel for more than 100 years, however, in 1986 it became New Zealand's first new generation brewpub and started brewing. The list of beers produced is almost endless and always changing, but usually the beers will have a Shakespeare-themed name. Indeed the brewer proclaims that "none of our beers are ever quite the same".

MONTEITH'S BLACK BEER
BLACK LAGER 5.2% ABV
Soft and sweetish, with coffee, chocolate, and nut flavours — and often a hint of banana too.

MONTEITH'S BOHEMIAN PILSNER
PILSNER 5% ABV
Mild for the style, this firm-bodied brew has a grassy hop note and a lingering, sweetish finish.

CAPTAIN COOKER MANUKA BEER
WOODY AMBER LAGER 5% ABV
Seasoned with leaves from native shrubs, this is a fairly sweet and perfumy brew.

MONKEY PUZZLE
BELGIAN ABBEY-STYLE ALE 10% ABV
A copper-coloured brew that's big, spicy, and warming, yet delicately balanced and remarkably suppable!

KING LEAR OLD ALE
ENGLISH OLD ALE 8% ABV
Full-bodied, ruby-hued brew, with orange, toffee, and chocolate notes. Long, floral, hop-driven finish.

HOP DOGGIE IPA
INDIA PALE ALE 5.3% ABV
Marvellous hoppy, a malt sweetness gives way to a pleasing, bitter finish.

BREWERY

STEAM BREWING

186 James Fletcher Drive,
Otahuhu, Auckland, New Zealand
www.steambrewing.co.nz

The brewery was set up in 1995 to produce beers exclusively for the Cock & Bull pub in Pakuranga. Nine years and five pubs later, the company acquired the much larger Auckland Breweries site, complete with a high-tech packaging line. In addition to the Cock & Bull beers, the company now produces several beers under license.

THREE BOYS BREWERY

Unit 10, Garlands Rd, Woolston, Christchurch, New Zealand
www.threeboysbrewery.co.nz

Microbiologist Ralph Bungard employs a broad range of yeasts to produce tasty Kiwi interpretations of classic beer styles. He is the senior "Boy" – the others are his sons Marek and Quinn.

BREWING SECRET The brewery's limited release seasonal brews include an excellent Oyster Stout in winter and a fragrant Golden Ale in summer.

TUATARA BREWING

7 Sheffield Street, Paraparaumu 5032, Kapiti Coast, New Zealand
www.tuatarabrewing.co.nz

Named after an endangered native reptile, the brewery is located in hill country, about an hour's drive north of Wellington. Its beers are widely distributed in the lower North Island, and the brewery's success prompted the installation of a larger, German-designed brewhouse in 2007. Tuatara beers are often served on hand pump at The Malthouse pub in Wellington.

THE TWISTED HOP

7B Parkhouse Road, Wigram, Christchurch 8042, New Zealand
www.thetwistedhop.co.nz

Its ales may be English in style, but The Twisted Hop is no typical English pub. A former warehouse set in a quiet back street with a pleasant kerbside drinking area, "The Hop" is bright, airy, and modern, with internal windows offering views into the brewery. The beer is also available at The Prince Albert pub in Nelson.

BEER

EPIC PALE ALE

AMERICAN PALE ALE 5.4% ABV
Robust interpretation of the style, with an explosion of hop resins (US Cascade) and sweet malt.

MONK'S HABIT

AMERICAN AMBER ALE 7% ABV
Brewed exclusively for the Cock & Bull pub chain. Sweet malt, balanced by floral and resiny hop flavours.

THREE BOYS WHEAT

WITBIER 5% ABV
Plenty of zesty lemon and coriander notes, with a hint of ginger.
A spritzy and quenching brew.

THREE BOYS PORTER

ROBUST PORTER 5.2% ABV
Rich mocha notes dominate a silky palate, while heavily roasted grains and hops compete in the dry finish.

TUATARA BOHEMIAN PILSNER

NEW WORLD PILSNER 5% ABV
Generous late hopping (with locally grown Motueka hops) results in a fresh, hessian-like, hopsack character.

TUATARA INDIA PALE ALE

INDIA PALE ALE 5% ABV
Although there's some nutty malt sweetness, earthy hops dominate the aroma and palate – a tasty ale.

CHALLENGER

ENGLISH SPECIAL BITTER 5% ABV
Copper coloured and full bodied, with a fragrant hop aroma, toffeeish palate, and a long, hop-driven finish.

GOLDING BITTER

ENGLISH BITTER 3.7% ABV
Light, crisp, and flavoursome golden-coloured session bitter, with a fresh, leafy hop character.

Little Creatures began in 2000, and its bottle-conditioned, American-style Pale Ale has proved hugely popular in Australia.

GLOSSARY

abbey ale Belgian family of strong, fruity beers inspired by monastery brewers.

ABV Alcohol by volume, expressed as a percentage. A measure of the strength of a beer.

adjuncts Strictly speaking, anything added to the brewing process other than barley, *hops*, *yeast*, and water. More usually refers to unmalted grains such as rice, barley, oats, and maize, added to increase alcohol content and lighten flavour.

ale A beer made with *ale yeasts*. Styles include golden ale, brown ale, *mild*, and *bitter*.

ale yeasts *Yeasts* used in traditional *top-fermenting* ales, originating from recycled yeast skimmed from the surface of the last batch. They ferment at room temperature.

alt, altbier German style of beer similar to British *bitter* or *pale ale*, especially associated with Düsseldorf.

aromatic hops A term used to distinguish the floral and fruitier *hops*, such as Cascade and Goldings, that are used to impart additional flavours and aromas to beer. Aromatic hops are added later in the boil, or even after the boil, than *bittering hops*, to maintain the subtlety of their attributes.

barley wine An extra-strong style of *ale*, originally English, but now produced by many US brewers.

Berliner Weisse A pale, *top-fermented wheat beer* from northern Germany.

bière de garde "Keeping beer" traditional to northern France. Brewed in winter and spring, then bottled and stored to be drunk later in the year by thirsty farmhands. The style is now brewed year round in several brewing nations.

bitter, best bitter English beer style, usually designating a well-hopped *ale*. Best bitter usually refers to stronger variants of the beer.

bittering hops *Hop* varieties such as Chinook and Fuggles that are rich in chemical compounds that result in the bitter taste sensation in beer and are used to balance the sweetness of *malt*. As distinct from *aromatic hops*.

blond, blonde A mainly French and Belgian term for a golden beer.

bock A German term for a strong beer – formerly seasonal, but not any more. Several variations include the even-stronger doppelbock and urbock, made in the original 13th-century style. *See also eisbock*.

bottle-conditioning The process by which beers are bottled with live *yeast* and sometimes fermentable sugars, extending storage life and allowing flavour and effervescence to develop further over time.

bottom-fermenting Term used to describe *yeasts* of the *Saccharomyces carlsbergensis* strain that are used to make lager. During lagering (storage), the *yeast* sinks to the bottom of the brew, producing a clean-tasting beer.

brettanomyces A semi-wild genus of *yeast* used in *lambic* beers and some *porters* and *stouts*. Provides a distinctive aroma and flavour.

brew kettle The vessel in which the *wort* is boiled with *hops* to combine their flavours, usually for about 90 minutes.

brewpub A bar or restaurant with its own small brewery on the premises.

broyhan *Top-fermented* pale *wheat beer* created in Hanover, Germany in 1526.

burton union A system of fermentation in galleries of linked casks, in which a stable *yeast* culture develops over time. Introduced in the 19th century in the brewing town of Burton upon Trent in England.

carbonation Carbonation is the cause of effervescence in beer, and is generated by the metabolic action of *yeast* or by the artificial introduction of pressurized gas.

cask conditioning, cask ale The practice of bringing draught beer to maturity in the cask, in the conditioning room of a brewery or in the cellar of a pub. Maturity time ranges from a week to a year or more.

C-hops Term used for *hops* with a very high aromatic potential, which convey especially grapefruit and resiny flavours. They are known by this term because many have names beginning with C (Cascade, Chinook, Cluster, Centennial, for example), but it also encompasses Amarillo and Simcoe.

contract brewing Commercial arrangement in which the creator of a beer contracts to have it produced at a brewery with spare capacity.

copper Alternative name for the *brew kettle*. Many copper kettles survive, but today a greater number are made from stainless steel.

craft brewer Term referring to breweries opened since the late 1970s that produce specialist beers.

curaçao A small, bitter orange grown in the former Dutch colony of Curaçao in the Caribbean. The dried peel is used in some Belgian *wheat beers*, most notably Hoegaarden.

decoction A process in which some of the *wort* is removed from the mash tun, heated to a higher temperature, then returned to the brew. It helps produce complex caramel flavours and clearer beers.

doppelbock *see bock*

dortmunder Pale golden, full-bodied, *bottom-fermented* beer from Dortmund in Germany.

double, dubbel A Belgian *abbey ale*, stronger than a pilsner but less so than a triple or trippel.

dry hopping The addition of *hops* to the finished brew to enhance its aroma and flavour.

dunkel, dunkler bock Dunkel means "dark" in German, and the term most readily applies to dark *lagers* though it can also be applied to dark *wheat beers*. A dunkler bock is a *bock*-strength dark lager.

eisbock The strongest type of *bock*, lagered in ice-cold cellars, with frozen water crystals filtered off to increase the strength of the beer.

ester, estery An ester is a natural chemical compound that imparts fruity and spicy flavours (banana, strawberry, clove). Consequently, estery is a tasting note associated with some beers.

export Term often used for a premium beer, except in Germany, however, where it indicates a *Dortmunder*-style beer.

extreme beers Term originating in the US to describe a wide range of beer styles that are extraordinary in some way. Unusual ingredients, wild *yeast* fermentation, bourbon-keg ageing, or very high alcohol content might earn a beer the title "extreme".

fermentation The conversion of malt sugars to alcohol and CO_2 by the action of *yeast*.

feistbeer German term for any beer that is traditionally brewed for a festival. Sometimes it refers to *märzen* and *Oktoberfest* styles, both strong variants of *Vienna lager*.

gose Distinctively salty style of *wheat beer* native to Leipzig.

grist Ground *malt* (or other grains) which, along with warm water, forms the basis of *wort*.

gueuze, geuze A blend of young and old *lambic* beers, blended to produce a sparkling, refreshing beer.

head The foam that forms on top of a beer when it is poured.

hefeweizen German term for *wheat beer* with *yeast* sediment. "Hefe" is a German word for yeast.

hell, helles German term designating a pale-coloured beer.

hops Hop flowers – in dried, pellet, or resinous form – are added to beer to give flavour, aroma, and a bitterness to complement the sweetness of *malt*. See also *aromatic hops*, *bittering hops*, and *Noble hops*.

hop back A sieve-like vessel through which a brew is filtered. Its purpose is either to remove *hop* petals, or, when pre-filled with fresh hops, to add more flavour to the brew.

imperial stout Extra-strong *stout* made for export; the name stems from the beer's popularity with the Russian Imperial court.

IPA India Pale Ale; a robust and heavily-hopped beer, which has nothing to do with being exported to India from Britain. The style is constantly evolving and is now produced worldwide.

kellerbier "Cellar beer" in German; usually an unfiltered *lager*, hoppy and only lightly carbonated.

kölsch Light style of top-fermenting golden *ale* first brewed in and around the city of Cologne (Köln).

krieken A Belgian *lambic* in which macerated cherries are fermented, giving a tart, fruity flavour.

lace Pattern of foam left clinging to the sides of the glass.

lactic, lactic acid An acid that imparts a sour flavour to beer, produced when *lactobacilli* metabolize sugars. A tasting note for some beers.

lactobacillus A family of bacteria, usually benign, that convert sugars to lactic acid. The resulting sourness defines certain styles, such as *Berliner weisse*.

lager Family of *bottom-fermented* beer styles. Examples range from black beers such as *schwarzbier* to the more familiar golden pilsner.

lambic Designates beers fermented by wild, airborne *yeasts* in small, rural breweries in the Payottenland region of Belgium.

late-hopping The technique of adding *hops* to the brew kettle in the final minutes of boiling, so imparting pronounced hop flavours.

lees *Yeast* deposits resulting from secondary fermentation in the bottle.

malt Barley or other grains that have undergone a process of controlled germination, which is arrested at a point when the seed contains high concentrations of starches. After drying, kilning, or roasting, the malt may be made into *grist* for brewing.

maltings A facility in which the grain is steeped in water, allowed partially to germinate, and then dried.

märzen Originally a German style of medium-strong beer brewed in March (März in German) and matured until September or October. These days, the style of beer may be brewed and drunk year round.

mash The mixture created when the *grist* is steeped in hot water. The mashing process breaks down grain starches into fermentable sugars.

mash bill A north American term for the proportion of different grains used in the mash.

méthode champenoise, méthode traditionelle A form of *bottle conditioning* that follows the method for creating Champagne. A secondary fermentation is achieved in the bottle by adding *yeast* and fermentable sugars. Beers made with this method are usually produced in Champagne-style bottles and the beer can usually mature for several years.

microbrewery Generic term for small breweries founded from the 1970s onwards producing relatively small quantities of beer. The US Brewers Association defines the term as a brewery that produces less than 15,000 US barrels (17,600 hl) per year.

mild A lightly-hopped and thus mild-tasting *ale*, usually of modest alcoholic strength. Traditionally associated with the industrial regions of Wales and the English midlands.

milk stout A sweet *stout* made with unfermentable lactose sugars, derived from milk, that sweeten the beer's final taste.

münchner (munich dunkel) A German style of dark *lager* that was developed in Munich.

Noble hops Term used specifically for a group of four traditional aromatic varieties of *hops* that are low in bitterness: Hallertau, Žatec (or Saaz), Tettnanger, and Spalter.

nonic glass A classic style of smooth-sided beer glass, typically made in half-pint and pint sizes. It is characterized by a bulge in its profile that aids grip.

Northwest hops Refers to the Pacific Northwest of the US – the country's main *hop*-growing region. Cluster hops were traditionally grown here, but now many other, especially aromatic, varieties are grown too.

oatmeal stout A revived style, popular in the USA, brewed with up to 5 per cent oats.

Oktoberfest A two-week beer festival held in the Bavarian city of Munich in Germany.

original gravity A measure of density of *wort*. High density indicates abundant fermentable sugars. The more sugar is present, the stronger the resulting beer will be.

oud bruin "Old brown"; a Flanders-style beer with a lengthy ageing period of up to a year.

pale ale A style of beer that originated in Britain, characterized by the use of pale *malts*. It mostly applies to bottled beers.

pasteurization Heat treatment process applied to beer to maintain its stability during storage. Arguably, pasteurization deadens the flavour of beer marginally.

pilsner, pils A popular style of golden *lager* pioneered in the Czech town of Plzeň, or Pilsen.

porter A family of very dark beers characterized by dark chocolate *malt* flavours and assertive *hop* bitterness.

priming The addition of sugar to a beer before it is bottled to encourage *carbonation*.

rauchbier A German style of *lager* made from *malt* that has been smoked over beechwood fires. The beer is a Franconian speciality.

reinheitsgebot The German beer purity law of 1516; now superceded by updated legislation but still a guiding principle in German beer-making. Under its ruling, beers must not contain anything but water, *yeast*, *malt*, and *hops*.

saison Originally a Belgian beer style; a dry, strongish *ale*, traditionally brewed in winter for drinking in summer. These days, the style can be produced year round, and it is usually *bottle-conditioned*.

schwarzbier "Black beer" in German. A dark, opaque style of *lager*.

seasonal beers Beers made for limited periods of sale, usually to suit climatic conditions at a given point of the year (such as *märzens* and *saisons*), or to celebrate a holiday or commemorate a historical event – a *festbier* for *Oktoberfest*, for example.

session beer Term describing an easy-drinking beer that is relatively low in alcohol and thus suitable for drinking in quantity.

sour ales, sour beer Originating in Flanders, these *ales* typically undergo ageing for between 18 months and two years in oak *tuns*, during which they gain a sharply thirst-quenching acetic character.

stein A traditional German tankard, made either of glass or ceramic (stein translates as "stone").

stout A dark style of beer, usually *top-fermenting*, that is made with highly roasted grain.

tap, taproom On-site bar or pub that serves a brewery's products directly to visiting drinkers.

top-fermenting Descriptive of all ale *yeasts* of the *Saccharomyces cerevisiae* strain, which produce a thick foam at the top of the *fermentation* tank.

tun A vessel in which mash is steeped.

triple, tripel, trippel Traditionally the strongest Belgian *abbey ale*; though there are now quadruples to exceed them. In more general use, it denotes a very strong *ale*.

urbock see bock

urtype "Original type" in German; term used to emphasize that a beer is an authentic example of an established style.

Vienna lager Bronze-to-red *lager* with a sweetish *malt* aroma and flavour. Pioneered by Austrian brewer Anton Dreher.

weiss, weisse "White" in German, denoting a *wheat beer*.

weizenbier German generic term for *wheat beer*.

wheat beer Beer containing a high level of *malted* wheat. Usually *top-fermented* and often *bottle-conditioned*. Pale and cloudy, with suspended *yeast* particles, creamy-textured and sweetish.

wild beer Beer that has been spontaneously *fermented* by wild *yeasts*, through being left exposed to the elements for a period of time. The classic example is Belgian *lambic*.

wit, witbier "White", "white beer" in Belgian: *wheat beer*.

wort An infusion containing fermentable sugars that is produced by the *mashing* process. The wort is filtered, boiled, and cooled before *yeast* is added to initiate the process of *fermentation*.

yeast A large family of unicellular fungal organisms, certain species of which are active agents in brewing and baking.

Yorkshire squares Square *fermenting* vessels associated with traditional brewing in the English county of Yorkshire. Still in use at Samuel Smith's Brewery and at Black Sheep. It is said to produce a remarkably well-balanced beer between sweet *maltiness* and *yeasty* sourness.

YOUR TASTING NOTES

You can use these pages to make your own notes about the appearance, aroma, flavour, and finish of different beers that you have the opportunity to sample. For more guidance about tasting beer, see pp36–37.

BEER	STYLE	BREWERY	CITY	STRENGTH

COLOUR	AROMA	TASTE	FINISH	VERDICT	
				AGAIN & AGAIN SAME AGAIN NEVER AGAIN	
				AGAIN & AGAIN SAME AGAIN NEVER AGAIN	
				AGAIN & AGAIN SAME AGAIN NEVER AGAIN	
				AGAIN & AGAIN SAME AGAIN NEVER AGAIN	
				AGAIN & AGAIN SAME AGAIN NEVER AGAIN	
				AGAIN & AGAIN SAME AGAIN NEVER AGAIN	
				AGAIN & AGAIN SAME AGAIN NEVER AGAIN	
				AGAIN & AGAIN SAME AGAIN NEVER AGAIN	
				AGAIN & AGAIN SAME AGAIN NEVER AGAIN	
				AGAIN & AGAIN SAME AGAIN NEVER AGAIN	
				AGAIN & AGAIN SAME AGAIN NEVER AGAIN	
				AGAIN & AGAIN SAME AGAIN NEVER AGAIN	
				AGAIN & AGAIN SAME AGAIN NEVER AGAIN	
				AGAIN & AGAIN SAME AGAIN NEVER AGAIN	

YOUR TASTING NOTES CONT.

BEER	STYLE	BREWERY	CITY	STRENGTH

COLOUR	AROMA	TASTE	FINISH	VERDICT	
				AGAIN & AGAIN	
				SAME AGAIN	
				NEVER AGAIN	
				AGAIN & AGAIN	
				SAME AGAIN	
				NEVER AGAIN	
				AGAIN & AGAIN	
				SAME AGAIN	
				NEVER AGAIN	
				AGAIN & AGAIN	
				SAME AGAIN	
				NEVER AGAIN	
				AGAIN & AGAIN	
				SAME AGAIN	
				NEVER AGAIN	
				AGAIN & AGAIN	
				SAME AGAIN	
				NEVER AGAIN	
				AGAIN & AGAIN	
				SAME AGAIN	
				NEVER AGAIN	
				AGAIN & AGAIN	
				SAME AGAIN	
				NEVER AGAIN	
				AGAIN & AGAIN	
				SAME AGAIN	
				NEVER AGAIN	
				AGAIN & AGAIN	
				SAME AGAIN	
				NEVER AGAIN	
				AGAIN & AGAIN	
				SAME AGAIN	
				NEVER AGAIN	
				AGAIN & AGAIN	
				SAME AGAIN	
				NEVER AGAIN	
				AGAIN & AGAIN	
				SAME AGAIN	
				NEVER AGAIN	
				AGAIN & AGAIN	
				SAME AGAIN	
				NEVER AGAIN	
				AGAIN & AGAIN	
				SAME AGAIN	
				NEVER AGAIN	

YOUR TASTING NOTES CONT.

BEER	STYLE	BREWERY	CITY	STRENGTH

COLOUR	AROMA	TASTE	FINISH	VERDICT	
				AGAIN & AGAIN	
				SAME AGAIN	
				NEVER AGAIN	
				AGAIN & AGAIN	
				SAME AGAIN	
				NEVER AGAIN	
				AGAIN & AGAIN	
				SAME AGAIN	
				NEVER AGAIN	
				AGAIN & AGAIN	
				SAME AGAIN	
				NEVER AGAIN	
				AGAIN & AGAIN	
				SAME AGAIN	
				NEVER AGAIN	
				AGAIN & AGAIN	
				SAME AGAIN	
				NEVER AGAIN	
				AGAIN & AGAIN	
				SAME AGAIN	
				NEVER AGAIN	
				AGAIN & AGAIN	
				SAME AGAIN	
				NEVER AGAIN	
				AGAIN & AGAIN	
				SAME AGAIN	
				NEVER AGAIN	
				AGAIN & AGAIN	
				SAME AGAIN	
				NEVER AGAIN	
				AGAIN & AGAIN	
				SAME AGAIN	
				NEVER AGAIN	
				AGAIN & AGAIN	
				SAME AGAIN	
				NEVER AGAIN	
				AGAIN & AGAIN	
				SAME AGAIN	
				NEVER AGAIN	
				AGAIN & AGAIN	
				SAME AGAIN	
				NEVER AGAIN	
				AGAIN & AGAIN	
				SAME AGAIN	
				NEVER AGAIN	

INDEX

The Contributors

Tim Hampson, Editor-in-Chief of this book, is a journalist and writer who for many years has travelled the world in pursuit of the perfect beer. His published works include *World Beer* (DK), *Eyewitness Companion Beer* (DK), *Great Beers* (DK), *101 Beer Days Out*, *London's Riverside Pubs*, *London's Best Pubs*, *London's Best Style Bars*, *Room at the Inn*, *The Oxford Companion to Beer*, and *1001 Beers You Must Try Before You Die*. He writes the news for *What's Brewing* newspaper and his work has been published in many periodicals including *The Telegraph*, *Guardian*, *Drinks International*, and *American Brewer*. He is a regular broadcaster on beer and pubs, is a judge at many beer competitions around the world, and is currently chairman of the British Guild of Beer Writers. In his writing for this book, he was assisted by **Adrian Tierney-Jones**.

Stan Hieronymus is a lifelong journalist who has made beer his "beat" since 1993, authoring four beer-related books, contributing to several others, writing hundreds of articles for scores of periodicals, and founding the Beer Oral History Institute. His work has won scores of awards and he was the USA Beer Writer of the Year in 1999. Since 1998 he has been editor at Realbeer.com, taking a leave of absence in 2008 to spend 15 months travelling – and more than occasionally visiting breweries – with his wife, Daria Labinsky, and their daughter, Sierra. For this book, Stan wrote the section on beers of the USA.

Werner Obalski has been a journalist for 30 years, specializing in spirits, wine, and of course beer. He also reviews bars and restaurants for several guides. Among his books are *365 Wine Tips* (Dumont Verlag, Köln), *Sherry* (Haedecke Verlag, Weil der Stadt), and *Tequila* (Haedecke Verlag Weil der Stadt). Werner is member in the organization Food Editor's Club, Germany, and he is also judge and member of the ISW (the International Spirits Competition in Neustadt, Germany). Werner lives and writes in Munich, and here contributed the section on Germany's beers.

Alastair Gilmour is one of Britain's leading regional journalists. He is Features Editor of *The Journal*, the daily newspaper for the northeast of England, where his specialist work on beer has an extensive and enthusiastic following. He was Glenfiddich Food & Drink Awards regional writer, 2004 and 2007, and has been the British Guild of Beer Writers' "Writer of the Year" on four occasions between 1998 and 2007. He has been a judge at several international beer competitions, including The Great British Beer Festival in London and the International Master Bartender Awards in New York and Prague. Alastair wrote the sections on beer in the British Isles and in the Czech Republic.

Joris Pattyn was a founding member of Objectieve Bierproevers (OBP) in the mid-1980s, since when he has helped organize and has spoken at many beer festivals, seminars, and competitions. He has also been a judge at several international competitions, including, most recently, the World Beer Cup, 2008, in San Diego. He has written for publications in the UK and USA, and co-authored *Lambic/kland* with Tim Webb and Chris Pollard. He is also soon to publish *100 Belgian Beers to Try Before You Die*. Joris is a member of Zythos in Belgium, PINT in the Netherlands, CAMRA in the UK, Les Amis de la Bière in France, and ABO in the Czech Republic. For this book, he wrote about Belgian beer.

Lorenzo Dabove was born in Liguria, though today he lives and works in Milan and Genoa as the Cultural Director of Unionbirrai. He is the foremost expert on Italian craft beer, and is internationally recognized for his efforts to promote Italian beer and traditional lambic brewing as well. He has judged in such prestigious contests as the World Beer Cup in 2004, 2006, and 2008, and the European Beer Star in Gräfelfing, Bavaria, in 2006 and 2007. He wrote the book *Le Birre*, published in 2005 by Gribaudo Editore, Savigliano. Lorenzo contributed the section on Italian beer.

Gilbert Delos is a French journalist and beerologist. For more than 20 years, he has tasted the beers of Europe – especially those of his native France. Among the books he has written on the subject are *Beers of the World* (Tiger Books, 1994) and *The Master Chefs and Beer* (Somogy, Paris, 2003). He is also President of The Friends of Beer in Ile-de-France – an organization of beer lovers located in Paris and its environs. He regularly leads tastings of beers. Gilbert wrote on French beer for this book.

Conrad Seidl was born in Vienna, where he lives as staff writer and political commentator for the daily newspaper *Der Standard*. For his beer writing he uses the "Bierpapst" moniker. His columns appear regularly in the gourmet magazine *Falstaff* and in the trade magazine *Der Getränkefachgroßhandel*. He has a monthly TV show, which can also be seen on the Internet (www.bierpapst.tv). His career as a beer writer started with a guide to Austrian beer (*Hurra Bier!*) in 1990, and he has now published more than 25 books. He is a member of the British Guild of Beer Writers in London, the Gesellschaft für Geschichte und Bibliographie des Brauwesens in Berlin, the Confrérie Gambrinus in Luxembourg, and the Bier Convent International in Munich. Conrad wrote about Austrian and Swiss beer for this book.

Ron Pattinson is a member of the British Guild of Beer Writers, and has written extensively about European beer. His pub guides, written in a gloriously chatty style, have been used by thousands of beer lovers. Bad jokes, a superfluity of statistics, and an obsession with Barclay Perkins, Dark Mild, and Leipziger Gose litter his many writings on the history of beer. He lives in Amsterdam. Ron contributed the section on beers of the Netherlands.

Laura Stadler-Jensen is an American freelance journalist based in Copenhagen, Denmark. She specializes in Scandinavian culture and writes on topics that include gastronomy, travel, and design. She is married to Lasse Fredrik Jensen, an accomplished Danish chef, who provides insight into exciting culinary trends such as beer pairing and molecular gastronomy. Laura wrote the sections on Denmark and Scandinavian beer.

Bryan Harrell is Californian by birth, but has lived in Japan since 1977. He has been a writer and correspondent for several US magazines, and has also extensively researched the beer scene in Japan for the late, eminent drinks writer Michael Jackson, contributing to several of Jackson's books. Bryan has written books on cycling and home brewing, currently publishes the monthly *Brews News* (www.bento.com/brews.html), and writes a regular beer column in Tokyo's *Metropolis* magazine (www.metropolis.co.jp/tokyo/recent/beer.asp). Bryan wrote the Japan section.

Willie Simpson lives in a one-pub town in northwest Tasmania and is regarded as Australia's foremost beer writer; he has been commentating on the amber nectar and other alcoholic beverages for the past 20 years. His writing appears regularly in the *Sydney Morning Herald* and *The Age* (Melbourne) and he is the author of three books: *Amber & Black* (New Holland Publishing, 2001), *The Beer Bible* (Fairfax Publishing, 2006) and *Home Brew* (Penguin, 2007). More recently, he has become a craft brewery operator, with the opening of Seven Sheds – a brewery, meadery, and hop garden. Here he has written about Australian beer.

Geoff Griggs is New Zealand's only full-time specialist beer writer, commentator, judge, and educator. He has written for many magazines, and, in addition to writing a weekly beer column in his local regional newspaper, Geoff reviews beers for the country's largest supermarket group. Having judged at New Zealand-based international beer competitions for the last decade, Geoff was invited to join the judging panel at the world's largest beer competition, the World Beer Cup, in 2008.

Picture Credits

The publisher would like to thank the following for their kind permission to reproduce their photographs:

(Key: a-above; b-below/bottom; c-centre; f-far; l-left; r-right; t-top)

20 Alamy Images: Visions of America, LLC (tl). **Corbis:** (tc, ca, cb). **20–21 Alamy Images:** Andre Jenny. **21 Corbis:** Mitsu Yasukawa / Star Ledger (crb, br). **49 Alamy Images:** M Itani (clb). **66–67 Corbis:** Mark E. Gibson. **88–89 Corbis:** Frank Leonhardt / dpa. **102–103 Alamy Images:** Yadid Levy. **158 Alamy Images:** Werner Dieterich (tc). **159 Alamy Images:** AR Photo (t). **209 Alamy Images:** Cephas Picture Library (l). **267 Alamy Images:** Marina Spironetti. **304–305 Alamy Images:** Travel Pictures. **316 Alamy Images:** Nic Cleave Photography. **322 Alamy Images:** Andrew Wheeler

Additional studio and location photography by Thameside Media, Quentin Bacon, Joe Giacomet, Tim Hampson, Catherine Harries, Michael Jackson © DK/Michael Jackson, Roger Mapp © Rough Guides, Ian O'Leary © DK, Michael Schönwälder, Mark Thomas © Rough Guides, Peter Anderson

Jacket: (on spine) Berg Brauerei Ulrichsbier, Kinshachi Red Miso Lager; (on back) Sierra Nevada Anniversary Ale, Hogs Back Brewery TEA, Žatec Pivovar Blue Label, Butte Creek Brewing Pilsner, Heineken Premium Lager, Diageo/Guinness ® brand, La Trappe Quadrupel, Little Creatures Pale Ale

Maps: Casper Morris, Paul Eames, David Roberts, Iorwerth Walkins

The publishers would also like to thank the following people and organizations for their help in the preparation of this book: Beers of Europe, Finn at Utobeer, Jeff at Cracked Kettle, Lithuanian Beer, Belgian Beer Shop, The Grove Tavern, Karen Heptonstall, Malini McCauley, Jennifer Crake at Tourmaline Editions, Florian Bucher, Dorothee Whittaker, Tina Gehrrig, Monika Schlitzer, Ina Melzer at DK Verlag, Dirk Kaufman at DK Inc, Rebecca Carman, Shawn Christopher, Katerina Cerna, Wojciech Kozlowski, Agnes Ordog, Jürgen Scheunemann, Yumi Shigematsu, Diggory Williams, Nora Zimerman.

For editorial and design assistance, thanks to Angelika Dunsmore, Anna Sanders, Aparajita Barai, Arani Sinha, Barbara Campbell, Divya Chandhok, Jennifer Chung, Ligi John, Neha Samuel, Nigel King, Omar Lee, Sajili Oberoi, Sourabh Challariya, and Tarun Sharma. Special thanks to Vikas Sachdeva for photography.

The publishers would like to thank all the breweries that provided their kind assistance in sending bottles or bottle images to be used within this book and related works:

1516 brewing company, 32 Via dei Birrai, A. Le Coq, Aass Bryggeri - Copyright Aass Brewery, Norway, Abbaye des Rocs, Abita, Åbro Bryggeri, Achel, Achouffe, Acorn, Adnams, Affligem, Airbräu, Aktien, Alaskan, Aldaris, Aldersbacher - Courtesy of Brauerei Aldersbach, Alesmith- Chris Myers of alcoholandaphorisms.wordpress.com, Alfa, Alhambra, Allagash, Allersheimer, Almond 22, Alpine, Alpirsbacher- Courtesy of Alpirsbacher Klosterbrau, Altenburg- Courtesy of Altenburger Brauerei, Altöttinger, Alvinne, Amber, Amsterdam Brewery, Anchor, Andechs – © Kloster Andechs – ARGUM Falk Heller, Anderson Valley, Anheuser-Busch, Ankerbräu Nordlingen, Antares, Apatinska Pivara, Appalachian, Arcadia, Arco, Arkell's, Asia Pacific Breweries, Au Baron, Auer, August Schell, Augustiner, Avery, Ayinger, Baird Brewing- Fumiaki Yamazaki, Baladin, Ballast Point, Baltika, Banks's, Barba Roja, Barley, Barre, Batemans, Bath Ales, Bathams, Bavik, Bayern, Bear Republic, Beartown, Beba, Beierhaascht, Belhaven, Bell's, Bellevaux, Berentsens Brygghus, Berg, Bergquell, Berkshire, Berliner Kindlschultheiss, Bernard, Biermanufaktur, Engel, Biervision Monstein, Big Lamp, Big Rock, Big Sky, Binding, BIP-Beogradska, Birra del Borgo, Birrificio Italiano, Bischoff (Winnweiler), Bischofshof, Bitburger, BJ's, Black Isle, Black Sheep, Blonder Sörgyar, Blue Point, Bockor, Bocq, Bøgedal Bryghus, Boon, Boon Rawd, Bootleg, Borsodi Sörgyár, Boscos, Bosteels, Boulder, Boulevard, Boundary Bay, Bourganel, Brains, Brakspear, Brand, Brasseurs de Lorraine, Braugold, Braustolz, Breckenridge, Brewdog, Brewer's Art, Brewery, Brewpub, Bridge Road Brewers, Bridgeport, Bright, Brinkhoff's, Bristol, Brooklyn, Broughton, Brouwerij 't Ij, Browarmia, Brunehaut, Brüton, Bucher Bräu, Budels, Budweiser Budvar, Buffy's, Burton Bridge, Butcombe, Butte Creek- Butte Creek Brewing, Cairngorm, Calanda, Caldera, Caledonian, Camba Bavaria, Cambridge, Camden Town, Camerons, Cantillon, Capital, Captain Lawrence, Caracole, Carib, Carlsberg, Carlsberg Sweden AB, Cascade, Castelain, Castle/SAB, Cerná Hora, Cerveceria Bucanero, Cervesur, Cesu Alus, Chimay, Chodovar, Church-key Brewing, Citabiunda, Cittavecchia, City of Cambridge, Coedo, Coniston, Contreras, Coopers, Copper Dragon, Cornelyshaff, Cotleigh, Creemore Springs, Cropton, Crouch Vale, Cuauhtémoc Moctezuma, Dachsbräu Weilheim, Daleside, Damm, Damm Portugal, Darmstädter, Darwin, De 3 Horne, De dolle Brouwers, De Koninck, De la Senne, De Landtsheer, De Molen, De Prael, De Ranke, De Ryck, De Schans, De Struise, Deschutes, Detenice, Deux Rivières, Diamond Knot, Die Weisse, Diebels, Diekirch, Dinkelackerschwaben Bräu, Distelhäuser, Dithmarscher, Dixie, Döbler, Dogfish Head, Domus Huisbrouwerij, Donnington, Drake's, Dreher, Drie Fonteinen, Dubuisson, Ducato, Duck-Rabbit, Dugges Ale & Porterbryggeri, Dupont, Durham, Duvel Moortgat, Dux de Lux, Duyck, Ecaussinnes, Echigo, Eel River, Eggenberg, Eggenberg, Eichhof, Eichhorn, Einbecker - Courtesy of Einbecker Brauhaus, Elgood's, Elysian, Emerson's Brewery, Erdinger, Erl, Everards, Exmoor, Falken, Fantôme, Fässla, Faust, Felinfoel, Felsen Bräu, Feral, Fiege, Finlandia, Firestone Walker, Fish, Flensburger, Flossmoor Station, Flying Dog, Flying Fish, Foothills, Forstner, Founders, Four Peaks, Freeminer, Freiberger, Freistädter, Friedenfelser, Füchschen - Courtesy of Brauerei im Fuchschen, Full Sail, Fuller's, Fürst Wallerstein, Fürstenberg, Fürstlichen Ellingen, Fyne Ales, Galbraith's, Galway Hooker, Gambrinus, Ganter,

Gayant, Geary's, Genesee, Georgetown, Gilde, Girardin, Glaab, Goacher's, Gold Ochsen, Göller, Goose Island, Gordon Biersch, Goslar, Gösser, Gotlands Bryggeri, Gottsmannsgrüner, Gourmetbryggeriet, Grado Plato, Grain, Grain d'orge, Grand Teton, Granville Island brewing, Great Divide, Great Lakes, Great Lakes brewery, Green Flash, Greene King, Greif- Courtesy of Brauerei Greif, Gritty Mcduff's, Grolsch, Growler, Grünbach, Grunn, Grupo Modelo, Guangzhou Zhujiang, Gubernija, Guinness, Gulpener, Gusswerk, Haake-beck, Haand Bryggeriet, Hacker-pschorr, Hadrian & Border, Hair of the Dog, Hale's, Hall & Woodhouse, Halve Maan, Hambleton, Hansa Borg Bryggerier, Hanssens Artisanaal, Härke - Courtesy of BrauManufaktur Harke, Harpoon, Hartwall, Harvey's, Harviestoun, Hasseröder, Hawkshead, Heavy Seas Beer, Heineken España, Heineken Hungária, Heineken Russia, Heineken Slovensko, Herforder - Courtesy of Herforder Brewery, Herold, Herslev Bryghus, Hertog Jan, Het Anker, Hideji, High House, High Point, Highland, Hilden, Hirter, Hitachino Nest, Hite, Hobsons, Hoegaarden, Hofbräu München, Hofbräuhaus, Hogs Back, Holba, Holden's, Holgate Brewhouse, Hook Norton, Hop Back, Hoppin' Frog, Hopworks/HUB, Hornbeer, Hue, Hurns, Hütt, Hutthurmer, Huyghe, Hydes, Innis & Gunn, Inveralmond, Ipswich Ale brewery, Iron Hill, Ise Kadoya, Isle of Arran, Isle of Skye, Ithaca, Iwate Kura, Jacobsen Brewhouse, James Boag's, Jämtlands, Jandelsbrunner, Jarrow, Jennings, Jettenbach, Jever, Ježek, John Smith, Jolly Pumpkin, Jopen, Joseph Holt, Kalnapilis, Kaltenhausen - Copyright: Brau Union Oesterreich AG, Karlovacko, Kauzen, Keiler Brauhaus- Courtesy of Keiler Brauhaus, Kelham Island, Keo, Kerkom, Kesselring, Khan Bräu, Kinshachi, Kirner, Kitzmann, Klein Duimpje, Knappstein, Kneitinger, Kompania Piwowarska SA, Kona, König Ludwig, Koszalin, Kozel, Krombacher, Krone Tettnang, Kronenbourg, Krušovice, Kuchlbauer, Kuhnhenn, Kulmbacher, Kulturbrauerei Heidelberg, L'olmaia, La Binchoise, La Choulette, La Rouget de Lisle, La Rulles, La Trappe, Lagunitas, Laitilan, Lake Placid, Lakefront, Lambrate, Lancaster, Lancelot, Landskron - Courtesy of Landskron Brau-Manufaktur, Landwehr-Bräu - Landwehrbräu, Germany, Lang-bräu, Lao Brewery, Lees, Lefebvre, Left Hand, Légendes/ Ellezelloise, Leibinger, Leikeim- Courtesy of Brauhaus Leikeim, Leinenkugel's, Lepers, Lervig Aktiebryggeri, Licher, Liefmans, Lindeboom, Lindemans, Lindenbräu, Lion, Lion Brewery, Little Creatures, Little Valley, Live Oak, Lobkowicz, Locher, Lonerider, Long Trail, Lord Nelson, Lost Abbey, Lost Coast, Loterbol, Löwenbräu, Lübzer, Mac & Jack's, Mac's, Mack's Brewery, Mad River, Magic Hat, Magnotta Brewery, Maisel, Malmgårdin Panimo, Malt Shovel, Maltus Faber, Marble, Marin, Marston's, Matilda Bay, Maxim Brewery, Maxlrain - Courtesy of Schlossbrauerei Maxlrain , Mcauslan, Mcmenamins, Mcmullen, Meantime, Mendocino- Mendocino Brewing Company, Meteor, Mettlacher Abteibräu, Michard, Michelsbräu, Middle Ages, Midnight Sun, Midtfyns Bryghus, Mikkeller, Millstream, Minhas, Minoh Aji, Mitchell's, Moa, Mohrenbräu, Molson Coors, Mommeriete, Montegioco, Monteith's, Moo Brew, Moonlight, Moorhouse's, Moosehead, Mordue, Mort Subite, Mountain Goat, Multi Bintang, Murphy's, Murray's, Mysore Breweries, Mythos, Náchod/Primátor, Nasu Kohgen, Nesselwang, Neumarkter Lammsbräu, New Belgium, New Glarus, New Holland, Nils Oscar, Ninkasi, Nøgne ø, Nokian Panimo, Nørrebro Bryghus, North Coast, North Yorkshire, Novopacké Pivo, Nymburk, Nynäshamns Ångbryggeri, Oakham, Obolon, Ochakovo, Odell, Okell's, Okocim, Old Dominion, Old Luxters, Olvi, Ommegang, Oriental Brewery, Orkney, Orlando, Orval, Oskar Blues, Ossett, Otley, Otter Creek, Palm, Palmers, Panil (Torrechiara), Pécsi Sörfözde, Pelican, Penn, Pernštejn, Piccolo Birrificio, Pietra, Pike, Pilsner Urquell, Pinkus Müller, Pivovar Samson, Plevna Brewery, Portland Brewing, Proefbrouwerij, Pump House Brewery, Pyramid, Quilmes, Radegast, Rch, Real Ale, Rebel, Red Brick Brewing, Redhook, Redoak, Refsvindinge Brewery, Regent, Reichenbrand - Tobias Rauche, www.bierverkostung. de, Reutberg, Ridna Marka, Riegele, Ringnes, Ringwood, River Horse, Robinson's, Rochefort, Rock Bottom, Rodenbach, Rogue, Röhrl- Courtesy of Rohlbrau Straubing, Roman, Rooster's, Rosenbrauerei Pössneck- Courtesy of Rosenbrauerei Possneck, Rostocker, Rothaus, Royal Unibrew, Rudgate, Rugenbräu, Russian River, Saalfeld - Courtesy of Brauhaus Saalfeld, Saint Arnold, Sainte–Hélène, Saku, Samuel Adams, Samuel Smith, Sankt Gallen, Saranac, Scarampola, Schaumburger, Scheldebrouwerij, Scheyern, Schlafly, Schlappeseppel, Schlenkerla, Schloderer, Schlossbrauerei AU/Hallertau, Schmucker - Courtesy of Private Brewery Schmucker, Schneider, Schönram, Schussenrieder- Courtesy of Schussenrieder Brewery, Schwarzbach, Schwechater, Schweiger, Shakespeare Hotel, Sharp's, Shepherd Neame, Shiga Kogen, Shipyard, Shmaltz, Shonan, Shongweni/Robson's, Siebensternbräu, Sierra Nevada- Sierra Nevada Brewing Co., Silenrieux, Silly/Mynsbrughen, Simon, Simonds Farsons Cisk, Sinebrychoff, Ska, Slaghmuylder, Slater's, Sleeman, Sly fox, Smisje, Smuttynose, Snake River, Sociedade Central de Cervejas, Sonnenbräu, Southampton, Southern tier, Speakeasy, Spendrups, Spoetzl, Sprecher, Springhead, St. Austell, St. Christoffel, St. Germain, St. Peter's, St. Sylvestre, St. Bernardus, Starobrno, Staropramen, Starr Hill, Steam Brewing, Steamworks, Steamworks, Sternquell, Stevens point, Stiegl - Copyright: Stieglbrauerei zu Salzburg GmbH, Stiftsbrauerei Schlägl, Stone, Stralsunder - Courtesy of Stortebeker Braumanufaktur, Straub, Streck, Sudwerk, Summit, Sun In Bev Rrussia, Sun Lik, Surly, Svaneke Bryghus, Svijany, Švyturys-Utenos, Teerenpeli, Terminal Gravity, Terrapin, Thaibev, The Kernel, The Mussel Inn, The Twisted Hop, Theakston, Theillier, Thiriez, Thisted Bryghus, Thornbridge, Three Boys Brewery, Three Floyds, Thurn & Taxis, Thwaites, Timmermans, Timothy Taylor's, Titanic, Topvar, Traditional Scottish Ales, Traquair, Traunstein, Triggerfish, Tring, Troll, Trotzenburg, Trumer, Tsingtao, Tuatara Brewing, Tucher, Two Brothers, U Medvidku, Uerige, Uherský Brod, Uinta, Unertl, Unibroue, Union, United Breweries, Ur-Krostitzer, Ursus breweries, Urthel, Utah Brewers, Val-Dieu, Van den Bossche, Van Eecke, Van Honsebrouck, Van Steenberge, Vancouver Island, Vapeur, Verhaeghe, Victory, Villacher, Wachusett, Wadworth, Waldschlösschen, Warka, Weideneder, Weihenstephan, Weilheim, Weitra Bräu, Wellington Brewery, Wells & Young's, Weltenburger, Wentworth, Westerham, Westheim, Westmalle, Westvleteren, Weyerbacher, Wickwar, Widmer Brothers, Wig & Pen, William Worthington's, William Brothers, Wismar, Wolf Brewing, Wolters, Woodforde's, Würzburger Hofbräu - Courtesy of Wurzburger Hofbrau, Wychwood, Wye Valley, Wylam, Wynkoop, Yoho, York, Yukon Brewing, Zagrebacka, Zahre, Žatec, Zillertal Bier, Zipfer, Zlatopramen, Zötler, Zubr, Zwettler, Żywiec.

All other images © Dorling Kindersley
For further information see: www.dkimages.com